Praise for
Clash of the Carriers

"Tillman, a longtime master of Pacific War naval history, has skill-fully combined a wealth of research into an unprecedented look into both sides of this pivotal sea battle....Tillman's narrative gives near-definitive coverage of its subject, from the usual view from the cockpit to less common perspectives from the command plotting station, the deck of an oiler engaged in underway replenishment, the bowels of the engine room, or a submarine periscope."

—Jon Guttman, *American Fighters Ace Bulletin*

"In this superb work, the greatest naval air battle of all time finally re-ceives the meticulous and comprehensive treatment it deserves. Whether you seek the view from the canopy or the sharp-eyed cri-tique, Barrett Tillman, with unmatched command of the subject, de-livers both in spades—and for both sides. His heroes are the aviators, whatever the uniform they wore, and he illuminates more warts on the U.S. side and the rare gems for the Japanese previously ignored or ob-scured."   —Richard Frank, author of *Guadalcanal* and *Downfall*

"I saw the war from the deck of a battleship, so I cannot render an avi-ator's view. But I can certainly recommend Barrett Tillman's definitive work on the subject. It does not replace the efforts of Admiral Mori-son, but amplifies them in a manner both instructive and entertain-ing."   —Lt. Col. Jeff Cooper, USMCR, USS *Pennsylvania*, 1944

continued...

CLASH
OF THE
CARRIERS

The True Story of the
MARIANAS TURKEY SHOOT
of World War II

BARRETT TILLMAN

Foreword by Stephen Coonts

NAL
CALIBER

NAL Caliber
Published by New American Library, a division of
Penguin Group (USA) Inc., 375 Hudson Street,
New York, New York 10014, USA
Penguin Group (Canada), 90 Eglinton Avenue East, Suite 700, Toronto,
Ontario M4P 2Y3, Canada (a division of Pearson Penguin Canada Inc.)
Penguin Books Ltd., 80 Strand, London WC2R 0RL, England
Penguin Ireland, 25 St. Stephen's Green, Dublin 2,
Ireland (a division of Penguin Books Ltd.)
Penguin Group (Australia), 250 Camberwell Road, Camberwell, Victoria 3124,
Australia (a division of Pearson Australia Group Pty. Ltd.)
Penguin Books India Pvt. Ltd., 11 Community Centre, Panchsheel Park,
New Delhi - 110 017, India
Penguin Group (NZ), 67 Apollo Drive, Mairangi Bay,
Auckland 1311, New Zealand (a division of Pearson New Zealand Ltd.)
Penguin Books (South Africa) (Pty.) Ltd., 24 Sturdee Avenue,
Rosebank, Johannesburg 2196, South Africa

Penguin Books Ltd., Registered Offices:
80 Strand, London WC2R 0RL, England

Published by NAL Caliber, an imprint of New American Library, a division of Penguin Group
(USA) Inc. Previously published in an NAL Caliber hardcover edition.

First NAL Caliber Trade Paperback Printing, November 2006
10 9 8 7 6 5 4 3 2

NAL Caliber Trade Paperback ISBN: 978-0-451-21956-5

The Library of Congress has catalogued the hardcover edition as follows:
Tillman, Barrett.
    Clash of the carriers: the true story of the Marianas turkey shoot of World War II / by Bar-
rett Tillman; with a foreword by Stephen Coonts.
        p. cm.
    Includes bibliographical references and index.
    ISBN 0-451-21670-9
  1. World War, 1939–1945—Aerial operations, American   2. World War, 1939–1945—Naval
operations, American.   3. Philippine Sea, Battle of the, 1944 (June 19–21)   I. Title.
    D790.T59 2005
    940.54'2599—dc22   2005013618

Set in Janson Text
Designed by Ginger Legato

Printed in the United States of America

For Jig and Ginger and Alex and Kay

CONTENTS

FOREWORD

ONCE UPON A TIME carrier decks were straight, Grummans had tail-wheels, and Pratt & Whitneys had props. In those days of yore, before free trade and NAFTA and the new world economy, America was the arsenal of democracy. She built her own ships, planes, guns, bombs, beans, bullets, uniforms, and electronics, and could, within three years of the declaration of war, field the largest, best-equipped, most modern military machine on the planet, one capable of fighting simultaneous wars in Europe and the Pacific and winning them both. Once upon a time . . .

In June 1944, the Japanese brought nine aircraft carriers to the sea battle off the Mariana Islands in the western Pacific; America brought fifteen, eight of which were small, *Independence*-class light carriers. The battle was a total rout, a disastrous defeat for the overmatched, outnumbered Japanese, who lost a third of their carriers and *90 percent* of the airplanes their ships brought to the fray. Their planes were shot out of the sky like . . . well, like turkeys . . . by better-trained American pilots flying better, faster, more technically advanced aircraft. This sea battle marked the first time that Japan felt the full weight of America's economic, population, and industrial superiority, which had in three short years been translated into an amazing military advantage that would, within fifteen months, leave Japan prostrate and in ruins.

The world has changed profoundly since 1944. For better or worse, American politicians have chosen to lower trade barriers that once protected domestic industries that paid living wages in peacetime and produced critical materials in times of war and national emergency. The American textile industry is now dead; the corpse was sent to India and China. The American steel industry is on its last legs. The American military carries pistols made in Italy. The only American shipbuilding concerns make U.S. Navy ships, and are not getting enough work to stay in business. No merchant ships are constructed in this country anymore. The remaining two American automobile companies face fierce competition from every automobile company on earth, yet are burdened with pension and health care obligations that will, one suspects, ultimately force them into bankruptcy, the same fate that has befallen the nation's legacy airlines. Today every American manufacturer is forced to "outsource" jobs, shipping them overseas to stay competitive. (Amazingly, an increasing number of hospitals are having their medical X-rays read on the cheap in India. How the hospitals will have the X-rays interpreted if the Internet goes down is something that hospital administrators don't talk about.)

It is always a mistake to plan the next war based upon the last. In the wars of the future, it is hard to see how fleets such as those that existed during World War II can be brought into being by current national economies, or how they could contend in battle upon the oceans of the earth as independent military entities.

Aircraft carriers are still with us, although one suspects they too are on the cusp of becoming obsolete. Equipped with jet fighter and attack airplanes, they control vast areas of ocean . . . yet since World War II they have been asked repeatedly to project their power ashore. That task they do well, at a tremendous cost in manpower and treasure. In fact, carrier airplanes have become so expensive that one type after another is currently scheduled for retirement, not to be replaced. The ships will not stay in service without airplanes.

I wish to leave you with a few questions: If America is ever again forced to fight a large-scale conflict that lasts more than a month or two, where are the electricians, welders, and steel going to come from to build more ships? Where will we get tanks, uniforms, rations, and weapons to equip our troops to fight our battles? Who will build the planes to launch and fight from aircraft carriers, if we still have any of those? And finally, where is the fuel going to come from to power the ships and planes and tanks?

Once upon a time we had all these assets. Once upon a time America was the arsenal of democracy that could vanquish tyranny. Once upon a time America's people believed that they had a duty to help make the world a safer place for democracy and the rule of law. Once upon a time . . .

Perhaps in the future we will not need what we have willingly surrendered or traded away in return for lower prices at Wal-Mart, lower prices at the automobile dealers and service stations, and lower taxes. At any rate, we can certainly hope so.

As you read Barrett Tillman's excellent work on the Marianas Turkey Shoot, reflect upon the dazzling courage and profound determination of those World War II naval airmen, pilots, and aircrew alike. Navigation consisted of a running dead-reckoning plot on a board each pilot carried on his lap, with the last-known position being the carrier from which he launched. When, or if, he managed to navigate his aircraft to that watery spot where the ship hoped to be at recovery time, the ship might or might not be there. There were no inertial nav systems, no GPS, no computers, not even a TACAN or Omni to home in upon.

If the aviator were shot down or his plane malfunctioned, he went into the great wide ocean, there to drown immediately or die slowly of exposure. Or become a meal for a shark. In that pre-helicopter age, finding lost airmen was haphazard at best, and no one expected the war to stop while a ship or ships went looking. There were no emergency transponder squawks, locator beacons, or handheld radios. Many Navy pilots and aircrewmen launched from carriers and were never heard from again.

I was fortunate enough to fly A-6 Intruders during the Vietnam War, and many a night, up there in the goo above a dark, lonely sea, I thought about those men with the big cojones who had gone before me.

The courage, teamwork, training, professionalism, and aggressiveness that the officers and men of the U.S. Navy exhibited during that battle in June 1944 will always be required of American fighting men and women. The World War II example is their legacy. These qualities in our war fighters are our real assets, and the only ones that will endure.

—Stephen Coonts

PREFACE

MARIANAS: THE WORD CONJURES different meanings to different audiences. To oceanographers it recalls the deepest spot on planet Earth. Located in the Pacific Ocean, the Marianas Trench bottoms out at 36,200 feet, nearly seven statute miles. Mount Everest would fit with about 7,000 feet to spare.

For comparison, the Pacific's average depth is 13,700 feet, while the Atlantic's average is 1,500 feet less. The steep-walled trench runs nearly 1,600 miles, but the deepest part is 210 miles southwest of Guam.

That island brings to mind another image of the Marianas. To historians it harkens the 1944 campaign for control of Guam, Saipan, and Tinian, which became coral nests for the B-29 firebirds that burned out the urban and industrial heart of Japan. But before the Superfortresses arrived, one of the world's most notable sea battles unfolded west of the Marianas. It was the fifth and last time in history that opposing fleets fought major engagements without ever steaming within sight of each other. It went into history as the Battle of the Philippine Sea, and so great was the American victory, it passed into legend as the Great Marianas Turkey Shoot.

For such a notable battle, surprisingly little literature has been devoted specifically to the Philippine Sea. As the world's largest aircraft carrier duel, it has been the subject of only four previous volumes in sixty years. In contrast, Midway and Leyte Gulf each spawned fifteen to twenty noteworthy studies and probably as many minor works. It's a curious situation, considering that the Japanese themselves regarded Saipan as the third nail in their imperial coffin, after Midway and Guadalcanal.

The first significant treatment of the Turkey Shoot appeared in 1953 with volume eight of Samuel Eliot Morison's monumental *History of U.S. Naval Operations in World War II: New Guinea and the Marianas*. Though the carrier battle occupies barely one-quarter of the text, it set the standard for all that followed, both in content and elegance of style. But such was Morison's reputation that some of his errors were accepted and repeated downstream.

Nearly fifteen years passed, and in 1967 one of the U.S. Navy's premier wartime leaders released his own survey. Admiral Charles W. Lockwood's *Battles of the Philippine Sea* (written with Hans C. Adamson) studied both the Marianas engagement and the Battle of Leyte Gulf, a.k.a. the Second Battle of the Philippine Sea. As commander of Pacific Fleet submarines, Lockwood was thoroughly acquainted with both engagements.

The Marianas Turkey Shoot was too significant for the naval-minded British to ignore, and in 1975 Ian Allan, Ltd., produced a fine little book: *The Battle of the Philippine Sea*, by former U.S. Navy officer W. D. Dickson. Crammed with data and illustrations, it took up where Morison had left off.

Six years later, U.S. Naval Institute Press published William T. Y'Blood's excellent *Red Sun Setting*. After Dickson's volume, *Red Sun* was only the second book devoted wholly to the carrier battle, an excellent work with the author's aviation insight as a former airline pilot.

Finally, in 1994 my monograph was published by Phalanx in tribute to the battle's fiftieth anniversary. However, "Phil Sea" had featured in several of my operational histories of tailhook aircraft.

Research for this book occupied decades, including the writing of previous histories. Along the way I was fortunate in knowing a few dozen veterans of the battle, walking the flight deck of USS *Hornet* (CV-12), squeezing into CIC and the ready rooms of USS *Yorktown* (CV-10), and even logging some cherished flight time with my father in our restored Dauntless dive-bomber.

Based upon previous experience, several conventions are observed here. As in most naval histories, the unit of measure is the nautical mile (2,000 yards). Occasionally English miles (1,760 yards) are cited for land distances, and are noted accordingly. Like ship speeds, airspeeds are cited in nautical miles per hour (knots). Occasionally metric distances are given for Japanese perspective.

Times are rendered in naval twenty-four-hour local "zone time," though Japanese ships maintained Tokyo time wherever they sailed.

Throughout the text and appendix, Japanese names are rendered in English order (surname second). While the names of Japanese ship captains were often more easily obtained than American, translations were another matter. For example, depending on context, a submarine skipper's given name could be read as Fumitake or Monmu. Another officer's surname was alternately Sakakura or Itakura. In most cases I have deferred to my Japanese-language authorities.

—Barrett Tillman
Summer 2004

CLASH
OF THE
CARRIERS

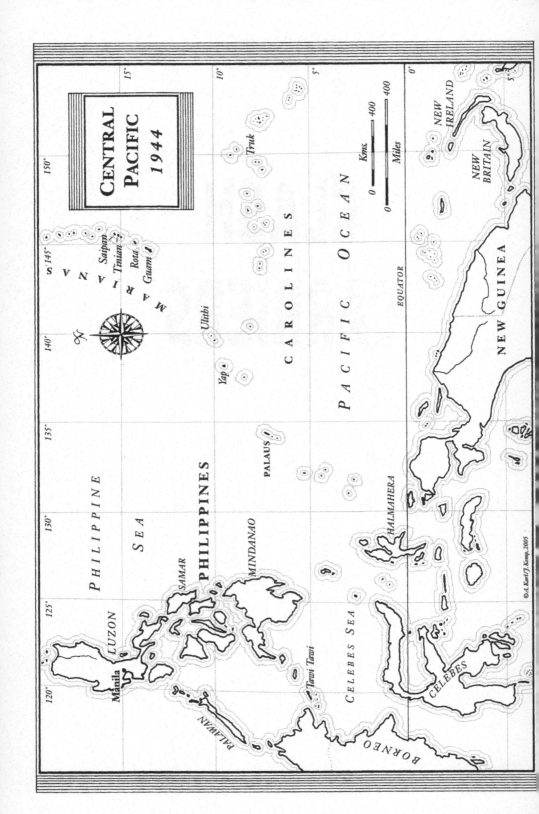

PROLOGUE

On Tuesday, June 6, 1944, a huge invasion fleet departed its various embarkation areas, formed up, and shaped course for a hostile shore. The armada included warships, supply vessels, attack transports, and landing craft of every description. The assault troops that would wade ashore through artillery and gunfire were fully trained and equipped with all the esoterica of an amphibious operation.

On the other side of the world, near the prime meridian running through Greenwich, England, it was Monday, June 5. Another fleet, nearly ten times larger, faced a vastly shorter trip to its destination: barely a hundred miles to the Norman coast. But Operation Overlord remained tentative, uncertain. D-day in Europe had been set for the fifth, while the weather—the worst in the English Channel in decades—forced a delay. General Dwight Eisenhower of Denison, Texas, and Abilene, Kansas, assembled his deputies of the combined chiefs and sought their counsel. Meanwhile, 173,000 soldiers from five Allied nations waited aboard five thousand ships and small craft, on airfields and staging areas. The world held its breath, focused on events pending in France.

In the Pacific the objective of Operation Forager lay 1,200 nautical miles south of Tokyo: an obscure island called Saipan in the Marianas. It was not large as islands go: only twelve miles long and less than half that at the widest point. San Francisco covered about the same area: 46.5 square miles.

Saipan featured little to draw tourists, other than wildlife enthusiasts. Green turtles nested on Tanapag Beach, and the island hosted several indigenous birds such as the Marianas Mallard, the Common Moorhen, and the Nightingale Reed Warbler.

However, Saipan had three Japanese airfields and room for more that could be leveled by the incredibly efficient U.S. engineers.

Next down the chain, almost ninety miles south, was Guam, over twice the size of Saipan and previously an American trust territory seized by Japan in December 1941. There the Chamarro islanders labored under the dubious mercies of the Greater East Asia Co-Prosperity Sphere for two and a half years.

The Pacific commander in chief was another Texan, but not a general. From his headquarters in Hawaii "CinCPac," Admiral Chester W. Nimitz, had provided Admiral Raymond A. Spruance with all that his Fifth Fleet needed for Operation Forager: 127,000 Marines and GIs in 535 ships and landing craft. Four and a half divisions were expected to overwhelm some 60,000 Japanese on Saipan. With the Marianas again in American hands, Tokyo would fall within range of B-29s.

The last fact was well-known to Imperial General Headquarters, ensuring a major naval battle. There had not been a fleet engagement since the fall of 1942, when some seventy American and Japanese ships clashed in the Battle of Santa Cruz. The U.S. lost the carrier *Hornet* (CV-8) but Japan's strategic goal—isolation of Guadalcanal—was stymied. Subsequent battles were mostly small surface duels: brief, bloody, nocturnal engagements fought with gunfire and torpedoes. The next battle was bound to be far bigger and bloodier.

To defend the Marianas, the Japanese Combined Fleet was committed to an all-or-nothing endeavor. To cede the islands to the Americans was unthinkable; to engage the Fifth Fleet was tantamount to suicide. The Imperial Navy's once-vaunted superiority in numbers, equipment, and fighting skill had dwindled precipitously since 1942. Now, in the third summer of the Pacific war, the emperor's armada was triple-damned. It was significantly outnumbered by superior ships and aircraft operated by more experienced men. Nevertheless, the forthcoming battle shaped up as something unique in naval history.

To place the Battle of the Philippine Sea in context, it remains the third-largest naval battle of the steel era, with 193 U.S. and Japanese combatant ships: carriers, surface types, and submarines. The three-day slugfest at Leyte Gulf four months later involved some 244 ships and subs plus 39 PT boats.

By comparison, the two biggest dreadnought battles of World War I were Jutland in 1916 (250 combatants) and Dogger Bank in 1915 (approximately 100). The first great clash of ironclads had occurred between Russia and Japan only ten years earlier, with eighty-one capital ships and destroyers plus sixteen Japanese torpedo boats.

A century before, off Trafalgar in 1805, Horatio Nelson's epic victory involved just 60 British, French, and Spanish ships of the line. Far greater numbers fought under sail in other battles, but seldom so decisively. Probably the most notable exception occurred in 1588, the year of the armada, when some 320 British and Spanish vessels contested mastery of the English Channel.

In terms of carrier battles, the Turkey Shoot exceeded everything that preceded it. None of the four carrier clashes of 1942 engaged more than seven flattops; excluding floatplanes and land-based aircraft, Midway involved just over 500 tailhook airplanes. Off Saipan, Vice Admiral Marc Mitscher embarked 905 aircraft in fifteen fast carriers; Vice Admiral Jisaburo Ozawa about 440 in nine flattops. (There existed an eerie symmetry between Philippine Sea and the surface battle planned by both navies. During war games in the 1930s, the U.S. Navy expected to commit fifteen battleships against nine Japanese.) In fact, Philippine Sea involved as many fast carriers as the total committed to all four 1942 carrier duels, and nearly as many total ships and aircraft.

For further difference of scale, the greatest naval battles against the western Axis occurred in the Mediterranean in 1940–42. In one of the largest engagements—off Spartivento in November 1940—none of the thirty-eight British or Italian ships were sunk.

Prior to 1942 the U.S. Navy's largest battles occurred in the Spanish-American War. The storied victories off Manila and Santiago in 1898 involved a total of thirty ships, evenly divided between the U.S. and Spain. Yet the combined tonnage of American and Spanish ships at Manila Bay barely matched the total of one *Essex*-class carrier.

Moreover, fully fueled and armed, the 905 aircraft in Mitscher's fifteen carriers outweighed any of Commodore George Dewey's ships.

Excepting Jutland, Philippine Sea was the greatest assemblage of warships in living memory. (Operation Overlord, with far more vessels, had fewer combatants.) But there were vastly greater differences than mere numbers. The very means of naval warfare had undergone a revolution in an astonishingly short time. In 1916 the contenders exchanged broadsides at ranges of no more than nine nautical miles; twenty-eight years later the distance reached three hundred miles. Carrier aviation represented the technical and tactical millennium of war at sea.

Philippine Sea was fought far from land, which made it rare in naval history, as most fleet battles occurred within sight of shore. For one or both combatants, Trafalgar, Tsushima Strait, Santiago, and Manila Bay all were fought within easy distance of one or more ports. Jutland occurred just eighty miles off the Danish coast, barely 300 miles from Scapa Flow and 275 from Wilhelmshaven.

All that changed at Coral Sea in May 1942, 2,500 nautical miles from Hawaii. Even in "home" waters at Midway, the U.S. Pacific Fleet deployed some 1,200 miles from Pearl Harbor; Japan's carrier force sailed nearly twice as far from home. Consequently, logistics factored hugely into carrier operations, as the ability to sustain task forces far at sea for weeks on end was crucial to prosecution of World War II. Neither Spruance nor Ozawa had a fleet base in the Mariana Islands, so both commanders brought everything with them to fight the battle.

The combat theater was huge. The advanced U.S. naval base at Majuro in the Marshalls lay 1,850 statute miles east-southeast of Saipan; Japan's Tawi-Tawi in Borneo was a similar stretch southwest.

Disregarding relative positions, that expanse would barely fit within North America. With Saipan centered on Minneapolis, Majuro lay on Miami and Tawi-Tawi on Watson Lake in the upper Rocky Mountains, a day's drive from the Alaskan border. Pearl Harbor, another 2,300 miles eastward, would alight somewhere in the mid-Atlantic.

In comparison, the 3,600 miles from Tawi-Tawi to Majuro equals the straight-line route between New York and London. In the European land war, Normandy to Moscow was barely 1,500 miles.

Because of the enormous oceanic distances, America's Pacific offensive could not be entirely supported by land-based airpower. That meant naval aviation at the tip of the spear.

Flying from aircraft carriers is probably the most difficult task that humans have ever routinely performed. So esoteric is the carrier art that only four navies have conquered the enormous design, production, and economic challenges to put those ships to sea. Britain, America, Japan, and France all accomplished the feat with indigenous efforts. The German and Italian navies never completed their carriers, and the last-minute Soviet attempt died aborning.

After World War II, Argentina, Brazil, Canada, India, and the Netherlands employed British-built carriers for fixed-wing aircraft, all long since retired. Subsequently, vertical/short-takeoff-and-landing ships have increasingly been used around the world, but the payload and performance of VSTOL aircraft remains a distant second to tail-hook jets, inheritors of the mission and the heritage of 1944.

In short, there had never been a battle like Philippine Sea. And there never will be again.

"The Great Marianas Turkey Shoot" remains by far the biggest day of aerial combat in American history. Carrier pilots claimed 380 aerial victories, of which two-thirds likely were valid.

But it's easy to become absorbed with the figures and the hardware: the magnificent ships and glamorous aircraft. Excluding the amphibious forces and support units, the Fifth Fleet's striking arm, Task Force 58, was manned by nearly a hundred thousand sailors and fliers, while the Mobile Fleet deployed almost thirty thousand. By World War II standards those men equaled seven U.S. Army divisions and two Japanese.

More important, the Turkey Shoot was fraught with drama, controversy, and consequences. Among other things, it marked the de facto end of the Imperial Navy's carrier force; afterward Japan's *Nihon Kaigun* retained aircrews for just four flattops with 115 planes at Leyte

Gulf. Consequently, after June 1944, the emperor's "sea eagles" were useful only as decoys—a role they fulfilled in the October clash.

At the strategic level, Philippine Sea inflicted the greatest strategic jolt to Japan thus far, as loss of the Marianas forced the resignation of Tokyo's warlord, Prime Minister Hideki Tojo. As the emperor's choice to lead the government since October 1941, the erstwhile general was held responsible for the course of the war, and soon B-29s would be perched within reach of Tokyo.

Tojo departed the scene, fated to die on the gallows in 1948. But before the hangman's noose snapped taut, thousands of Japanese would pay with their lives for Tojo's ambition and Hirohito's folly. Many of them plummeted to the depths of the ocean off Saipan that summer of 1944.

PART ONE

A Precarious Honor

USS *Lexington*, 1005 hours, June 19, 1944

THE ATMOSPHERE WAS LITERALLY ELECTRIC in the air-conditioned steel confines of the room called "radar plot." Radio circuits crackled and phosphors glowed green on radar screens in the subdued lighting of the flagship's combat information center (CIC).

Vice Admiral Marc A. Mitscher's senior fighter direction officer (FDO) was Lieutenant Joseph R. Eggert, a thirty-one-year-old reservist. He had been a New York stockbroker in a previous life, but now he shouldered a responsibility that no Wall Street merchant ever imagined. Eggert oversaw the air defense of more than a hundred American warships deployed in four task groups, each with its own FDO who would conduct a localized battle of survival.

Mitscher's carrier fleet was nearly a century removed from the age of sail, but every officer and sailor understood what was pending that clear Pacific morning. Task Force 58 was standing by to repel boarders.

The only thing that seemed peculiar about Joe Eggert was his preference for tea. In Uncle Sam's Navy, coffee was the brew that fueled the fleet.

The preliminaries had been under way for more than a week. Since June 11 Mitscher's fighters had claimed more than two hundred kills in Marianas skies, not counting a foray against Iwo Jima. Earlier this Monday morning, elements of nine squadrons splashed fifty Japanese planes near Saipan, Guam, and Tinian, so the eastern flank was secure. Now the threat winged out of the west.

The "boarders"—nearly seventy Japanese fighters and torpedo planes—approached beyond human vision but within sight of the

Argus-eyed sentinel called radar. Launched at 0830, they advanced at the rate of two and a half sea miles per minute, and they had been plotted by the westernmost U.S. task group minutes before. At 0957 the battleship *Alabama* had reported the initial contact at 140 miles. Eggert approved: Atmospherics were unusually good. A "skin paint" at that range—without enhancement by transponders—was excellent performance. The long-range SC radars were working exceptionally well.

Eggert ran the time-distance equation in his mind. He had nearly an hour to marshal his forces and assign fighters in relays to intercept the bandits, for they were surely no longer bogeys. Early in the war the Navy identified stockbrokers as prime FDO material: They managed expendable resources (fuel and ammunition) in a fluid situation requiring coolness and judgment. In wartime, with the lethal game played in three dimensions, Joe Eggert was one of the best.

Now the enemy formations appeared on *Lexington*'s scopes. The primary radar operator made the call: "Contact! Two groups, one-twenty-one and one-twenty-four miles, bearing two-six-zero."

Eggert handed off to the task group director, Lieutenant J. H. Trousdale. Behind a Plexiglas screen a sailor marked the plot on the circular grid radiating outward from the center. The FDO assigned the day's first plot as raid one, then called the flag bridge. Vice Admiral Mitscher, his ruddy face concealed beneath the long brim of his lobsterman's cap, responded with an esoteric order: Broadcast "Hey, rube!"

Eggert knew what it meant: the old circus call for "Everybody come help." He keyed his mike and relayed the message to Grumman F6F Hellcats "capping" Guam's airfields. Japanese planes had been landing there, funneled in from the Carolines and elsewhere, building strength for the coming battle. But the F6F pilots had shot them down in growing numbers; now the main event shaped up at sea. Most of the Grumman fighters turned their blunt noses westward, returning to their respective ships to refuel, rearm, and await an air battle of unprecedented scale.

Things began to happen with accelerating speed. Those ships not already at general quarters sounded the klaxon or bugle call that sent sailors sprinting to battle stations. Hatches were dogged, helmets donned, trousers tucked into socks to reduce flash burns. Gun crews trained their weapons toward the westerly threat, setting ready ammunition nearby. One of the four carrier group commanders, Rear Admiral John Reeves, cautioned his gunners, "Try to avoid shooting down our fighters. They are our best protection."

On carriers the red diamond Fox flag was hoisted to indicate flight quarters. Pratt & Whitney engines belched blue-gray smoke, emitting loud, hollow coughs as three-bladed propellers turned over. The wood-planked flight decks—Oregon pine or Douglas fir—trembled with the sensation.

In fourteen minutes between 1023 and 1037, Task Force 58 had 220 Hellcats airborne. The big, angular fighters from Grumman's Long Island hatchery already had proven themselves the masters of Pacific skies. Now their pilots anticipated their greatest battle yet.

Sitrep: June 1944

JUNE 1944 WAS A WATERSHED month in World War II, and not only in France and the Marianas. On the fourth (east longitude date), Allied forces entered Rome, liberating the Eternal City after nine months of muddy, bloody slogging up the Italian boot. The U.S. Fifth Army gained the credit, but the victory also belonged to men of at least a dozen other nations: Britons, New Zealanders, South Africans, Frenchmen, Poles, Indians, and Gurkhas; even some Brazilians. In case proof were needed, the Italian campaign reminded everyone that it would take the rest of the world over five years to defeat Germany.

Farther east on the Eurasian landmass, the Soviet Union prepared to launch a massive blow. Along the Donets the *Wehrmacht* still occupied land several hundred miles east of Kiev, holding prepared positions in anticipation of what was coming. Four Soviet Army groups—124 divisions with 1.2 million men—were poised to strike, a cocked fist with an armored avalanche of 5,200 tanks and massive artillery on a scale that only Russians have ever managed. Half a million Germans awaited the blow on Army Group Center.

In northeastern India, British Empire forces shot it out with determined Japanese attackers (the only kind the emperor possessed) at a place called Imphal. It was valuable more for its position than anything intrinsic: Imphal controlled the only all-weather highway on the Burmese frontier. In a dank, jungly world perennially wet, soldiers on both sides watched their uniforms mold and weapons rust almost before their eyes.

Ironically, there were Indians among the attackers and defenders. The latter included members of the British Indian Army with hardy little Gurkhas, pound for pound among the best fighters on earth. Opposing them, Subhas Chandra Bose's National Army consisted of anticolonial troops siding with Japan. With roughly a hundred thousand men on each side, casualties ran around 30 percent, including fifty thousand Japanese. Tokyo's hope of seizing the crown colony died in the rot and decay of Manipur Province.

Events at home did not escape notice, either. For soldiers, sailors, and Marines, one of the greatest events that month was signing of the Servicemen's Readjustment Act, better known as the GI Bill of Rights. It provided for postwar education loans to veterans as well as additional discharge pay, unemployment benefits, and Social Security credit for time in uniform.

Federal spending reached $91.3 billion in 1944, raising the national debt to $204 billion. But unemployment rated merely 1.2 percent, and more than a few servicemen reckoned that at least 1 percent of the population was unemployable.

Rationing was now a way of life in America. Gasoline was thirty-five cents a gallon, when available, and the public groused about meatless Tuesdays while counting sugar coupons, contributing to scrap drives, planting victory gardens, and buying billions of dollars in war bonds. On the other hand, first-class postage was three cents, and V-mail became a staple of wartime correspondents.

Among the Americans bound for Saipan, some yearned for baseball news. At month's end St. Louis retained the lead in both leagues, leading to the crosstown World Series that fall. Ultimately the Cardinals defeated the Browns 4–2.

Entertainment reflected escapism from the war. The year's top tunes were "The Trolley Song" by Judy Garland, plus Bing Crosby's "San Fernando Valley" and the Andrews Sisters' "Shoo Shoo Baby." In early June the Mills Brothers' mellow tones debuted "You Always Hurt the One You Love," which remained on the *Billboard* chart for thirty-three weeks.

Popular films that month included Jimmy Durante's *Two Girls and a Sailor, Once Upon a Time* with Cary Grant and Janet Blair, and an equine tearjerker, *Home in Indiana*, with the prematurely aged Walter Brennan. More forgettable cinema fare was *Cobra Woman*, with Lon Chaney Jr.

Two Oscar winners premiered in May, most notably *Going My Way*, which would garner 1945 Academy Awards for Bing Crosby, Barry Fitzgerald, and director Leo McCarey. George Cukor's *Gaslight* yielded an Oscar for Ingrid Bergman.

Meanwhile, Crosby, Bob Hope, Dorothy Lamour, and a host of other stars were selfless in touring the war zones with Les Brown's Band of Renown. Hope, a keen judge of audiences, gazed at a khaki-filled Pacific amphitheater and quipped, "Wow, look at all these Republicans."

At the GOP convention in Chicago that June, former president Herbert Hoover paid tribute to the troops, noting, "Older men declare war. But it is youth that must fight and die." The convention nominated two governors, New York's Thomas E. Dewey and Ohio's John Bricker, who lost to the dying Roosevelt in November.

But much as they craved news of home, Fifth Fleet sailors and airmen had an insatiable appetite for everything else, notably consumables. Food, ammunition, and fuel topped the list. Especially fuel. In the fourth era of naval propulsion (after oars, wind, and coal), that meant fuel oil.

Bunker C

OIL. IT ALWAYS CAME DOWN to the viscous, black lifeblood of the fleet. The entire war was about oil, though five decades later blow-dried "war correspondents" would insist with arrogant ignorance that the Mesopotamian live-fire exercise was the first ever waged over petroleum. But that was the 1990s. In the 1940s Japan needed the South Seas' oily wealth to feed her imperial ambition.

Tokyo's conquest of the Dutch East Indies remains one of the most underrated victories of the Pacific War. In less than ninety days—between the December 16 attack on Borneo and the March 9 conquest of Java—Japan gained its major strategic objective, ensuring itself almost unlimited oil reserves. Such was the importance of the objective that Japan's only significant airborne operations of the war occurred there, with some units taking 80 percent casualties.

Most World War II ships ran on bunker fuel, so called because it was stored in large tanks called bunkers. The standard fuel, known as Bunker C, was a sludgy, malodorous substance almost the texture of molasses ("too thin to walk on and too thick to swim in"). Unlike gasoline, it was easily obtained and in some cases could be used almost raw.

Bunker C was what the petroleum industry calls a heavy distillate: fuel oil number six. A light distillate is gasoline, while middle distillates include diesel and kerosene. Bunker fuel begins as crude oil, but in refining the lighter fractions such as gasoline, kerosene, and diesel are removed by distillation. That leaves the residuals, heavier materials not distilled because their boiling points are too high. Therefore, they survive the refining process, as do contaminants such as salts and sediment, not unlike seawater when it evaporates.

Because bunker fuel had to be preheated before burning, most Navy ships were built with fuel oil heaters in the fire rooms and steam heating coils in the tanks to facilitate pumping Bunker C. At fifty degrees Fahrenheit it emitted an unpleasant odor similar to asphalt paving material.

The war could not be fought without it.

Power Base

IN THE PREVIOUS THIRTY-ONE MONTHS, much had happened to bring the Fifth Fleet into being and to position it for Operation Forager. If not at the time, certainly in retrospect Japan's attack upon America seems insane. Had the Allies not hanged some of Tokyo's leading criminals, the Japanese people would have been justified in lynching them for the misery they inflicted.

In 1941 Japan attacked a nation with nearly twice the population, though that was almost irrelevant: The Imperial Army had conquered much of China. But the U.S. was a burgeoning industrial giant that eventually produced five times Japan's steel, seven times the coal, five times the aircraft, and eight times the merchant ships. One wonders if Japanese economists ran the figures and compared America's with their own. Nevertheless, Tokyo outraged a nation with more factories, a newer and more automated industrial plant, and a population attuned to machines and technology: the nation that invented mass production, and the lightbulb, telegraph, telephone, machine gun, and airplane. Not to mention Japan's favorite sport: baseball.

Even before partial mobilization, the U.S. possessed nearly as much wartime potential as the rest of the world combined. Analysts at the Office of Economic Warfare concluded that before 1939 America's war-making potential was nearly 42 percent of its peacetime economy. Germany and Russia came second at 14 percent each; Britain with 10 percent; and France barely led Japan 4.0 to 3.5 percent. The greatest growth after 1939 occurred in Germany and the Soviet Union, but despite the prolonged effects of the Depression, the U.S. economy had enormous "stretch." It also possessed a greater workforce, opening manufacturing jobs to women long before the Axis powers. Rosie the Riveter became an American icon, with women accounting for nearly 10 percent of the manufacturing pool by war's end.

By any measure, the United States would dominate its Pacific enemy, yet Tokyo's warlords convinced themselves that *Bushido* warrior spirit would defeat steel, expertise—and rage.

In 1941 America outproduced Japan in every category. That year the U.S. Navy commissioned forty-four warships and thirteen submarines—a further investment in Franklin Roosevelt's two-ocean navy. In comparison, Japan managed twenty-four: three carriers, one battleship (the world's largest), two cruisers, and seven destroyers, plus eleven subs.

Three years later the U.S. launched more than nine million tons of cargo vessels, while Japanese yards produced less than eight hundred thousand: a twelve-to-one disparity. And that figure did not account for the attrition that U.S. submarines inflicted upon the empire's vulnerable merchant marine. Excluding escorts, in 1944 America commissioned 762 warships, Japan barely 200. America built 93,000 aircraft versus 28,000 "made in Japan."

Yet for all its egregious folly, Japan enjoyed breathtaking success in the five months after December 7. In an unrelenting litany of Allied gloom, Imperial forces seized the coveted oil fields of the Dutch East Indies; humbled Britain at Singapore; took the Philippines from America; swept through Indochina and Southeast Asia. The Anglo-American navies were humiliated everywhere: Hawaii, the Indian Ocean, and the Java Sea. Even Australia lay vulnerable, her brawny youth committed to the defense of North Africa.

The reasons for Japan's early dominance were varied. In Clausewitzian terms they included mass—the ability to concentrate superior forces at a desired point—whereas the Allies were spread thin across a huge part of planet Earth. Additionally, the emperor's forces were well organized, thoroughly trained, and generally well led. The Americans, British, and their allies had seldom operated together and frequently lacked cohesive leadership. Combined with Japanese technical superiority, the early innings could only go one way—Tokyo's way.

Admiral Isoroku Yamamoto, commander of the Combined Fleet, had spent time in America between the wars. He attended Harvard, traveled widely, and briefly flirted with prospects of entering the oil business in Texas. In a manner of speaking, twenty years later he did deal in oil, and went permanently bankrupt. But unlike his Army counterparts, Yamamoto was a realist. Although apparently he never said anything about awakening a sleeping giant, he did predict six months of victories, after which he could guarantee nothing.

The admiralissimo proved prescient. Pearl represented his only significant victory—ironically, in an operation he opposed. At Midway in June 1942—right on schedule—his grand scheme to win the war came unhinged. Four Imperial carriers went to the bottom in one day, with many of their crews and airmen, an irreplaceable loss.

On the first anniversary of the Doolittle raid, Yamamoto had a fatal rendezvous with Lieutenant Rex T. Barber, an Oregon farm boy flying a Lockheed P-38 named *Miss Virginia*. By then, Japan was permanently forced on the defensive, first at Guadalcanal, then in the Gilberts and Marshalls. At each waypoint on the road to victory, American carriers led the way: the honed steel at the tip of the spear pointing inevitably to Tokyo Bay.

Murderer's Row

THEY CALLED IT MURDERER'S ROW: a lethal array of fifteen aircraft carriers basking in the harsh sunlight seven degrees above the equator. The ships bore historic fighting names such as *Enterprise*, *Lexington*, *Princeton*, and *Cowpens*. Their crews knew them by nicknames either affectionate or comic: the Big E, Lady Lex, Sweet Pea, and Mighty Moo.

More than a quarter million tons of carriers swung at anchor in beautiful Majuro Atoll, their gray-painted hulls contrasting with the vivid beauty of their surroundings. In 1889 Robert Louis Stevenson had visited the Marshall Islands and proclaimed Majuro "the pearl of the Pacific." And so it was: white beaches, swaying palms, and multi-hued aquamarine waters.

The Marshalls are composed of some sixty islands and islets, but Majuro's land area amounts to less than four square miles. However, the lagoon covered 114, enough for a fleet. Nearby Kwajalein's anchorage was huge, eight times larger.

Majuro was wonderfully situated, lying almost equidistant between Hawaii and the Marianas. Japan had acquired the Marshalls from Germany after the Great War and fortified most of the atolls, especially Kwajalein and Eniwetok. But the Japanese left Majuro in November 1943, and the U.S. Navy arrived in February 1944, turning it into an advanced base.

Besides the fifteen flattops of Task Force 58 arrayed at Majuro was a screen of four heavy cruisers, thirteen light cruisers, and fifty-three destroyers: eighty-five ships in three task groups. The battleship group, 58.7, involved seven battlewagons, four cruisers, and fifteen destroyers for a task force total of fifteen flattops, seven battleships, eight heavy and thirteen light cruisers, and sixty-eight destroyers. The total was 111 surface combatants, not counting submarines from Hawaii and Australia. There had been larger assemblies, but for range, mobility, and pure striking power the world had never seen anything like the Fifth Fleet.

America's awesome production capacity had delivered an armada that had not existed in 1941. Fifth Fleet was largely wartime construction: 76 percent of the combatants had entered service in the two and a half years since Pearl Harbor. Fourteen of the carriers had been commissioned in wartime. Four of them—*Hornet, Wasp, Bataan*, and *San Jacinto*—were barely six months out of the builder's yard, their two-tone Measure 33 camouflage still fresh.

The rest of the fleet was nearly as new. Of the two task forces' twenty-one cruisers (eight heavy), just five were prewar construction. Ten had been commissioned in 1943, and one, light cruiser *Vincennes*, had just hoisted her pennant in January. Only nineteen of sixty-eight destroyers predated 1942, the oldest from 1934.

Commanding the Majuro armada was Admiral Raymond A. Spruance, victor of Midway two years previously. Spruance bore a deserved reputation as one of the brightest officers in the U.S. Navy. He had graduated twenty-fifth of 209 in the Annapolis class of 1907 and earned superior ratings from ensign to admiral.

A cruiser officer for much of his career, Spruance started the war leading William F. Halsey's screen in the *Enterprise* (CV-6) task force. He was everything Halsey was not: quiet, modest, cautious—and bright. Where Halsey smoked cigarettes, Spruance abhorred tobacco and seldom missed a chance to exercise. Halsey's nickname, appropriately, was "Bull." Spruance didn't have a nickname; the closest thing was his Fifth Fleet call sign, "Blue Jacket." Where Halsey relished the limelight (he appeared twice on the cover of *Time* and wrote a splashy postwar memoir), Spruance shunned publicity. When Spruance also made the cover of *Time*, a week after the Marianas battle, he placed the magazine facedown in his quarters and declined to look at it. He never wrote his memoirs.

After Midway, Spruance became Admiral Chester Nimitz's chief of staff at CinCPacFleet. A year later he was made commander of the Central Pacific Force, which became Fifth Fleet in April 1944. Spruance's command alternated with Halsey's Third Fleet, using the same forces. Efficiency drove the arrangement, as it permitted the respective staffs ample planning time between operations. But a dividend was strategic deception, as only at the end of the war did the Navy announce that Third and Fifth Fleets were essentially one and the same.

In June 1944 Raymond Ames Spruance wielded more power than any seagoing admiral in history. Though subordinate to "CinCPac" Chester Nimitz in Hawaii, Spruance had overall command of Operation Forager. From his flagship, the cruiser *Indianapolis*, he choreographed the geopolitical ballet in all its iterations: the amphibious operation to seize the Marianas; the carrier striking arm protecting the amphibious force; the enormous logistics group supporting the whole endeavor. Each component had its own commander, but they in turn answered to Spruance.

Greatest of Spruance's strengths was risk assessment. If he lacked Bull Halsey's headlong, damn-the-torpedoes attitude, neither did he ever commit a serious error—something that cannot be said of William F. Halsey. Spruance summarized his philosophy thusly: "I believe that making war is a game that requires cold and careful calculation. It might be a very serious thing if we turned the wrong way, just once."

Leading Spruance's carrier striking arm was Vice Admiral Marc A. Mitscher at the helm of Task Force 58. His call sign reflected his appearance: "Bald Eagle." Slight, wiry, and wrinkled, "Pete" Mitscher looked a decade older than his fifty-seven years. He spoke so softly that sometimes he could not be understood, yet he loathed the very thought of the Japanese empire and devoted himself to its extinction. Briefly stated, his attitude toward the Japanese had to do with good ones and dead ones.

Though six months younger than Spruance, Mitscher graduated from Annapolis three years later. In 1916 he had become only the thirty-third aviator in the U.S. Navy. He had piloted the NC-1 flying boat on its 1919 transatlantic attempt (the NC-4 succeeded) and helped develop early carrier procedures.

Apart from duty as a fleet pilot, Mitscher had two tours at the Bureau of Aeronautics in Washington. He was captain of USS *Hornet* (CV-8), which launched Jimmy Doolittle's B-25s against Tokyo in April 1942, but was overshadowed by his flamboyant superior, Halsey. Two months later Mitscher badly mishandled *Hornet* in the crucial Battle of Midway, effectively forcing Admirals Spruance and Frank Jack Fletcher to fight four enemy carriers with two of their own. Intimates later acknowledged that Mitscher felt his career was ended after Midway, where he relied on former Bureau of Aeronautics cronies who had no business leading squadrons in combat.

Nevertheless, Mitscher had already been selected for flag rank and became a rear admiral. He commanded Air Forces Solomon Islands (ComAirSols) during 1943, and in March 1944, as a vice admiral, he assumed command of Task Force 58 under Spruance.

Spruance and Mitscher were a study in contrasts. Spruance was quick, analytical, cerebral: He graduated in the top 12 percent of his Annapolis class. Mitscher finished near the bottom of his class; ironically, for a technically minded professional he could be sloppy and inattentive. (Several of his pilots splashed at Midway because, unaccountably, he launched his short-legged fighters before his bombers.) Largely uninterested in details, Mitscher relied heavily upon his brain trust, and seldom bothered reading a task force operations order. He much preferred a verbal condensation from his chief of staff.

As much as he relied upon his staff, Mitscher surprised some astute observers with his reluctance to accept advice. Whether he was overly confident or simply indifferent is hard to say, but his apparent stubbornness was noted by no less an authority than Commander John S. Thach, the Navy's preeminent fighter tactician. After serving briefly with Mitscher, Thach said that the admiral "had his own convictions and he didn't see the need to hear from anybody else much."

But there were similarities between Mitscher and Spruance: Both were soft-spoken, courteous, and thoughtful of subordinates. Neither sought publicity, though both received much. Both thoroughly disliked "navalese." Mitscher would seldom read official documents and Spruance preferred to write or rewrite his own.

If Mitscher's failings were known, so were his strengths, especially his leadership. Few commanders were so devoted to their men, and Task Force 58's fliers and sailors knew that Marc Mitscher had their welfare on his mind every waking hour.

When Guam was secured he arranged for two Chamorro mess stewards to go ashore and search for relatives. He loved his aviators, and they returned the sentiment. Seldom one for pep talks, he often invited a squadron leader or air group commander to the flag bridge for a firsthand strike report. But he was fond of ensigns, too. He said, "You can train a combat pilot for fifty thousand dollars. But never, ever tell a pilot that. We can't buy pilots with money . . . each of these boys is captain of his own ship. What he thinks, his confidence in what he is doing, how hard he presses home the attack is exactly how effective we are. Such pilots are not cheap." Thus, for reasons of morale as well as economy, Mitscher placed tremendous importance on search-and-rescue operations.

Mitscher's strength as a leader was also his greatest fault—a pathological loyalty to his subordinates. Apparently it never occurred to him that someone he liked could prove inept or deceitful. After Midway he retained *Hornet's* incompetent air group commander through two subsequent assignments, ensuring that the officer received the Navy Cross and endorsing falsehoods in the ship's action report.

By 1944 Nimitz's faith in Mitscher had been restored, perhaps because of his own misplaced sense of loyalty. Long after the war, naval historians argued the wisdom of CinCPac's retaining Bull Halsey after the Leyte Gulf debacle and losses in two hurricanes. However, Mitscher was clearly at his best with a seagoing command, and both Nimitz and King considered him indispensable conning the fast carriers.

The magnitude of Mitscher's command is evident in the numbers. In June 1944 his fifteen fast carriers represented half of those afloat; America had seven more thirty-knot flattops on the way, while Britain and Japan possessed six and three, respectively. In total carrier strength, the U.S. Navy's eighty-five represented almost 60 percent of the world total.

But Task Force 58's strength was reckoned in far more than tonnage and aircraft. Whereas Mitscher's subordinates at Midway included service politicians, now he had a superb chief of staff in Captain Arleigh Burke, who graduated seventy-first among 412 in the Annapolis class of 1923. A distinguished "blackshoe" surface officer, in contrast to aviators who wore sporty brown shoes, "Thirty-one Knot Burke" had reversed Japan's dominance of nocturnal torpedo fighting in the Solomons. His 1943 victories at Empress Augusta Bay and Cape Saint George were heralded as textbook examples of the destroyer-man's trade.

Nevertheless, Mitscher resented the policy requiring a surface officer as chief of staff for aviation commands. At first Mitscher ignored Burke, almost as if hoping the blackshoe would go away.

Mitscher's previous chief of staff had been Captain Truman J. Hedding, a scholar who stood fifth among 522 in the class of 1924.

Mitscher had known "Duke" Hedding at BuAer almost a decade before and respected his ability. So did those who worked with him: He
had a reputation as an intelligent, thoughtful planner. Nevertheless,
although Mitscher had inherited Hedding as chief of staff upon taking
over Task Force 58, King's directive requiring a blackshoe forced a
role reversal. Mitscher was so upset that he refused to name a replacement, leaving that chore to Hedding. At length Burke was selected,
and Hedding temporarily stepped down.

Arleigh Burke was astonished when he received his new orders.
He said "they came out of the blue." Though familiar with Mitscher, he
knew absolutely nothing about aviation and could not imagine why he
had been selected. He felt that he should begin his aviation appren-
ticeship as "tail gunner in a TBF."

When Hedding returned to the flagship as operations officer,
Burke's chilly reception was a natural topic of discussion. He resented
being treated as an outsider, and said so. Hedding sought to calm him:
"It's a job of great importance," he began, stating the obvious. "In fact,
it's one of the best jobs in the Pacific. He's hard to understand at first,
but he's a great man."

Arleigh Burke puffed on his pipe and smoldered some more. But
over time Burke's intellect and common sense became evident; the ultimate brownshoe and blackshoe officers forged a strong, lasting alliance.

Captain Ernest W. Litch kept a taut line on board *Lexington*, as
would be expected of an admiral's flagship. Frankly, morale on "the
Blue Ghost" was not merely good; it was stratospheric.

One reason was the West of Tokyo Missionary Society, open to
self-styled "evangelists" who had carried "the Word" west of the
140th Meridian, which runs through Tokyo. Since Air Group 16 had
attacked the Palaus in March, "Lady Lex" was eligible, though the target lay twenty-four hundred statute miles south of the enemy capital.
Membership card number one was held by now–Lieutenant General
Jimmy Doolittle; number two belonged to Marc Mitscher. "Priests" of
the society formally forswore liquor and women while aboard ship—
an oath easily kept in the latter instance but less fervently observed in
the former.

Morale also touched the overhead in flag country, as *Lexington*'s flag plot was the nerve center of Task Force 58. Manned around the clock, it was the focus of twelve to twenty men at a time among the 140 total, rotating in and out of the watch bill. But flag plot was always crowded: A large chart table dominated the compartment, while the bulkheads sported status boards (friendly, enemy, and unknown), repeaters for compasses and radar scopes, and high- and low-frequency radio sets.

Mitscher kept his finger on Task Force 58's pulse within a small area of the ship. He lived on the "03 level," three decks above the main (hangar) deck and two tiers up from the flight deck. His usual haunts were flag plot and the wing of the bridge, though occasionally he visited radar plot aft of flag plot. His tiny sea cabin also was nearby. It was an extraordinarily efficient system: Mitscher ruled much of the Pacific Ocean from an area that could be covered on foot in less than a minute.

Mitscher's subordinates were, with one exception, longtime aviators. Most had been flying since the 1920s and knew their trade thoroughly. Their leadership styles ranged from low-key to explosive, but they got results. And that was what counted.

Mitscher shared *Lexington* with Rear Admiral John W. Reeves, commanding Task Group 58.3. Reeves (Annapolis 1911) was a latecomer to aviation, winning his wings at age forty-eight in 1936. Previously captain of the first *Wasp* (CV-7), he ran the Northwest Sea Frontier before rising to task group command. "Stern, steady, dependable" was how Samuel Eliot Morison described him, though "stern" may have been understatement. Reeves's nickname was "Black Jack" for his temperament. In addition to Lady Lex he had the veteran *Enterprise* plus light carriers *Princeton* ("Sweet Pea") and *San Jacinto* ("San Jack" or "Flagship of the Texas Navy").

A year junior to Reeves was Alfred E. Montgomery, a Nebraskan commanding Task Group 58.2. He was a rarity: a "double-dipped" specialist rated to wear submariner's dolphins and aviator wings. He learned to fly in 1922 and eventually commanded *Ranger* (CV-4), the first American carrier built as such from the keel up. Reeves was commander of the huge naval air training complex at Corpus Christi, Texas, before gaining his task group command in August 1943. He did well at Kwajalein with *Essex*, then hoisted his flag in *Bunker Hill* ("Holiday Express") with *Wasp, Monterey,* and *Cabot* ("Iron Woman").

Leading Task Group 58.1 was the colorful, combative Joseph J. Clark, at fifty the youngest of Mitscher's commanders. "Jocko" Clark hailed from Oklahoma, boasting a proud Cherokee heritage. Few people would have taken Clark for an Annapolis man. Loud, profane, and dogmatic, he was said to resemble a frontier desperado more than a naval officer. He graduated from Annapolis in 1918 and, though he waited seven years to win his wings, he was all aviator. He had an escort carrier in the invasion of North Africa, then placed the new *Yorktown* (CV-10) in commission in April 1943. Jocko Clark placed his stamp on his ship as few captains ever did. Though he was promoted to task group command in January 1944, "the Fighting Lady" remained Jocko's boat. Even after moving his flag to the second *Hornet* (CV-12), he would gaze wistfully at CV-10 and mutter, "Gosh, that's a beauty-ful ship!" His two light carriers (CVLs) were *Belleau Wood* and *Bataan.*

Commanding Task Group 58.4 was William K. Harrill, a courtly Tennessean out of the class of 1914. An aviator since 1921, like Montgomery he commanded *Ranger* and organized carrier replacement squadrons on the West Coast. Harrill proved technically competent, but his tenure was short-lived. Known as a worrier tending toward indecision, he came down with appendicitis on June 28 and was replaced. Meanwhile, "Keen" Harrill's bobtailed group contained only *Essex, Cowpens* ("Mighty Moo"), and *Langley.*

As a group, the fifteen captains who conned Mitscher's flattops were an impressive lot. Eleven had finished in the upper half of their classes (1918–21), while the median figure was the twenty-ninth percentile. Two were academy superstars: Ralph Ofstie of *Essex* and *Enterprise's* Matt Gardner finished tenth and thirteenth among 199 ensigns in the class of 1919. However, academic excellence did not guarantee leadership ability (Mitscher was 108th of 131 in his class). Inevitably there were goats among the rams.

A case in point was the second *Hornet*'s (CV-12) original skipper. Captain Miles Browning was an abrasive officer out of the class of 1918, known for his intellect and ego. He had been Halsey's chief of staff in 1942 and remained to serve under Spruance at Midway. But Browning was a driver, an egomaniac convinced of his own infallibility. After failing to follow procedure looking for a sailor missing from *Hornet*, he was beached. "Horney Maru" did not miss him in the least.

Browning's successor was a breath of fresh air to CV-12. William D. Sample, who graduated well up in the class of 1919, came aboard in May and began turning the ship around. He kept his men informed, looked after their welfare, and brought morale up from the keel where it had sulked under Browning. In a speech to the crew he later said, "You came up to my expectations in every way in our recent operations. You did a great job. You delivered the goods to the satisfaction of our task group commander, Rear Admiral Clark."

Vice Admiral Willis A. Lee commanded seven fast battleships in Task Group 58.7, none over three years old. "Ching" Lee was a sharpshooting Kentuckian who acquired his nickname for his vaguely Oriental features and wire-rim glasses. In May 1944 he had just turned fifty-six but had lost none of his prowess. According to NRA legend, Midshipman Lee joined a pickup revolver team at the 1907 national championships and walked off with the trophy. He also won the rifle championship that year, the only shooter ever to claim both honors. He had finished Annapolis in 1908 and, as per regulations in those days, he was commissioned two years later and continued shooting. An international marksman, he won five gold medals in the 1920 Olympics. In the 1930s he headed the Navy's gunnery and tactics boards, a rare instance of the right man in the right job.

Off Guadalcanal in November 1942, Lee fought a memorable engagement in defense of hard-pressed Marines ashore. Leading two battleships and four destroyers that had never worked together, he tackled thirteen Japanese ships in a nocturnal slugfest. He lost three "tin cans" but sank a battlewagon and a destroyer, the first major U.S. surface victory in forty-four years. Receiving his third star in March 1944, he trolled the Pacific in search of another gunfight.

The crucial fleet auxiliaries—oilers, supply ships, and transports—were similarly fresh from America's teeming, nonstop maritime industry. On both coasts, shipyards worked what a later generation would call "twenty-four/seven." Three shifts, around the clock, with few vacations. Ringing with pneumatic hammers and sparking with welding torches, they were a Neptune's Vulcan forge. No other nation came close to matching U.S. naval construction: probably no combination of nations. Assembly-line production was the specialty of industrial genius Henry Kaiser, whose Pacific Northwest yards produced fifty-two CVEs in twelve months. Liberty ships were welded together in as little as five days. Japan simply could not compete.

Mitscher's staff began pulling together before departing on Forager. The biggest change was the admiral's attitude toward his chief of staff.

After his frosty reception, Arleigh Burke began seeking a way to increase his credibility with the brownshoes. He decided to cadge some hops and valiantly flew on two combat missions: a TBF mining operation to close a harbor in the Palaus and an "inspection" tour of Hollandia, New Guinea, in the backseat of an SBD. The latter caught some flak, and though Mitscher chastened his venturesome chief of staff, the admiral was pacified when the "blackshoe" declared that the flying machine was here to stay.

Burke also did some adjusting, especially toward a lowly reserve lieutenant (junior grade) named Charles A. Sims. Almost from the day he reported aboard the flagship, Burke noticed that Sims bypassed the usual protocol, ignoring the chain of command and walking straight up to Mitscher. Sometimes they stepped into the flag spaces where no one could hear them. The admiral obviously approved of the nonregulation arrangement, and finally Burke could hold his tongue no more. Essentially, he asked Mitscher, "What's with this reserve jaygee?"

Mitscher regarded Burke, then said, "I have orders not to discuss this with anybody who's not already cleared." He paused to consider the situation, then decided that his chief of staff needed to be cut into the loop. Mitscher hailed Sims, informing the secretive young officer that Captain Burke should be cleared for full disclosure. Sims blanched; the more people who knew a secret, the less likely the knowledge could be preserved. But Mitscher was insistent, and Sims disappeared into his arcane spaces to send coded messages up the naval food chain.

A prompt reply descended from CinCPac, Nimitz's domain in Hawaii. Arleigh Burke was let in on one of the fleet's major secrets. Sims was Mitscher's window on the enemy. He was a double-dipped golden boy despite his junior status: a linguist and cryptanalyst who consulted all manner of sources to compile a comprehensive picture of Japanese capabilities and intentions. While signals traffic, prisoner interrogations, and captured documents were invaluable, Sims could do even more. He had the ability to eavesdrop on Japanese radio frequencies and provide real-time information on enemy activities. Burke immediately recognized his enormous value, and regarded the impertinent youngster with new respect.

In other cases, Mitscher still needed convincing. Despite his extensive aviation background, he remained skeptical of carrier-based night fighters, which sometimes forced overworked plane handlers to "respot" the deck after each evolution. It was not an unusual attitude among carrier captains and group commanders. Finally PacFleet established full-time night air groups and the concept was proven beyond doubt. In the meantime, each big-deck carrier had a small night-fighter detachment that rubbed the air department the wrong way.

However, the night owls had a friend at court. The task force air operations officer, Commander William J. Widhelm, had commanded a land-based night fighter outfit in the Solomons and was evangelic in his support. Finally he stage-managed a convincing display. He got Mitscher onto the wing of the bridge one night while a snooper droned overhead, seemingly untouchable. Widhelm picked up the mike and said, "Now!" Twenty thousand feet up, a Night Hellcat pilot heard the word and pressed his trigger. The Betty he had been stalking erupted into flames, torching toward the water.

Pete Mitscher was suitably impressed.

The Gargoyle

IN THE SAME MONTH THAT Mitscher assumed command of Task Force 58, his opposite number also "fleeted up." On March 1, 1944, Vice Admiral Jisaburo Ozawa established the First Mobile Fleet: an optimistic title, considering that there was never a second.

Actually, Ozawa was counterpart to both Spruance and Mitscher, wearing two hats as fleet and a task force commander. It was not an enviable situation. Apart from far fewer assets, Ozawa commanded a force ill prepared for a major engagement.

Ozawa was a moon-faced officer of imposing appearance; at two meters tall, he was huge for a Japanese. One of his carrier skippers said, "Ozawa was probably the most courageous officer in the Imperial Navy. He . . . interpreted Horatio Nelson in terms of the Samurai code and lived accordingly."

Though Ozawa's colleagues considered him one of the three ugliest admirals in the Imperial Navy (his nickname was "Gargoyle"), few criticized his intellect. He was fifty-seven in 1944, product of the thirty-seventh naval academy class (1909), two years behind Spruance at Annapolis. Ozawa's professional credentials were solid: A torpedo specialist, he had commanded two destroyers, a destroyer division, a cruiser, and a battleship.

Ozawa was known as a capable, thoughtful commander, but history consistently underrates him. He knew his enemy: He spent most of 1930 touring Europe and America. He was Combined Fleet chief of staff in 1937–38, gaining position and influence that he used to excellent effect.

Despite his conventional career path, Ozawa was extremely open-minded toward aviation. In 1939–40, urged by subordinates such as Lieutenant Commander Mitsuo Fuchida, he advocated concentrating Japan's carriers into a unified striking force—something that had never been done in any navy. Prophetically, Admiral Isoruku Yamamoto granted approval in December 1940 and got the accolades. But Ozawa helped make it happen, and seldom received credit for his strategic vision.

Upon promotion to vice admiral in 1940, Ozawa became president of the Etajima academy but received a fleet assignment the next year.

With war looming in 1941, the Gargoyle returned to sea with a major command: the Southern Expeditionary Fleet that seized Malaya and the Dutch East Indies. A year later he relieved Vice Admiral Chuichi Nagumo—victor at Pearl Harbor, loser at Midway—as ComThirdFleet, including most of Japan's carriers.

As fleet commander, Ozawa showed the same type of freethinking as he had four years previously, when he advocated consolidating six carriers under one command. Now, instead of remaining tied to the usual "type command" structure, he integrated battleships and cruisers with his carrier groups. In 1940 Ozawa had been a world-class innovator. But in 1944 he was following the American example, with good reason: The U.S. fast carrier task force had become the global standard for a balanced naval striking arm.

Ozawa organized the Mobile Fleet into three units that Americans would recognize as task groups, each with three flattops. He personally led A Force, built around Carrier Division One, including his flagship *Taiho* (Great Phoenix), at 34,600 tons the biggest Japanese carrier. CarDiv One also included the 20,000-ton Pearl Harbor veterans *Shokaku* (Flying Crane) and *Zuikaku* (Auspicious Crane).

Few of Ozawa's subordinates possessed anything resembling the aviation experience of Mitscher's task group commanders or carrier captains. Influenced by the Royal Navy, *Nihon Kaigun* did not require carrier skippers to be pilots. However, the deficit in flying experience was partly bridged by high-time staff officers to handle the aviation side of things.

Leading B Force with CarDiv Two, Rear Admiral Takaji Joshima had more varied experience than most of his contemporaries. He had led the transport group that landed reinforcements on Guadalcanal in 1942 and later commanded the Eleventh Air Fleet, a land-based organization in the Solomons. In May 1944 he had the 26,900-ton sisters *Junyo* (Wandering Falcon) and *Hiyo* (Happy Falcon), with 16,700-ton CVL *Ryuho* (Dragon Phoenix).

Though Vice Admiral Takeo Kurita led the vanguard, C Force, he was largely a figurehead. Carrier Division Three was in the capable hands of Rear Admiral Sueo Obayashi, who had commanded the 14,000-ton light carrier *Zuiho* in the Santa Cruz battle. Now she was part of his new command with two other CVLs, *Chitose* and *Chiyoda* (15,000-tonners named for cities). Additionally, Obayashi had conned the battleship *Hyuga*, a rare combination in any navy.

Most carrier skippers were from the forty-fifth to forty-seventh Etajima classes, graduated in 1917–19. Apparently only three of Ozawa's nine carrier captains were aviators. Tomozo Kikuchi of *Taiho* and Toshiyuki Yokoi of *Hiyo* were former flight-school classmates, while *Chiyoda's* Eiichiro Joh was a fighter pilot of slightly later vintage. In fact, Joh had placed her in commission in December; she had known no other skipper.

Some captains were new to carrier command. Two officers— *Chitose's* Yoshiyuki Kishi and *Zuiho's* Takuro Sugiura—had led cruiser and destroyer divisions, respectively. Captain Takeo Kaizuka had been a gunnery specialist in cruisers before taking command of *Hosho*, Japan's training carrier, in mid-1943. At year end he took over *Zuikaku*.

Unlike the Americans, the Japanese Navy relied heavily upon non-commissioned aviators. In 1940 officers represented only about 10 percent of *Kaigun* pilots, either regulars (naval academy graduates), reserves (college graduates) or special service (former enlisted men). The academy men had spent three and a half years at Etajima and another year as midshipmen, whereas others passed almost directly to flying. Consequently, much of the aviation expertise in the Mobile Fleet lay in the hands of warrant officers and senior petty officers.

Sometimes even the rank-conscious Imperial Navy made allowances. In Cruiser Division Four, assigned to Kurita's C Force, Captain Ranii Ooe's *Maya* had an unofficial crew member. The ship's air department had acquired a mascot: a monkey donated by the Kure

Zoo. Being aviators, and noncommissioned aviators at that, the fliers taught their simian shipmate to render a smart salute to senior officers. It is not recorded how Captain Ooe reacted to the gesture, but presumably he was more concerned that his two Aichi floatplanes remained operational.

Two Years from Midway

IN JUNE 1944 JAPAN HAD been losing the war for two years. Since Midway the Imperial Navy had been able only to respond to American initiatives; *Nihon Kaigun*, the emperor's fleet, ventured no major offensives of its own.

During those twenty-four months the war had steamed westward across forty-eight degrees of longitude: from 177 West to 45 East. That's 2,880 nautical miles measured at the equator, an average advance of 120 miles per month. At that rate, Tokyo lay another nineteen months westward. (As things developed, it was fourteen.)

Nevertheless, Japan still controlled much of the Pacific Ocean and the Asian mainland. Its army remained dominant in China, Burma, the East Indies, and the Philippines. Its navy controlled the Western Pacific, though increasingly the area became a hunting ground for PacFleet submarines.

Japan had been unable to sustain its burgeoning population for more than forty years; food imports were essential. That fact was well-known to Admiral Chester Nimitz, who directed growing numbers of long-range fleet submarines to sink Japanese merchant shipping. By mid-1944 the strangulation was beginning to take hold. But not only food was affected. As hundreds of ships went to the bottom, so did strategic materials scarce or lacking in the home islands, including oil, rubber, iron ore, and copper.

Though Japan's industrial base had accelerated production of everything from bayonets to bombers, it was not enough: Tokyo had managed to outrage a nation with seventeen times its gross national product. But aside from the industrial deficit was the human element. Japan entered the war with about thirty-five hundred trained naval aviators; America had about eight thousand. The disparity only increased over the next two years.

Meanwhile, the rate of material attrition was unrelenting. In the thirty-six weeks between April 1943 and February 1944 the Imperial Navy lost thirty-three warships. Furthermore, new construction was hampered by valuable shipyard space devoted to repairing damaged vessels. In short, Japan started at a deficit and lagged farther behind with each passing month.

Though fighting a two-ocean war, the U.S. Navy still brought enormous power to the Marianas. The U-boat war required destroyers and escort carriers in the Atlantic, where battleships and fast carriers were unnecessary. And although American amphibious groups supported invasions in Morocco, Sicily, Italy, and northern and southern France, more than seventy opposed landings were executed in the Pacific. It says a great deal for American productivity that major "'phib" operations were made on opposite sides of the globe within nine days of one another.

In June 1944 the United States Navy counted 46,032 ships (over two hundred feet in length), vessels, and small craft to fight a global war. The Navy itself disposed of 2,981,365 men and women, augmented by 472,582 Marines and 169,258 Coast Guardsmen. The Navy and Marine Corps possessed 47,000 pilots for 34,000 aircraft. Overall, the 3.6 million naval personnel amounted to about one-third of America's military strength.

On Japan's side, *Bushido* spirit and a martial culture were expected to make up the deficit. They did not.

The path to the Marianas involved a separate battle of its own. It was fought furiously, passionately, and sometimes bitterly. It pitted two old rivals against each other: the United States Army and the United States Navy.

Admiral Ernest J. King and the Navy hierarchy favored seizing Formosa (now Taiwan), by far the largest island between the Philippines and Japan. King, with Nimitz, argued that a naval attack on Japan's shrinking perimeter was best served by taking Formosa, partly because that route was logistically more supportable than a circuitous approach from the south. En route, it was necessary and desirable to take the Marianas.

As early as January 1943, King had told the Allied Combined Chiefs that the Marianas were "key to the situation" because of their position to interdict Japanese sea-lanes. The Army Air Forces chief, General Henry "Hap" Arnold, was supportive: He knew that his growing fleet of B-29s could make good use of Marianas airfields.

General Douglas MacArthur, the former Army chief of staff and prewar Philippine field marshal, insisted on keeping his 1942 pledge to return to the islands. In support of his personal ambition, the vainglorious general found more practical reasons for his plan. Like Formosa, the Philippines were strategically positioned, but their people had direct ties to America. Formosa, on the other hand, had belonged to the Japanese empire since 1895. MacArthur insisted that American honor required early liberation of the Filipinos, who had suffered under Tokyo's brutal oppression for two years.

Though the interservice feud continued into the summer, the calendar required a decision about the Marianas. On March 12 the Joint Chiefs issued MacArthur and Nimitz their running orders. MacArthur was to drop his planned attack on Kavieng in the northern Solomons and further reduce Rabaul, New Britain, by aerial siege. His amphibious forces were aimed at Hollandia, New Guinea, with the landings slated for April 15. The size of the undertaking would require intratheater cooperation, so Nimitz was obliged to provide his support. Consequently, he would bypass the enemy bastion at Truk in the Carolines. But MacArthur was required to return the naval forces to PacFleet control no later than May 5.

Subsequently, Nimitz was directed to seize the southern Marianas, preferably beginning June 15. The islands of Saipan, Guam, and Tinian were sufficient for operating large numbers of Boeing B-29s, which would transfer from China, where the logistics problems were debilitating.

Nimitz's staff wasted no time preparing for the Marianas conquest, dubbed Operation Forager. In barely a week his planners had the basics on paper.

On a map, the American plan became obvious. With Nimitz advancing across the Central Pacific and MacArthur upward through New Guinea, the two theater commanders would be poised to merge at Douglas MacArthur's self-appointed destiny: liberation of the Philippines. That campaign was expected to commence in the fall.

A Full-contact Sport

As IN ANY MILITARY ORGANIZATION, each sailor and airman fit into an orderly, disciplined framework, but some were better trained; others were better led and likely more motivated. And as in any drama, motivation counted for a great deal off Saipan. The Japanese were defending the outer rampart of their empire: Drawing a straight line almost due north, only Iwo Jima in the Bonins stood between the Marianas and Tokyo.

For most of the Americans, whether "snipes" in the engineering spaces, lookouts perched topside, or shooters in Hellcats and Avengers, Saipan represented "another damned island." It was one step closer to the ultimate battle expected on Japanese soil sometime in 1945 or 1946. What distinguished the upcoming battle as Task Force 58 drew nearer the Marianas was a chance to come to grips with the Imperial Navy. Two of the six carriers that had committed the Sunday murders on December 7 were still afloat. Off Saipan in June 1944, the youngsters manning Admiral Raymond Spruance's warships anticipated their appointment with history.

Aboard ship, pilots and aircrews spent most of their downtime in the squadron ready room. Generally located beneath the flight deck, ready rooms were at once the operational and social center of each squadron. Padded leather chairs resembling theater seats were provided with folding trays that could be laid across the arms as a writing platform. Beneath the seat was a built-in drawer for assorted gear and personal items.

At the head of each ready room was a large screen that clacked out Teletype messages: everything from navigational and weather data to current events and the latest "hot dope" from Rumor Central. From the overhead frequently dangled one-seventy-second scale models to sharpen fliers' recognition skills. The bulkheads were festooned with flight gear, squadron emblems, and leggy Vargas pinups with saucy smiles, sculpted derrieres, and perfect breasts. Today they seem quaint; sixty years ago they were considered racy. Overall, the ambience was a cross between a locker room whose team played an especially violent full-contact sport, and a fraternity house where admission was based on surviving more than a year of intense training, and acceptance was ceded only to those who could "hack the program." A pilot or gunner who couldn't hold his own in the crucible of the ready room was ill prepared to fly and fight for any star-spangled banner.

Ready rooms also offered pleasant diversions: endless card games (acey-deucy was almost de rigueur), bull sessions (women and flying and women), a coffee urn and cold cuts in the back, and occasionally air-conditioning. Good squadron skippers worked hard at building and maintaining morale, and some advocated old-fashioned sing-alongs. The topics of ready room doggerel often took two forms:

Oh, those who want to be a hero, they number almost zero.
Those who want to be civilians—Jesus! They number in the millions.

Then there was flying:

Oh, I wanted wings and I got the damn things and I don't want them anymore.
I want my hand around a bottle, and not around a throttle. Oh, I don't want to fly anymore.

Some flying songs were specific:

> *Oh, Mother, dear Mother, take down that blue star,*
> *Replace it with one that is gold.*
> *Your son is a Helldiver pilot;*
> *He'll never be thirty years old.*
> *The people who work for Curtiss*
>   *are frequently seen good and drunk.*
> *One day with an awful hangover,*
>   *they mustered and designed that clunk.*

House of the Setting Sun

THE IMPERIAL NAVY RECOGNIZED THE impending clash but could not convince the Army. General Hideki Tojo, jointly prime minister and army minister, dismissed naval concerns as "feverish" or "hysterical." Convinced that the Americans could not muster the necessary strength, he declined to allot any Imperial Army units to the Marianas.

Tojo's attitude was all too familiar to his navy counterparts. Interservice rivalry—virtually a full-contact sport in Japan—led in amazing directions. The Japanese Army developed its own aircraft carriers, actually ferries not intended to launch or recover planes. Additionally, the Japanese Army established its own submarine school (for supplying cutoff islands) at a port called Hiroshima.

The Imperial Army's and Navy's differences extended to techniques and equipment that had long since been standardized in other nations. Perhaps the best example was the throttle operation in Japanese aircraft. Heavily influenced by Britain and the Royal Navy before World War I, *Nihon Kaigun* adopted the standard "push to go" arrangement. But the Japanese Army Air Force, impressed with early French aviation, copied the reverse "pull to go" method. It made for interesting viewing when army and navy pilots swapped cockpits.

Ultimately, the Imperial Navy was forced to rely upon its own resources for all but garrison troops. One option was assigned Vice Admiral Kakuji Kakuta, commanding land-based naval aviation in the area. His First Air Fleet contained nearly a thousand planes dispersed throughout the Marianas, Carolines, and Bonins.

The Imperial Navy's institutional background was at once a blessing and a curse. Undefeated in the 350 years prior to Midway, the emperor's fleet dramatically burst upon the world scene in 1905. Admiral Togo's lopsided defeat of the Russian Navy in Tsushima Strait reinforced the concept of the decisive battle: the single blow toward which strategy was aimed to decide a war. Seemingly it had worked, until the morning of June 4, 1942. Since Midway had come other defeats, most notably at Guadalcanal. Yamamoto had presided over Pearl Harbor, Midway, and Guadalcanal: One out of three was not a winning record.

On March 8, 1944, Yamamoto's successor, Admiral Mineichi Koga, set in motion Tokyo's preparation for the Marianas campaign. From his flagship *Musashi* at Palau, five hundred miles east of the Philippines, Koga issued orders for Operation Z, anticipating a decisive battle somewhere in the Central or Western Pacific. The most likely arenas were the Marianas, New Guinea, or the Palaus.

Near month's end, Koga and his staff boarded two long-range flying boats en route to new headquarters at Mindanao. In heavy weather over the Philippines, the big Kawanishis became separated. Koga's plane disappeared in the storm; his fate remains unknown.

Koga's chief of staff also went down as Vice Admiral Shigeru Fukodome's aircraft stalled and spun into the water off Cebu. Fukodome and some crewmen survived the crash but were picked up by Filipino guerrillas who delivered the admiral and his briefcase to Lieutenant Colonel James Cushing, a freewheeling American of Irish-Mexican extraction who had married a Filipina before the war.

Fukodome's injuries prevented quick evacuation, and the Japanese Army spared no effort to retrieve the errant admiral. In typical fashion, the Japanese threatened to kill hostages and burn villages unless the officers were returned. Given the Imperial Army's reputation, the threat was easily believed. Moreover, the vastly outnumbered guerrillas on Cebu had no chance of winning a stand-up fight.

Therefore, Cushing released Fukodome but sent the briefcase to MacArthur in Brisbane. MacArthur was livid: From three thousand miles away he radioed a scathing message reducing Lieutenant Colonel Cushing to private. Nevertheless, Cushing remained the popular leader of his band and was reinstated after the war.

Succeeding Koga as Combined Fleet commander was fifty-nine-year-old Admiral Soemu Toyoda, simultaneously counterpart to Nimitz as CinCPac and the U.S. chief of naval operations, Admiral Ernest J. King in Washington. Toyoda and King shared more than responsibility for their respective navies—both were abrasive, hard-nosed officers, drivers more than leaders. It was said of King that he shaved with a blowtorch; Toyoda was known for driving his subordinates to nervous breakdowns.

Toyoda had helped build the prewar Imperial Navy, serving as director of construction from 1939 to 1941. He was well regarded as a naval academy instructor, a position befitting his intellect. Yet for all his brains, Toyoda lacked saltwater experience during the war. Consequently, his chief of staff was selected from a distinguished naval family. Rear Admiral Ryunosuke Kusaka and his cousin Junichi Kusaka both were stationed at Rabaul, New Britain. But Rabaul was besieged by Allied aircraft, limiting an evacuation to a nocturnal flight. Toyoda's future chief of staff boarded a bomber after suitable fortification: a toast with Johnnie Walker Black Label, once the symbol of Japanese conquest of the Anglo-Saxons.

A predawn fighter sweep nearly caught Kusaka's bomber in its 0400 takeoff. The Americans passed so closely that the admiral glimpsed the enemy pilots in their cockpits, but they failed to spot him. Thanking his lucky stars, he continued to Truk in the Carolines, then onward to Saipan. There Kusaka was briefly reunited with his former commander, Vice Admiral Chuichi Nagumo, victor at Pearl and vanquished at Midway. Kusaka was dismayed at the minimal assets at Saipan and Guam. The area was mainly garrisoned by the army, which seemed largely disinterested. Upon arrival in Tokyo he made a priority of bolstering the defense of the Marianas.

Kusaka spoke with the authority of thirty-one years' service. An early aviator, he had commanded two carriers and an air flotilla. Prime Minister Tojo finally recognized the enormous threat posed by the most lethal bomber of the Second World War, and pledged himself to the defense of Saipan.

Meanwhile, American plans were well in hand. In late April and early June, Liberators flew long-range reconnaissance missions from Eniwetok. The four-engine bombers returned with valuable photos of Saipan. So thorough was the recon scheme that the PB4Y crews flew at low level off the beaches, taking oblique shots that represented the view from a ship offshore.

After further planning, the Imperial Navy satisfied itself with a defensive strategy for holding the empire's inner circle. In early May Toyoda distributed his orders: The Palaus were to be the decisive area, but if the Americans sailed for the Marianas, the enemy should be enticed southward to save the Imperial Navy increasingly rare fuel and to retain the advantage of land-based air.

Toyoda's May 4 dispatch positively reeked of forced optimism. He lauded officers and men who "voluntarily sacrificed their lives and inflicted great damage on the enemy" while conceding that the selfsame "crushed" enemy had somehow recovered and "moved over to a full-scale counterattack."

Conceding that "the issue of our national existence is unprecedentedly serious," Toyoda saw the upcoming engagement as opportunity for yet another decisive battle. After putting an Olympian spin on an impending disaster, the commander in chief finished with a Nelsonian exhortation: "Realizing the gravity of responsibility for the fate of our Empire, with its history of more than twenty-six hundred years, full of reverence for the glory of the Imperial Throne and trusting in the help of God, I will endeavor to comply with the Emperor's wishes."

Whether the CinC believed any of his rhetoric, he clearly recognized that the upcoming battle was of enormous importance.

* * *

On May 10 Operation A-Go was set in motion. At Singapore the ships of Carrier Division One fired their boilers and got up steam, the capstans rolling in fathoms of anchor chain. In a matter of hours Vice Admiral Jisaburo Ozawa's force of three carriers plus escorts hoisted anchor and departed Lingga Roads for a harbor called Tawi-Tawi.

In 1944 Tawi-Tawi was among the most obscure places on earth. The southernmost harbor in the Philippine archipelago, it bordered the Sulu Sea between Mindanao and Borneo. In fact, the name Tawi-Tawi derived from the Malay word *jaui*, meaning "far." It truly was far—far from anyplace most Americans or Japanese had heard of, having been settled by Muslim evangelicals in the fourteenth century. It was much better known to turtles, dolphins, and whales.

Meanwhile, well to the north, Rear Admiral Takaji Joshima's CarDiv Two and Rear Admiral Sueo Obayashi's CarDiv Three, with six more carriers, left home waters a day or so later, refueling en route off Okinawa. The fleet was formed at Tawi-Tawi on the sixteenth, ultimately comprising nine carriers, five battleships, thirteen cruisers, and twenty-plus destroyers. The crucial fueling group totaled six oilers and seven escorts.

One advantage of Tawi-Tawi was proximity to nearby oil fields, a fact that Ozawa knew well: He had supervised the Borneo landings in 1941–42. Two years later, the attentions of American submarines upon Japanese shipping had made Tawi-Tawi of more than geographic interest, as its Tarakan crude oil was capable of being used "raw" without refining. Though heavy in sulfur that could damage boilers, it was an important factor in Ozawa's planning. Lacking sufficient refined bunker oil, Japan welcomed unprocessed fuel. Presumably the ships' engineering plants could be repaired after the battle.

There was a downside, however: Tarakan crude was highly volatile, posing a serious risk in the event of battle damage.

Warm-ups

ON MAY 15 REAR ADMIRAL Alfred E. Montgomery left Majuro with the impromptu Task Group 58.6, a temporary organization composed of three new carriers plus five cruisers and a dozen destroyers. Mitscher wanted his newest air groups to gain some experience before the Saipan showdown, so Marcus Island was targeted in "warm-up" strikes with the fleet carriers *Essex* and *Wasp*, and the light carrier *San Jacinto*.

Marcus was a Pacific waypoint: a thousand miles southeast of Tokyo and a similar distance northeast of Saipan. As such, it represented a crossroads that drew repeated visitations from American carrier groups.

Launch commenced early on the nineteenth beneath a breezy overcast, led by the skipper of *Wasp*'s air group, Commander Walter Wingard Jr. There was little opposition, though several planes were struck by automatic weapons fire. The second attack was directed by Commander David McCampbell, *Essex*'s new air group commander (CAG). This time the Japanese were better prepared: They shot down McCampbell's wingman and a VB-15 Helldiver.

Following en route strikes against much-bombed Wake Island on the twenty-third, the carriers proceeded to Majuro, where they rejoined Task Force 58.

While Montgomery was exercising at Marcus, in Tokyo Admiral Toyoda put his forces on six-hour notice for A-Go. Ozawa used the opportunity to convene a meeting for his Mobile Fleet commanders. His staff and the division commanders' staffs met aboard the flagship *Taiho* to discuss plans for the Marianas engagement.

Various options were considered, including the typically Japanese policy of dispersing forces to confuse and possibly trap the enemy. But Ozawa was wiser than that: He knew that dispersion had been the major flaw of Yamamoto's Midway plan, and it was difficult enough coordinating task groups without spreading them over the Pacific. He decided on a compromise: Vice Admiral Kurita's C Force with Rear Admiral Obayashi's CarDiv Three would form the vanguard, drawing the Americans' immediate attention. Trailing about a hundred miles astern would be the main body: Ozawa's and Joshima's A and B Forces built around CarDivs One and Two, respectively.

Beyond that, the fleet commander had some sober comments. He told his subordinates that their units undoubtedly would become "expendable" against the might of the Americans.

The Americans did not allow Tokyo much breathing space for Operation Z/A-Go. On May 27 they landed at Biak in the Schouten Islands, across the entrance to Geelvink Bay in Dutch New Guinea. The Japanese responded with Operation Kon, seaborne reinforcement of Biak's garrison that, while partly successful, could not retrieve the situation. Elements of the U.S. Sixth Army slogged through the jungles and swamps for two months before securing Biak. By that time A-Go had been launched, fought, and lost.

Antisubmarine Actions

MEANWHILE, AMERICAN DESTROYERS savaged the Japanese submarine force.

Vice Admiral Takeo Takagi commanded the Sixth Fleet, Japan's primary submarine command. In late May his order of battle listed two dozen big I- and smaller RO-class boats deployed throughout the Central and Western Pacific.

Japan produced some of the most capable submarines of World War II—and used them less efficiently than almost any other navy. Submarine doctrine was oriented toward supporting the surface fleet with attacks on enemy warships, in contrast to the U.S. and German philosophies, which targeted the merchant marine.

Nevertheless, a few of Takagi's subs were extremely successful. Among his ace boats was *I-10*, commissioned in October 1941 and immediately assigned to the Oahu task force. The big 2,400-tonner had exceptional range—16,000 miles on the surface—and could operate one or two small aircraft for reconnaissance flights. But with a succession of skippers, *I-10* made an enviable record against Allied shipping. From 1942 onward she sank sixteen vessels from six nations, totaling nearly 90,000 tons. Her current skipper was Commander Seiji Nakajima, who had not scored since taking command in January. Her two sister boats already had been sunk; she would follow before long.

Nine boats were deployed in two patrol lines extending 250 miles north and east of the Admiralties. Losses, already heavy, were about to reach disastrous proportions.

Fortunately for the Americans, among the submarines sunk en route to the Marianas that spring was one carrying a cargo far more lethal than torpedoes. The Japanese Army's notorious Unit 731 had brewed a devil's smorgasbord of biological weapons, including bubonic plague. Containers full of fleas carrying the bacteria were dispatched with seventeen men of the Manchurian unit, intended for Saipan. The porcelain containers were to be air-dropped on American troops coming ashore, though Tokyo had signed the 1925 Geneva Protocol prohibiting offensive use of chemical and biological weapons. Fighting for its existence, the Tojo government felt no constraint against using banned weapons. Only after the war did the horrific nature of Unit 731's experiments become known.

Though the identity of the submarine carrying the plague weapons is unknown, its loss may have saved more Japanese lives than American. Had Tokyo pulled the stopper off the biological weapons bottle, the American genie would almost certainly have been loosed as well.

Seven of Admiral Takagi's boats were sunk from mid-May to early June; six in fourteen days by the destroyer escort *England* under Commander Walton B. Pendleton, an Annapolis man.

Pendleton was an old-timer—class of 1921—but he was one of just two regular officers aboard. *England* was still new, only five months in commission, but the skipper worked his 185-man crew into a well-oiled machine. A hunting, killing machine. Upon joining Escort Division 39 in the Solomons, the cocky, aggressive crew cheerfully went to work slaying imperial submariners.

Five of the victims were RO-class subs, two hundred feet long with seventy-five-man crews. The other was *I-16*, first of the prewar class of big, capable boats some 350 feet in length with a hundred-man crew.

England favored the hedgehog projector, which had tactical advantages over depth charges. With forward-firing salvos of sixty-five-pound hedgehogs, the destroyer could maintain sonar contact with the target, whereas tracking was lost when rolling depth charges off the stern. Though much smaller than DCs, the hedgehogs' thirty-five-pound warheads had the advantage of striking the submarine rather than detonating hydrostatically.

England's feat was an unexcelled achievement in antisubmarine warfare. Three months earlier, when Britain's ace hunter-killer group claimed six U-boats in nineteen days, the force was showered with honors and attention. Walt Pendleton eventually received the Navy Cross while Chief of Naval Operations (CNO) Ernie King declared, "There'll always be an *England* in the U.S. Navy."

In all, during May and June the Japanese lost seventeen of the twenty-five subs deployed in the Southwest and Central Pacific. Consequently, A-Go was largely deprived of its submarine arm before the carrier battle was joined.

Though surface hunter-killers did most of the execution, two sinkings were accomplished by aircraft. Lieutenant Commander Yasuo Enomoto's *RO-117* had left Truk for Saipan, but early on the seventeenth he was surprised on the surface by a VPB-109 Liberator out of Eniwetok. The patrol plane commander, Lieutenant William B. Bridgeman, conducted an attack that yielded questionable results, resulting in a "possible damage" claim. After the war it was evident that Bridgeman's aim had been lethal: The boat took all fifty-five men to the bottom.

Two days later—the same day as the fleet engagement off Saipan—the escort carrier *Suwannee* got on the board. A Torpedo Squadron 60 pilot, Ensign Guy E. Sabin, was patrolling twenty miles southeast of Saipan but wanted better visibility. He got it. When he descended beneath the cloud deck he sighted *I-184* and made the most of a rare opportunity. He dived to the attack, but Lieutenant Commander Matsuji

Rikihisa saw the Avenger coming and ordered a crash dive, submerging just before Sabin got in range. Undeterred, the aviator dropped his depth charges forward of the swirling foam and ended the big boat's eight-month career for all ninety-six men aboard.

With his buccaneers hunted to destruction, Toyoda had almost no prospect of a coordinated sea-air strategy. Reportedly one or two imperial submarines made attacks on a U.S. carrier group during the battle, but their efforts went undetected and unrewarded. Unfortunately for the fortunes of Tokyo's warlords, the same would not apply to their enemy.

Fleet Boats

AT THE TIME OF FORAGER the U.S. Navy counted forty-four years' experience with submarines. The many technical problems had been solved in an evolutionary process that sometimes lasted decades. On top of the more immediate concerns were long-term disputes regarding doctrine, tactics, and even politics. In 1941 international conventions still required submarines to operate like commerce raiders of old, stopping merchant ships and searching them before sending them to the bottom. Clearly, that was impractical, even suicidal. On December 7 the U.S. Navy issued an order comparable to Admiral Karl Doenitz's policy from 1939: "Execute unrestricted submarine warfare." In other words, sink on sight.

World War II subs have been accurately described as "submersibles." They were underwater craft capable of diving to three hundred feet or more, but they patrolled and frequently attacked on the surface. They were fast, long-range commerce raiders with the ability to disappear.

Because they operated independently, submarines attracted a contradictory type of officer. The Navy had often been the most conservative service, dominated by generations of admirals from the "gun club." Battleships had been the undisputed instrument of sea power until early in the twentieth century, when German submarines posed a serious threat to Great Britain's lifelines. When America found itself without deployable battlewagons in 1941–42, subs and carriers were the only means of offensive action.

Prewar sub skippers were Annapolis graduates who had served two years in surface billets before entering submarine school. Promoted to command their own boats, they were largely free to fight as much or as little as they liked. Early in the war an unpleasant discovery appeared in form of the "skipper problem": captains who were technically competent but lacked a warlike attitude. Additionally, peacetime training had produced a gamesman mentality among some of the motivated officers. Winning commendations in fleet exercises did not always translate to shooting for blood.

Eventually the problems were solved. Younger, more aggressive officers were promoted to command and began showing results. Whereas the mid-1942 COs hailed from the academy classes of 1925–30, by mid-1944 the skippers were typically from 1931–35. Moreover, at war's end only two of the top twenty captains had graduated before 1930.

Life on a fleet submarine was not for the timid or the claustrophobic. All submariners were selected after thorough psychological screening, but that was only a start. For nearly two months at a time, as many as eighty men lived within the confines of a 312-foot steel tube with far less habitable space than the overall length. The atmosphere stank of varied odors including diesel fuel, sewage, and unwashed bodies. There was never enough water for crew showers (usually cooks got priority), so once in a while the captain held "swim call." A dip in the Pacific was always welcome, but the bathers dived and splashed under the eyes of lookouts and manned deck guns.

Frequently food contributes to morale, and submariners ate well early in a patrol. But the best food went fast because of limited refrigeration space. After that, it was mostly canned or dehydrated fare, which is why innovative cooks and bakers were eagerly sought after. The one constant was coffee—the U.S. Navy ran on "java" nearly as much as fuel oil.

Leadership perhaps counted for more in submarines than anywhere else in the war. The skipper set the tone for the entire crew, and there was simply no way to bluff. Living cheek by jowl for several weeks at a time, often under lethal stress, submariners quickly gauged a man's worth based on his competence and judgment. As in any military organization, a commander didn't have to be popular to be effective, but it's noteworthy that many of the star skippers were beloved by their men: Sam Dealey, "Mush" Morton, and Dick O'Kane, to name a few.

Submariners pursued a dangerous calling, drawing a 50 percent hazardous duty bonus. The seventy- to eighty-man crews were all volunteers, and despite fearsome losses, there was never a shortage of applicants.

Fifty-two American submarines were lost during the war (three in the Atlantic): the highest casualty rate of any U.S. branch. But the appeal of belonging to an elite manifested itself elsewhere. At the end of the European war, when U-boat losses exceeded 75 percent, Admiral Doenitz's boats never lacked for volunteers. Unlike the kaiser's navy, there was no mutiny in Hitler's *Kriegsmarine*.

While Japan's submarine ranks were being thinned, American boats were growing fat on merchantmen and warships alike. The *Gato-Ballao*-class fleet submarine was largely responsible for sinking Japan's merchant marine.

Like the Fifth Fleet, the submarine force also was mainly wartime construction. Sixteen *Gato*-class boats constituted the majority of the twenty-eight supporting Forager, with seven similar vessels of the deeper-diving *Balao* class. The balance were three S types and one each G and P types.

Four diesel engines driving two shafts could call up 6,500 horsepower to make twenty knots surfaced, or, alternately, 240 electric batteries propelled a *Gato* at eight knots submerged. The *Gato*s had a proven 300-foot test depth with a theoretical 50 percent safety factor, meaning 450 feet in an emergency. The sub's "main battery" consisted of six bow and four stern tubes, for a load-out of two dozen twenty-one-inch torpedoes.

In May 1944 twenty-six PacFleet subs departed Pearl Harbor;

thirty-two left in June. Two of the fifty-eight were lost, while thirty-four were successful, sinking eighty Japanese ships of nearly 350,000 gross tons.

American subs based in Australia also were active. Departing Fremantle and Brisbane in May and June were thirty-two boats, of which one never returned. Among the others, twenty-two boats put thirty-nine ships on the bottom, representing 173,500 tons.

By far the most successful skipper was *Tang*'s Richard H. O'Kane out of the class of 1934. In just thirty-six days he claimed eight ships, but postwar assessment upped his tally to ten for nearly 40,000 tons. He made *Tang* a masterkill in the sub force, even though she was lost with most of her crew in October. O'Kane survived to receive the Medal of Honor.

The sub force never sank as many ships as it claimed: typically 70 percent of the sinkings and about half the tonnage. The errors were unavoidable in combat, owing to incomplete information, necessary speculation, and the natural optimism of aggressive young males under lethal stress. However, the results were real enough, especially when damaged ships were added to those destroyed. During May and June, Pearl Harbor boats claimed 107 ships of 659,000 tons and actually got eighty-one for 348,000 tons. Meanwhile, Australia-based subs got thirty-nine of fifty-three claimed sinkings while typically estimating tonnage at more than twice actual.

The undisputed star of SubPac was Commander Samuel D. Dealey, a hard-charging Texan from the class of 1930. He made *Harder* one of the most successful boats of the war, claiming five Japanese destroyers off Tawi-Tawi. Actually he sank three, but few sub skippers relished tangling with enemy destroyers. Sam Dealey scarfed them up and asked for seconds.

Thirty-two-year-old Herman J. Kossler (class of 1934) had a Silver Star from his time as executive officer of *Guardfish*, when skipper Thomas B. Klakring sank ten ships of 33,000 tons. The affable Kossler then took *Cavalla* on her first war patrol in May 1944. He would sink just one ship in a sixty-four-day sortie, and it was a beaut.

Cavalla was probably the newest sub in the fleet. Kossler had placed her in commission in late February and reached the Pacific in early May. He remained her skipper for all six war patrols, sinking three more ships before VJ-day. In mid June she was among the "Speedway" wolf pack patrolling the eastern exits from the Philippines.

In contrast, watching the "Pentathlon" area west of the Marianas was *Albacore*, a veteran boat. Commissioned two years previously by Lieutenant Commander Richard C. Lake, she had sunk five ships in her seven previous patrols from Pearl and Brisbane. Her new skipper, Commander James W. Blanchard (upper half of the class of 1927), had spent most of the war at the New Haven submarine school, "hollering like hell to get out." He had assumed command in late 1943 and took "Applecore" on her next three patrols, sinking six ships versus a wartime claim of eleven. Her forty-eight-day May and June patrol would net two sinkings. One would gain him fame.

During May, U.S. intelligence sniffed out Ozawa's departure from Singapore and concluded that a logical destination was Tawi-Tawi. Therefore, Rear Admiral Ralph C. Christie sent some of his Australian-based boats to investigate the Celebes Sea. Surfaced west of Borneo on May 13, Commander Lowell Stone's *Lapon* got visual confirmation: three carriers, five cruisers, and many destroyers. Stone (class of 1929) pulled the plug at six miles, hoping to line up a shot, but couldn't close inside two and a half miles. He bided his time, surfaced after dark, and radioed the vital contact.

Christie's designated sniffer was *Bonefish* with Lieutenant Commander Thomas W. Hogan, class of 1931. He had found good hunting in the Sulu Sea, sustaining some damage, but was available for reconnaissance. Consequently, Christie ordered Hogan to look at Tawi-Tawi. In the wee hours of the fourteenth he came across a juicy convoy: three big tankers with three escorts. *Bonefish* worked into position and fired five of her last six fish. One speared a tanker and another blew up the destroyer *Inazuma*. The twelve-year-old veteran of Java, the Aleutians, and the Solomons went down with her skipper and 160 men. Another "can" rescued survivors.

Remaining in the area, Hogan trolled forty miles northwest of

Tawi-Tawi in the morning. His periscope revealed the same force that *Lapon* had reported, with the addition of two battleships. *Bonefish* bided her time and surfaced that night, getting off a confirming report to Christie.

The following morning, the fifteenth, the persistent Hogan was back off Tawi-Tawi, nosing close enough to the entrance to get a look. He gawked at what he could see: six carriers, "four or five battleships," eight cruisers, and "many" destroyers. (Actually the Mobile Fleet was fully assembled on the sixteenth.) Again he surfaced after dark to report his find, though the Japanese apparently got a direction-finding fix. Two destroyers charged out of the anchorage to hunt down the intruder. With only one defective torpedo left, Hogan evaded and awaited orders.

On May 22, on a surveillance mission near Tawi-Tawi, *Puffer's* skipper, Lieutenant Commander Frank G. Selby, got an eyeful. He happened across one of Ozawa's periodic training sorties, finding two carriers in the periscope. Selby made an approach on one when the other crossed his stern at only five hundred yards. Switching targets, he turned to engage the latter. Before a firing solution emerged, the range had extended to fourteen hundred yards, but *Puffer* fired a full spread: six torpedoes. *Chitose* was the target, and Shelby connected. One fish, maybe two, struck her hull. Neither exploded. In turn, enemy escorts pummeled *Puffer*, but she got away. Two weeks later she got some retribution, sinking two of Ozawa's repair and supply ships.

June 6

SOME ENTERPRISING SUB SKIPPERS WERE not content simply to track and report the enemy. And none was more enterprising than Commander Samuel David Dealey, the confident, charismatic Texan. In four patrols over the previous eleven months, Dealey had thrust *Harder* to the top of the SubPac ladder. He scored every time out, claiming fourteen victims of some seventy thousand tons. In reality he'd bagged eleven totaling forty-six thousand, but it was still an impressive performance. However, Dealey was about to set a new record as his crew basked in the boat's motto, "Hit 'em again, *Harder!*"

Approaching Tawi-Tawi on the sixth, Dealey found repeated opportunities. He achieved the unprecedented feat of sinking two destroyers in two days, picked up friendly guerrillas in northeastern Borneo, and got away clean. Then he killed a third destroyer, claiming possible damage to a fourth.

Still trolling off Tawi-Tawi on June 10, Dealey spotted two giant battleships. They were *Yamato* and *Musashi*, the biggest things afloat, steaming to join Ozawa. But a Japanese plane sighted *Harder*'s periscope and directed a destroyer to attack. Dealey fired another spread of torpedoes in his patented "down-the-throat shot," but all missed. Nevertheless, *Harder*'s morale, already stratospheric, went through the overhead. The submarine force rejoiced.

More important, Ozawa's forces were being depleted. In addition to *Harder*'s victims, U.S. Army planes sank a destroyer on the eighth, and another was lost in a collision six days later.

SubPac cast a wide net to track the Mobile Fleet's sortie. Six boats patrolled the Bonins, watching the northern flank, while six more were deployed west of the Marianas. Other subs were positioned off the Philippines, in the Carolines, and in home waters of Japan itself.

Wherever the Japanese appeared, they would be found, tracked, and trailed.

In a Rainstorm

Task Force 58's sortie from Majuro was a drizzly departure, both grim and grand. Beneath low, gray skies, 111 gray-painted warships steamed slow ahead in stately procession, emerging from the anchorage one at a time at roughly two-minute intervals. From first to last, the exit took almost five hours.

On the flight decks and hangar decks of fifteen fast carriers reposed the latent violence tacit in nearly a thousand warplanes. The 96,618 men in TF-58 existed for one reason: to put those technical-scientific marvels in the air for the purpose of placing ordnance on target.

Nor was that all. The disparate elements of Operation Forager got under way from other ports as distant as Hawaii and Guadalcanal, as near as Eniwetok and Kwajalein. Assault troops (127,571 Marines and soldiers), fire support forces (seven veteran battleships and eleven cruisers plus destroyers), two escort carrier groups (seven "jeep" carriers), and scores of attack transports, stores ships, hospital ships, escorts, and oilers all added to the total: 535 ships and vessels.

All were en route to the largest sea battle yet fought in World War II.

PART TWO

"Cut Their Damned Throats"

IN THE EARLY DAYS OF June, Task Force 58 bore down upon the Marianas with a single-minded purpose. The immediate objective was Saipan, with D-day scheduled for the fifteenth. In truth, the initial landings would inaugurate a two-month campaign to wrest Saipan, Guam, and Tinian from the Japanese and convert the islands into coral airfields for a mammoth aerial fleet of Boeing B-29s to torch Japan. But before the Army bombers could alight on their newly won fields, Marines and GIs had to seize the nascent bases, provisioned and sustained by Fifth Fleet logistics ships and protected by carrier airpower. The enterprise called Operation Forager was therefore the product of a symbiotic relationship: sailors who delivered soldiers to the beach, supported by airmen prepared to fight one of history's major sea battles.

June 10

IT WAS LIEUTENANT JOHN WHEATLEY's sixty-second patrol in Consolidated Coronado flying boats. Operating with VP-13 out of Eniwetok Atoll, he lifted the PB2Y named *Good Body* off the lagoon and began a 550-mile sector search to the west. Wheatley, a highly capable reservist, declined to send the obligatory "outbound" message that could alert the Japanese to his presence. He had assassinated a Betty bomber four weeks before and earnestly hoped to do so again—a rarity for a PB2Y.

About four hundred miles out, searching at 350 feet, the crew of *Good Body* spotted something on the horizon. Wheatley climbed for a better view and counted four task groups with an estimated fifteen carriers. He heaved a sigh of relief. "Thank God, those are ours," he told his crew. "The Japs don't have fifteen carriers!" His recognition was soon confirmed when an SBD nudged alongside, canopy open for the crew to appreciate "the naked lady painted on the side of our aircraft."

Taking a heading westerly from Task Force 58, Wheatley decided to scout ahead of Mitscher in case the Japanese also were searching. About a hundred miles farther on he spotted an aircraft approaching in the distance; radar gave a range of seven miles. Wheatley suspected it was another Betty and prepared to engage, though he held little hope of catching the speedy Mitsubishi.

The *Rikko* was from 761 *Kokutai*, the Tinian-based "Dragon Unit" rebuilt after its near destruction attacking U.S. carriers in February. Now, with the Japanese skimming the water, Wheatley shoved his four throttles ahead. Splashes appeared behind the Betty as the Japanese jettisoned their bombs. The Coronado followed suit, cutting the corner as the Mitsubishi made a dogleg northerly turn.

Good Body gained more ground when the Japanese realized their error and turned westerly again. After a forty-minute tail chase, the lumbering patrol plane hauled into range. Wheatley, a noted scrounger, had traded the Army some booze for extra ammunition boxes and cadged twenty thousand rounds of armor-piercing incendiaries.

As the distance narrowed, the Japanese gunners opened up, their tracers spiraling through the bright sky. But they underdeflected, putting just two rounds into the PB2Y.

Descending from his altitude perch, Wheatley wrapped the big Coronado into a pylon turn three hundred feet over his quarry. The nose and top gunners, AOM1c Thomas D. Murphy and AOM2c Duane H. Smith, opened fire. Their aim was excellent: Bright motes of light played across the Betty's dark green form as the APIs struck home. "It was all over in five seconds," Wheatley reported. "On fire, the Betty made a high-speed 'landing.' Only a wingtip and a wheel remained visible." Later, Wheatley's crew received a commendation for protecting the task force from early detection.

In truth, the Japanese knew of Mitscher's approach, but that knowledge was not yet evident to the visiting team. Two Eniwetok-based Liberator squadrons, VPB-108 and -109, also lent a hand, splashing three of their opposite numbers within seventy miles of the task force. Later *Bataan*'s combat air patrol downed a bomber identified as a "Fran" only fifty miles out. It was only the third splash for VF-50 since breaking into combat in April. The new pilot on the scoreboard was the skipper, thirty-two-year-old Lieutenant Commander Johnnie C. Strange.

Planning for the air phase of Forager involved some astute headwork by Mitscher's staff. His brain trust believed that the Japanese would expect the usual dawn fighter sweep as the first step toward air superiority. Therefore, the Task Force 58 staffers decided to false-foot the enemy by launching the first sweep in the afternoon. Accordingly, plans were laid for 208 Hellcats, guided by Avengers, to descend upon Marianas airfields on the afternoon of June 11.

June 11

DESPITE WHEATLEY'S SUCCESS, AND THAT of some long-range Liberators, the task force was snooped on June 10, approaching the Marianas from the east. Consequently, Mitscher ordered high-speed steaming to be within range half a day early.

During the task force's approach, more Japanese patrol planes poked around. But radar controllers were alert, and again *Bataan* got the call. On the morning of the eleventh, *Yorktown*'s FDO, Lieutenant Alexander Wilding Jr., directed VF-50 Hellcats to splash a snooper. Rear Admiral Ralph Davidson, Jocko Clark's understudy, showed his gratitude with a box of cigars.

Proving that the first kill was no fluke, during the noon hour Wilding vectored his own fighters onto two more snoopers, one within seventy miles of the force. Moments later *Yorktown*'s teammate, *Hornet*, controlled Fighting One in another splash only thirty miles south.

Most Hellcat pilots eagerly anticipated the fighter sweep, especially *Yorktown*'s Fighting One, which awaited its first big fight. The CO, Commander Bernard M. "Smoke" Strean, had flown missions from Tarawa but had never tangled with Japan's first team. He was so distracted that he was almost to his Hellcat when a VF-1 troop caught up with him, carrying the skipper's parachute harness.

As Hellcat pilots manned their aircraft for the first CAP, some pilots noticed unusual gestures in "vulture's row," the gallery on the carrier's island overlooking the flight deck. Some sailors conducted pantomime rooting sections, holding up five fingers, meaning "Make ace!" Not every fighter pilot was so inspired. One said, "To hell with that. I might run into a Jap looking for his fifth one."

All four task groups contributed to the massive show of airpower. At 1300 the carriers' helmsmen spun their wheels, turning into the fourteen-knot wind in preparation for launch. The F6Fs' Pratt & Whitney engines coughed blue-gray smoke as starter cartridges kicked the big cylinders into motion. Three-bladed propellers turned reluctantly by fits and starts, then blurred to invisibility as 2,800 cubic inches of raw power took hold.

In surprisingly few minutes the carriers steadied up on their heading, and launch officers waved the tricolored fighters off the decks. The Hellcats quickly formed up: fighting pairs of section leader and wingman; two pairs to a division; three or four divisions to a squadron. Each *Essex*-class ship launched sixteen fighters; the *Independence*-class ships contributed a dozen each.

Depending on their assigned targets, the pilots launched between 180 and 230 miles east of the Marianas. Jocko Clark's Task Group 58.1 drew the plum assignment at Guam. Saipan and Tinian were the venue of Al Montgomery's 58.2 and Black Jack Reeves's 58.3, while Keen Harrill's 58.4 shared Tinian and staked out Pagan for itself.

Before launch, Mitscher sent a message to the Hellcat squadrons: "Cut their damned throats. Wish I could be with you."

Flying low over the gray-tossed sea, the top cover F6Fs avoided Japanese radar until thirty minutes out. Then the pilots adjusted throttle and prop controls for a fast climb through the two thousand-foot overcast. Successively the midlevel and low fighters slanted upward at five-minute intervals.

Some of the pilots had been to the Marianas before. In late February Task Force 58 raided Saipan and Tinian, expecting a shoot-out, as Mitscher had said, "We will fight our way in." But Japanese air strength there was still building: Two days of strikes netted only thirty-six Japanese planes splashed. Mitscher's force also was growing at that time. He tackled the islands with six fast carriers: *Essex*, *Yorktown*, *Bunker Hill*, *Monterey*, *Cowpens*, and *Belleau Wood*. Among the February shooters still embarked in June were Mighty Moo's Air Group 25 and most of the night-fighter detachments.

That had been the third time Mitscher took the fast carriers against a land base and emerged the winner. Now February's exercise was a dimming memory, as few of the same squadrons remained.

The Big E

BY FAR THE MOST EXPERIENCED of Mitscher's carriers was neither an *Essex* nor an *Independence*. She was *Enterprise* (CV-6), widely known as "the Big E." Commissioned in 1938, she was the only prewar carrier in Task Force 58. She was seven thousand tons smaller than her *Essex*-class teammates, embarking seventy planes to their ninety. However, *Enterprise* remained "the fightingest ship in the U.S. Navy." Her captain was Matthew B. Gardner, but her fighting heart came from the former air operations and executive officer, Commander John Crommelin. The pilots adored him: At forty he left the youngsters awestruck at the things he could do with an airplane. But more than that, he knew the value of loyalty down. It was repaid in kind; Crommelin's spirit remained aboard after he departed.

Carrier Air Group Ten was the senior unit in Task Force 58. Joined at the hip with *Enterprise*, CVG-10 had been aboard for six months in 1942–43, fought the Santa Cruz battle, then rode her to Bremerton for repairs. After turnaround, the ship and air group were reunited and benefited from a high degree of institutional experience. The air group commander (CAG) was William R. Kane, Annapolis 1933, better known as "Killer." He had been stationed at NAS Pearl Harbor on December 7, and it would be an understatement to say that he disapproved of the Japanese empire. Now thirty-three, he had succeeded the legendary Commander Jimmy Flatley as skipper of VF-10, and though now CAG, he remained de facto leader of the Grim Reapers. Officially Lieutenant Commander Roland "Bud" Schumann was ComFitRon Ten, but in spirit and in fact the Hellcats still belonged to Killer Kane.

Torpedo Ten was a going concern run by big, ebullient Lieutenant Commander William I. Martin, who insisted that CV-6 was "a long and teedjus journey from Booger County, Missouri." Bill Martin was an extraordinary individual, like Killer Kane a thirty-three-year-old trade-school professional widely recognized for his innovative leadership. As a junior officer he had written the first instrument flying manual for carrier aviators, and it was said his middle initial (for Inman) stood for Instruments. He firmly believed in night attack aviation and proved his point by training VT-10 to a razor's edge in that mission. TorpRon Ten's nocturnal low-level strike against Truk Atoll in February resulted in a dozen ships sunk or damaged for loss of one Avenger—an exceptional ratio. Eventually Martin held the record for night carrier landings for forty years.

Martin's partner in the precision esoterica of night flying was Lieutenant Commander Richard E. Harmer, skipper of Night Fighting Squadron 101. A Solomons veteran from the Annapolis class of 1935, "Chick" Harmer had an unusual command. NightFitRons were small by any measure, but Harmer's four planes were half the original outfit. The other detachment had been aboard *Intrepid* (CV-11) when she caught a torpedo at Truk, and "Evil I" wasn't back yet. So Harmer and his night owls pressed on with their Vought F4U-2s, radar-equipped Corsairs. It was an odd situation, as the U-Bird was notoriously hard to land aboard ship in daytime, let alone at night. Under other circumstances, it might have remained beached until year end. But Harmer and company paid no heed to the bad press and kept flying with a perfect record.

Skipper of Bombing Ten was Lieutenant Commander James D. Ramage ("Rampage without the P"), at twenty-seven one of the youngest squadron commanders in the navy. A Buckeye from the class of 1939, he was known in the fleet as "Jig Dog" after the phonetic alphabet for his initials. Ramage had spent most of his five-year career in *Enterprise*, his first ship after graduation. He won his wings in 1942 and returned to the Big E, where the competent, egotistical Lieutenant Commander Stockton B. Strong told him, "Ramage, I'm going to make you the second-best bomber in the Pacific Fleet."

It was a matter of perverse pride with Jig Ramage that during his Annapolis tenure he consistently ranked in the lower half for "grease," or military protocol. He had little regard for his classmates who became "draft dodgers"—those who wrangled noncombat assignments—and he was characteristically vocal about it. Finally he became so disgusted at the ratio of no-shows that he took off his academy ring and never wore it again. In later years he said, "I had more use for those who could make their hands and feet work than for those with friends in high places." He identified more with the reservists than the "trade-school boys," and he looked out for his whitehats—a trait not always shared by academy graduates.

Crafty, battle-wise, and hungry, *Enterprise* eyed the Marianas and licked her chops.

On June 11 the strike leader over Saipan was *Enterprise*'s CAG, Killer Kane, with fifty-eight Hellcats at his back. He led four divisions of his own Grim Reapers guided by two Avengers flown by VT-10's skipper, Lieutenant Commander Bill Martin, and his exec, Lieutenant Van V. Eason. Each fighter division leader had an assigned target or operating area on the island, with its checkerboard pattern of paddies and fields.

The carrier pilots achieved almost immediate air superiority. "It was a losing battle from the start," gloomed Commander Masatake Okumiya, as Kakuta's carefully garnered strength was continually eroded.

Ninety minutes after launch the Hellcats rolled in on Saipan's three airfields: Marpi Point in the north, Aslito on the south, and a dirt strip at Chalan Kanoa on the southwest coast. A dozen Japanese fighters were up, drawing the attention of Kane and company. The CAG latched onto a green-painted bandit; he thought it was an Oscar, but no Japanese Army planes were present. The Zeke pilot recognized a no-win situation and shoved his throttle against the stop, diving for cover. At three thousand feet Kane astutely gave up the chase—it wasn't worth the risk of being drawn into a flak trap.

Kane's division hunted along the periphery of the target area, seeking fresh game. He was in luck: He flushed a covey of Zekes, including two dogging the tail of a pair of Hellcats. Kane knocked down one; Lieutenant Junior Grade Alfred Taddeo claimed the other. Still hungry, Killer went for altitude and spotted another Zeke below. He took Lieutenant Walter R. Harman down with him and destroyed the A6M with one carefully sighted burst from six o'clock.

Meanwhile, Taddeo refused to be skunked. He turned up a lucrative target: a Kawanishi flying boat. The big four-engine patrol plane absorbed a considerable amount of .50 caliber before splashing.

Other Reapers went after grounded planes and shot up several. But the Japanese AA gunners scored hits, too. Harman downed a Zeke, then took damage and limped away.

Extroverted Ensign Lester E. Gray Jr. had also claimed a kill, then came across Harman's damaged plane. Gray was escorting Harman toward the designated rendezvous between Saipan and Tinian when three Zekes appeared overhead. Caught at an altitude disadvantage, Gray was circling protectively between Harman and the Japanese when another damaged F6 appeared with two more Zekes in tow. It was a shot-up *Bunker Hill* recon plane flown by Lieutenant Edward L. Feightner. "Whitey" Feightner was an old *Enterprise* hand: He'd flown Wildcats under Flatley in 1943.

Recalling the adage about best defenses and good offenses, Gray hopped over Feightner's limping Hellcat, turned into the pursuers, and drew a bead on the nearest. He triggered a burst head-on and saw the Zeke pitch up dramatically. It stalled and spiraled into the water.

Back on course for the Big E, Gray found yet another Mitsubishi. This enemy pilot was more skilled than most. Try as he might, Gray could not get a clear shot as the agile Zeke unveiled its full aerobatic repertoire. But Gray was determined and grimly hung on through loops, rolls, and violent, uncoordinated skids. Finally, in evident frustration, the Japanese abandoned his slippery tactics and turned back for Saipan. Gray chased him over the south coast and sent him crashing onto the perimeter of Aslito Field. The twenty-one-year-old Missourian had scored a triple in his first combat.

Even the Avengers got some action. Lieutenant Van Eason, one of the Big E's navigation pilots, downed a Mitsubishi Betty bomber over Tinian.

Still, it was not all one-sided. Lieutenant Junior Grade Merle P. Long's Hellcat couldn't carry the load of flak it absorbed, and splashed down fifteen miles off Saipan. Mitscher was ready for such contingencies: Long was fetched back by a floatplane from the cruiser *Indianapolis*, Spruance's flagship.

Hornet's Fighting Two had the best of the hunting over Guam. The skipper, Commander William A. Dean, directed his divisions against known airfields but soon was diverted when Lieutenant Junior Grade Howard B. Duff was shot down by flak. Duff went down offshore, and Dean circled overhead trying to direct air-sea rescue to the scene. While cruiser-based floatplanes went inbound to attempt pickups, SB2C Helldivers were available to drop large inflatable rafts. Dean was focused on Duff's predicament when Lieutenant Junior Grade John T. Wolf called, "Heads up."

An estimated thirty Zekes dropped onto Fighting Two beneath the cloud deck, prompting a dandy dogfight. When two bandits descended toward Dean's tail, he led his wingman into a climbing turn to meet the threat. Firing nose-to-nose, the two Grummans and two Mitsubishis closed at more than five hundred miles per hour. The Americans' aim was superior: Dean and Lieutenant Junior Grade David R. Park each flamed his opponent.

Next Dean latched onto a Zeke that he identified as an army "Tojo." Nevertheless, the Japanese climbed rapidly, and Dean, eager for another kill, shoved his throttle through "the gate": He pushed the lever past the safety-wire stop on the quadrant, engaging the water-methanol mixture that boosted his engine's power. The water injection feature added two hundred horsepower to the usual two thousand, accelerating the big Grumman beyond normal performance. It was good for only five minutes: Afterward, the Pratt & Whitney would begin to burn itself out. But Dean's Hellcat ate up the distance, reeling in the Zeke until he shot it into flames.

Retarding his throttle, Dean turned back toward the main combat area and bounced another Zeke to become the squadron's first ace. Lieutenant Junior Grade Wolf also claimed three; the other *Hornet* pilots ran the day's total to twenty-six.

The second sweep claimed a dozen more kills, paced by Fighting Eight CO William M. Collins Jr., with three Irving night fighters. *Bunker Hill* Hellcats also claimed the last victories of the day, splashing a pair of snoopers within forty-five miles of the task force late that afternoon.

Nearly half the claims were made by CVL squadrons, paced by VF-31 with thirteen over Tinian's Ushi Airfield. Lieutenant Junior Grade Vincent Rieger bagged three Zekes in a half hour's hunting. His only previous claim was a damaged on April 1.

Among the big-deck air groups was *Essex*'s. The CAG, Commander David McCampbell, spotted a Zeke descending from the overcast over Saipan. "Dashing Dave" added power, closed the range, and triggered three bursts. The Mitsubishi went down smoking.

It was anticlimactic to the former NCAA diving champ from Annapolis: He had trained long and hard as a fighter pilot, possessing an extraordinary amount of experience. With some two thousand hours in his logbook, he was supremely confident: "I knew I could shoot him down, and I did." McCampbell regarded his CAG tour as much more satisfying than his previous cruise: As LSO aboard the first *Wasp* (CV-7) he had swum away from the ship after she was torpedoed by a Japanese submarine in September 1942.

Meanwhile, the "Fabled Fifteen" pilots, in combat less than a month, added nine more kills in their first dogfights. The skipper, Commander Charles Brewer, shared a big Emily flying boat with one of his ensigns, Richard E. Fowler Jr. Another flying boat was splashed by VF-15's celebrity pilot, Lieutenant Bert D. Morris. The husky blond Californian was better known as actor Wayne Morris, star of

1937's *Kid Galahad*. Low on flight time, Morris had pulled strings to get into fighters, and he knew just the string to pull. His wife, Patty, was Dave McCampbell's niece.

In exchange for nearly a hundred claimed shoot-downs, eleven Hellcats were lost. Three of the pilots eventually were saved from the sea, including *Cowpens*'s CAG, Lieutenant Commander Robert H. Price. Shot down while attacking a convoy, Price drifted in his one-man raft for eleven days, sustained by one pint of water and thoughts of his wife and baby daughter. When finally rescued he was gaunt, sunburned, and emaciated—with a huge smile on his reddened face.

Another pilot rescued was Ensign R. G. Whitworth, a *Cabot* flier who survived "only" three days in the water.

Whatever the extent of the June 11 claims (ninety-eight victories credited against Japanese admission of twenty-two), there was no doubt that the sweeps were effective. Local air superiority largely had been achieved, and at least twenty-two Japanese fighter pilots were killed.

Finally, night fighters "capped" Orote and Agana fields in the wee hours of the twelfth, keeping the Japanese grounded and awake. Task Force 58 was now a round-the-clock operation, "Mitscher and Company: Open all night."

June 12

THE NEXT DAY ONLY TWENTY-TWO Japanese planes were claimed destroyed in the air, half by *Hornet* Hellcats over Agana and Orote Point. With local air superiority already achieved, the carrier bombers went to work. They had three days before the landings to sink coastal shipping and reduce many of Saipan's strongpoints. Mitscher's aircrews put the time to good use. On D minus three, *Enterprise* alone launched 169 sorties that dropped fifty-two tons of bombs.

Support of the still-seaborne assault troops also began that day. Gauging the wind, Avenger pilots dropped incendiary bombs on the upwind side of Saipan's sugarcane fields, depriving the defenders of cover and concealment.

During strikes against the islands, the bombers found few airborne bandits but plenty of flak from positions reportedly knocked out. Observed one Helldiver pilot, "The Japs had a lot more fun than we did."

June 13

SNOOPERS CONTINUED PROBING the task force on June 13, and six were spared the tedium of a return flight. The first shoot-down was logged at 0900 as *Essex* CAG Dave McCampbell led a forty-six-plane strike against a Japanese convoy spotted the day before. However, early that morning only one of the dozen enemy vessels could be found, and the Fabled Fifteen used its sledgehammer weight to smash one peanut.

En route home, Ensign Walter Fontaine looked down from his Helldiver and glimpsed a twin-engine aircraft. He knew it had to be hostile and called out the sighting. McCampbell investigated with his four-plane division and immediately pounced. After repeated gunnery runs he made his second kill, identified as a Nakajima "Helen" bomber. If the CAG's recognition was correct, the Japanese Army aircraft was well off its usual range.

The Japanese were persistent, however. They kept sniffing around the periphery of Task Force 58, with VF-15 and -25 executing the last three Bettys late in the afternoon.

Meanwhile, the Americans also were searching. On a morning three-hundred-mile search four *Hornet* Helldivers ran low on fuel and had to "pancake" aboard *Bataan* in the same task group. It was a mismatch, as the big dive-bombers didn't operate from CVLs' narrow flight decks. The first three "beasts" got aboard, but the fourth rebounded off the deck, bounced over the barrier, and smashed onto the other three. All four were write-offs. It was just part of the price of doing business in carrier aviation.

While searchers probed the oceanic expanse to the west, preinvasion strikes continued ashore. At 0500 Task Group 58.3 launched an attack on Chalan Kanoa Airfield that proved costly: three aircraft and six fliers from *Enterprise* and *Lexington*. Lieutenant Commander Bill Martin of Torpedo Ten coordinated with Lieutenant Commander Robert H. Isely of VT-16; both were knocked down by AA fire, as was a VF-10 Hellcat. The only survivor was Martin. With flames searing the cockpit, he parachuted into the shallow water off Saipan, skinning himself on the coral reef.

Cool and professional, Martin made mental notes of the water depth—only chest high—and the width of the reef, but allowed himself time to remember his two aircrewmen, ARM1c Jerry T. Williams and AOM2c Wesley R. Hargrove. He later conceded that the tears in his eyes were not from salt water.

Martin could not remain there for long. Barely two hundred yards offshore, he soon came under small-arms fire. He heard the *snap-crack* of 7mm bullets and gauged that the shooters were getting the range as splashes came ever closer. Looking toward the beach, he could see khaki-clad figures standing and gesturing. Their intentions were not hard to infer, and spurred him on: "I knew how Japs treated prisoners." He struck out for the reef about a thousand yards away.

Bill Martin was a big, powerfully built man, but he could only dog-paddle so far. Swimming was somewhat difficult with his Mae West uninflated, and his progress was impeded by his parachute canopy, which he had retained for survival purposes. When he looked back to check his progress, his heart sank. Two small boats were chugging toward him. He began alternately swimming and diving to avoid the gunfire that seemed relentless.

Nearly exhausted, the Missourian came up for air again, half expecting to be dragged aboard a boat. Instead, he heard the blissful clatter of Wright engines: Two Avengers flew low overhead, drawing some flak. Shell splinters spattered the water all around him, but Martin welcomed the risk: The boats had turned back.

Upon reaching the reef, Martin collapsed onto the jagged coral. It felt as welcoming as a feather bed. Regaining his breath, he gathered his few supplies under one arm and splashed across the reef, perhaps fifty feet wide. Once in the water on the ocean side, he allowed himself to believe he might survive. The Japanese owned Saipan; America owned the sea.

Hours later, the Big E's torpedo skipper was retrieved by a Curtiss SOC floatplane. The Seagull delivered him to *Indianapolis*, where Martin gave Spruance the most recent information possible. Later that day, returned to the Big E, Martin immediately got fitted with new flight gear; he had no intention of remaining grounded.

That same day Jocko Clark launched a long-range strike against six ships that scouts located west of Saipan. Guided by radar-equipped night fighters, twenty-one *Yorktown* and *Hornet* fighter-bombers flew seven hundred miles round-trip, claiming two destroyers and a freighter set afire. Japanese reports indicated damage to one vessel.

Far to the west, at Tawi-Tawi, the Mobile Fleet was getting up steam. That afternoon the order was given: "Prepare for A-Go decisive operation."

Ozawa's fleet upped anchor, en route to the advanced base at Guimaras, between Panay and Negros. But almost immediately the Kon operation to relieve Biak was canceled, requiring the powerful surface force to rejoin Ozawa. Supersisters *Yamato* and *Musashi*, plus three cruisers and five destroyers, were directed to rendezvous with the Mobile Fleet en route to the Marianas.

Ozawa's departure did not go unnoticed. Among the submerged sentries watching the exit was *Redfin*, conned by Lieutenant Commander Marshall H. Austin. On his inaugural patrol the month before, "Cy" Austin had put three ships on the bottom for ten thousand tons. Now he was positioned to add some serious tonnage if only he could maneuver for a decent shot. The leading elements—cruisers and destroyers—followed a vigorous zigzag pattern and got past at extended range. However, things looked better a couple of hours later when Austin saw most of Ozawa's main body. But again *Redfin* was unable to close the distance and could only log the observation: at least six carriers, four battlewagons, six cruisers, and an impressive number of escorts.

Meanwhile, ill omens beset Jisaburo Ozawa. Upon leaving Tawi-Tawi, *Taiho*'s flight operations were interrupted when one of his rookie pilots crashed while landing. Six planes were destroyed.

Unharried, the Mobile Fleet transited Sibutu Passage into the Sulu Sea, bound for replenishment. Lying at Guimaras overnight, the force took on fuel and provisions before heading for the ultimate confrontation.

That evening *Redfin* surfaced and sent a contact report. Major enemy fleet elements were now at sea.

June 14

IF POSSIBLE, A RESCUE ATTEMPT nearly as dramatic as Martin's occurred a day later. A *Hornet* fighter pilot, Ensign Donald C. Brandt, was shot down by gunners at Agana Field. Brandt got his flakked-up Hellcat over the water before bailing out, but he parachuted only about a mile offshore. He went over the side at twelve thousand feet, finding himself inverted when his canopy opened.

As per standard procedure, a Helldiver flew low overhead and dropped an inflatable raft. The VF-2 pilot pulled the CO_2 cartridge and hauled himself aboard.

That was the good news.

The bad news: He was visible to enemy gunners, who began firing ranging shots, dropping explosive shells ever closer.

Fortunately, more immediate help was at hand in the form of a lifeguard submarine. *Stingray* was a veteran boat with ten war patrols dating from December 1941. In March Lieutenant Commander Sam C. Loomis Jr. became her fourth wartime skipper, and logged a sinking on that first patrol. But now he was confronted with a challenge that few submariners had ever contemplated, let alone attempted.

Notified of Brandt's peril, Loomis rang up full speed and left his patrol station for Orote Point. When he reached the area during the noon hour, he noted explosions in the water, which helped him locate the downed aviator. Shortly another shell burst less than a quarter mile from *Stingray*; Loomis dived but he had no intention of giving up. He continued his approach, manning the periscope. He had a plan.

The technique was called PRP: periscope rescue procedure. It was a new concept that likely had never been tried in combat, but both submariners and airmen had received briefings. The object was to bring the submerged boat alongside the downed flier so that he could grab the raised periscope and hang on long enough for the sub to tow him to safety. It was a twentieth-century version of the nineteenth-century whaling experience known as "the Nantucket sleigh ride."

Making a slow approach, with his attack scope on high power, Loomis coached his helmsmen onto the course to intercept Brandt. Five minutes later, while ducking shell bursts, Brandt saw the periscope moving toward him. He waved in acknowledgment, permitting Loomis to note a bad gash on the youngster's left hand.

Thirty minutes after spotting the *Hornet* pilot, *Stingray* was ready to try the rescue. Loomis approached with both periscopes raised to improve chances of a "catch." But Brandt didn't have a line ready to secure to a scope.

The first attempt failed.

With shells occasionally dropping nearby, Loomis maneuvered *Stingray* for another try. It took nearly an hour to reposition for a second slow approach, but Brandt failed to spot the scope. Loomis and his crew subdued whatever frustration they felt and prepared for a third attempt. Though the skipper was gratified to see blue airplanes bombing the airfield and nearby shore batteries, the air attacks did not prevent half a dozen shells from dropping nearby in barely one minute.

At 1453, one hour after the second pass, *Stingray* went in again. It appeared as if Brandt made a grab for the scope, but in any case, he missed. Loomis confessed that he was "getting damn disgusted, plus a stiff neck and a blind eye."

Still determined to effect a rescue, Loomis swung his boat hard about and was repositioned only twenty-three minutes later. Despite more shell fire, *Stingray* bore straight down on the flier and collided with him. Somehow Brandt hung on, maintaining his grip literally for dear life for fifty-seven minutes.

Upon surfacing at 1613, the good ship *Stingray* completed more than three hours under near-constant shell fire to retrieve one thoroughly waterlogged ensign. Profuse in his thanks, Brandt admitted that on the first and third passes he feared he would be run down and actually tried to avoid the periscope.

As if in anticipation of the main event the next day, D minus one was notable mainly for inactivity. Two Bettys were splashed that morning, one by *Bataan*'s fighter skipper, Lieutenant Commander Johnnie C. Strange. The other fell to *Lexington*'s Lieutenant Junior Grade Alex Vraciu, forty miles northwest of Saipan. It was the twelfth career victory for the former DePauw premed student.

The task groups refueled in turn that day, anticipating events on the morrow.

The assault troops also lived with anticipation, as soldiers have always done, whether sharpening spears or oiling machine guns. They spent the day conducting inspections and preparing their weapons and gear. Then they settled down for the hard part: waiting.

Logistics and planning for Forager were immense undertakings. Three infantry divisions were allotted to Saipan: borne to battle aboard thirty-two transports, supported by ten cargo ships carrying everything from shoelaces to artillery shells.

The amphibious forces had a sober idea of what to expect from recent experience. The first atoll assault had occurred in the Gilberts seven months previously. Tiny Tarawa, covering just three square miles, had turned into a three-day killing spree with nearly 1,000 Marines dead and 2,100 wounded. Fewer than 150 of the 5,000 defenders surrendered.

In contrast, the smooth-as-silk Marshalls operation in February and March was practically a cakewalk. Kwajalein, for instance, cost 173 American dead and 793 wounded versus 8,400 Japanese dead. As always, precious few Japanese surrendered, and some of the prisoners were taken only because of crippling wounds. Tarawa had been conquered with 1,000 American casualties per square mile. By comparison, Eniwetok had cost 325 per mile.

Saipan was likely to fall somewhere in the middle.

The preinvasion ammunition expenditure was awesome: nearly 6,400 rounds of fourteen- and sixteen-inch from battleship main batteries; 19,000 rounds of cruisers' six- and eight-inch; and 140,000 five-inch, mainly from destroyers. And those figures represented the usage only up to July 10, D minus five. The weight of those projectiles approached 12,000 tons.

During the campaign, consumption of Bunker C was over 40 percent greater than estimated. Yet the deficit was made good by the tireless efforts of the fleet service squadrons and use of chartered civilian tankers.

"ServRons" of the Pacific Fleet Service Force made possible the Navy's strategic reach. It was achieved by Vice Admiral William L. Calhoun, one of the least appreciated officers of the war. A gregarious Floridian, "Uncle Bill" Calhoun had graduated twelfth in the class of 1906, a stellar group including Pacific war fighters such as Bob Ghormley, Frank Jack Fletcher, Jack Towers, and John "Slew" McCain. Eventually Calhoun earned submariner's dolphins and commanded battleships, but he excelled at logistics. From 1939 through 1945 his command grew to vast dimensions, finally comprising 455,000 men aboard 290 ships. Ray Spruance knew his value, saying, "There was nothing the fleet wanted that Uncle Bill couldn't get."

Delivery of vital supplies to the end users was conducted in phases. ServRon Eight transported matériel from the West Coast to the forward areas, while in late 1944 ServRon Six was established as a dedicated unit to operate with Spruance's and Halsey's striking forces.

Other elements of Calhoun's far-flung empire included ServRon Two's hospital ships and repair vessels; ServRons Four and Ten, eventually consolidated to support fleet anchorages; and ServRon Twelve, which worked closely with Seabees to keep harbors dredged.

Like the fleet oilers, the service squadrons' contribution to the Pacific war remained largely unheralded—and absolutely essential.

Meanwhile, Lieutenant Junior Grade Sims had been deciphering enemy radio traffic and concluded that significant aircraft reinforcements were going to be shuttled southward via the Bonins. Therefore, Mitscher ordered Clark's and Harrill's groups to hit Iwo Jima, midway between Saipan and Tokyo. Not without reason, neither Clark nor Harrill was eager to divert far northward with a fleet engagement in the offing. But Mitscher wanted to interdict enemy aircraft possibly funneling southward from Japan proper, and Iwo Jima was the only waypoint. Rather than simply saying "Do it," the astute Arleigh Burke passed the word while exercising some psychology. Conceding that the operation was "a very difficult and dangerous mission," he "admitted" that the Task Force 58 staff shared Clark's concern.

Mitscher and Burke knew that Jocko Clark could not resist a challenge. They were right.

The two groups refueled that day, preparing for their seven-hundred-mile run to the north. Three oilers serviced each group, with *Cimarron* joining her sisters *Sabine* and *Kaskaskia* in topping off Harrill's 58.4. Meanwhile, the escort carrier *Copahee* delivered replacement aircraft, bringing the air groups up to strength.

Unreps

THE EVOLUTION WAS CALLED "UNREP," naval shorthand for underway replenishment. Without it, the Pacific war could not have been conducted as it was.

Though methods had existed for passing coal from one ship to another, unreps became more common after World War I, when navies changed to fuel oil. There were two basic methods for transferring fuel while under way: rigging lines bow to stern or side by side, known as "riding abeam." The latter became standard.

The oiler and its "customer" steamed alongside each other, usually at eight to twelve knots. One or both ships deployed bumpers or "fenders" of heavy manila hemp to protect the hulls in the event of collision.

With forward motion stabilized, "messenger" or "pilot" lines were propelled across the fifty feet or so separating the two ships. Sailors secured the ropes, which became the means of passing "distance lines" heavy enough to support the fuel hoses under pressure. Once the distance lines were in place, the oiler crew rigged out the booms holding the fuel lines, which were then hauled across the expanse separating the two ships. With the hoses secured in receptacles leading to the recipient's fuel tanks, the oiler then began pumping thousands of gallons of Bunker C.

However, even in ideal conditions it was almost impossible for two ships to maintain an even strain on the lines. A twenty-five-thousand-ton oiler fueling a ten-thousand-ton cruiser imparted a good deal of inertia from normal movement through the water. In moderate wind or tossing seas, lines alternately went taut or slack, requiring power winches to adjust line tension. Sometimes gangs of sailors had to compensate by muscle power. It was especially difficult for the oiler crews, who often worked on exposed well decks with low freeboards. They grew accustomed to being drenched as Pacific swells whipped up saltwater crests that cascaded onto the deck and swirled calf-high around them.

Inevitably, there were errors. Suspension lines sometimes parted, which complicated the process, but four-inch fuel hoses also could snap under violent strain. In that case, there was nothing to do but shut off the pumps to prevent loss of additional bunker fuel into the sea. But by and large, the complex evolution was accomplished so often that it became routine.

Because oilers could not always operate with the combatant units, large men-of-war also had the ability to pump Bunker C. Battleships and fleet carriers frequently fed the precious fuel to cruisers and destroyers, using largely the same techniques as the dedicated tankers. The ability of battlewagons and flattops to top off the "smallboys" was doubly beneficial, as it permitted independent operations for two or three days at a time, until a tanker rendezvous could be arranged.

One of the major unrep innovations was attributed to Captain Duke Hedding, who became Mitscher's operations officer. While serving as chief of staff to Rear Admiral Charles Pownall in 1943, Hedding thought he saw a better way to perform underway replenishment. During the Gilbert Islands operation in November, the decision already had been made to refuel the entire fleet at sea rather than rotate task groups back to the New Hebrides, a thousand miles and five days out of the way.

Previously, the operating technique required the oiler to approach the carrier. During the Tarawa landings, Hedding watched a tanker linked to a cruiser make an approach to a carrier. The procedure struck him as silly. The aviator remarked to his boss, "We all know how to fly formation. Let's set the tanker up there and let everybody come up and make an approach on the tanker and just run the fuel lines across." Pownall thought a moment, then replied, "Let's try it."

Duke Hedding's idea worked. Dispensing with the prewar method of rigging breast or spring lines, oilers and recipients alike learned that they could conduct unreps without heading into the wind.

After the war, officers of the U.S. Strategic Bombing Survey (Pacific) questioned Japanese strategists about the reasons for America's victory. Apart from the obvious industrial disparity, ranking high on the list was the ability to keep task forces at sea for weeks at a time. That meant oilers. If the American public had little idea of their contribution, the warlords in Tokyo fully knew their worth.

Among the hundreds of ships that departed the Marshalls on June 6 was a particular auxiliary vessel, a noncombatant. Though she carried four five-inch, .38-caliber guns plus eight antiaircraft mounts, her weapons were more a contingency than a practicality. She was a fleet oiler: bulky, wallowing, unglamorous. And absolutely essential.

She was USS *Cimarron*, first of eight T-3 oilers in her class. She was designed for one purpose: to transfer Bunker C–type fuel to other ships while at sea. Built for the Maritime Commission by Sun Shipbuilding in Chester, Pennsylvania, *Cimarron* was acquired by the Navy, designated AO-22, and commissioned at Philadelphia in March 1939, six months before the Europeans launched themselves into another Great War.

Cimarron was christened for a river that sprang from Oklahoma and drained into Kansas. Other than perhaps the Sabine, her sisters bore riverine names that most Americans had never heard, such as *Salamonie* (Indiana), *Kaskaskia* (Illinois), and *Chemung* (New York–Pennsylvania).

Almost three years after *Cimarron*'s commissioning, war had come to the other side of the planet, conferring unexpected importance upon the small family of naval oilers. Her nearest sister, *Neosho* (AO-23), also with Kansas–Oklahoma roots, had survived Pearl Harbor, only to die in the Coral Sea five months later.

In March 1942, three months after the Pearl Harbor debacle, *Cimarron* transited the Panama Canal to join the Pacific Fleet. There she found a supporting role in the legendary operation called the First Special Aviation Project. Departing with Vice Admiral William F. Halsey's task force, *Cimarron* and her sister *Sabine* (AO-25) pumped bunker fuel to USS *Hornet* (CV-8) under Captain Marc Mitscher and Halsey's flagship *Enterprise* (CV-6). Aboard *Cimarron*, the three-hundred-man crew gawked at *Hornet* the first time they saw her: Sixteen Army B-25 Mitchell bombers were lashed down in place of the familiar slate-gray Navy aircraft. On April 18 Lieutenant Colonel Jimmy Doolittle's Mitchells flew off *Hornet*'s rain-lashed deck six hundred miles from Japan, and Halsey's task force hauled off. The oilers had played an obscurely vital role in America's response to Pearl Harbor.

Less than sixty days later *Cimarron* refueled several ships before and after the crucial Battle of Midway. For much of 1942 into 1943 she was involved in the Guadalcanal campaign. She had even dodged enemy submarines. No other oiler had seen as much action.

By June 1944 *Cimarron* was an old Pacific hand. Though she remained unheralded, the headline-making Fifth Fleet would have gone nowhere without Commander A. H. Koostria's oiler and her sisters.

That month *Cimarron* belonged to Unit Three of Task Group 50.17 under Captain Edward E. Paré, a Bay Stater who had graduated in the top 20 percent of the Annapolis class of 1920. With two other tankers—her old partner *Sabine* plus *Kaskaskia*—she was protected by the new *Fletcher*-class destroyer *John D. Henley* (DD-553) and two destroyer escorts, *Riddle* (DE-185) and *Waterman* (DE-740). Paré's fueling group included six other such units plus four escort carriers, two with the standard complement of Wildcat fighters and Avenger bombers; two ferrying P-47 Thunderbolts for the Army.

Four hospital ships accompanied Task Group 50.17 to tend the inevitable casualties of an opposed landing on a hostile shore. In all, the task group boasted two dozen oilers and eighteen escorts: a sizable fleet in itself. It was an assembly worthy of an admiral, but Paré accepted the honorific of commodore: a captain in a rear admiral's billet.

When *Cimarron* stood out of Majuro that Tuesday, Commander Koostria had conned her through the channel, feeling the pulsing power of 30,400 horsepower thrumming through the deck plates. Geared turbines driving twin screws could push the oiler through the water at eighteen knots, but she seldom needed to make that speed, especially with a full load. And today she rode low in the water. Her empty weight measured some 7,500 tons, but fully loaded, as now, with 146,000 barrels of fuel on board, she ran close to 25,000.

Oilers were a growth industry. Only four of Commodore Paré's twenty-four AOs had turned a wake before Pearl Harbor; three others were less than six months in service. At war's end the U.S. Navy owned three times as many as at the start, and that did not include gasoline tankers (AOGs). Nor did it include munitions ships or other auxiliaries necessary to sustain task forces at sea for months at a time.

Other unheralded but essential auxiliary ships belonged to Vice Admiral William L. Calhoun's service force. His vessels included provision ships (AFs), better known as "reefers" for the dry goods they carried. The Pacific Fleet counted only nine that summer, owing to considerations on the other side of the globe. They were augmented by Merchant Marine hulls to meet the ceaseless needs of a fleet at sea as well as for corps-sized operations ashore, a thousand miles from the nearest base.

Stores munitions ships (AKSes) were called "floating general stores," carrying everything from typing paper to steel plate. Even so, they could provide only about five thousand of the forty thousand inventory items required at a given time. Ammunition ships (AEs) provided reloads for everything from small-arms ammo to one-ton bombs and sixteen-inch main battery rounds.

How important were the auxiliaries? It's indisputable that, without firing a shot, the supply force helped win the war.

The Reluctant Admiral

WILLIAM KEEN HARRILL WAS NOT so keen on the Bonins. He used the replenishment lull to inform Clark of his doubts about the enterprise. That was too much for the combative Jocko, who had himself flown to *Essex* for a "conference." In truth, it was a showdown. Clark climbed out of the Torpedo Two Avenger in no mood to negotiate.

The outcome was seldom, if ever, in doubt. Between them, Clark and Harrill's chief of staff, Captain Herbert Ed Regan, went to work on the reluctant admiral. His concerns about fuel, weather, and the upcoming main event were clearly a smoke screen: He simply did not want to leave Mitscher. Finally, Clark played his ace: "If you do not join me in this job I will do it myself." Harrill was outmaneuvered and he knew it. Clark flew back to *Hornet*, and Harrill trailed in his wake.

The episode was further evidence of Mitscher's command dilemma. Instead of designating Clark as commander of the Bonins strike, "CTF-58" gave both admirals joint command: poor policy and a tacit slap at Harrill. Certainly Mitscher knew that Clark was by far the more aggressive. If the task force commander wanted to hit Iwo and environs, he could have averted Harrill's queasiness by placing Clark in charge, though it would have been discomfiting: Clark (class of 1918) was four years junior to Harrill (1914).

Meanwhile, *Yorktown*'s radar officer, Commander Cameron Briggs, put out the word: "Get the shootin' irons ready and maintain a keen lookout."

That night, while Clark and Harrill were pounding north through heavy seas, Mitscher passed the word: Ozawa was out. He was en route to the Marianas.

* * *

Ozawa's unrep force had problems of its own. During the midnight watch, ninety miles beyond Surigao Strait, a lookout shouted a warning: torpedo inbound. Among the escorts was the eight-year-old destroyer *Shiratsuyu*, veteran of Coral Sea, the Aleutians, and Guadalcanal. Actually there was no torpedo, but *Harder's* depredations clearly had the imperial destroyermen jittery. In avoiding the "danger," *Shiratsuyu* swung across the path of an oiler with predictable results. The ten-thousand-ton *Seiyo Maru* smashed into the sixteen-hundred-ton escort, cutting her in two forward of the fantail. Concerned about the omnipresent American submarines, *Shiratsuyu's* captain had already ordered her depth charges armed, and she sank before they could be safed. Reaching their set depth, the charges exploded beneath the floundering survivors, killing 104 men, including the captain, Lieutenant Commander Kuro Matsuda.

Seiyo Maru continued with the rest of the First Supply Force, her crew doubtlessly pondering the irony of having sunk one of the ships assigned to protect her.

Fleet Opposed Landing (June 15)

BARELY A WEEK AFTER D-DAY in Normandy, American landings began on Saipan's southwest coast. The assault troops—two Marine divisions with an Army division in reserve—were assigned eleven beaches designated Red, Green, Blue, and Yellow, north to south. The latter beaches lay less than two miles from Aslito Field, a major objective.

The amphibious tractors (amtracks) churned into the water at 0542. Each beach was assigned a dozen amtracks supported by gun-toting LCIs (landing craft, infantry). Overhead, seventy-two Grummans from the escort carriers strafed and rocketed the beaches and inland areas, suppressing Japanese gunfire.

But not all of it. At 0845 the first wave of tractors grounded, encountering automatic weapons fire, but offloaded their Marines and returned for more. In twenty minutes eight thousand men were ashore, with twelve thousand more not far behind. It was the American way of war, from the sea and from the sky.

Resistance was toughest on the southern beaches. It was worst on Blue Two, where the Marines were stymied only a hundred yards inland. Consumption of "consumables" increased: ammunition, water, and plasma.

Though twenty months had passed since a fleet battle, some Americans were optimistic, none more so than Mitscher's air operations officer, the flamboyant Commander William J. Widhelm, an exceptional pilot and awesome gambler who had flown from the previous *Hornet* in 1942.

Gus Widhelm was an archetypal aviator: big, loud, and just as good as he claimed. He quipped, "When you brag as much as I do, you gotta live up to your words!"

Hailing from the class of 1932, Widhelm was an accomplished hustler, frequently winning bets that he could outdrive other golfers with his putter. Aboard *Lexington* he haunted the squadron ready rooms, swapping rumors, cadging bets, and looking for a poker game. Only the valiant sat at Widhelm's table: When Air Group 19 relieved Air Group 16 in July 1944 he announced, "Welcome, Air Group Nineteen. When Air Group Sixteen was aboard I won sixteen thousand dollars. So I repeat: Welcome, Air Group Nineteen!"

As the landings progressed, Widhelm offered a $1,000 bet to all comers: a fleet engagement before the twentieth. There were few takers, as some officers had learned to their cost that Gus Widhelm was plugged into the intelligence pipeline. However, *Life* magazine correspondent Noel F. Busch noted that some aggressive fighter pilots hoped that the "ops O" was right: They told one another, "The Jap fleet is where the meatballs grow thickest." While stalking Fighting 16's ready room, Widhelm found Lieutenant Junior Grade Alex Vraciu, just down from a CAP, who took the last $125 of the bet.

* * *

Sooner than the Americans expected, several Japanese aviators appeared willing to wager their lives for a chance to sink American ships. That morning a small air attack developed on Task Group 58.3, and some Guam-based planes penetrated the CAP and destroyer screen. A handful survived to drop torpedoes, one of which seemingly had *Lexington* bore-sighted. Captain Ernie Litch timed his evasive turn nicely, prompting Arleigh Burke to lean over the rail to watch it pass. Burke, who knew everything worth knowing about torpedoes, appreciated the display.

Though no ships were torpedoed, the task force did not escape damage. Low-angle antiaircraft fire inevitably was misdirected, striking friendlies. Three sailors were killed and nearly sixty wounded.

Meanwhile, Clark's and Harrill's task groups proceeded to hit the Bonins with three CVs and four CVLs. The plan called for strikes on just one day, returning Task Force 58 to full strength back "home" off Saipan for the impending battle. Though holding joint command with Harrill, Clark stretched his orders and rang up more steam, pounding north through the Pacific swells to arrive off the Bonins a day early.

It was typical Clark, once described as "part Cherokee and part Southern Methodist but all fighter." He wanted two days to maul the Bonins, reckoning that one would be insufficient.

Still skittish, Harrill wanted to limit his operations to ForceCAP through most of the day, leaving 58.1 to do most of the job.

However, Harrill's flagship air group led the Iwo parade. Commander Dave McCampbell headed twenty-two *Essex* fighters, the largest contingent among forty-six Hellcats in the afternoon's first fighter sweep, 140 miles from Iwo.

The weather, in aviation terminology, was "dogshit," the kind that caused enthusiastic pilots to doubt their calling. Low ceilings prevented the planned approach under the radar, so McCampbell led his formation up to eight thousand feet before letting down again.

Among the defenders was Air Group 301, a new outfit. Established at Yokosuka in November, the group included two *hikotai*, or squadrons, one of which deployed to Iwo on June 11. Largely composed of former floatplane pilots, *Hikotai* 316 logged a disastrous combat debut. Lieutenant Shigeo Juni scrambled with eighteen A6M5s to intercept the raiders; Juni and sixteen others were killed. Similarly shredded was *Hikotai* 401 from Group 341; thirteen launched and three returned.

The Hellcats claimed forty and got twenty-seven—a better figure than normal—losing two.

Half the American victories were credited to Fighting One. A twenty-seven-year-old veteran of North Africa, Lieutenant Paul M. Henderson Jr. announced that he had nailed four to make ace, then answered a call for help from a *Yorktown* squadron mate. He chased after some Zekes and was never seen again.

Lieutenant Junior Grade John R. Meharg also claimed a quadruple, despite insisting he made "all the mistakes in the book." It was his only score of the war.

Yorktown's Ensign Jack Hogue also was lost. He bailed out of his flak-stricken Hellcat and was seen in the water, drifting toward shore, but was never rescued. It may have been a blessing: the Bonins garrison became notorious for ritual cannibalism.

Among *Hornet*'s eight pilots was Lieutenant Lloyd G. Barnard, who, in his first combat, joined the elite ranks of the aces in a day. The young Texan fired at six Zekes and missed just one, running his tally from zero to five in twenty-five minutes. It was more than 90 percent of all fighter pilots accomplished in as many weeks. Using water injection for his Twin Wasp engine, the former flight instructor employed speed and climb to retain the advantage. Three of his victims exploded: the second so abruptly that Barnard's Hellcat was singed when he flew through the fireball.

Two other VF-2 aviators did nearly as well. Lieutenant Junior Grade Mervyn E. Noble gunned five Zekes, getting three kills and two probables; Lieutenant Junior Grade Charles H. Carroll went three for three.

Their squadron mate, Lieutenant Junior Grade Earling W. Zaeske, found himself the meat in a Mitsubishi sandwich. Cornered by four Zekes, the midwesterner wriggled port and starboard in a sustained climb, spoiling his pursuers' aim each time. When the chase topped out at seven thousand feet he reversed course, accepting a nose-to-nose confrontation, and gunned his erstwhile tormenter.

The *Hornet* pilots had little regard for their opponents, who were described as "erratic and disorganized." When they had an advantage, the Zekes often failed to press an attack. Though locally outnumbered, the eight Grummans kept up the pressure, scoring flamer after flamer. One pilot later exclaimed, "They were blowing up all over the place." Fighting Two sustained two planes damaged and one written off in a hard landing.

Lieutenant Commander George C. Duncan got the first of *Essex*'s three Zekes. Hailing from Tacoma and the Annapolis class of 1939, Duncan had been a floatplane pilot in another life and lied his way into Hellcats. After "a goddamned Jap fighter" shot his SOC full of holes in the Aleutians, he insisted that next time he would do some shooting himself. Upon reporting for reassignment Duncan insisted: "I'm a fighter pilot, damn it!" Despite lack of documentary evidence, his detailer chose to believe him and sent the Washingtonian to VF-15. Duncan's kill was the first en route to a baker's dozen.

After the dogfight, those Hellcats with ammo or fragmentation bombs remaining dropped down to attack parked aircraft and anything else that looked worthwhile. Carrier aviators counted eighty-six grounded planes, mostly claimed destroyed. Some pilots made as many as six passes, but they didn't have it entirely their own way.

The carrier bombers arrived half an hour after the fighter sweep. However, rain squalls and low visibility hindered navigation, and some dive-bombers spent sixty minutes over the target, seeking a cloud layer high enough to permit a useful attack.

The Bonins' AA gunners knew their business. They concentrated their fire on obvious gaps in the clouds, knowing that was where the blue airplanes would appear. Consequently the flak gunners knocked down four planes over Iwo while two more were lost at Chichi-Jima and Haha-Jima. In exchange for twenty or more floatplanes and seaplanes thought destroyed there, none of the fliers downed near the islands was recovered from seas that crested at eight feet.

Fifty miles south of Chichi, VT-1 pilot Lieutenant Junior Grade Johnny Keeler ditched his shot-up TBM. His friends circled overhead, optimistically dropping rafts into a forty-knot wind, calling for the lifeguard submarine. But the carriers' early arrival got ahead of the briefed target date, and the lifesaving sub was not there.

Keeler's *Yorktown* shipmates spent half an hour alternately dropping supplies and waving to one another before the dwindling fuel supply forced a return. Even then, the margin was razor thin. The sun had set beneath the obscured horizon as the last Avengers arrived overhead Coal Base. One pilot taxied clear of the arresting gear, then ran out of fuel. Another had four gallons to spare.

Ensign John Delmore reached the groove with several gallons remaining, but the deck was dancing, forcing two wave-offs. It looked like third time lucky. Then the big Wright quit, out of gas. Delmore made a safe water landing; a destroyer fetched the crew from the sea.

Back at the carriers, the weather was just as tough as the Japanese. Four Hellcats were wrecked or lost during landings on jitterbugging flight decks, as were a Helldiver and an Avenger.

Harrill determined that, having stuck it out thus far, he had discharged his obligation. Over the TBS line-of-sight radio net he told Clark of his intention to withdraw after recovering his planes. Characteristically, Clark boomed back that Task Group 58.4 could do what it wanted; his 58.1 was going to stay and finish neutralizing the Bonins.

Harrill had painted himself into another corner. With most of the two task groups' radio operators listening in, the courtly Tennessean again had been trumped by the blunt Oklahoman. Harrill briefly held his head in his hands, the soul of despondency, then allowed that he would stay.

Back in the Marianas, D-day at Saipan went largely unopposed in the air. Only thirteen Japanese planes were downed, with *San Jacinto*'s fighters claiming seven that evening. Three went to Lieutenant Robert Maxwell, formerly a land-based Wildcat pilot who had been shot down in the Solomons a year before. He had survived the bailout and encounters with crocodiles, determined to even the score. That he did, becoming VF-51's only ace.

The snoopers came out after dark, and most were harried away by night fighters. Late that afternoon Lieutenant Commander Evan P. Aurand dropped a Judy nine miles from *Bunker Hill.* Normally soft-spoken, Pete Aurand was another aviator who had asserted himself to "convince" his way into fighters. After flying SBDs in early 1942 he insisted that he was qualified in fighters and took the first slot available: Project Affirm, the then-new night-fighter program. After nearly two years of nonstop experiments, trial and error, and something called radar, the project bore fruit. In January 1944 Aurand worked a succession of minor wonders, getting VF(N)-76 from Quonset Point, Rhode Island, to combat in twenty-six days. Much later he confessed, "I would have had the honor of dropping the first bomb on Kwajalein had I remembered to arm the bomb rack switch!"

That same day Chick Harmer's *Enterprise* Corsairs got hits on two more bandits just south of the force.

With Bill Martin, Harmer and Aurand were among the small band of true believers in nocturnal carrier ops. They fought a relentless two-front war literally around the clock: one against the Japanese empire, the other against an ingrained conservatism in the United States Navy. Despite repeated success in both offensive and defensive operations, the pioneering night fliers still encountered resistance from senior officers. Some dissenters were carrier operations officers who conceded the night owls' worth, but were reluctant to work their deck crews beyond the normal twelve- to fourteen-hour day. Furthermore, few task group commanders wanted to maneuver their ships for one flattop's night launch and recovery. Clearly, the solution was a dedicated night task group, but that remedy lay months downstream.

In the Marianas that day the 22nd Air Attack Force (*Kushu Butai*) put up eleven Jills of Air Group 551 that attacked a "convoy and task force," reporting with world-class optimism the sinking of four transports and a cruiser. For good measure they claimed torpedoing a battleship with unknown results.

* * *

On D-day Nimitz had more than forty submarines spread throughout the Pacific. Neptune-like, they cast a huge net almost certain to catch any Japanese ships en route to the invasion beaches. Operating in groups and singly, the latter-day buccaneers were deployed from the Home Islands to New Guinea with wolf packs concentrated off Borneo, the Philippines, and the Bonins.

Well west of the Marianas were six subs deployed on a north-south patrol line: four boats grouped west of Saipan with two more opposite Guam. The crews set watch and watch (six hours on and six hours off), taking the odd freighter that crossed their bows, but mainly they bided their time and waited.

They were patient hunters, and their quarry was on the way.

Late that afternoon, off the Philippines, *Flying Fish* caught sight of a major unit exiting San Bernardino Strait, separating Samar from Luzon. Lieutenant Commander Robert Risser edged closer to count three flattops, three battlewagons, and numerous escorts. Though he would have liked to attack so lucrative a target, he knew where his priority lay. After the parade steamed by he waited till dark, then surfaced to transmit the news. *Flying Fish* briefly trailed the unsuspecting armada, then broke contact when low fuel dictated a return to Australia.

Farther south, another sub skipper got an eyeful. He was Lieutenant Commander Slade D. Cutter of *Seahorse*, who had sunk fifteen ships of sixty-seven thousand tons during three previous patrols.

Cutter was a man of many parts. He had ditched a music scholarship as Illinois's champion flautist in favor of Annapolis, where he became the academy boxing champion. More notably, he kicked the winning field goal in the 1934 Army–Navy game, giving the Middies their first victory over West Point since 1920.

Now, two hundred miles off Surigao Strait, his lookouts noted smoke on the horizon and he sped to investigate. Four large warships were prominent in the Japanese force: enough to draw any aggressive submariner for a closer look. Cutter's attack team began establishing the enemy's base course and speed, calculating where to zig when the target zagged. Things were looking good for an end-around to attack from the flank.

Then *Seahorse* threw a shoe. One of her main motor's brushes started sparking, and there was no choice but to shut it down. A reduced speed of barely fourteen knots snuffed any hope of an intercept, so Cutter bided his time. He surfaced after dark but dived again to avoid an aircraft. It was early the morning of the sixteenth before he could transmit a position report about "plenty of battleships." He had seen the Kon force, belatedly headed to Biak, where MacArthur's troops were already ashore. Though he didn't know it, the unit he tracked included sisters *Yamato* and *Musashi*, the biggest ships in anyone's navy. With Kon called off, they were en route to link up with Ozawa for Operation A-Go.

That same day Spruance asked MacArthur to extend Liberator searches to max range: twelve hundred miles from Wakde and Los Negros in the Admiralties. The previous day Spruance had Vice Admiral John Hoover's Eniwetok patrol wing send a tender with six Mariners to Saipan. The big Martins, with extensive range and powerful radar, could probe deep into the Pacific recesses where carrier planes could not. Fighting the longest-ranged war in history, Ray Spruance needed reach.

June 16

For Clark's and Harrill's task groups, weather off the Bonins only worsened after the first afternoon, which hardly seemed possible. But it was true: Aerology examined the evidence and concluded that a typhoon was inbound. Consequently, flight ops were canceled the morning of the sixteenth, allowing many sailors and all aircrews to get some additional sack time after dawn GQ.

Clark had capped Chichi-Jima with a pair of Hellcat night fighters, preventing any takeoffs before dawn. With miserable weather at sunup the Japanese, not illogically, concluded that no sane aviator would fly during the day, but they reckoned without the combative juices of Joseph J. Clark. Things improved marginally after noon, permitting launches of local patrols and a small strike. Fifty-four planes surprised Iwo, bombing and strafing some sixty aircraft on the field. This time the AA gunners were not so vigilant as before, and they dropped only one Yorktowner. No "meatballs" got airborne, to the disappointment of some Hellcat pilots who missed the previous day's melee.

Though Harrill stayed, he reckoned he didn't have to fly. His group launched no strikes.

Getting aboard was another risky venture, but the 58.1 tailhookers were up to the challenge. Just one plane crashed—likely from battle damage—though some staffers attributed the success partly to Jocko Clark's intercession. Normally twitchy anyway, he watched the recovery from *Hornet*'s bridge, employing subtle body language to nudge a pilot into the proper groove. Whatever other incantations he employed, they worked. All planes were back by 1710, and the two groups proceeded independently to rendezvous off Saipan.

Preparing for the run south, during the day Clark astonished everyone by ordering his carriers to refuel the "smallboys." Underway replenishments probably had never been accomplished in a storm approaching typhoon dimensions, though the destroyers bucked the pitching seas and got away with it. Some lines and hoses parted under inordinate strain, but the exceptional seamanship of the U.S. Navy was seldom better demonstrated.

Around the task force that day only one snooper was splashed: an Emily by *Langley*'s VF-32. Farther north, up near Guam, escort carrier fighters bagged a Betty.

Meanwhile, *Enterprise*'s Killer Kane was shot down by American gunners. Launched early that morning with four fighters and seven bombers, Kane was designated Strike Able's airborne target coordinator. He took the violent catapult shot into the predawn darkness and, running lights illuminated, joined with wingman Lieutenant Junior Grade Robert F. Kanze for the hundred-mile trip to Saipan.

Approaching the U.S. ships twenty-five miles offshore, Kane and

Kanze doused their lights but kept their IFF transponders on: electronic beacons identifying them as friendly on radar. It was still dark below, but wakes were visible beneath the morning clouds.

Then Kane's world exploded. A five-inch shell erupted beneath his port wing, jarring him so hard that his goggles were knocked off. Obviously radar controlled, the destroyer guns continued firing; nasty gouts of explosions rent the dark sky around him.

Kane prepared to jump. He released his safety harness and slid back the canopy. Then he noticed that he was still flying and his engine was running. Standard procedure took hold: Don't bail out except for a fire or structural failure. Kane poured the coal to the abused R2800, diving westward to get out of the flak zone, hollering with profane eloquence over the air support net. He even identified himself with his day's call sign, Cherokee. No good: The flak kept bursting.

Then the Pratt & Whitney died. With zero oil pressure, Kane had no choice but to put the stricken Hellcat down in the water. He hit hard, skipped, then splashed to a stop. He'd been too busy to refasten his restraints and was tossed forward into the gunsight. Nevertheless, the CAG abandoned ship, inflated his small raft, and nursed a bleeding forehead. While awaiting rescue he reviewed everything that had occurred and found no fault of his own. The destroyer crew that hauled him aboard found Commander William R. Kane one cranky aviator. With his head bandaged, he was highlined back to the Big E that afternoon, off flight status until further notice.

That same day the Japanese continued their optimistic ways. One Betty of Naval Air Group 755 and four Jills from Air Group 551 attacked, claiming they sank one cruiser, damaged another, and probably torpedoed a third.

Latitude 11 North, longitude 130 East: rendezvous of the far-flung elements of the Mobile Fleet. Some 250 miles east of Samar, well into the Philippine Sea, the first order of business was fueling. Oilers maneuvered into position alongside Vice Admiral Matome Ugaki's battleships, exchanged pilot lines, then rigged out the big hoses and transferred thousands of barrels of fuel oil. The loss of a destroyer and damage to a tanker two days before did not significantly affect the operation.

With the first phase completed, the tankers turned toward Ozawa's carrier force. It was a long, laborious process, lasting until the evening of the seventeenth, some 220 miles along the northeasterly track toward Saipan. That chore accomplished, the First Supply Force then diverted to the designated point to link up with the Second Force's two oilers and escorts, about five hundred miles from the Philippines.

The geometry of the battle was taking shape, proceeding at the stately pace of a fleet oiler.

American submarines continued dogging Ozawa's trail; he simply could not shake them. One was Herman Kossler's *Cavalla*, running surfaced late the night of the sixteenth. Radar contact showed a small formation: two oilers and a pair of escorts. Kossler had found Ozawa's Second Supply Force and turned up the RPMs to get ahead of his quarry. Early in the morning he dived and was ready to shoot, but the alert destroyers were on to him. They drove him down long enough for the oilers to escape.

Kossler reported the contact, expecting to proceed with his patrol. But ComSubPac, Vice Admiral Charles Lockwood, had other ideas. He regarded fleet oilers as worthwhile targets and sent *Cavalla* back on the hunt. Kossler reversed his helm and gave chase.

It was a valiant but fruitless effort. Aside from an hour's head start, the supply force was unknowingly aided by Japanese aircraft that twice forced *Cavalla* under. Kossler and his officers made other plans that would yield spectacular results.

"Blue Jacket"

EVERYONE WHO KNEW HIM AGREED: Raymond Spruance had one of the finest minds in the U.S. Navy. Which was fortunate, because he had to keep the concerns of several subordinates and his main opponent properly ordered at the same time. Now, with the Saipan landings and the fleet engagement almost certain, his mental juggling act needed to remain nearly flawless.

First his subordinates. Though riding *Indianapolis* with Mitscher's carriers, Spruance's primary concern was with Vice Admiral Richmond Kelly Turner's amphibious force. "Terrible Turner" (his temper was legendary) had put the assault troops ashore to wrest Saipan from the Japanese, always suicidally tenacious in defense. But it was a given that Tokyo would respond violently to the attempt, and a major naval battle seemed inevitable.

Consequently, Spruance faced a dual concern at sea: Protect the 'phibs while taking advantage of the rare opportunity to sink the enemy fleet. As usual, his operations plan included a "major action annex," describing the contingencies he anticipated, but it lacked the decisive quality advocated by the Naval War College. Spruance knew that plans were only starting points: The conventional wisdom held: "No battle plan survives contact with the enemy." Still, certain assumptions were necessary, and the annex laid them out.

Spruance and his chief of staff, Captain Charles J. Moore, considered a surface engagement most likely. Certainly the past two years pointed in that direction, since Japan's carriers had not been committed since late 1942.

That afternoon Spruance sent his thoughts to Mitscher and Lee. ComFifthFleet envisioned the carriers doing most of the fighting, with the battleships and surface forces mopping up: "Our air will first knock out enemy carriers then will attack enemy battleships and cruisers to slow or disable them. Battle line will destroy enemy fleet if enemy elects to fight or by sinking slowed or crippled ships if enemy retreats. Action against the enemy will be pushed vigorously by all hands to ensure complete destruction of his fleet. Destroyers running short of fuel may be returned to Saipan if necessary for refueling."

The directive caught Mitscher off guard. It sounded as if Spruance were assuming command of the upcoming battle, maneuvering Mitscher's queens and Lee's bishops around the oceanic chessboard with squares defined by degrees of latitude and longitude. To avoid any confusion, Mitscher requested amplification as to who was calling the shots. Spruance's reply confirmed that Task Force 58 was to conduct its own fight in accordance with his overall policy.

That evening, some six hundred miles west of Guam, *Cavalla*'s radar strobed with some major blips. There were at least seven big ships ten miles to the east.

Closing the distance, Herman Kossler mentally smacked his lips: The procession crossing his viewfinder was unlike anything he had ever seen. He counted at least fifteen ships steaming east at nineteen knots. In the darkness he was unable to see many more, but *Cavalla* had found the First Mobile Fleet.

With the discipline of an Annapolis professional, Kossler passed up the chance to add major tonnage to his score. He avoided attacking in favor of notifying Lockwood of Neptune's jackpot. Subsequently ComSubPac ordered *Cavalla* to pursue and attack, even if it meant running his fuel to near exhaustion. Many hours in trail, Kossler exercised his initiative. Beneath a fourth-quarter moon, he headed for a point in the Pacific Ocean where he suspected he might resume the trail. In *Cavalla*'s engine room, four sixteen-cylinder General Motors diesels sucked fuel from her ninety-four-thousand-gallon tanks. She would be heard from again.

Meanwhile, the aggressive Lockwood signaled all skippers: "The . . . list of enemy ships does not frighten our varsity. We have all that and plenty more ready and waiting, and they are all rough, tough, and nasty."

June 17

VICE ADMIRAL KAKUTA REMAINED UNDERSTANDABLY curious about Task Force 58's activities, and continued dispatching reconnaissance flights to their doom. In war's grim ledger, it made sense: If one crew survived long enough to get off a useful report, that was ample use of assets. Consequently, snoopers were splashed routinely throughout the day. Of ten kills, eight went to the escort carrier pilots, mainly east of Saipan.

Other shore-based units were more proactive. Five Jills of Naval Air Group 551 attacked a "transport convoy" in the invasion area. They allegedly set afire a light cruiser, which "listed heavily and is considered to have sunk." A destroyer was claimed afire and probably sunk. For good measure, one tanker was reported blown up. The only U.S. record of damage on the seventeenth occurred when an escort carrier group was attacked by a large formation south of Saipan. *Fanshaw Bay* took a bomb through her aft elevator and withdrew to Pearl Harbor with fourteen men killed.

Later in the day the first Martin PBMs arrived from Eniwetok, as per Spruance's request. Supported by the seaplane tender *Ballard*, almost immediately PatRon Sixteen began flying six-hundred-mile searches—nearly twice the distance possible with carrier planes, though of course the flattops operated well out to sea.

That evening *Cavalla's* crew was still disappointed after the thirteen-hour stern chase of the oilers. But at 2000, some 350 miles off Samar, Herman Kossler's radar got a long-range contact: "a faint, fading pip at 30,000 yards." It was definitely worth investigating.

Kossler began a high-speed run-in, then reversed course to slow the closure rate for better identification. At twenty-two thousand yards the radar picture showed seven large blips zigzagging easterly at a nineteen-knot rate of advance. Taking position ahead of the force, *Cavalla* gleaned more radar data that seemed promising. From fifteen thousand yards the disposition was a large bogey with six smaller blips in two columns, obviously escorts.

It looked a lot like a carrier group.

Anticipating a possible setup, Kossler dived, leveling off to continue radar tracking. As the unidentified task group bore down on her, *Cavalla's* sonar operators began picking up distinct screw noises—lots of them. Before long the sharp-eared listeners had identified at least fifteen acoustic signatures. Obviously, something big was passing overhead.

Herman Kossler decided to take his boat to a hundred feet, allowing the topside parade to proceed on its way. However, two "trailers" remained in the area, keeping *Cavalla* down for about an hour. After they departed, Kossler surfaced and reported his find to ComSubPac.

Ozawa had been found.

Meanwhile, aboard *Taiho*, Ozawa held a strategy session with his staff. He reviewed the latest intelligence updates, which largely confirmed his previous estimates. By now he knew that he was facing Spruance and Mitscher: information obtained from captured American documents and interrogation of downed pilots without undue concern for the strictures of the 1929 Geneva Convention.

The certainty that Fifth Fleet was in Spruance's hands shaped Ozawa's approach to the impending battle. He felt confident that because of Spruance's conservative nature, the American carriers would likely remain within a hundred miles of the invasion beaches. That seemed even more likely now that the amphibious operation was under way, with U.S. troops ashore on Saipan.

Information from Naval General Headquarters was disappointingly incomplete. While two carrier groups had been savaging Iwo Jima (Harrill's reluctance was likely unknown), Tokyo only alluded to one other group somewhere west of Guam.

Hedging his bets as much as he felt justified, Ozawa decided to hold back CarDiv Two on the day of battle, and not without reason. He knew that American carriers had outflanked *Kido Butai* at Midway and Santa Cruz, appearing from an unexpected quarter. He wanted to be able to respond to that contingency, so Air Group 652 would be held in reserve.

Ironically, therefore, both opposing admirals based their strategy partly on the mistaken assumption that each would seek a way around the other's flank. Raymond Spruance and Jisaburo Ozawa were steaming into a long-range face-off, bow-to-bow, while casting a wary eye to port and starboard.

The enemy composition was known with startling accuracy in Task Force 58. Correspondent Noel Busch developed a close rapport with Mitscher's staff (a later generation would recognize the thirty-eight-year-old *Life* reporter as "embedded"), partly because of his knowledge of Japan and the Far East. Since he could not possibly divulge any secrets, he had free access to "flag country" and routinely jotted down information for future reference. He correctly recorded that the Mobile Fleet was composed of about fifty ships, including nine carriers embarking some 450 aircraft: figures that were exactly right.

June 18

As NEAR AS ANYONE COULD tell, Arleigh Burke didn't sleep. Before 0400 he roused Mitscher with word of *Cavalla*'s sighting several hours before. The admiral pulled on some khakis and joined Burke with Duke Hedding in flag plot. Setting his dividers to the map's scale, Burke walked off the distance and concluded that the Mobile Fleet likely would be 660 miles west of Saipan at dawn.

After some back-and-forthing, reinforced by competent speculation, Mitscher guesstimated that he could take a shot at Ozawa before sunset. The Mobile Fleet would be within range by late afternoon, assuming that Task Force 58 took the logical move and started steaming west right away.

Licking his chops at the prospect, Mitscher began laying plans. He radioed Lee, asking the old gunfighter if he would seek a night surface battle. Lee's response came as a surprise: "Do not, repeat not, believe we should seek night engagement."

Nobody yearned for a shoot-out more than Ching Lee, but his reasoning was impeccable. His force, though the most powerful surface unit afloat, was not well trained in group tactics. His beautiful battlewagons were most useful as high-speed antiaircraft platforms to protect the carriers, and that was where their experience lay. Additionally, Lee anticipated nocturnal radio problems that were typical in the area, and he retained a healthy respect for the Imperial Navy's night-fighting skills. If there were to be a surface battle, he much preferred that it take place in daylight.

* * *

War correspondent Noel Busch jotted another memo to himself: "Church services were held today, apparently which is Sunday." The uncertainty reflected the often humdrum pace of life at sea. The indicator of the Sabbath was deduced by conduct of divine services aboard *Lexington*, including standby hymns such as "Lead, Kindly Light." The service ended with "the one about the perils of the sea." Busch might have deduced that the latter was none other than "The Navy Hymn," upgraded to the twentieth century with addition of a passage "for those in peril in the air."

That morning, job one for Task Force 58 was locating the Mobile Fleet. Consequently, two- and three-plane search teams were launched to scout to a distance of 325 miles west of the force. Most were airborne by 0530, winging their way on the outbound leg of their wedge-shaped sectors. Inevitably, American and Japanese scouting sectors overlapped.

The skirmishing between opposing scouts was not surprising. At 0600 Mitscher's and Ozawa's flagships were roughly 420 sea miles apart—well beyond the normal U.S. search radius but within reach of the longer-legged Japanese. Furthermore, the Imperial Navy benefited from land-based recon, including the very capable Bettys that had skirted Mitscher's aerial picket line. Whether the Mobile Fleet received timely reports from the *Kokutai*s ashore is uncertain, but Ozawa's organic recce birds certainly fetched back something useful when they roosted.

The first search wave that morning comprised fourteen Kates and two Jake floatplanes sniffing the easterly wind from north-northwest to east-southeast: 350 to 110 degrees. Their orders took them to the very edge of Mitscher's widely deployed groups: 425 miles. At least two scouts radioed contact with American aircraft, but three dropped off the edge of the earth. Ozawa never knew what happened to them; Mitscher did.

Enterprise contributed four teams, including one of the most re-markable aviators in Task Force 58. Lieutenant Junior Grade Charles English Henderson III was a torpedo pilot known as "Hotshot

Charlie." Possessed of a bulletproof optimism, Henderson wasn't completely fearless, but he gave that impression. Despite his unspritely Avenger, he thrived on air-to-air encounters; in the first he outfoxed a persistent Zeke pilot at Truk Atoll, timing his breaks so artfully that the Japanese ran out of ammo and disengaged with a sporting tilt of the wings.

After that close call, Henderson swore off playing fighter pilot. His resolve lasted until this day, June 18. While flying a sector search with a wingman, Henderson spotted a floatplane. For a moment there was consternation in the TBF cockpit. "Suddenly there was a Jake—fat, dumb, and happy, cruising along far off my port wing. I too was fat, dumb, and happy. In fact, I had my shoes off, feet on top of the instrument panel, smoking a cigar. I still don't know what happened to the cigar. All I do know was that I was shortly 90 degrees port, full throttle, guns charged, and hands sweating. I knew I'd only have one chance. Ensign Cliff Largess was flying my wing, a very eager young man."

Making artful use of clouds, Henderson closed almost to rock-throwing distance from the right rear. He sweetened up the sight picture, barely touched the trigger, and executed the Aichi with seventeen rounds of .50 caliber.

Essex teams made two of the three contacts that morning. Just before 0800 Lieutenant Junior Grade Raymond L. Turner was leading in his Helldiver when he made the cross-leg turn at the 325-mile limit of his outbound leg. At that point he noticed a single-engine aircraft perhaps five miles off, flying at roughly his own altitude of a thousand feet. It had to be hostile.

Turner had helped sink a Japanese transport on June 12, but aerial encounters were new to him. Nonetheless, he decided to engage. He added power to his big Wright engine, climbed up beside his Hellcat escort, and pointed out the stranger. Ensign James E. Duffy immediately got the message. Forming up, the Hellcat and Helldiver gave chase.

As they closed the distance, closer examination revealed a hostile: one of Obayashi's scouts. The *Essex* pilots were inside five hundred yards before they were spotted; then the chase was on. Though they identified the enemy as a Jill, it was certainly a Kate, the older Naka-jima torpedo plane now most useful in reconnaissance.

Whatever the bandit's identity, Turner approached it below and be-hind while Duffy went wide, trapping the Nakajima in a three-dimensional squeeze play.

Both Americans opened fire, with Duffy scoring .50-caliber hits from the beam. Turner had armed his two wing-mounted 20mm can-non and triggered about a hundred rounds, knocking off chunks of aluminum. Caught in an unavoidable cross fire, the enemy scout bomber gushed flames. Turner drove in close enough to see the gunner apparently dead, slumped over the side of the rear cockpit, while the pilot tried to escape. In stop-frame motion, the ghastly details revealed themselves: The Japanese flight suits had caught fire. Then the Kate slid off on one wing and dived into the Pacific's extinguishing embrace.

Though both pilots scored telling hits, back aboard *Essex* the credit for the kill went to Duffy.

Ninety minutes later another Air Group 15 team had a near-identical experience in a sector to the northeast. Bombing 15's Lieu-tenant Junior Grade William S. Rising also was first to sight the enemy, alerting Ensign Kenneth A. Flinn to the Betty bomber. Flinn took over, chasing the fast Mitsubishi in and out of some low clouds. After four firing passes he set the port wing afire—a typical reaction, as Japanese land attack crews sardonically called their aircraft the "Type One Lighter." Descending to attempt a ditching, the Betty snagged a wingtip on the waves and cartwheeled to destruction in a montage of flames, smoke, spray, and debris.

It was Ken Flinn's second victory. That October, with five notches, he was shot down and captured near Okinawa. He died of starvation in a Japanese prison camp the following July, age twenty-one. Three weeks later the emperor announced Japan's surrender.

Another intercept was logged by *Monterey*'s VF-28. Patrolling near the force at 0855, Lieutenant Oscar C. Bailey's division was vectored onto a Betty and immediately pounced. He and his wingman, Ensign John R. Bicknell, dropped it within several miles of *Monterey*.

Other scouts and snoopers were intercepted throughout the day, including two Judys scared or splashed by Fighting 25 and 28. Meanwhile, Fighting Eight bagged a Betty 120 miles west of Guam, and a *Hornet* search team interrupted a Jake's recon flight 240 miles from Task Force 58. Sniffing around the edges of the American carrier fleet was increasingly hazardous duty.

Though the early searches turned up no Japanese ships, there was reason for grins in flag country. At midmorning Task Groups 58.1 and 58.4 topped the northern horizon. Clark and Harrill had returned from the Bonins chore in good time; Marc Mitscher had his full force available for the showdown with Jisaburo Ozawa.

But the Mobile Fleet remained undetected by American aircraft—carrier-, land-, or sea-based. In a 165-degree arc, northwest to south, Mitscher's search teams flew to the extent of their range—325 miles—but despite good visibility nothing was seen. Pieced together later, the two plots came about sixty miles short. The mantra went, "Find, fix, and strike." Until Task Force 58 had a solid contact there was no prospect for an attack.

At that point, Jisaburo Ozawa knew more than Marc Mitscher. Realizing that he was within recon range of Task Force 58, Ozawa ordered another search during the noon hour. This time he dispatched thirteen speedy Judys and two more Jakes. Then he changed course more northerly, shifting fleet axis to 030, keeping ample salt water between the Americans and himself. Then he awaited word from his minions.

The first contacts were not what Ozawa anticipated. Several reports mentioned enemy aircraft, including one of a "flying boat," probably a Liberator from the Admiralties. Eight Zekes were sent out to catch it but they came up empty: There was too much sky and too little time. Some of the searching fighters never returned from the oceanic expanse.

However, the number fifteen scout struck gold. Shortly past 1500 he was flying the northerly cross-leg of his sector when he saw flat-tops steaming southwest. The closest U.S. carrier group was then 180 miles west-northwest of Guam. However, the report was probably disappointing to the staff in *Taiho*, as it included no information of enemy composition or numbers. But amplification soon arrived from other sectors to the north. At 1500 precisely, the number thirteen scout broadcast its finding: carriers headed west.

A little over an hour later, scout number seventeen discovered the naval Big Rock Candy Mountain: three American carrier groups, each with two visible flattops and ten or more escorts. One report was specific if not entirely accurate: two "regular" *Saratoga*-class carriers. "Sara," second of the prewar *Lexington* class, was nowhere near the Marianas that day (she was undergoing an overhaul in Bremerton, Washington), but no matter: U.S. carriers had definitely been spotted. The other groups contained "seemingly regular carriers."

Then, for the frosting on the recon cake, the very astute young men in scout number seventeen added a local weather report: seven-tenths coverage with cloud decks at a thousand and nine thousand meters. Wind was reckoned at ten knots from a hundred degrees true.

Whatever His Imperial Japanese Majesty paid his carrier scout crews in 1944, they earned every yen.

Ten minutes after receiving number fifteen scout's report, Ozawa began shaping the geometry of the next day's battle. Surely June 19 would see the opposing fleets exchanging air strikes, and Ozawa intended to keep his enemy at arm's reach, just within the radius of his own aerial haymakers. Mitscher, though an intuitive counterpuncher, would find himself outdistanced.

Therefore, the Mobile Fleet's base course was shifted from northeasterly to southwesterly: from 060 to 200. By opening the distance during the night, the Japanese would preserve their advantage of range when the Americans were relocated again in the morning.

During the day, Japanese dive-bombers attacked oilers in Task Group 50.17 some thirty miles southeast of Guam. The attackers, identified as eight Judys in two groups, were more determined than the torpedo planes repelled by gunfire the previous day. Though destroyers splashed three raiders, the others hit *Neshanic*, *Saugatuck*, and *Saranac*. The latter lay dead in the water until tugs arrived that night.

The "jeep" carriers continued their winning ways on the eighteenth, downing twenty-three of the thirty-one Japanese planes claimed. In barely an hour that afternoon *Coral Sea*'s pilots earned their keep, splashing ten bandits twenty-five miles east of Saipan. Eight more were credited as probables or damaged.

On the evening of the eighteenth another submarine turned in a report. *Finback*, under Lieutenant Commander James L. Jordan, spotted searchlights to the south and laid on knots in that direction, hoping for radar contact. It was not to be.

What *Finback* saw was Carrier Division Three. Around 1630 Obayashi's radio watch monitored number fifteen scout's report describing part of the U.S. fleet. Taking the initiative, he ordered an attack, against the better judgment and advice of his staff. With sixty-seven planes already armed and warmed up on his three flight decks, Obayashi gave the launch signal at 1637. But as his squadrons were forming up he received Ozawa's order to turn southwesterly, keeping the distance between Task Force 58 and the Mobile Fleet. Since Ozawa did not know of Obayashi's aggressiveness, the strike was recalled.

Chiyoda's *Hikokitai* 332 had just launched twenty-one aircraft (mostly Zero fighter-bombers) when the recall was issued. One fighter crashed on takeoff, but the others safely got back aboard.

Air Group 653's aircrews were generally disappointed at the aborted mission. In their blissful ignorance, they felt that a night attack would achieve surprise, and by proceeding on to Guam they would be in position for a restrike in the morning. Whether any regarded the marginal state of their training to accomplish either goal—let alone both—is uncertain but dubious at best.

In their defense, Obayashi's enthusiastic fliers knew nothing of the U.S. Navy's eye-watering air defense capability. The next morning they would painfully learn just how effective the combination of radar, radio, and powerful fighters really was. But that night, returning to their ready rooms, they undoubtedly griped in the manner of all military subordinates at the unfathomable ways of those with braid on their hats.

Having preserved his distance advantage for the morrow's battle, Ozawa then negated much of his edge. He had told his subordinates, "I will pound the American fleet with carrier-based planes, land-based bombers, and the guns of my surface vessels. I will give them no time to counterattack." Therefore, he broadcast a request to Kakuta's land-based air force to coordinate with carrier strikes the next day. American signals intelligence got a rough bearing via direction finder, but no range. However, the radio monitoring stations in Hawaii, Alaska, and elsewhere could triangulate and provide a decent position fix.

Ozawa's staff knew that Task Force 58 would operate in four task groups, presumably with twelve carriers (there were in fact fifteen). Deploying only nine flattops, the Mobile Fleet nevertheless felt confident. Said Masatake Okumiya, "We had never assembled in one striking force so much carrier aviation, and our pilots were convinced that they would shatter the attacking American fleet. It appears, however, that these people who enjoyed such premature success thought only in terms of the total available aircraft carriers and their planes, failing to give due consideration to the human factor."

Okumiya was from the fifty-eighth (1930) Etajima class, so he enjoyed some perspective. He had spent the early months of the war with a carrier division staff and, following reassignment, fetched up at Rabaul. He left that isolated garrison in early 1944 and joined the Mobile Fleet. Consequently, he was one of a handful of experienced aviators on Ozawa's staff.

Noting the decline in Imperial Navy tactical leadership, Okumiya compared the Midway air group commanders from the 1924 class with the 1934 to 1936 classes. "In only the two short years . . . the average age of the senior air group leaders had dropped by at least ten years. Unfortunately, too, the skill of the air crews which flew in the Marianas conflict had deteriorated in direct proportion to the average reduced age of their commanding officers."

Reportedly some in the Mobile Fleet felt that Ozawa's force would surprise the Americans off Saipan. If so, they ignored the evidence: Four destroyers were sunk by U.S. subs and aircraft around Borneo, and boats like *Harder* had been attacked while tracking the force after it sortied. One believer was *Hiyo's* skipper, Captain Toshiyuki Yokoi, who said, "We were completely undetected, we were sure of it; sure also we would sight the American fleet before it sighted us, and destroy it. Fighting morale was at fever pitch from the supreme commander right down to the lowest mess hand."

The Americans also had erred in their original assessments, but those mistakes had been recognized. By June 18 Raymond Spruance knew that his original estimate was wrong. Not only did the Japanese plan to fight: They were forcing a carrier action. As he later related to Nimitz, "Their attitude about risking their fleet had not changed. Their methods of operation had changed, in that they were using carriers again. . . . They had no intention of throwing everything at us by coming in to Saipan at high speed to fight it out."

Spruance realized that Ozawa meant to fight at arm's length—four hundred miles if possible—thus denying the "meleeist" theory espoused by Alfred Thayer Mahan and more recent naval strategists. Studious as ever, Spruance fetched something he had written long before the war. During his 1926 War College tour he had studied the Russo-Japanese War and came away admiring Admiral Junichi Togo, who had patiently awaited arrival of the Black Sea Fleet virtually on Japan's doorstep. The historic victory at Tsushima Strait in 1905 struck a chord that resonated in Raymond Spruance's analytical brain: "The way Togo waited . . . for the Russian fleet to come to him has always been on my mind. . . . We had somewhat the same situation, only it was modified by the long-range striking power of the carriers."

That settled it: Task Force 58 would stand by and absorb whatever blows the Mobile Fleet threw. As Burke expressed it, "We knew we were going to have hell slugged out of us in the morning." With the shield of radar and the sword of Hellcats, the Americans would block, parry, and counterthrust Ozawa's aerial kendo. Simultaneously, the potentially vulnerable troop transports would be protected.

To say that Spruance's decision did not sit well in Task Force 58 was akin to saying that J. Edgar Hoover disapproved of crime. Mitscher and his staff seethed at what they saw as a lost opportunity of historic proportions. Even Arleigh Burke, the dedicated surface warrior, was steamed. He spent part of the night drafting one scorching message after another, hoping to convince Spruance to permit the carriers to steam westward and engage the Mobile Fleet in the morning. His co-conspirator was newfound friend and soul mate Commander "Jim-mie" Thach, who later confessed that the early drafts fit the legal description of mutiny.

But the evening dragged on, and each succeeding version found its way into the "burn before reading" file. Eventually all hands acknowledged the inevitable and gave up the fight. It was Ray Spruance's call, and if the fleet commander was concerned about a Japanese end run, so be it. Nobody could dispute that in naval warfare, flanks could move at thirty miles per hour: two hundred miles in perhaps eight hours. Never mind that the transports were well guarded; never mind that Task Force 58 had the enemy in numbers, personnel, and equipment. As Sunday night rolled over to Monday morning, it was advent of the greatest air battle in American history.

Balance of Forces

THE FORCES COMMITTED TO THE forthcoming clash were enormous: They represented more than the combined carriers involved in all four previous battles.

Arrayed against Spruance were Ozawa's three carrier divisions with nine flattops, five battleships, thirteen cruisers (two light), and twenty-eight destroyers. However, Ozawa lost five destroyers en route to the Marianas, leaving forty-six surface combatants plus nineteen of an original twenty-four submarines.

Both fleets also had logistics groups including oilers and ammunition ships not reflected here. The numbers were impressive, historically so, but the totals can be deceiving.

	Fleet Carrier (CV)	Light Carrier (CVL)	Battle-ship (BB)	Heavy Cruiser (CA)	Light Cruiser (CL)	Destroyer (DD)	Sub-marine (SS)	Total
USN:	7	8	7	8	13	68	27	138
IJN:	5	4	5	11	2	23	19	69

The defense of the Marianas would be an air battle, and warships were the smaller part of the equation. Mitscher embarked some 900 planes in his fast carriers, leaving two Seventh Fleet escort carrier groups to devote nearly 200 more aircraft to other duties. Ozawa embarked almost 440 planes, while nominally 630 more waited ashore in the Marianas and other bases within range.

Ozawa's nine carriers were generally comparable to Mitscher's; a few were bigger and in some ways more capable. But despite world-class organization and equipment in 1941, the Imperial Navy had slipped badly in the next two years.

Though big and capable, with fairly recent carriers, the Mobile Fleet was showing its age. Of twelve cruisers and five battleships, only three vessels had been commissioned since 1941, a startling contrast to the much larger Fifth Fleet. Ozawa's oldest was battleship *Kongo* from 1913. Yet, despite the superiority of some vessels such as the superbattleships *Yamato* and *Musashi*—the biggest ever built—the Imperial Navy was a fleet in decline.

Arguably the most prestigious carriers were the veterans *Shokaku* and *Zuikaku*. The prewar sisters had been commissioned in the summer of 1941, and by mid-1944 they were the only survivors of the six that launched the Pearl Harbor attack. They had made every carrier battle but Midway. However, Ozawa flew his flag in *Taiho*, at 34,600 tons the second biggest carrier afloat. She was brand-new, having been completed only in March.

Joshima's CarDiv Two was built around the 26,900-ton sisters *Junyo* and *Hiyo* and 16,700-ton CVL *Ryuho*, all completed in 1942. *Junyo* and *Hiyo* were merchant conversions; *Junyo* fought at Santa Cruz in October 1942, while *Hiyo* had an undistinguished career. She'd been torpedoed in June 1943, repaired, and returned to service.

Three light carriers comprised Obayashi's CarDiv Three: *Chitose* and *Chiyoda* with *Zuiho*. The latter was completed a year before hostilities and had been damaged at Santa Cruz in October 1942. *Chitose* and *Chiyoda* were constructed as seaplane carriers but converted to CVLs in 1943.

Four of the Mobile Fleet's flattops had fought carriers previously: the big sisters *Shokaku* and *Zuikaku* plus *Junyo* and *Zuiho*, nearly as large. But that had been in 1942. There had not been a fleet engagement since, and the Japanese experience level had continually declined while America's steadily increased.

Most of Ozawa's carrier captains were new to their commands, with two or three months' experience. The flagship's commander, Captain Tomozo Kikuchi, had just put *Taiho* in commission, though he previously commanded *Zuikaku*. *Shokaku*'s Hiroshi Matsubara and *Chitose*'s Yoshiyuki Kishi were senior in tenure, having commanded since November.

The emperor's veteran carriers were sisters *Shokaku* and *Zuikaku*, 1941 ships that debuted at Pearl Harbor. "Flying Crane" and "Auspicious Crane" had been laid down in 1937 and 1938 by the Kawasaki shipyard at Kobe, benefiting from previous carrier experience. They were big, handsome ships grossing some twenty-nine thousand tons, embarking nearly seventy planes.

Together the "Cranes" had constituted CarDiv Five, in 1942 regarded with moderate scorn by CarDiv One's veterans *Akagi* and *Kaga*. "Sho" and "Zui" fought at Coral Sea, giving and receiving damage in the world's first carrier battle, prompting senior airmen to sniff, "Son of concubine won a victory." In truth, Coral Sea was a strategic defeat for Japan, as the objective (Port Moresby, New Guinea) was not seized. Additionally, Sho took heavy damage, and Zui's air group was mauled so they were knocked out of the Midway lineup, with fatal consequences for Japan's ambition.

Following the post-Midway realignment, Sho and Zui were redesignated CarDiv One, now reinforced with the spanking-new *Taiho*.

Thus, Ozawa concentrated his three largest carriers in one powerful task group.

Though neither side knew for sure, certainly they suspected another rematch with old opponents. *Shokaku* and *Zuikaku* had tangled with *Enterprise* twice before, off Guadalcanal. At Eastern Solomons in August 1942, their respective air groups stalked each other in a largely inconclusive duel, only the third ever fought by flattops. Two months later in the sanguinary Santa Cruz battle, Sho and Zui had helped put *Hornet* on the bottom, leaving the Big E to limp away. *Enterprise* aviators were eager for another shot at their perennial rivals.

Not only had Japan's technological advantage disappeared in two years, but the human factor was, if anything, even more deficient. Ozawa had lost the combat edge that Chuichi Nagumo had enjoyed in 1941–42. By mid-1944 Japanese aircrews were far less experienced than their predecessors, let alone their enemies. Most American aviators now entered combat with five hundred to six hundred hours of flight time, confidently competent in carrier operations. Many of the Japanese pilots had never deployed; the simplicity of their planes and procedures kept them out of the water.

As a nonaviator, Ozawa matched Spruance in background and intellect, but institutionally there were major differences in the two navies. Like the British, the Japanese did not require pilots to command aircraft carriers, and both fleets did well. However, by U.S. law, only aviators could become carrier captains, the result of bitter experience in the 1920s when some ill-considered orders by "paddlefeet" commanders led to airmen's deaths. Consequently, some senior officers were sent to quickie "aviation observer" courses, and later men in their forties were given pilot wings in the 1930s: Ernest King and William Halsey being the most notable. Gradually the "real" aviators like Pete Mitscher gained enough seniority to walk a carrier's bridge on their merits rather than tenure.

Forager also shaped up as another rematch of sorts, as several of Ozawa's ships had sailed in the Pearl Harbor task force. Besides carriers

Shokaku and *Zuikaku* were cruisers *Chikuma* and *Tone*, and four destroyers. Since then, fifteen of the twenty-seven ships in the Pearl Harbor force had been lost, and only one destroyer would survive the war.

There were also 1941 veterans with Mitscher. Two cruisers and ten destroyers had been at Pearl that Sunday: *San Francisco* and *New Orleans*; *Bagley, Conyngham, Dewey, Helm, Hull, MacDonough, Mugford, Patterson, Ralph Talbot,* and *Selfridge. Indianapolis*, Spruance's flagship off Saipan, had been at sea on December 7, as was *Minneapolis* and the homeward-bound *Enterprise.*

Now the Pearl Harbor survivors would meet again, more than two thousand miles west of Hawaii. They would clash in a battle whose size and nature were almost unimagined thirty months previously—a battle that would determine the fate of an empire.

On the U.S. side, the mind and muscle behind the Fifth Fleet's machinery represented nearly every age, origin, and attitude that midcentury America could produce: healthy males from their teens to their late fifties. There were riflemen, airmen, and frogmen; kids too young to drink and seadogs too old to quit. There were hard-shell Baptists, evangelical Mormons, recovering Catholics, and confirmed atheists. There were athletes and scholars; bigamists and rapists. There were men who had written books and those who could barely read. There were nascent heroes and practicing cowards; those who would exceed all expectations and a few who would disappoint their shipmates and themselves. Some would die far too young; others would live far too long with maladies yet unnamed.

All were bound for one destination.

Next stop: Saipan.

PART THREE

"Your Signal: Buster"

TWO FLEETS STEAMED THROUGH THE midnight darkness, occasionally trailing phosphorescence in their wakes. Task Force 58 bore 230 miles west-southwest of Saipan while the Mobile Fleet lay some 300 miles farther southwesterly.

For the infantrymen of V Amphibious Corps, that evening had brought reason for optimism and concern. Heavy resistance on Saipan had resulted in two thousand American casualties in four days, prompting Marine lieutenant general Holland M. Smith to commit his reserve, the 27th Infantry Division. Of his two Marine divisions, the Fourth had reached the island's east coast, while the Second had repulsed a Japanese attack supported by tanks—a rarity in Pacific combat. Meanwhile, the GIs were securing the south end of Saipan, with more fighting clearly to come.

Knowing that a Japanese "end run" was possible, Admiral Raymond Spruance was concerned with filling his primary mission: protecting the beachhead. Vice Admiral Marc Mitscher with his carriers believed the best way to do that was to find and sink Ozawa's Mobile Fleet.

June 19

BOTH SIDES KNEW THAT IT WOULD be a day of battle. It started early.

At 0100, Japanese aircraft droned through the darkness near Mitscher's flagship. They dropped float flares and turned away, undoubtedly making for Guam. One of the 58.1 screen, Commander Donald T. Eller's *Burns*, attempted the innovative technique of depth-charging the floating flares, but they stubbornly kept burning.

Shortly before 0200 Spruance learned of *Finback*'s sighting: search-lights northeast of the direction-finder "fix." Not until much later did Spruance receive a potentially confirming report from PBMs, just prior to the sub report. Flying from Garapan Roads, the Mariners snooped six hundred miles in the westerly quadrant, making good use of search radar. Lieutenant H. F. Arle's operator was astounded by a huge return: some forty ships only seventy-five miles from the HF/DF plot. Proper assessment would have shown that a mere three hundred miles separated the U.S. and Japanese forces. Assuming that Ozawa continued steaming east, and Mitscher maintained the distance, a major strike could have caught Ozawa in early daylight.

However, the opportunity vanished in the fog of war. The contact report was not received, apparently owing to atmospheric conditions, though reportedly another aircraft monitored the message and failed to relay it. Consequently, the report had to await Arle's return, and Fifth Fleet staff did not read the report for seven and a half hours.

In the meantime, other intelligence reached the flagship. Spruance got *Finback*'s sighting report just before 0200 on the nineteenth. Later he monitored a SubPac response to *Stingray*'s garbled contact report amplifying *Finback*'s contact.

As Task Force 58 continued easterly, the possible geometry began coming together. Based on submarine reports and radio direction finding, Spruance and Mitscher arrived at different conclusions. The carrier commander reckoned that if he turned west, daylight would bring the two forces close enough to exchange air strikes. He put his staff to work with that in mind. Gus Widhelm and company burned the midnight oil.

Aboard his flagship *Indianapolis*, Spruance's intel shop also worked late. His Japanese linguist was Commander Gilven Slonim, who benefited from PacFleet's excellent cryptanalysts. Armed with a list of Ozawa's ships and most of their call signs, Gil Slonim could keep Fifth Fleet advised of enemy actions as long as the Japanese unlocked their Morse code keys and began tapping.

However, the fleet commander dismissed the available intelligence as too sketchy. He dwelled on a possible end run by one or more of Ozawa's carrier groups and decided to stick to his priority: guarding the invasion beaches. The orders remained unchanged. Mitscher sulked in his cabin.

According to *Enterprise* legend, when Captain Matt Gardner heard the news, he threw his cap on the deck. Then he stomped on it.

In the wee hours of the morning, both fleets began probing the Pacific blackness, feeling their way toward each other beneath the night's dark cover.

Ozawa's fingers were longer than Mitscher's.

At 0200 Bill Martin's fourteen Avengers departed the Big E, spreading out to scan the 240- to 270-degree sector. They were aimed in the right direction but fell about sixty miles short of the enemy van force.

Meanwhile, Ozawa continued closing the distance. At 0300 he ordered the Mobile Fleet onto its attack course, 050, and the three groups turned northeasterly, working up to twenty knots.

Ninety minutes later the van was in position to launch a two-phase search. Throughout the war the Imperial Navy relied upon battleship and cruiser floatplanes for much of its scouting, contrary to the Americans, who used carrier aircraft almost exclusively.

Much had been learned at Midway—all of it the hard way—and there was evidence that the battle had turned on a balky catapult that prevented a cruiser from launching her plane in time. That delay added thirty minutes to *Tone*'s number four scout in spotting one of the two American carrier forces.

Consequently, Ozawa and Kurita agreed that a one-phase search entailed excess risk. The double approach used more assets but presumably eliminated the possibility of nasty surprises—the nastiest being enemy dive-bombers rolling in over the flagship, unannounced.

At 0445 Kurita's floatplanes banged off their catapults, the crews punched in the back by powerful black-powder charges. Phase one involved sixteen Aichi E13As (Jakes) scouting 315 to 135 degrees to 350 miles. It was extraordinarily cautious, as 315 true lay to the west-northwest, behind the Mobile Fleet. The Americans were not the only ones concerned about an end run.

The first launch was briefed to fly eastward 350 miles, reaching the cross-leg about 0700. At that point the scouts would turn ninety degrees and fly another thirty miles before returning. It was obvious that they found something: Only six returned. Eight fell afoul of American searchers or combat air patrols, and another was caught by VF-50 while trying to get into Guam. The other simply disappeared.

At 0515 fourteen more recon aircraft (all but one from carrier decks) were winging into the morning sun. The Nakajima B5N Kates from Obayashi's division scoured three hundred miles to the eastern hemisphere, north to south, and found nothing. The recon mission was important enough that the division's senior torpedo officer took the flight. Lieutenant Commander Masayuki Yamagami led eight Kates westward; neither he nor the others were ever seen again.

Ordinarily floatplanes would augment antisub patrols around the task force, but today they were needed for searches. It was a matter of allocating limited resources, and something had to give. Besides, in two and a half years of war, American submarines had never sunk a fleet carrier.

In order to avoid any gaps in the pattern, Ozawa dispatched a third search wave at 0530. It was the most ambitious of the battle, with eight CarDiv One Judys and three Jills plus two Jakes from *Mogami*, stretching their fuel (and maybe their luck) to a kidney-straining 560 miles, 020 to 105 degrees true. It meant at least six and a half hours round-trip.

Whatever *Nihon Kaigun*'s failings, reconnaissance was not among them. In the hour before sunrise, forty-three scouts were airborne with the rust-red *hinomaru* on their wings.

Floatplanes

BOTH NAVIES USED FLOATPLANES FOR reconnaissance and gunfire spotting, but Japan far more than the U.S.

Carried on battleships and cruisers, floatplanes had been used for more than twenty years. Sitting on swivel-mounted catapults, the planes had their noses turned into the prevailing wind, the engines run up to max rpm, and then were flung into the air. The slingshot effect was unpleasant: a sudden kick in the small of the back as a hefty black-powder charge sent the observation plane on its way down a sixty-foot track. The violent acceleration shoved the pilot back in his seat as airspeed spiked from zero to fifty knots or more in about two seconds.

Getting off the ship was one thing; getting back was quite another.

Upon return from a scouting or spotting mission, the floatplane pilot faced one of three options. In the U.S. Navy the procedures were Able, Baker, and Cast recovery (Charlie for *C* came postwar). Able was employed when the parent ship lay at anchor, in which case the airplane taxied up to the stern, where it was hoisted aboard.

Baker recovery came with the ship under way in calm seas. Much like Able, it involved overtaking the ship and being craned back on deck.

Cast recovery posed a test of seamanship as much as airmanship. Floatplanes were vulnerable to high seas, requiring the ship to steam in a wide circle, creating a smoother landing surface in its wake. Simultaneously the crew rigged booms over one side to trail a hemp sled or mat resembling a cargo net. The pilot landed as close to the mat as possible, added power to overtake the ten-knot advance, and drove his plane onto the mat.

On the bottom of the center float was a hook to engage the latticework pattern of the mat. Once it was engaged, the pilot cut his throttle and the aircraft was reeled in. A hoist cable was lowered from the crane, with pilot and observer standing in their seats to affix the hooks to the lifting shackles. Once secure, the plane was lifted aboard and placed back on the catapult or on a dolly.

Task Force 58 had two types of observation aircraft: twenty-three Curtiss SOC biplanes and thirty-four Vought OS2U monoplanes, both prewar designs capable of about 165 mph.

The Mobile Fleet embarked some sixty-five floatplanes, mainly Aichi E13A1 monoplanes. Exceptionally long-ranged, with a three-man crew, the Jake was arguably the best recon floatplane of the war. Its combat debut had involved scouting ahead of the Pearl Harbor strike force. Additionally, Ozawa also had nine less-capable Mitsubishi F1M2 "Pete" biplanes with two-men crews.

Eyesight was crucial to the Imperial Navy's reconnaissance and targeting. Cruising at thirteen thousand feet (four thousand meters), their scouts could see 130 miles to the horizon on a cloudless day without haze. But seeing the far horizon was one thing: Making out ships was another. High-powered binoculars were far more common in Japanese cockpits than surface-search radar.

Airborne radar was perhaps the most significant failure of Japanese naval aviation. Though the advantages were obvious, and some land-based bombers possessed sets with a sixty-mile range, there was little impetus in the carrier realm. Partly the reason was bureaucratic: The Navy Technical Department assigned the Naval Air Arsenal the task of developing and acquiring airborne radar but provided too few technicians, funding, or support.

Sea Eagles

WITH ITS LARGEST FLEET YET formed during the war, *Nihon Kaigun*'s prized possession was not its enormous *Yamato*-class battleships, nor even its powerful aircraft carriers. The jewel in the Imperial Navy's crown was its carrier air groups.

Naval aviators always considered themselves elite. One peculiar manifestation in the Imperial Navy was permission for all aircrew to grow a full head of hair, as officers usually did. But every other non-commissioned member of His Majesty's armed forces maintained a shaven head.

Nihon Kaigun hatched its "sea eagles" in a variety of aeries: a complex of flight training programs recruiting budding aviators from various educational and age backgrounds. Commissioned officers were widely sought, but aviation expansion demanded acceptance of sailors already serving in the fleet. Consequently, petty officers and enlisted men went to the *Hei* program; eventually they formed the core of experienced aircrew.

However, direct enlistment for aviation was essential to maintain the force structure. The *Yokaren* programs included *Ko* for boys with at least three years of academic or vocational schooling beyond the elementary level. *Otsu* cadets possessed the minimum schooling.

By 1944 the razor-sharp prewar cadre of some eight hundred pilots had largely been expended at Midway and in the prolonged Guadalcanal meat grinder. Many of the second wave, competent but far less experienced, had perished in further Solomons action and the campaign to reduce Rabaul.

The current crop of carrier airmen would face appalling attrition. In many flight school classes—perhaps most—combat and operational losses reached 85 percent, with some approaching 100 percent. For example, among fighter pilots in the *Hei* second class, graduated in November 1941, only six among thirty-seven survived the war. The twelfth *Otsu* class of January 1943 sustained fifty-one killed from fifty-eight graduates. In the eleventh *Yokaren* class, winged in November 1943, four of thirty-seven survived.

Owing to such catastrophic losses, Japanese naval aviation had twice been rebuilt in the war: beginning in 1942 and then after the grinding attrition of the Solomons and Rabaul in 1943. Thus, in its third iteration the emperor's carrier air arm offered a pale reflection of itself. The glory days of Pearl Harbor and even Guadalcanal were long past, the ranks dreadfully thinned. While the numbers looked impressive, the quality had plummeted. With more and more rookie pilots and aircrew, the burden increasingly fell on the scarce supply of combat-experienced leaders: men like Zenji Abe.

By mid-1944 Lieutenant Zenji Abe was among the Imperial Navy's most experienced aviators. One of the dwindling group of Pearl Harbor attackers, he was appointed commander of Air Group 652's bombers in March. As a product of the IJN's rigorous prewar selection process, he knew the value of training and recognized the Mobile Fleet's lack of same. There had been very little flying in the forty days since leaving the Inland Sea. He wrote, "This unbelievable situation was causing various disadvantages in service to our aircraft and capability of the pilots." He was also concerned about the extreme ranges Japanese search pilots would face: four hundred nautical miles over open water was clearly beyond the ability of most newly winged airmen.

Abe's concern went farther up the chain of command. *Hiyo's* Captain Yokoi was typical in his concern about his green airmen. He felt that a combat aviator needed a full training cycle and two years of carrier duty to be effective. He considered "Wandering Falcon's" junior birdmen as products of poorly equipped schools with ideological fervor filling the gaps in technical training. Few had seen a carrier at sea before 1944.

"Yet, to my amazement, these men got their planes safely off the flight deck and, often as not, even got them back down—at least, in broad daylight, on calm seas, and without the tension and distraction of being under fire."

The lamentable situation predated arrival at Tawi-Tawi. After formation, Ozawa's three divisions devoted as much time to training as possible, but it wasn't nearly enough. His own CarDiv One benefited the most, receiving nearly six months of workups for the big-deck ships and air groups. But Joshima's CarDiv Two and Obayashi's Division Three had time for only two and three months, respectively. In masterful understatement, the after-action review conceded, "The degree of training was not sufficient to meet the demand of an actual battle."

Despite the institutional emphasis on reconnaissance, many Mobile Fleet scout crews were raw beginners. In CarDiv Two, the recon units completed their aircraft checkouts only just before deploying, and almost none had flown more than a hundred nautical miles over water.

Joshima's men also lacked equipment familiarity. While hastily organizing at Tenzan, no one had logged any test flights to check radio function or learned how to gain best performance from the gear. The few original radars issued were "totally unusable."

Aside from too many fliers who were recently cadets, Ozawa faced other problems. Most notably, the promised airfields ashore had not been completed, so his nine air groups received little proficiency flying while anchored at Tawi-Tawi. Most units could fly only twice a month—insufficient for routine operations, let alone for sharpening combat skills. The Mobile Fleet therefore began the campaign at a serious disadvantage in training, as well as in numbers.

Imperial Navy carrier operations were unlike any other during World War II. The differences were apparent in the alpha and omega of tailhook aviation: from launch to recovery.

One of the first things an American or British aviator would notice on an imperial carrier was the absence of catapults. Few *Kaigun* flattops had them, owing to Japan's lightweight aircraft design. Because of their low wing loading, most *Nihon Kaigun* carrier aircraft made "deck run" takeoffs without artificial assistance.

But the larger distinction became apparent in the groove prior to landing. Where American LSOs and British "batsmen" stood on a platform port-side aft, wielding paddles or batons, the Imperial Navy had no one. Instead, an ingenious system of lights was installed that anticipated the mirror visual landing system of the postwar U.S. and Royal navies.

On either side of the flight deck, about one-fifth of the way forward, was a red light ten to fifteen meters aft of a green light. Each light had a refracting mirror that projected a narrow cone to the desired point in the air astern of the ship. The heights were variable according to the optimum glide slope for various aircraft; typically 5.5 degrees for fighters and five degrees for bombers.

When the pilot approached the flight deck's red-and-white-striped ramp, he centered himself between the port and starboard lights. That was lineup. Glide slope was determined by keeping the green light tangent above the red. If he saw red over green, he was too low; green over red meant a potential overshoot. The pilot made whatever corrections were necessary to keep the lights in tangent.

The Japanese system had two potential flaws. First, there was no indicator of proper speed, whereas landing signal officers (LSOs) could give "fast" or "slow" signals. Secondly, just before crossing the ramp, the pilot lost sight of the lights owing to their offset from each deck edge. However, if he held his previous attitude and lineup, he was in the groove and usually landed straight ahead.

The closest thing to an LSO was a sailor on the bridge, wielding a large red flag. In event of a fouled deck, the *hikocho* waved the banner, indicating a mandatory aborted landing.

By 1944 the Japanese system had been in use for a decade. It was well proven and in many ways superior to the American and British system. Fortunately for the Mobile Fleet, it was mastered by novice aviators with precious little flight time.

Whatever the paint on their airplanes, carrier aviators felt themselves one notch (or two, or three) above land-based pilots. A Pearl Harbor veteran was Lieutenant Iyozo Fujita, who said, "We practiced landing on and taking off from aircraft carriers. You had to be a more skillful pilot in order to do that."

Fujita's sentiment was reflected by one of his opponents, Captain Roy M. "Butch" Voris. The Hellcat ace said, "There's a camaraderie in carrier aviation that you'll find no other place in the world. The carrier itself is your home. It's where you eat, where you sleep. Then you have the flight deck and the sky. You leave the carrier, you do your mission, and you come back to home, really."

For the upcoming battle, Ozawa's assets included greater "reach" for his aircraft and initial use of land bases in the Marianas. His command was numerically impressive, including two brand-new carriers, one larger than the U.S. *Essex* class. But he was outnumbered two to one in carrier planes, and counted heavily upon those based in the Marianas.

A staff officer, Commander Masatake Okumiya, wrote after the war, "The Marianas defense was to be a maximum effort; we would greet the Americans with an impenetrable wall of fire and steel. To make certain that our planes would be flown by veterans as well as novices, the Navy drew instructors from its training air corps and assigned them to the front. Every serviceable plane and ship moved into the area of decision."

Composition of Japanese air groups was a mixture of new and old.

Japan's signature aircraft of the Second World War was Mitsubishi's A6M series of Type Zero fighters (for the Japanese year 2600, or 1940). When first flown in 1939 it established a landmark: No carrier fighter had ever exceeded the range and performance of its land-based counterparts. In 1941–42 the Zero (later code-named Zeke by Allied intelligence) stunned its opponents, flying a thousand-mile round-trip missions and establishing air superiority along the way. Eventually more than eleven thousand were built—by far the most-produced Japanese aircraft in history. But for all his flash and aura, Zeke could be beaten. Allied fighter pilots learned to avoid turning with the nimble Mitsubishi, keeping their airspeed above two hundred knots and using altitude for "boom and zoom" tactics.

There was also a role for older model Zeroes, notably the A6M2. Armed with a 250-kilogram (550-pound) bomb, the "Zeke 21" was intended to augment genuine bombers such as the prewar Aichi D3A and Yokosuka D4Y (Val and Judy to the Americans).

Nine A6M2s went aboard each carrier of the Joshima force, while each of Obayashi's three flattops received at least fifteen, and Ozawa's *Zuikaku* embarked eleven. Thus, a total of eighty-four modified Zeroes deployed in seven of Ozawa's nine carriers. But despite their numbers, the A6M2 pilots were ill trained in *shosho*, or battle tactics; they would function more as shallow-angle glide bombers than high-angle dive-bombers.

When the Mobile Fleet deployed for the Marianas, more than half the total carrier aircraft were Zeroes. It was as if Mitscher's force contained 450 Grumman Wildcats.

The Imperial Navy's dive-bomber pilots were as good as those flying anywhere in 1941. Though their aircraft was the ungainly-looking Aichi D3A of 1938, it was a proven ship killer. The U.S. Navy knew the fixed-landing-gear silhouette as "Val," and while Wildcat and Hellcat pilots snacked on D3As, sailors respected them. Off Saipan, nearly one-quarter of Ozawa's dive-bombers were the same type that had pummeled Pearl Harbor.

Val's successor was known to her enemies as "Judy." Designed by the naval arsenal at Yokosuka and built by Aichi in 1942, the D4Y *Suisei* (Comet) carrier bomber was a rara avis: distinctive for her twelve-cylinder, liquid-cooled engine in a generation of air-cooled radials. Capable of an honest 300 knots (340 mph), she boasted nearly 2,000 nautical miles' range with drop tanks, which endeared her to admirals who valued reconnaissance. However, despite her strengths, Judy was vulnerable. Like so many Japanese combat aircraft, the D4Y lacked self-sealing fuel tanks and armor plate.

In 1941 Nakajima's B5N was the best shipboard torpedo plane on earth. Reasonably fast for its 1937 first flight, it came as a nasty surprise to the U.S. Navy, not least because of its notoriously effective torpedoes. "Kate" was showing her age by 1944 but remained an important asset, especially for scouting with a three-man crew of pilot, observer, and radioman-gunner.

Nakajima's follow-up was the B6N *Tenzan* (Heavenly Mountain). Carrying its torpedo externally, Jill was first tested in 1941 and, after two years of development, entered service in time for the Marianas battle. However, the *Tenzan* was limited to Japan's big-deck carriers due to its relatively small wing area and fairly high landing speed. In fact, its forward-canted vertical tail was a concession to the eleven-meter elevators on most carriers.

Despite the capability of Judy and Jill, Ozawa's force was hugely reliant on Zekes, Vals, and Kates. In other words, nearly two-thirds of his planes had entered service before Pearl Harbor. It was a technical deficit that could not be overcome.

A major lapse in Japanese aviation was air-to-air communication. Voice radios were generally unreliable, often due to unshielded ignitions, so pilots developed *ishin denshin*, or a mutual sixth sense. Fliers of all nationalities shared the intuition that comes with long hours of flying together, but that was a function of time, and time was never in Ozawa's favor.

Electronics greatly favored the U.S. Navy. Radar direction of fighters had proved decisive in the Battle of Britain four summers previously, and Task Force 58 operated radio and radar almost seamlessly. Even in mid-1944 the Japanese had almost no idea of their opponents' awesome capability. In fact, evidence indicates that the Imperial Navy did not fully tumble to the unpleasant facts until after Leyte Gulf.

Reinforcements

WITH THE BATTLE SHAPING UP well before dawn, the defenders summoned help from far afield.

Eager to reinforce his units on Guam and Saipan, Vice Admiral Kakuji Kakuta directed all operational aircraft at Truk in the Carolines to fly to the Marianas. However, only seventeen planes (including thirteen Zekes and two night fighters) were operational that morning. They made the 580-mile northwesterly trip without difficulty, taking off just ahead of fifty-six U.S. Army Liberators that ravaged Truk. Upon arrival the Zekes claimed shooting down three or more American planes, though the only victories were made by Grummans. Throughout the morning F6Fs and FMs—mostly from CVLs and CVEs—took a dozen scalps over the islands.

Welcome as the newcomers were, they did not compensate for the grinding attrition of Kakuta's squadrons in recent days. Their arrival boosted his strength to about fifty operational aircraft plus perhaps thirty under repair.

Whatever disappointment Kakuta must have felt about the paltry response to his call, he still had assets close at hand. Some of his land-based fighter-bomber pilots were called to their briefing tents and provided with vague descriptions of the invaders' location and composition. Unfortunately for the imperial cause—whether by chance or design—they found the one American task group that was largely invulnerable to their ordnance.

At 0550 half a dozen Zero bombers assailed Destroyer Squadron 53 in Lee's screen. *Stockham* came under attack as a Zero missed her with a 550-pound bomb, but her partner *Yarnall* shot down the assailant. Ten minutes thereafter, other Task Group 58.7 escorts splashed a Val, undoubtedly from Guam.

But there were too many Japanese fingers probing the American blanket for Mitscher to escape detection. About a half hour after making the cross-leg turn, Kurita's number seven Jake got a hit. On Imperial Navy maps the position was NA-SO-4TE, bearing 160 miles almost due west of Saipan. The radioman reported two large carriers, four battleships, and ten other ships. Minutes later, at 0734, number nine scout confirmed the contact, minus carriers. Most likely the Japanese observers glassing the Americans saw parts of 58.7 and Harrill's 58.4. It's easy to understand any confusion—Task Force 58 spanned forty sea miles northwest to southeast.

Remaining unbothered, the number seven scout went on the prowl, seeking additional information. Twelve miles east, he reported four "large" carriers—likely Clark's 58.1—and amplified with a weather report: eight-tenths cloud cover at three hundred meters, clear on top.

Jisaburo Ozawa now held the initiative.

Fighter Pilots

THE FIGHTER PILOT WAS A twentieth-century invention. He never existed before 1915, but despite his latecomer status, he quickly assumed the mantle of the most glamorous warrior of his era. The fact that he was bred for the purpose of clearing the sky for his overlooked reconnaissance and bomber compatriots mattered not at all.

Fighter pilots were widely regarded as prima donnas: individualists who sought out their counterparts to engage in single combat. That image reflected some reality in the era of Roland Garros and Max Immelmann, but thirty years later the profession had become a corporate enterprise. The loner, let alone the glory hunter, was nearly extinct, in both the operational and the Darwinian sense.

Air combat was about teamwork. And nobody practiced teamwork better than the U.S. Navy.

The basic building block was the section, a two-plane unit with a leader and wingman. Two sections constituted a division (a flight in the Air Force), and though squadron-strength missions of twelve planes or more were occasionally flown, it mattered little. World War II was a division leader's war. In combat, it was nearly impossible to keep track of a dozen other planes, let alone coordinate their actions.

Before the war, most of the world's air arms flew three-plane sections and six-plane divisions, or flights. But it was merely a carryover from the Great War. The fact was, in combat the two wingmen in a "vic" (V formation) spent far more time concentrating on their leader than looking for the enemy. The RAF learned that lesson the hard way during the Kentish summer of 1940, fighting the disciplined professionals in Messerschmitt 109s who hunted and killed in groups of four.

Before long, the four-plane flight became the global standard, though the Japanese were the last major nation to change. In a four-plane division there were two shooters and two wingmen: a 50 percent increase in shooters over the six-plane vics. The wingmen typically flew echeloned on their leader, slightly behind and offset.

But in 1941 the commanding officer of Fighting Squadron Three went even further. Lieutenant Commander John S. Thach, a lanky Arkansas pheasant hunter, conducted some experiments at NAS San Diego. He found that by positioning the wingman abreast of the leader, the offensive dynamics increased substantially. His scheme converted all Wildcat pilots into potential shooters. Regardless of rank or seniority, the first pilot to eyeball a bandit immediately assumed the lead. The mutual support afforded by the abeam position meant that each pilot could clear the other's tail. The wingman was no longer a bullet magnet to protect the leader.

If either member of the pair was attacked from behind, he immediately turned toward his partner. Depending on altitude, the abeam position was equal to turn radius at cruise speed. The bandit now had two choices: abort the attack, or pursue his intended victim across the partner's nose. Naval aviators lived and breathed deflection gunnery: Before the war only the tiny, highly efficient Finnish air force came close to the American standard. Consequently, a Japanese pilot pressing his run now exposed himself to a deflection shot at bore-sight range: roughly a thousand feet, where the Grummans' guns were aligned. Fighting 3 initiated the "beam defense maneuver" at Midway in June 1942, and it worked splendidly. It went into history as the Thach Weave.

(In June 1944, now-Commander Jimmie Thach rode *Lexington* as liaison officer between Mitscher's staff and that of Vice Admiral John S. McCain when the Fifth/Third Fleet switch occurred after Forager.)

The Japanese learned to respect if not admire their opponents, as expressed by Lieutenant Junior Grade Kazuo Tsunoda, whose seven-year combat career included China, the Solomons, New Guinea, the Philippines, Formosa, and Iwo Jima: "The American tactics were very practical and efficient. During the war I thought that the Americans were very sly. Their way of fighting was not fair, but their teamwork was very good."

In turn, U.S. aviators quickly overcame any misplaced disdain of the Imperial Navy. Said Lieutenant Commander E. Scott McCuskey, an ace in both the F4F and F6F, "I respected the Japanese pilots. If you didn't give them some respect you'd get your butt shot off. They had some marvelous fliers but sometimes they didn't seem to have the team concept that we had."

Whatever the tactics employed, they were aimed at a single goal: bringing the fighter's guns to bear on enemy aircraft. The trick to aerial gunnery was smooth flying and correct lead. Immediately below the slanted glass plate with the gun-sight reticle was a ball in an arced housing. The fighter pilot did whatever was necessary to keep the ball centered: "Step on the ball" was the technique. If the ball slewed to the right, he'd add right rudder. That way the bullets went straight ahead rather than askew.

Proper lead was extremely difficult to judge by eyeball. Consequently, the Mark VIII reflector sight superimposed a pattern of concentric rings upon infinity. Wherever the pilot's head was positioned, the sight pattern or reticle remained in focus. There were 50- and 100-mil rings around the aiming dot, or pipper. Since one mil subtended one foot at a thousand feet distance, pilots could quickly gauge their range and lead angle by comparing the target aircraft to their mil rings. It was three-dimensional geometry: The correct lead was the sine of the angle, shortened to "the two-thirds rule." If a fighter was pushing three hundred knots at full deflection (ninety degrees), at bore-sight range the correct lead was 200 mils. At lesser angles the lead was reduced by the sine of the angle-off: full deflection down to sixty degrees; three-quarters at thirty; half at twenty; and one-quarter value below that.

Though all fighter pilots received the same training, some excelled for a variety of reasons. A few were naturally imbued with the physical gifts: keen vision, hand-eye coordination, and a feel for gunnery. Others achieved the same level of skill through hard practice. But not all of the ablest pilots were motivated; many simply wanted to do the least that was required without embarrassing themselves. Others were extremely competitive from childhood. Aces tended to be eldest sons or only children, usually with sports backgrounds.

Whatever their particular credentials, a handful of fighter pilots were disproportionately productive. Service to service, nation to nation, usually one-tenth of those credited with kills accounted for one-third of the total score.

Despite the flamboyant, bon-vivant image, not all fighter pilots were Hollywood stereotypes. In fact, the "producers" tended toward a quiet demeanor on the ground that changed when they strapped into a Hellcat or Corsair. For instance, Alex Vraciu of VF-16, Mitscher's ranking ace, was a practical joker who spoke with a smile-when-you-say-that earnestness.

Vraciu became semifamous for a prewar prank at DePauw University. During a dull classroom lecture he feigned dementia, declaring, "I can't take this anymore!" Then he jumped from a second-story window, astonishing the students and professor. They did not know that he landed in a tarpaulin held by his fraternity brothers.

Vraciu's successor as top gun would be *Essex* CAG Dave McCampbell, a garrulous "trade school" professional nine years older. An Annapolis diving champ, "Dashing Dave" speculated on how he would abandon ship if he were ever sunk. He had considered executing "a layout and maybe a pike or tuck," but when he looked over the side of the previous USS *Wasp* (CV-7), torpedoed off Guadalcanal in 1942, "I grabbed my nose with one hand and the rest of myself with the other and went in feetfirst."

At war's end the service's third-ranking ace was a quiet, considerate South Dakota schoolteacher named Cecil Harris who splashed "meatballs" in threes and fours.

Fighter pilots often resembled the boys about whom mothers warned their daughters: You had to watch out for the quiet ones.

Steel in the Sky

ON THE DAY OF BATTLE, the American advantages were substantial. They included well-trained personnel; superior numbers and quality of ships and aircraft; plus far better radar and communications. Task Force 58 was receiving new four-channel VHF radios, but in June there was still not full commonality. Fortunately, each task group had two radio frequencies available to all ships, as communication was essential to task force air defense.

That defense took two forms: combat air patrols consisting of radar-directed fighters, and massive amounts of shipboard antiaircraft guns. Both were sophisticated endeavors backed by enormous funding, research, and production.

While Americans had been fighting in climes as diverse as Tunisia, Italy, and the Aleutians, the U.S. war effort also was conducted on the home front. Over the previous two and a half years, science and technology had forged a single-minded alliance dedicated to the proposition that America's enemies deserved the most efficient destruction possible. Significant advances had been made in communications (VHF radios), electronics (shipboard and aircraft radar), and ordnance (the proximity fuse). The latter was one of the marvels of the war: Scientists at Johns Hopkins and other organizations worked with Navy technicians in perfecting a tiny radio transmitter that fit into the nose of an antiaircraft shell. The VT (variable timed) fuse sensed a target aircraft and detonated the shell within lethal range. When combined with radar-controlled fighters and conventional AA guns, the VT fuse rendered the Fast Carrier Task Force nearly immune to conventional air attack.

The American task force was composed of four task groups, each nominally operating two big-deck carriers and two light carriers. Typically each group's screen comprised four cruisers and about a dozen destroyers.

Task group defense was based on a scientifically determined cruising disposition calculated to put the most flak in the sky between the ships and attacking aircraft. With the carriers in the center of a four-mile circle, cruisers and destroyers were deployed to force Japanese pilots to run a gauntlet of airborne steel: five-inch dual-purpose guns plus twin and quad 40mm mounts and a chattering array of single and twin 20-millimeters.

Four dedicated antiaircraft cruisers belonged to the *Atlanta-Oakland* class: swift six thousand-tonners with twelve to sixteen "five-inch 38s" in six or eight turrets. The 5.38 was the standard dual-purpose naval weapon, firing a five-inch-diameter shell from a barrel thirty-eight diameters long (190 inches or 15.8 feet). The 5.38s fired fifty-five-pound shells tipped with the radio-activated proximity fuse. The variable-timed fuse sensed reflected radiation off the target and detonated within lethal radius of some thirty feet. It wasn't foolproof—at one point a 50 percent dud rate was considered acceptable—but when radar directed, the shell could be deadly. Combat analysis showed roughly five hundred rounds of VT shells were fired to destroy one enemy aircraft—four times better than timed or impact fuses on the same projectiles.

Experience and logic dictated that some attackers would penetrate the heavy gunfire. Consequently, the cruisers' upper decks were arrayed with six or seven Swedish-designed 40mm Bofors mounts and as many as sixteen 20mm Swiss-designed Oerlikons. Every ship in the task force carried similar weapons in a daunting variety of configurations. The rapid-fire weapons, though smaller than the five-inchers, splashed far more "meatballs" because of the necessarily shorter ranges.

Task groups usually steamed in a formation with twelve miles between centers; about eight miles screen-to-screen. It was no coincidence: Eight miles was the effective range of heavy antiaircraft guns. That disposition accomplished several aims simultaneously. It afforded enough latitude for individual maneuvering when needed, but presented a dense pattern of flak to any attacker. It also afforded overlapping radar coverage, filling in the blind spots so that fighter controllers usually did not have to consult their fade charts when a blip disappeared from the scope. Radar and reliable radio communications were essential to task force operations, especially in defense.

Radar early warning and control of fighters was conclusively proven in the Battle of Britain during 1940. Thereafter, the mating of radio and radar worked a revolution in naval warfare. Not only did radio permit shipboard control of fighters over the task force, but with reliable radar it permitted timely identification of bogeys (unknown aircraft) and interception of bandits (confirmed hostiles).

Consequently, fighter direction officers (FDOs) were handpicked specialists for one of the most important jobs in the Navy. At one time the FDO program's priority ranked second only to the Navy's part in the Manhattan Project that built the A-bomb.

Early in the war it was felt that the best FDOs would be aviators with communication backgrounds. However, as demand quickly outstripped supply, the program was opened to alumni of the Quonset Point indoctrination center.

Whether regulars or ninety-day wonders, FDOs carried enormous responsibility on their young shoulders, and they were chosen accordingly. In drafting criteria for FDO candidates, the Navy determined that anyone who had earned $30,000 in three years was a good prospect because he had demonstrated management ability and sound judgment. Therefore, FDO ranks contained a large proportion of lawyers, bankers, and stockbrokers. Teachers and journalists also were welcomed, being exempt from the financial aspects in favor of good organizational and communication skills.

Communication was vital to effective fighter direction. As early as 1941 the Navy established an FDO vocabulary and incorporated it into a curriculum eventually three months long. Fledgling FDOs were trained to think spatially, managing consumable assets (fuel and ammunition) in three dimensions. Graduates of St. Simons Island, Georgia, and the Pacific Fleet Radar School in Hawaii were then mated with other specialists and sent to the fleet, grown as a team from the ground up. Carriers had priority, but eventually every warship in Fifth Fleet had at least one FDO aboard with a supporting cast of radar operators, plotters, and talkers. In fleet carriers they formed the CIC team of perhaps seven men, working in the tight confines of a combat information center. There was one advantage to CIC duty: The necessity of cooling the electronic gear made air-conditioning mandatory, especially in the tropics.

"Radar plot" could feature a great deal of activity in a very small space. (Some wags insisted that CIC meant "Christ, I'm Confused.") But FDO teams worked hard at perfecting their technique; repeated practice runs were part of most watches en route to the war zone.

Describing some of the esoteric skills necessary, fighter director Richard Morland said, "One of the things I learned in the Navy was how to print upside down and backwards with a grease pencil."

By mid-1944 FDO equipment, doctrine, and training had come together. Fleet and light carriers usually had two SK air-search radars with an earlier SC-2 as backup. SC and SK radars pulsed at about ten microseconds, an output that left a void of only five miles or so from the source. To fill the gap, surface-search SG sets were employed.

Temperature inversions could cause "channeling" of radar beams at sea, varying with moisture and air temperature. Therefore, in extreme cases SG provided a hundred-mile coverage over a narrow front, and those were "skin paints" without the enhancement of more modern sets.

Radar waves need to be smaller than their target; otherwise the object is lost in the width of the beam. Early ground-based radars emitted ten-meter wavelengths, which, like every magnetic pulse, expanded as they radiated from their origin. Though most twin-engine bombers' wingspans were eighteen to twenty-three meters, many fighters spanned less than ten, so scientists realized that a small, tight beam would be more useful at longer ranges. Therefore, centimetric radar became one of the war's great technical achievements. Developed by Britain and America in 1940, its beam was directed by a small parabolic reflector affording greater range and better resolution than long-wave sets. Eventually all the main combatants developed centimetric radar, but only the U.S., Britain, and Germany produced them in quantity. They were especially useful in air search and night-fighter direction.

Nevertheless, long-wave radar continued in use, and the island structures of U.S. carriers sprouted a bewildering "radar farm," with as many as eight antennae of half a dozen types: SG surface search; midsize SC and large SK long-wave air search; Mk-12 forty-centimeter and Mk-22 three-centimeter combos for aircraft range and altitude; and YE homing beacons.

Another knife in the FDO's drawer was four-channel VHF radio, which considerably eased the constant threat of jammed voice frequencies. It had been one of the causes of the first *Hornet*'s (CV-8) loss at Santa Cruz. Additionally, the VHF deck-condition code provided current status of a carrier's flight deck in the constant cycle of launches and recoveries while the dead-reckoning tracer (DRT) provided navigation and surface tracking at a glance. Finally, identification, friend or foe (IFF) transponders in U.S. aircraft helped reduce the number of bogeys requiring visual identification.

Mitscher's force FDO was Lieutenant Joseph R. Eggert Jr. The erstwhile stockbroker had been aboard *Lexington* since March 1943 and served as senior FDO the previous four months. Additionally, each subordinate task group had its own senior director. For instance, in Task Group 58.3 the CIC officer was Lieutenant Commander E. E. Haverstick Jr. He had an assistant and six other FDOs plus four radar maintenance officers.

Force, group, and individual ship FDOs learned to work together, handing off contacts to whomever had the better radar picture of a developing situation. The system was not foolproof—it could be overwhelmed and occasionally jammed—but it rendered the fast carriers almost invulnerable to conventional air attack.

In contrast, Japan's radar program was barely adequate. The Imperial Navy's Type 13 was the most common air search set, in service barely a year during A-Go. Operating on the 200-centimeter wavelength, it was a fairly short-range set capable of detecting aircraft formations at a hundred kilometers and single planes at fifty. Only about a thousand sets were produced, in contrast to the massive American output.

Perhaps forty Type 21 sets were made: 150-centimeter designs that were little better than the Type 13. Evidently Japanese carriers did not begin receiving Type 21 radars until early 1943, and there was little improvement throughout the war.

The H-6 was Japan's primary airborne search radar. Weighing 110 kilograms, it was suitable for single-engine aircraft as well as patrol bombers, performing comparably to the ship-based radars. Some two thousand were produced—again, a tiny figure compared to the U.S. Navy.

Turkey Shoot

IT WAS A GORGEOUS DAY for a battle.

The nineteenth dawned at 0430, casting its semitropical light over the enormous expanse of the Philippine Sea. At that hour Mitscher's group lay a hundred miles northwest of Guam. Not quite ninety minutes later the sun appeared behind Saipan, revealing beautiful flying conditions: a warm morning with the evening's clouds dissipating before noon. Temperatures ran in the low to mid-eighties, causing vapor trails to stream from aircraft wingtips at altitude. It worked to the advantage of attackers and defenders alike: There was no weather to cloak the ships' location, but almost unlimited visibility permitted early visual detection of the inbound raiders.

The wind—the all-important component of carrier operations—held easterly throughout the day. At only nine to twelve knots, the breeze forced the carriers to accelerate to about twenty knots to give pilots the necessary thirty for launch. Zigzagging throughout the day, turning in and out of the wind to launch or land aircraft, Task Force 58 eventually came as close as within twenty-five miles of Guam that afternoon.

Mitscher deployed his fleet in an ordered formation with Task Group 58.3 and flagship *Lexington* in the middle. Twelve miles north and south were Clark's 58.1 and Montgomery's 58.2. A similar distance astern (west) of Clark was Harrill's 58.4, while Lee's 58.7 trailed Reeves's 58.3 some fifteen miles. Picket destroyers several miles astern of the battleships further enhanced radar coverage.

With the sun tangent to the horizon around 0600, the American force lay 330 miles east-northeast of Kurita's van force and another hundred from Ozawa's Carrier Division One and Joshima's CarDiv Two.

Unlike Mitscher, who placed all his battleships under Lee, Ozawa distributed his heavies between CarDivs Two and Three. *Nagato* screened Joshima, while the other four steamed with Kurita. In a way, it was ironic: four battleships (including the world's two biggest) protecting three light carriers. However, it made sense. The Americans were most likely first to detect Kurita and Obayashi in the van, and among them *Yamato, Musashi, Kongo,* and *Haruna* packed a lot of AA.

Additionally, by "front-loading" the van force with battleships, Ozawa placed most of his recon planes well forward for the predawn launch. But in so doing, he deprived himself of several destroyers that would have been extremely useful trolling for American submarines around the heavyweight flattops of Carrier Division One.

It was the start of a bad day.

Nor was it a good start for the Americans.

Early that morning four Hellcats attacked a twin-engine seaplane near the task force. They shot it up considerably before recognizing the distinctive inverted-gull-wing configuration. It was a Martin Mariner. One VP-16 crewman was killed.

First Kill

THE DAY'S FIRST INTERCEPTIONS BEGAN on the periphery of the task force. In 58.2, the most southerly group, *Cabot*'s radar plotted multiple bogeys at 0515, plus a single five minutes later. Hellcats were vectored out for a look, but the snoopers made a clean getaway.

At 0547 Fighting Squadron 28 logged the first kill of the Great Marianas Turkey Shoot. Lieutenant Junior Grade Walter T. Fitzpatrick and his division were up on CAP early that morning, receiving a radar vector shortly after dawn. The fighter director was accurate, putting the *Monterey* pilots onto two Judy scout bombers thirty miles west of the ship. Leaving his second section as top cover, Fitzpatrick led Ensign Russell P. Granger in a high-side run from starboard. Their APIs lit up the lead Judy ahead of the cockpit and sent him spinning into the ocean. The Japanese wingman half rolled, pulled through, and dived into a cloud deck at four thousand feet.

It was the start of a fourteen-hour day.

Fifteen minutes later other CVL aviators were taking scalps over Guam. Gus Widhelm's operations plan for the day included "capping" enemy airfields, and *Belleau Wood* drew the first slot. Fighting 24 killed three Zekes in the start of a series of CAPs over the island.

Most productive overland was *Bunker Hill's* VF-8. The exec was Lieutenant Commander Elbert "Scotty" McCuskey, a lively, enthusiastic veteran of Coral Sea and Midway. He gunned a Zeke over Apra Harbor—his seventh kill of the war—while his junior birdmen claimed thirteen more. Three went to the credit of Lieutenant Junior Grade John D. Vanderhoof in his first fight.

Almost simultaneously, Mitscher's scouts were warming up their engines, ready to launch. Five *Lexington* and three *Essex* search teams cleared the decks, sucked up their wheels and tucked up their flaps, and turned onto their assigned headings from 185 to 345 degrees.

None of the Air Group 15 or 16 searchers found any ships, but they came across several land- and cruiser-based scouts. In the hour after 0700, searchers and CAP splashed ten Japanese scouts, including at least five Jakes.

Ozawa's second-phase search turned in only a report of some destroyers—likely part of Lee's screen. That scant intelligence cost half of the fourteen scouts. It was a big hunting ground—the ocean area spanned nearly 400 miles northwest of the Mobile Fleet to 330 southwest—but they had the enormous bad luck to fall afoul of Mitscher's own search teams. Hellcats from *Essex*, *Lexington*, and *Yorktown* dispatched nearly all of Kurita's lost scouts.

Meanwhile, Kurita's battleship- and cruiser-based Jake floatplanes came across something worthwhile. Reaching the limit of their range about 0700, the pilots reversed course, no doubt at once disappointed and relieved. But at 0730, some 130 miles along its return track, one floatplane crew spotted something to the south. The pilot rolled into a hard port turn and proceeded twenty-five miles southwesterly. There, on his nose, were two American task groups: Harrill's carriers and Lee's battlewagons. The contact was designated "7 I" and became the focus of Ozawa's attention. It was the most accurate report that the Mobile Fleet received during the day.

Carrier War

THE PRINCIPLES OF CARRIER WARFARE were well-known in 1944. Both navies had been experimenting with flattops since 1922, when America converted the collier *Jupiter* to USS *Langley*, named for aviation experimenter and Wright Brothers rival. "The Covered Wagon"—so named because of her flight deck superimposed on the hull—was small (12,700 tons, 542 feet long), but she showed the way ahead. Most of the generation of flying admirals who fought World War II had trapped on her short, narrow deck in fabric-covered biplanes.

America's first combat-capable carriers were the original *Lexington* (CV-2) and *Saratoga* (CV-3), which emerged from the Washington Naval Treaty of 1922, permitting unfinished battleships and battlecruisers to be converted. (Among the Japanese delegates was one Isoroku Yamamoto.) Commissioned in 1927, "Lex" and "Sara" were among the biggest flattops of the era, displacing thirty-eight thousand tons and capable of thirty-two knots. *Lexington* was slain at Coral Sea; *Saratoga* was torpedoed twice and kamikazed, surviving to be expended in the Bikini atomic bomb test.

In contrast, Japan's first carrier was, if not designed from the keel up, largely built so. HIMJS *Hosho* was of comparable size to *Langley*, with far less displacement (seventy-four hundred tons), but yielded large dividends. For starters, she could make twenty-five knots, in contrast to *Langley*'s fourteen. With lessons learned, the Imperial Navy emulated the Americans by converting surface ships to carriers. Thus were born the big *Akagi* and *Kaga*, completed the same years as the two *Lexington*s. Both Japanese ships went down in the Midway massacre.

Ironically (in view of later developments), the Imperial Navy owed much of its early expertise to the Royal Navy. In fact, the cordial relations between the two services went beyond operational matters. Earlier in the century some of Japan's most powerful battleships had been designed by British architects and built in British yards. But inevitably the situation changed from cooperation to combat. Thus far, the Japanese had outdone their U.K. instructors and matched their U.S. rivals.

For a decade or more after the Great War, Britain had led the world in carrier operations, though the RN was hampered for most of that time by a pesky reliance upon the RAF for aircrews. In the 1930s America grasped the winged trident of seagoing airpower, and seemingly gained the lead. Then things changed, literally overnight. In 1941–42 Japan seized dominance with a stunning display of technical and organizational innovation, fielding by far the most powerful carrier force yet assembled. America was desperately pressed to catch up, but the hard-fought battles of 1942 yielded hard-won lessons that bore fruit. From 1943 onward no nation or alliance of nations could match America's seagoing airpower.

Because of their powerful, volatile nature, carriers were like champion middleweights: fast on their feet with dynamite hands, exceptional reach—and glass jaws. Their hulls were three-eighths-inch steel; their flight decks usually were wood. Douglas fir and Oregon pine were used in huge quantities to lighten the upper works and reduce risk of sparks amid high-test avgas. Before the war, teak was preferred for its exceptional strength, but from 1941 onward Tokyo controlled much of the world supply. However, considering other demands, even the Japanese Navy opted for ancient pine.

Carrier warfare placed a premium on landing the first punch, and a one-two combination was preferred. Knowing just where to send the punch meant reconnaissance, which took two forms. Carriers had their own scouting planes (dive-bombers or torpedo planes assigned the role), while battleships and cruisers embarked observation floatplanes launched off catapults. Doctrinally, Japan differed from America in placing most of its scouting eggs in the latter basket, reserving the bombers and torpedo planes for strike missions. Occasionally long-range seaplanes scouted for carriers, but often efficiency suffered due to separate command and communication nets.

The primary instrument of American seapower was the fleet aircraft carrier: a large, fast ship with three squadrons of aircraft. After the Darwinian winnowing of 1942, only two prewar flattops remained in the Pacific Fleet. Consequently, wartime construction had to pick up the slack.

Enter the *Essex*-class (CV-9) carrier: 27,100 tons of seapower. An *Essex* accommodated 360 officers and 3,088 men to operate as many as ninety planes. She was propelled by four Westinghouse steam turbine engines fired by eight Babcock-Wilcox boilers burning Bunker C oil. The geared turbines produced 150,000-shaft horsepower turning four screws that propelled the ship to thirty-three knots. At economical cruising speed of sixteen knots, the CV-9 boats had a range of nearly seventeen thousand miles.

More *Essex*es were built than any other class of fleet carrier in history: twenty-four in all, seventeen during the war. None was ever sunk, though two—*Franklin* (CV-13) and *Bunker Hill* (CV-17)—sustained horrific damage in 1945. Others were mauled but bounced back. *Essex*es were the DC-3 of aircraft carriers: incredibly long-lived and versatile. Suitably modified for jets, they served in the Korean and Vietnam wars.

Yet even with round-the-clock schedules at U.S. shipyards, the supply always trailed demand. Consequently the 11,000-ton light carrier was born. The *Independence*-class (CVL-22) ships, with smaller plants and less fuel than their *Essex* teammates, could cruise ten thousand miles. Built on light cruiser hulls, they were wartime expedients, all commissioned in 1943 and surprisingly rugged. In nearly two years of constant operation only one of the nine was sunk. Complements of nearly sixteen hundred were typical for the *Independence* boats: half as many men as the *Essex*es. Light-carrier air groups embarked about thirty-three aircraft.

Some essential items were common to all U.S. carriers. To assist launching heavy bombers, or to generate artificial wind over the deck, catapults were used. Two hydraulic "cats" launched laden planes off the forward portion of the flight deck while transverse arresting wires snagged homing planes' tailhooks. In event of hook skip or a poor landing, steel-wire barriers protected aircraft parked forward. It could be a sporty course. In the days before angled flight decks it was said that carrier aviators either logged an arrested landing or a major accident.

For offensive operations the senior air group commander (CAG) in each task group usually was designated target coordinator, but the job necessarily was taken in rotation. By mid-1944 most CAGs were veteran professionals: a decade or more out of Annapolis with as much as eight years of flying in their logbooks. As commanders or lieutenant commanders, CAGs were subordinate to carrier captains but largely ran their own show. The big-deck air groups boasted three squadrons: fighters, dive-bombers, and torpedo bombers. *Independence*-class CVLs were limited to fighters and "torpeckers"; in both ships the CAG usually flew a Hellcat with an extra radio for command and control.

Carrier air groups flew a variety of missions, offensive and defensive. The latter included combat air patrols and antisubmarine patrols. The former could generate considerable excitement on occasion; the latter were notoriously dull . . . most of the time.

Offensive missions included strikes by bombers and torpedo planes as well as pure fighter sweeps. Hellcat pilots preferred sweeps to clear the air of Japanese aircraft, but strike escort also offered the prospect of combat. Far more mundane, but of crucial importance, were longrange searches for enemy ships. Various methods were employed, but during the Marianas campaign a typical search element involved two Avengers with a Hellcat escort. The wedge-shaped search sectors often extended 325 miles out, a fifty-mile cross-leg and return.

The Wind

PERHAPS THE GREATEST IRONY of twentieth-century naval warfare was that carriers were tied to the wind as were warships in the days of sail. Not for propulsion—Bunker C precluded that—but to conduct air operations. Unless catapults were used, it was necessary to turn a carrier's bow into the wind to generate enough lift to raise a laden aircraft from the deck. But "cats" involved a complex, time-consuming option, and for maximum safety it was still advisable to launch upwind. A "deck run" was much easier and faster. Thirty knots' relative wind was usually sufficient to get a plane airborne.

However, in a carrier duel inevitably one side or the other enjoyed "the weather gauge." Off Saipan the advantage was Ozawa's: He could continue steaming into the easterly breeze throughout the day, closing the distance on Mitscher if he desired. Conversely, Task Force 58 steamed a zigzag track, reversing into the wind for every launch or recovery.

Ozawa's Shuttle Service

OZAWA'S BATTLE PLAN CALLED FOR repeated carrier strikes against the American task force, augmented by attacks from land-based units. He even envisioned a sort of shuttle service, with his Mobile Fleet aircraft striking Task Force 58, landing on Guam to rearm and refuel, then making a return trip. The concept proved not only optimistic, but unworkable. Hellcat pilots prowled Guamanian skies, eagerly attacking enemy planes in the air and on the ground. In fact, throughout the day 160 kills were claimed over Guam or close offshore—nearly half the total.

From the American perspective, the air battle revolved around four strikes from the Mobile Fleet, totaling 326 aircraft launched between 0830 and 1130. It was an impressive figure in mere numbers: The two Pearl Harbor strikes involved 350 from six big carriers. Off Saipan, Ozawa had nine flight decks, including three CVLs, and presumably he could have put up more planes. However, reconnaissance sorties—not a major factor at Pearl—drained off some of his strike aircraft, and others were down for maintenance. He also needed to retain sufficient fighters for combat air patrol, protecting the fleet.

Upon receiving the 7 I contact, Ozawa lost little time. He turned southerly with his A Force and Joshima's B Force, preserving his planned distance advantage. Knowing that he enjoyed greater reach than his opponent, The Gargoyle sought 380 to 400 nautical miles between himself and Mitscher.

Meanwhile, what went into history as Raid I began launching from CarDiv Three. Beginning at 0800, Obayashi lofted sixty-nine planes from his CVLs, *Chitose*, *Chiyoda*, and *Zuiho*: forty-five Zero fighter-bombers (Lieutenant Keishiro Ito), sixteen escorts (Lieutenant Kenji Nakagawa), and eight Jill torpedo planes (Lieutenant Michijiro Nakamoto). By 0845 the strike group was airborne, trailing two Kates from *Chitose*, flown by experienced crews who could navigate accurately. The Japanese referred to them as "contact aircraft" to validate the original scout report. The British and American term was "pathfinder," which was just as accurate.

Obayashi then turned out of the wind, heading northwest to open the distance again. He retained a token reserve in the form of seventeen torpedo planes and a handful of fighters—too few to provide adequate CAP.

Air Group 653 droned eastward, formation leaders keeping track of their fuel. Uncharacteristically, they had been briefed to act independently after attacking the Americans: Return to CarDiv Three or, if shy of gas, proceed to Guam to refuel and rearm there. In either case, Obayashi now was effectively out of the battle.

In his flagship, Ozawa sensed a growing spirit of optimism from his subordinates. Soaring spirits also were evident elsewhere. In CarDiv Three, *Chiyoda's* fighter-bomber leader was Lieutenant Takashi Ebata, who stepped into the operations center with a bounce in his step. He confidently announced that Midway was about to be avenged.

In Task Force 58's combat information centers, where radio and radar frequencies were monitored, arcane rituals were being performed. "Radar plot" was a popular place—it was one of the few air-conditioned compartments—but visitors were not allowed. Phosphors glowed on radar screens, imparting esoteric information that was translated into meaningful English. Radar operators tweaked their sets, seeking optimum information from "skin paints" on bogeys—unidentified aircraft. American planes carried IFF (identification, friend or foe) transponders that distinguished between friendlies and potential hostiles. The distance and bearing was passed to sailors behind Plexiglas grids who had mastered the art of swiftly printing backward. Viewed from the FDO's side of the Plexiglas, the renderings made sense. The grease pencil marks indicated "Hostile One" comprised of "many" bogeys or, occasionally, "ten plus" or "thirty plus." Fighter directors took in the data, keyed their mikes, and sent Hellcats out to intercept.

Shipboard radar antennae rotated in their sweeps, the large "bedspring" SKs and round parabolic SK-2s, and the older, rectangular antennae of the SCs, still useful as backups.

Deployed west of the carriers, Ching Lee's battleships got the first electronic whiff of Ozawa's leadoff strike. Raid I showed on Task Force 58's screens beginning about 1000, distance 150 miles. Launched ninety minutes before, it contained sixty-nine Zeroes and Jills. But tactical cohesion had broken down. The Japanese orbited for a precious fifteen minutes, regrouping for the run-in to the American fleet, and Mitscher used that time well. All four groups swung into the ten-knot easterly breeze as the carriers worked up to thirty knots of wind over the deck. Signal flags snapped and flapped on their halyards as the diamond-design Fox flag was hoisted: Commence flight operations.

Just before 1000 Mitscher received Joe Eggert's radar information and pilot reports of Japs taking off from Guam. The admiral concluded that Task Force 58 was "probably due for a working over by both land-based and carrier-based planes." Consequently, FDOs began recalling the roving CAPs from the islands with the old circus phrase "Hey, rube!" That call alerted 450 of the world's best-trained fighter pilots.

In each carrier the word was passed: "Pilots, man your planes!" Aviators and aircrewmen trooped out of their ready rooms, laden with parachute harness, Mae West, and survival gear. Pilots cradled their plotting boards with the latest navigation data penciled on the plastic circular grids. The atmosphere was expectant with anticipation: a heady mixture of excitement and enthusiasm tinted with fear. Some physical fear, yes, but far more often the persistent dread of letting down one's friends. It always defaulted to the aviator's most heartfelt prayer: "Please, Lord, don't let me . . . foul . . . up."

At 1023 task group FDOs scrambled every available fighter while clearing the decks of bombers. Those planes not assigned targets ashore flew easterly, orbiting on the disengaged side of the disposition. In fifteen minutes some 200 Hellcats were airborne or climbing to their assigned patrol stations.

The Flight Deck

SIXTY YEARS AFTER THE BATTLE a World War II sailor, Otis Kight, penned a colorful description of the carrier environment. It bespeaks an era and an attitude long gone:

> Back in time, there was a definite difference between "sound" and "noise." Sound (aka rhapsody) was a Pratt & Whitney tuning up after a 240-hour check. Just pure purr, and no clank or clink. On the flight deck the sound was really that good. Purr, roar.
>
> It was the burp, cough, chug that gave you the pucker factor of twenty-six. For the pilot and crew, you gave a quick prayer, then held on to a wooden chock with two hanks of Manila number nine hemp, and fought your way up the flight deck alongside your aircraft. To me, the sound (not noise) was pure harmony. Overwhelming, inspiring, like "The 1812 Overture."
>
> This audio was the ultimate end of many hours of hot, sweaty, sometimes painful labors of love—like changing the five-o'clock plug on the rear bank of cylinders. All planes taxiing forward, "Foxtrot" flying, then the klaxon and "Launch aircraft!" Not Men against the Sea, but Us with the Wind, the Sea, and Nature.
>
> It was beautiful.

"Working the deck" was two parts science, three parts technology, and five parts choreography. Plane handlers and directors coordinated with catapult and arresting-gear crews, keeping aircraft moving forward of the woven-steel barriers to the parking area. It was an incredibly noisy, violent, and dangerous routine. Men walked within a few feet of spinning propellers, idling at twelve hundred rpm. Occasionally the unwary or unlucky crossed into the prop arc with lethal consequences.

Aircraft elevators also were important to the deck cycle. With limited space on the flight deck, many planes were taken below to the hangar deck for postflight inspection, servicing, or maintenance. For instance, *Shokaku*'s elevators could be raised or lowered in fifteen seconds, with a plane delivered to the hangar deck every forty seconds. It was a factor that mattered in combat when maximum sortie generation was needed.

To the landlubber, or even to a "blackshoe" sailor, the organized pandemonium of a flight deck appeared roughly ordered chaos. The first thing a stranger noticed was the rainbow of varicolored tunics, each denoting a particular function. The colors were keyed to various parts of the air department, with divisions signified by the V prefix, indicating heavier-than-air craft. The V-1 division included catapult and arresting-gear crews in green, while blue-clad plane handlers pushed aircraft, directed by "yellowshirts." LSOs also wore yellow, if they wore much at all. In tropic climes many sported skivvy shorts or swimsuits.

Fuel crews—purple-clad "grapes" in V-2—trailed hoses to waiting gas tanks. V-5 was the realm of plane captains in brown who inspected their aircraft, conducting preflight and postflight checks. Red-shirted "ordies" of V-12 uploaded ammunition, bombs, rockets, and torpedoes, as well as flares and sonobuoys. They also inserted bomb fuses in nose and tail positions, ensuring they were safety-wired against premature detonation.

V-3 comprised air plot, flight control, and aerology (weather). V-4 was the realm of radar plot, later called CIC. V-4 was far different from V-1: CIC was seven-tenths science, 1940s style.

Deckloads

MITSCHER HAD ANTICIPATED (OR MORE aptly, craved) sighting of the Mobile Fleet and had deckload strikes warmed up, ready to launch. The CVs had each uploaded twenty-eight bombers and torpedo planes; the CVLs four Avengers. Each flattop had three or four divisions of fighters ready as well. Black Jack Reeves felt that his strike groups should head west, trailing *Enterprise* Avengers who might find enemy carriers within 250 miles. Therefore, he hailed Mitscher, suggesting that most of the SBDs and TBMs head outbound as soon as possible. Mitscher readily approved, but with overloaded radio circuits the message got lost.

Apart from following doctrine, Reeves's idea was good headwork. However, Ozawa remained out of range the entire day, and the effort would have been wasted. But Jack Reeves was not the only American admiral indulging in some shrewd thinking. Ray Spruance had already issued a contingency order for strike groups to attack enemy airfields even though the ordnance favored ship attack. The bombers holed runways and destroyed some grounded planes, preventing the coordinated attacks that Ozawa and Kakuta envisioned. As at Midway, the blackshoe fleet commander was proven right.

The task force's fifteen torpedo and seven bombing squadrons were active during the day, logging some 260 sorties. However, six Torp-Rons were either retained as a ready reserve or assigned to searches and routine patrols.

Meanwhile, ships not already at general quarters sounded "Boots and Saddles," sending sailors scrambling to their battle stations. Hatches were closed, guns were trained outboard, and helmets were buckled on. Except for Pete Mitscher. He considered a steel helmet too uncomfortable, even for combat conditions, and steadfastly refused to exchange his duckbill for a "tin hat."

On *Belleau Wood*'s bridge, Quartermaster John M. DiFusco fidgeted in anticipation of what was inbound. Despite his youth, DiFusco was a "plank owner." He had enlisted as an eighteen-year-old from Providence, Rhode Island, and was assigned to the ship's precommissioning detail. He recalled, "Radar was picking up large groups of planes from all over, headed for our task group. I made mention to an ensign, 'I guess this is our last day in this world.' He did not help when he agreed with me."

More information came via the fighter director net. Battleship *Alabama*, with Lee's 58.7, got a solid radar contact: fifty-plus bearing 265 true, distance a hundred miles. It was "good dope," as Obayashi's sixty-nine-plane strike was inbound at eighteen thousand to twenty thousand feet.

From Mitscher's perspective, the bright sky eased the defenders' chore. Said *Lexington* fighter director Richard Morland, "The day was so clear that all we had to do was give the fighters a heading and they did the rest."

On some ships the scramble order was more literal than figurative. In Task Group 58.2, *Cabot*'s CAG, Lieutenant Commander Robert A. Winston, was a thirty-six-year-old professional with a book and four planes to his credit. When the launch order was sounded, Winston found himself in a footrace with two of his youngsters for the last available F6F. He barely won and hastily strapped in, started the R2800, allowed minimum warm-up time, and shoved everything forward with his left hand.

When he finally lifted off the deck and retracted his wheels, Winston noted that the fight was already under way: He was nearly hit by two Japanese planes dropping into the water. Six of his pilots claimed fifteen kills among them, paced by Lieutenant Junior Grade John L. Wirth with four. The skipper eagerly sought a target—he'd not scored since March—and was nearly apoplectic when all he could find was some orbiting Dauntlesses.

The Hellcats already airborne were pointed west in high-power climbs. The big R2800s growled at 2,700 rpm, pulling 52.5 inches of manifold pressure for an indicated 130 knots airspeed. At 7,000 feet the low blowers kicked in, holding 49.5 inches to 22,000 feet. The Japanese strike leader's concern for pulling his squadrons together may have enhanced tactical cohesion, but it gave precious minutes for Mitscher's fighter pilots to gain three unbeatable assets: numbers, altitude, and position.

Above ten thousand feet the F6F pilots snapped on their masks, checked the regulators, and began inhaling pure oxygen. Some pulled their goggles over their eyes, turning the world crisply amber or green. All ran their precombat checklists: six guns armed, Mark VIII sight's rheostat adjusted, shoulder harness tight or loose according to individual preference. Some—usually the more aggressive—would accept less safety in exchange for more mobility in the cockpit, the better to see potential threats or targets.

Fighter directors allotted their assets according to doctrine: While the interceptors were vectored outward, high and low CAPs were maintained over each group. The arrangement in Montgomery's 58.2 was typical: *Bunker Hill's* Fighting 8 took high CAP at eighteen thousand feet, while *Monterey's* VF-28 covered the enemy approach course lower down.

Some sixty miles out, the pilots of Air Group 653 were just tidying up their formation. The long flight from C Force had strung out some squadrons, and the leader circled to allow the stragglers to catch up. He double-checked the formation: fighters deployed on both flanks and in the vulnerable six-o'clock-high position. The brief period of circling also afforded time to finalize attack orders.

Then the sky fell in.

The Hellcats had nearly half an hour to work over the inbound strikes. It was more than enough time.

Shoe Clerks

RALPH CLARK WAS A GRUMMAN "tech rep," a field service representative who worked with Navy squadrons who were, in effect, his clients. The young New Yorker had signed on with the expanding Grumman firm in 1941 and stayed more than forty years. During four of those years he kept Hellcats and Avengers flying, and learned firsthand of America's war-winning secret.

Shoe clerks.

Clark believed fervently in what he called "the shoe-clerk approach to aviation." He said, "We had shoe clerks building airplanes, we had shoe clerks repairing airplanes, and we even had shoe clerks flying airplanes. That's not taking away anything from shoe clerks, but 90 percent of the people involved in aviation had never touched an airplane before the war."

The massive changeover to wartime production and training was unlike anything previously seen. Men and women with no mechanical experience became expert riveters and welders. Farm boys and city slickers were turned into aircraft mechanics who could troubleshoot problems and repair them quickly.

Pilots had to be trained in production-line numbers while retaining the touch of the artisan. The aviator curriculum was force-fed with a fire hose: theory of flight, navigation, communications (including the dreaded and seldom-used Morse code), meteorology, instrument flying, formation, aerobatics, gunnery, and much more. To say nothing of the esoteric, dangerous routine of carrier landings.

The Hellcat

LEGEND INSISTED THAT THE HELLCAT was designed to beat the Zero. It wasn't true, at least not specifically. Wartime scuttlebutt had it that a Zero force-landed in an Aleutian bog was dismantled, flown, and studied with the information going to Roy Grumman's firm on Long Island. In truth, the prototype XF6F-1 was first tested in June 1942, weeks before the captured Mitsubishi was even discovered. But once the nature of the enemy was known, Hellcat pilots began practicing to exploit their advantages against the Zeke's weaknesses.

The secret to beating Zeke in a gunfight was speed: not just being fast on the draw to get the first shot, but keeping more than two hundred knots on the dial. Flight tests revealed that the Zero's astonishing maneuverability was optimized below 230 mph. At much above that speed the controls began to stiffen, especially the ailerons. Since the F6 was faster at all altitudes from the deck to thirty thousand feet, it made no sense to play the Zeke's game in a turning contest. Instead, Grumman pilots used superior altitude (Zekes had no superchargers) to dive on the enemy, fire as the opportunity allowed, then zoom-climb back to the "perch" to reposition for another pass.

If a Zeke got on a Hellcat's tail, the solution (absent a wingman) was to shove everything forward and point the nose down. With airspeed building toward three hundred knots or more, the F6F retained aileron effectiveness and could execute a rolling pullout that the Japanese could not follow.

The F6F-3 Hellcat carried twenty-four hundred rounds of ammunition for its six Browning .50-caliber machine guns. Belted in sequence of armor-piercing incendiary, tracer, and ball, the combined firepower of six "fifties" was enough to destroy any Japanese single-engine aircraft in one well-placed burst. Cycling at about eight hundred rounds per minute, each gun's four hundred rounds could be emptied in thirty seconds, but half a minute's trigger time was more than ample. Throughout the war, some forty Hellcat pilots claimed five or more kills in one mission.

By VJ-day the Hellcat produced more aces than any American aircraft and claimed some 5,200 kills for 270 losses in aerial combat: a nineteen-to-one win-loss ratio over Japanese aircraft. Even allowing for inevitable errors and combat confusion, the lopsided statistics bespoke the superiority of the Grumman Iron Works and the training of the United States Navy.

Raid I

THE KEY TO AIR DEFENSE was adequate time to work over the attackers. Radar gave Mitscher's controllers the ability to concentrate squadron-strength fighters against the inbound raiders sixty to seventy miles out. At typical cruising speeds, that translated to nearly half an hour in which to deplete Ozawa's formations. The Japanese survivors were stunned—they had no idea that they would repeatedly be intercepted beyond visual distance of Task Force 58.

First to intercept Raid I were eight *Essex* F6Fs, led by VF-15's Commander Charles W. Brewer, class of 1933. He tallyhoed Zekes and Judys, and if his recognition was off (the strikers were Jills), his shooting eye was not. He and his wingman, twenty-year-old Ensign Richard E. Fowler, splashed four planes apiece.

But even their hot pace was bettered by Lieutenant Junior Grade George R. Carr, a Floridian who had joined the RCAF in 1941. Though he had never scored, his experience made him a division leader. Carr trailed Brewer into the Jills, selected a victim, and set it afire. Before he could shift targets the D4Y exploded, forcing him to dip his nose as he flew through the debris. Adding power, Carr climbed, found another Jill, and sent it spinning in a graveyard spiral.

By now the Japanese escorts were at work. One latched onto Carr's tail, but he was too astute to turn with the more nimble Zeke. Instead, he shoved his stick, throttle, and prop controls full forward. In a headlong plunge reaching 430 knots (nearly 500 mph) he pulled ahead of the Mitsubishi and, with adequate separation, laid the stick over to the right. The Zeke's controls were far too heavy to cope; Carr lost his assailant.

That battle had been won in the Hellcat factory on Long Island.

As he pulled out of his dive, Carr's windscreen fogged up in the moist tropical air. But he could see another Zeke tackling him head-on. Closing at perhaps six hundred mph, neither pilot had much time to aim. Both fired; both hit. But Carr's sextet of .50-calibers produced a denser pattern. He set the Zeke afire, then checked his own airplane. A 7.7mm round had starred the thick glass of his windscreen, but he could still see ahead.

What he saw was two more Zekes, and he didn't wait. He jumped on one and flamed it from astern. Quickly sliding behind the second Zeke, Carr pressed his trigger and got hits. The A6M5 gushed smoke and fell off on one wing. Not willing to let it go, Carr split-essed to stay behind it. He was lining up a finishing shot when it exploded.

Five down. George Carr pulled up and circled the area, counting wrecks and oil slicks on the surface. He quit at seventeen, preferring to join a section of Hellcats headed for *Essex*.

Carr's wingman was enthusiastic, crew-cut Ensign Norman Berree. In the first pass he selected a Hamp on the fringe of the formation and, leopardlike, he took the opportunity to cull the herd. Apparently the Japanese pilot never saw him coming; the determined Pennsylvanian closed in, pressed the trigger, and kept the pipper on target. His method was uneconomical but undeniably effective. Absorbing hundreds of rounds, the Mitsubishi exploded.

Like Carr, Berree found himself with a vengeful Japanese at his six-o'clock, so he applied standard procedure: full power and a hard, diving turn to starboard, away from the enemy's torque side. It worked.

Recovering at ten thousand feet, Berree and a Zeke found themselves abreast of each other. Each turned into the threat, firing as soon as their sights came to bear. The Zero gushed flame, rolled inverted, but kept on track. Just before colliding, it dropped away and exploded.

Berree checked his vital signs; his F6 had taken hits that damaged his water injection system. But it didn't stop him from splashing a Judy.

By the time reinforcements arrived, the "Fabled Fifteen" had claimed twenty kills.

Elements of six more squadrons piled in during the next half hour, shredding Air Group 653's ranks. Close behind Brewer and company was Lieutenant Commander Ronald W. Hoel of *Bunker Hill*'s Fighting 8. His division had a dandy dustup, each pilot dropping a Zeke apiece, while Hoel also shot down a bomber. In the process he was beset by a vengeful Zeke that thoroughly perforated his F6F, and Hoel was saved only by the timely intercession of his wingman.

Overhead 58.2, Hoel found his controls badly damaged. Then his stick jammed full forward. The stricken Hellcat nosed over and fell into an inverted spin. There was nothing to do but ring up the for-sale sign. Hoel slid back his canopy, pulled his oxygen and radio leads, and flipped his seat-belt release. Pitched out of the doomed fighter, he pulled his rip cord and floated to a watery landing. A destroyer fetched him before long.

Next up was Commander Bill Dean's Fighting 2, whose eight Hellcats claimed nine Zekes and three Jills that broke off from the main formation. The *Hornet* pilots found they could not stay with the speedy attackers in a high-speed descent, though two *Cowpens* divisions tried without success.

Five CVL squadrons conducted most of the remaining execution, mauling the Japanese for some twenty sea miles. Prominent among them was Fighting 27.

Princeton's Hellcats were the most distinctive aircraft in Task Force 58. During predeployment workups the squadron had designed a "shark mouth" motif that was commercially produced as a large decal. Transferred to the cowling of each F6F, the design featured white fangs dripping with blood that presumably would terrify any Japanese aviator. On the Hellcat's blunt nose the rendering lacked the fearsome snout of a Curtiss P-40, but one advantage was instant recognition in the heat of combat.

Lieutenant Fred Bardshar had been relaxing after an uneventful CAP, sunbathing on *Princeton*'s open forecastle. His reverie was shattered with an immediate call to FitRon 27's ready room. After a hasty briefing, "Sweet Pea's" Hellcats were launched to intercept the raiders. "I remember passing through ten thousand feet and only then getting around to fastening my harness to my parachute," Bardshar said.

Fighting 27 met "a large number of escorted single-engined Japanese bombers while still climbing, at about fourteen thousand feet. Several planes among my group had dropped out due to overheating engines or failure to shift into high blower. I was fascinated by the general inactivity of the Japanese escort fighters who continued to weave above the bomber formation. . . . A melee followed; one of several. The escort fighters did not oppose the intercept, nor were they effective after the melee began."

Still operating beneath the Zekes, VF-27 had no altitude advantage. So the white-fanged Hellcats slammed into the Japanese bombers in "flat-side" gunnery runs that degenerated into tail chases.

Bardshar quickly gunned one bomber, than chased another downward, where it flamed at about seven thousand feet. When he looked around, the fight was over. But he remembered the aftermath three decades later:

"The sky was marked with numerous burning and falling aircraft and some chutes as well as AA over the force directed at the few Japanese who delivered an attack. I believe this one hit on the main body was on the *South Dakota*.

"Air and communication discipline had been emphasized in VF-27 and was evident in the engagement. Section integrity was, generally, maintained; transmissions were limited and to the point."

Lieutenant William B. Lamb already had splashed two Jills (he called them Kates) when he latched onto a formation of twelve more "torpedo planes." Pacing the speedy Jills with their external loads, he radioed their position and called for help before attacking—with one gun working. He claimed another kill, raising his one-mission tally to three "Kates" and a Zeke.

(This event well illustrates the confusion common in air combat. There were no Kates among the attackers, and CarDiv Three launched only eight Jills. Most of Lamb's opponents had to be Zero fighter-bombers.)

The *Princeton* Hellcats proved their mettle, though two pilots were killed, including the air group skipper. Commander Ernest W. Wood, class of 1938, was lost when his empennage failed during a steep dive pullout. He was missed: An accomplished pianist, he often serenaded "Sweet Pea's" company with renditions of "Claire de Lune."

By the time the preceding FitRons were finished, *Bunker Hill* and *San Jacinto* pilots picked over the scraps: a dozen Zekes, "Judys," and "Tonys." The latter was a Japanese army fighter with the same engine as the Messerschmitt 109. Intelligence reports led aviators to expect the sleek Kawasakis, and pilots reported what they expected to see. Meanwhile, several Grim Reapers off *Enterprise* broke up a torpedo attack on the battleships.

Two *Monterey* divisions got in some of the last shooting on Raid I. Lieutenant Oscar C. Bailey had split a Betty the day before, but now he notched four Zekes in a matter of minutes. His first fighter went down smoking after a stern attack; then he sped after another. Though Bailey overshot, making himself vulnerable, the Japanese aviator decided to tackle the American wingman. Ensign Alan C. Persson tagged him with a half deflection shot, then rejoined Buck Bailey, who spotted another "dance partner."

This Japanese pilot was more alert and more competent than the others. He engaged Bailey in a horizontal scissors, each fighter passing and quickly reversing, trying to gain a favorable angle for a shot. Bailey used the Hellcat's effective ailerons to advantage, closing on his opponent's tail and triggering a telling burst. The Japanese pilot abandoned ship.

With no further bandits in sight, Bailey and Persson turned for home. But the battleship group lay between them and 58.2, and the gunners were jittery after the previous several minutes. They opened fire on the two Hellcats, scoring multiple hits on Persson's plane. With his radio shot out and his port wing holed, he followed Bailey back to *Monterey* and entered the landing pattern. Though unable to lower his flaps, he got aboard safely. However, his flakked-up fighter was assessed with "strike" damage. It was stripped of useful equipment and given the deep six.

Meanwhile, Buck Bailey had other ideas. He turned westward, hunting additional opportunities, and he found them. Though flying without a wingman was never a good idea, the aggressive Texan was hungry and competent. With two years as an instructor under his belt, he reckoned that he could fly about as well as anyone, and he felt safe if he kept his head on a swivel.

Topping out at "Angels 20," Bailey looked down and spotted two Zekes cruising about four thousand feet below. He rolled over, making a high-speed attack, and surprised his intended victims. Centering one in his reflector sight, he opened fire at four hundred yards—a little beyond bore-sight range—and closed with a rapid overtake. At 250 yards the Zeke burned and went careening toward the water.

Using his momentum, Bailey dived well below the second Zeke, then honked back on his stick in a vertical yo-yo. He opened fire at the enemy's belly, got no visible hits, and watched the Zeke dive away. It was folly for a Zeke to attempt outdiving a Hellcat. Bailey gave chase, reeled in the fleeing Japanese, and executed him from astern.

The main phase of the battle involved fifty Hellcats against nearly seventy Japanese planes. It wasn't even close. Following the initial intercepts, the surviving raiders went after the battleship group and thereby squandered their prospects. Two *Essex* divisions and one from *Bataan* hunted most of them to destruction, while others expended themselves against the gray castles of American warships.

Whatever the novice Japanese fliers lacked in ability, they did not want for courage: A handful took a shot at Lee's battleships. Lieutenant Don Gordon, a second-tour *Enterprise* pilot, described Task Group 58.7 as "an attractive, lethal target."

He was right: One Zero pilot scored a hit on *South Dakota* that blew a large hole in the deck, killing twenty-three men and wounding twenty-seven, but otherwise did no harm. "SoDak's" gunners put in a claim for the "Judy," though sailors on *Alabama* insisted that the plucky Japanese escaped. Two *Zuiho* fighter-bombers likely were responsible.

To "Flash" Gordon, the view of *Indiana* steaming in the center of a six-mile circle of twenty-three other warships beneath a twenty-thousand-foot flak umbrella was "my most memorable scene in World War Two." The blue sky, pocked with brown-black antiaircraft bursts, occasionally was lit by the flaming gout of a Japanese aircraft caught in the lethal radius of a VT-fused shell.

Steaming alongside "SoDak," keeping station at twenty-two knots, was *Hudson*, conned by Lieutenant Commander Richard R. Pratt, class of 1936. When one of the raiders penetrated the outer screen, everybody in range opened fire. Inevitably some of the rounds intended for Japanese aircraft impacted American ships. *Hudson*'s port 40mm mount took a direct hit, killing two sailors and jamming primary steering. Pratt quickly passed control to the aft engine room, and the veteran "can" maintained station.

Other Zero fighter-bombers broke through to attack *Minneapolis* and *Wichita* in Cruiser Division Six. Both were spattered with splinters and splashed with water, but the near misses resulted in war stories rather than results.

The massive AA barrage over 58.7 made an impression on the Japanese. Mitscher's language officer, Lieutenant Junior Grade Charles Sims, monitored a broadcast advising the follow-on attacks to circumvent the battleship group. Later, Mitscher's staff said that, judging by the approaches of subsequent raids, the advice was heeded. However, the different Japanese approaches more likely resulted from navigational concerns.

For Raid I, American claims of a hundred kills far exceeded actual Japanese losses of forty-two. But though three F6F pilots were killed, the fighter pilots and their controllers performed superbly, concentrating more than sixty Hellcats against sixty-plus raiders, who lost two-thirds of their number. More important, not one Japanese plane penetrated to the carrier groups. Raid I went into the books as a near-perfect example of fleet air defense.

The aircraft attrition for Air Group 653 was bad enough; worse yet were losses among formation leaders. Eight of the nine squadron commanders were killed, the only survivor being fighter leader Kenji Nakagawa. The senior fighter-bomber pilot, Lieutenant Keishiro Ito, disappeared with thirty-one of his men, while CarDiv Three torpedo skipper Masayuki Yamagami perished on the morning search.

Against its crippling losses, Air Group 653 had some good news, optimistically claiming that its planes "definitely scored hits on a large aircraft carrier and on a large cruiser." Ozawa endorsed that assessment, citing Air Group 601 aircrews who observed a carrier and a heavy warship afire during their approach to Task Force 58. In truth, no 653 planes penetrated the American carrier screen.

Meanwhile, the third phase of Ozawa's search had turned up more American ships. Shortly before Mitscher concluded that he was due for the "working over," one of the *Shokaku* scouts spotted a task group and reported three carriers accompanied by five "battleships" and ten other escorts. The find was possibly Task Group 58.2, but a gross error was committed. Whatever the cause of the new contact, designated "15 Ri," it was plotted more than seventy miles southwest of Guam. Actually, Montgomery's group was 120 miles to the north.

The sighting came from the number fifteen scout, a radar-equipped Jill in the 105-degree sector. The observer and aircraft commander was Lieutenant Keizo Kitao, who established the "15 Ri" position that led to so much confusion later in the day. With the radar contact established, Kitao coached his pilot within visual range and put his binoculars on the Americans. He counted eighteen ships, then proceeded a half hour to Guam. He avoided the diminished island CAP, landed and refueled, and returned to *Zuikaku* that evening.

At 1000, fifteen minutes after Kitao's sighting, the third-phase search made yet another "discovery." Far to the north yet another scout reported a similar find: three carriers plus escorts some 150 miles northwest of Guam. That became the "3 Ri" contact, which must have provoked some consternation in *Taiho*'s flag plot. Multiple American carrier groups operating across a two-hundred-mile front!

Within half an hour of Obayashi's left jab, Ozawa threw his right hook. At 0900 the cocked fist on CarDiv One's three flight decks represented 128 planes: fifty-three Judys, each with a 550-pound bomb; twenty-seven torpedo-packing Jills; and forty-eight Zeke escorts. No fighter-bombers were included in the second strike.

The flagship contributed something else: a special-mission D4Y1-C armed with bundles of aluminum chaff. Like so much in the Imperial Navy, it proved a good idea that arrived too late.

Though the Japanese jammed some U.S. radars as early as the Guadalcanal campaign, they never seriously pursued the practice. Reportedly some electronics specialists were drafted, while Japan suffered from a lack of adequate materials for even passive deception measures. Strips of aluminum that the British called "window" and the Japanese *giman-shi* ("deceiving paper") could be effective, but the material was considered too valuable for such purposes.

After forming up near the A Force, Air Group 601 proceeded on course to attack. But an hour after launch the formation encountered unexpected trouble over the van force. It was due in part to poor planning—the contingency should have been expected—and partly to poor discipline. In any case, Kurita's gunners opened fire on the Car-Div One squadrons. Never mind that they approached from the west—opposite the enemy's location. The damage was done: Two planes were destroyed and eight forced to abort.

Perhaps Takeo Kurita consoled himself that while his crews flunked aircraft identification, they passed gunnery.

The AA barrage threw 601's fighters into confusion, and it took a while to sort things out. By the time the survivors regained formation, events accelerated at the closure rate of about 150 knots.

Almost simultaneous with the overflight of the van force, Ozawa learned of the 3 Ri report. Not unreasonably, he concluded that, being two and a half hours later, it must be more accurate than the 7 I plot. Joshima's aircrews had been briefed on the earlier location and had just begun launch when the new information arrived, so at 1030 Ozawa broadcast the information to CarDiv Two. Thus did Raid III emerge: forty-seven planes of Air Group 652.

The Periscope View

WHILE RAID I WAS ATTACKING and dying, events accelerated in the Japanese operating area, unknown to Ozawa. American submarines had been astutely deployed, and they stalked his A Force. Because he had allotted most of his escorts to Kurita's van force, Ozawa retained only six destroyers to protect his three carriers. It was not nearly enough.

Observing with rapt attention was Commander James W. Blanchard, peering through *Albacore*'s periscope. He was almost perfectly positioned to intercept Ozawa's Carrier Division One.

It had been a long, frustrating journey to combat. Blanchard had been stuck at the New Haven sub school since 1941, howling that he needed to get in some shooting. Earlier that morning an enemy plane had forced him to dive, but the persistent Blanchard had stuck around, rightly figuring that something interesting was coming his way.

Persistence definitely counted in submarines. Three days before, some 350 miles off the Philippines, Lieutenant Commander Herman Kossler's *Cavalla* had tracked a Japanese fueling group but was delayed by escorts. After a prolonged stern chase, the following night he got radar contact on fifteen-plus ships. That information was gratefully received in Task Force 58.

Now Blanchard had a dream setup: a Jap carrier group squarely in his sights. He let the first flattop pass, then settled on the next one, closing from almost five miles to barely two. Then his target data computer malfunctioned. Damning his luck, Blanchard stayed on the periscope, established a firing solution visually, and launched six torpedoes.

Then Blanchard saw three destroyers charging his position. He folded the periscope handles and went deep, telling the crew to brace for depth charges.

The submariners counted two dozen or more "ash cans" that exploded close aboard, testing the boat's eleven-sixteenths-inch mild steel plates. They badly rattled *Albacore*, but she held together; no serious leaks penetrated her nine watertight compartments.

Blanchard's firing team checked its stopwatch and heard an explosion timed to the sixth "fish."

Topside, Ozawa knew the facts. *Taiho*, his flagship, was speared forward. At some thirty-three thousand tons, she was one of the biggest carriers afloat, largely impervious to one torpedo. A second torpedo would have struck but for the exceptional courage of Warrant Officer Sakio Komatsu, who had launched on Raid II about 0900. Spotting the spread of torpedoes, he instantly nosed over in his dive-bomber to intercept the closest one. His timing was perfect: His Jill impacted the water and detonated the Mark 14, taking him and his observer to the Yasukuni Shrine. But his valiant act of *tai-atari* could not save *Taiho*.

The explosion blew a hole big enough to flood the lower portion of the forward elevator well. Tons of water gushed in, weighing the bow down about four feet. Worse, for the moment, was damage to the elevator itself, which fell six feet, interrupting flight operations. Nevertheless, *Taiho* continued making twenty-six knots, and in half an hour repair crews had laid planks over the gaping elevator hole.

For a time, Ozawa remained confident enough to stay aboard. Initial damage appeared limited, so "Great Phoenix" launched her contribution to the third and fourth raids. However, a silent disaster was under way. The torpedo explosion fractured an aviation fuel storage tank, which leaked into the partly flooded elevator well. Concerned about accumulated gasoline vapors, a junior officer opened *Taiho*'s ventilation system, thinking he would dissipate the fumes. Instead, he turned *Taiho* into a floating time bomb as vapors spread throughout the ship. The volatile Tarakan crude oil taken on at Tawi-Tawi only added to the lethal brew.

The fuse burned for perhaps four hours. Then at 1530 *Taiho* erupted. From the bridge, Ozawa's staff watched in awe as the armored flight deck bulged upward from the interior blast. With her hull blown out below the waterline, she quickly began sinking. Ablaze, without power, the huge carrier began settling on an even keel, down by the head.

Heartsick, Ozawa expressed his intent to die with his flagship. However, his chief of staff did some fast talking. Captain Toshikazu Ohmae, a longtime friend, mixed fact and fantasy in one phrase: "The battle is still going on and you should remain in command for the final victory." Thus, he convinced the admiral to continue the fight rather than ride the ship to the bottom of the Marianas Trench. He reluctantly shifted his flag, temporarily transferring to the destroyer *Wakatsuki*.

With the fleet commander departed, Captain Kikuchi followed protocol. He ensured that the emperor's portrait was safely removed, then ordered his men to abandon ship.

Albacore escaped the subsequent pounding and reported damage to a carrier. Upon return to Majuro, Blanchard erroneously claimed damage to a *Shokaku*-class ship and was awarded a commendation ribbon. Intelligence analysts caught no word that *Taiho* might have sunk, and not until a prisoner was interrogated months later did the U.S. Navy suspect that *Albacore* may have struck it rich. Even then, skeptics remained, and Blanchard reportedly quipped that the POW should be treated kindly until he convinced his interrogators. Eventually Blanchard's commendation was elevated to a Navy Cross.

Less than three hours after *Albacore* mortally wounded *Taiho*, Herman Kossler put *Cavalla*'s crosshairs on another big carrier. He was justifiably concerned that she might be friendly, as *Cavalla* did not know Mitscher's location. The ONI recognition manual was hauled out, and several watch officers pondered the similarities between *Essex*-class ships and some Japanese flattops. Kossler asked his exec and the torpedo data officer to take a look through the periscope, but neither could say for certain yea or nay. The skipper took the scope again and then saw the flag: "There was the rising sun, big as hell." She was *Shokaku*, veteran of Pearl, Coral Sea, and the Guadalcanal battles. *Cavalla* made a stealthy approach while "Sho" was busy launching aircraft.

Kossler retracted the scope, proceeding toward a firing point, announcing that he would shoot on his next observation. The forward torpedo room prepared to empty all six tubes.

Kossler's communications officer was Ensign Ernest J. Zellmer, who made an eye-watering scholastic record at Annapolis. When the class of 1944 graduated a year early, "Zeke" Zellmer stood thirteenth among 766. He immediately applied for sub school and joined *Cavalla* two months before she was commissioned.

Zellmer, keeping the plot in the conning tower, worked with Lieutenant Junior Grade James "Jug" Casler on the torpedo data computer. They translated Kossler's periscope observations into numbers for the TDC to crunch, arriving at a firing solution. With *Shokaku*'s course and speed determined, the mechanical computer transmitted gyro angles to the forward firing room, where torpedomen set the values in the "fish." Then they emptied all six tubes from twelve hundred yards.

Fired at eight-second intervals, three Mark 14s and three single-speed Mark 23s leaped from their tubes, accelerating to full speed in eight seconds. The alcohol-fueled, steam-powered weapons, each weighing three thousand pounds, churned through the water, tracking toward the spot where the TDC reckoned the carrier would be forty-eight seconds later: some 650 feet along her track. The torpedo spread was 125 percent: four fish calculated to hit with one passing ahead and one astern for insurance. But the destroyer off *Shokaku*'s starboard beam was alert and competent. Whether he spotted the periscope or the torpedo wakes, the escort instantly pivoted and charged down the tracks.

Zellmer recalled, "On the last observation the destroyer was about fifteen hundred yards away with zero angle on the bow. Rather intimidating for a sub skipper getting ready to fire torpedoes!"

With the destroyer coming head on, after the fifth launch, *Cavalla* flooded negative and started to go deep. The sixth was fired with a down angle on the boat. It hung up briefly until released by the impulse pressure and the weight of the weapon itself.

The firing data was accurate. At the last moment, *Shokaku*'s lookouts spotted the wakes in the water, sixty degrees off the starboard bow. Captain Matsubara ordered hard a-starboard, hoping to "comb the spread" so the torpedoes would pass along each side.

It was too late. Kossler's shots bracketed the 845-foot-long target. Smashing into *Shokaku's* hull at forty-six knots, the Mark 6 detonators each ignited 668 pounds of Torpex. The result was devastating.

Cavalla's crew heard three hits through the boat's hull; then helmsmen pushed the bow planes down.

The destroyer that Kossler glimpsed was Lieutenant Commander Saneho Maeda's *Urakaze*, which jumped on the offending submarine so quickly that her first depth charge exploded almost simultaneously with *Cavalla's* first torpedo. Other persistent destroyers, obviously outraged at being skunked, dropped more than a hundred depth charges over a three-hour period. "Zeke" Zellmer, assigned to plot depth charge patterns, reckoned fifty-six were close.

Kossler's aim had been excellent: Probably four of his six "fish" scored, tearing the living guts out of *Shokaku*. She was hit at the most vulnerable moment, refueling recently recovered aircraft. Most of the hits were forward to amidships, near the aviation fuel tanks. A gas main erupted in a huge explosion that showered burning gasoline onto the flight deck, where the ghastly deluge incinerated a group of pilots and observers idling forward of the island. The force of the explosion blew her forward elevator nearly three feet upward; then it collapsed into the well, crushing men in the process.

Badly holed along her starboard side, the veteran carrier quickly began listing. Her boilers on that side were flooded, reducing speed and headway. Captain Matsubara ordered counterflooding to port, but his engineers overdid it. With alarming speed they managed to shift the list from starboard to port.

Shokaku had more experience with battle damage than almost any ship afloat. She had taken bomb hits at Coral Sea and Santa Cruz in 1942, but recovered both times. Now, however, the conventional wisdom fully applied. Submariners and torpecker ("carrier attack" plane) pilots said, "If you want to let in air, use bombs. If you want to let in water, use torpedoes."

With nine planes on the hangar deck, the conflagration there quickly worsened, hampered by efforts to pump aircraft fuel overboard. The ensuing fires and secondary explosions destroyed generator panels, depriving Matsubara of the electric pumps he badly needed. His hard-pressed crew was so desperate that bucket brigades were formed. Despite some of the primitive methods, the stricken carrier remained afloat. Ozawa turned his attention elsewhere.

"Sho" lingered about four hours until, just past 1500, a bomb "cooked off." It ignited the fuel vapors trapped on the hangar deck, resulting in a "terrific" explosion. At that point the carrier died very quickly. As she settled by the bow, the rate increased as water flooded the forward elevator well, and in minutes she stood nearly vertically on her bows and disappeared from the world of men. "Happy Crane's" career lasted two months under three years.

The toll was two-thirds of the crew: 1,263 men, including 376 from Air Group 601. Matsubara and 569 others were saved, but few if any would fight again.

Two imperial carriers had sunk within thirty-one minutes and twenty-five miles of each other.

Meanwhile, Herman Kossler had problems of his own. After firing, *Cavalla* went deep with full left rudder, changing course and slowing for silent running. Approaching test depth of three hundred feet as more depth charges erupted close aboard, her nose came up but her depth increased. The "up bubble" was not checking the descent.

Zeke Zellmer recalled, "It was necessary to increase the propeller speed and carry a four-degree up angle to stop the descent. Negative tank had been blown, but we were still heavy, and the depth charge salvos continued. We were nearly a hundred feet below our test depth."

After the second salvo a loud hissing sound had been heard in the crew's mess. Murphy's Law had kicked in: The main air induction trunk had flooded at the worst possible moment. *Cavalla* had taken on twelve to fifteen tons of unwanted water.

The school solution was to drain the flooded trunk to the engine-room bilge, then use the drain pumps to vent the water overboard. But that wasn't an option: The noise would help Lieutenant Commander Maeda and his vengeful partners find *Cavalla* and kill her. Kossler decided to compensate by running with a little extra speed: At eighty rpm the propellers turned at less than cavitation velocity, which would pinpoint the boat for enemy sonar.

But there were more problems: *Cavalla* also ingested water in the forward torpedo room bilges. One of the poppet valves had stuck, allowing the "water round torpedo tank" to overflow. Consequently, the sub's up angle sent bilgewater rearward, rising to a foot deep at the after bulkhead, flooding the motors controlling the JK, QC, and QB sonars. Only the JP set was functional, and it had to be trained by hand.

As if that weren't enough, one of the destroyers was back. Every man aboard *Cavalla* heard its high-speed screws. The high, screechy tone grew in pitch and volume as the hunter-killer passed directly overhead—the best pass yet, absolutely perfect alignment. All hands braced themselves as best they could, knowing what was coming.

It never came.

For reasons that will never be known, the Japanese skipper didn't roll his depth charges. Perhaps there was still ambient noise in the water from previous attacks, concealing *Cavalla*'s presence. Whatever the reason, it seemed providential. If Saints Brendan, Christopher, and Michael were the benefactors of sailors and mariners, United States ship *Cavalla* must have received their unanimous blessing.

But the crisis was far from over. As Zeke Zellmer noted, "For the next one and a half hours the three destroyers took turns trying to obliterate us. Finally only one destroyer remained. By this time we had planed up to our test depth and tensions eased."

Cavalla waited for the screw noises to vanish, then began pumping the excess water. Simultaneously, the five intact tubes in the forward torpedo room were reloaded.

Sending his contact report, Kossler informed headquarters, "Heard four terrific explosions in direction of the target two and a half hours after attack. Believe that baby sank."

Herman Kossler had bagged a carrier on his first patrol in command. Besides Kossler and Blanchard, only six other U.S. sub captains ever sank a carrier, while three Japanese and five German skippers also shared the honor.

Raid II

OZAWA'S SECOND STRIKE, LAUNCHED FROM his own A Force at 0900, originally numbered 128 aircraft. It was the only strike without Zero fighter-bombers, and therefore represented Japan's strongest punch, with fifty-three dive-bombers and twenty-seven "carrier attack" planes (torpeckers) from *Taiho, Shokaku,* and *Zuikaku.* In all there were eighteen aborts plus Komatsu's valiant sacrifice.

Proceeding to the 7 I contact, Air Group 601 flew outbound on 064 degrees, following two Jill pathfinders from *Zuikaku.* Additionally, a *Taiho* Judy constituted the "radio countermeasures" capability. The D4Y1-C was armed with strips of aluminum chaff that would be dropped northeast of the American task force. Presumably the large blip generated would siphon off some of the CAP and improve chances for the attackers to get through the fighters and flak.

By the time Raid II strobed on *Lexington*'s radar at 1107, aborts and casualties reduced the effectives to 109 Zekes, Judys, and Jills. As with the first raid, this one squandered precious minutes by orbiting briefly before resuming its eastward run-in. Joe Eggert's fighter directors used that time to advantage.

The first sighting of probable hostile aircraft was made in Task Group 58.4, as Harrill's five-inchers opened fire. Their target may have been one of the pathfinders, which in any case reversed course to the south.

Though Commander Paul Buie's VF-16 "Airedales" were vectored outbound, *Essex* Hellcats got there first. Led by Commander Dave McCampbell, three VF-15 divisions were ordered southwest, heading 245 true en route to Angels 25.

Fighter pilots called the tallyho seventy-two miles out at 1139, barely an hour after the fight began against Raid I. The fighting, along a track thirty miles eastward, was over in several minutes.

The *Essex* fighters jumped on Air Group 601 about forty miles west of the battlewagons. While four Hellcats tied up the Zeke top cover at twenty thousand feet, McCampbell took his other six into the lower Judys, stacked in a formation some twelve hundred feet deep. Flying two-plane sections, making fast high-side runs, Fighting 15 began depleting the raiders.

McCampbell, an old man at thirty-four, was arguably the finest aerial marksman in the U.S. Navy. On his last gunnery flight before deploying, he shot the tow cable in two, sending the target sleeve flopping to earth. "I practiced until I just couldn't get any better," he said.

In the next several minutes the Alabaman demonstrated his exceptional skill. Despite repeated gun jams, he made alternating port and starboard runs on the Judys, blasting five into the water. Finishing at the edge of the battleship disposition, he kept his distance from Ching Lee's avid AA gunners. The CAG reckoned he had emptied his guns and could do no more, so he reported to his controller, stating that the lead Judy (probable strike leader) was a splash. Then he returned to orbit base, "ammo minus."

Six other VF-15 pilots claimed nine more bombers and at least four Zekes. But it was not all one-sided. After bagging two Judys, McCampbell's wingman, Ensign Ralph Foltz, had to push his throttle "through the gate" for water injection to outrun a threatening Zeke. With fluctuating oil pressure he turned homeward, but the Pratt & Whitney continued its patented purr.

Ensign Claude Plant had an even tougher time. He gunned four Zekes; then a skillful Japanese pilot bore-sighted him, putting 7.7- and 20mm rounds in the Hellcat's tough hide before another F6F shot the assailant off Plant's tail. When Plant trapped aboard *Essex*, he counted 150 holes in his plane, including one through each propeller blade. One VF-15 pilot, Ensign George H. Rader, never came back at all.

By the time the combat drifted eastward, the Hellcat pilots were treated to the unforgettable sight of varicolored parachutes dangling in midair or mingling with oil slicks and wreckage on the surface of the sea. But the persistent Japanese tightened formation, plugged the gaps, and continued their approach to Task Force 58.

Forty-three more Hellcats piled in minutes later, half from *Lexington*. Climbing at full power, pulling fifty-two inches of mercury from their big R2800s, not all the F6Fs could keep up. Lieutenant Junior Grade W. C. B. Birkholm was anticipating some trigger time when his propeller governor failed: "My wingmates left me standing still." It was the height of frustration: the biggest opportunity yet afforded the Airedales, and Birkholm had to abort. He called Buie, saying he would return to the vicinity of the task group and orbit at eighteen thousand feet "just in case a stray Jap came by."

Then a viscous blackness clouded the windscreen. Birkholm realized his flight was over; he tried to make Sapphire Base but the Hamilton Standard prop lurched to a halt. Birkholm began a ten-thousand-foot glide to the water. He briefly considered ditching near the battlewagons, but he knew their formidable AA and their trigger-happy tendencies.

Down to the last few feet, Birkholm had the canopy open, shoulder harness locked tight, flaps up. He nudged the stick back, felt the tail drag in the water . . . and blacked out.

The shock of the landing temporarily stunned him, but Birkholm quickly scrambled out. "Fox 36" floated just a few seconds, then nosed under. With difficulty, the pilot shucked his heavy chute harness but retained the rubber seat pack for flotation. When he realized that his Marine "boondockers" were pulling him down, he pulled the CO_2 tabs, inflating his Mae West prior to deploying his one-man raft.

Once aboard, Birkholm took in the scenery. As the battle continued overhead, he counted flamers, then remembered to spread some bright green dye marker in the water. Shortly a division of F6s arrived, circled twice, and proceeded on course. Then Birkholm saw blood on his flight suit and realized he had cut his head exiting the Hellcat. However, the wound was minor and soon clotted.

Bill Birkholm sat back, contemplating his future as he drifted west, fifteen hundred miles upwind from land.

Another pilot in Buie's prop wash was Lieutenant Junior Grade Alex Vraciu, the leading Navy ace still in combat. His supercharger was stuck in low blower, and oil splattered his windscreen. But rather than miss the fight he called *Lexington*'s controller and requested a vector for himself and some other stragglers.

"The FDO directed us to vector 265 degrees. There was something in his voice that indicated he had a good one on the string," Vraciu recalled. "The bogies were seventy-five miles away when reported, and we headed out, hopeful of meeting them halfway."

Initially, Vraciu was disappointed at eyeballing just three bogies. Then, spot-gazing intently, his hazel eyes picked a formation out of the atmosphere: "A large, rambling mass of at least fifty planes two thousand feet below us, portside and closing. My adrenaline flow hit high C!" He thought, "This could develop into a once-in-a-lifetime fighter pilot's dream."

The bandits were less than forty miles from the task force screen; there was no time to lose. Vraciu was crowded out of his first run by another eager Hellcat pilot, so he slipped beneath the raiders, assessing their composition. He identified them and called an amplified report to his FDO, then went after a Judy maneuvering on the edge of the formation. Closing from astern, Vraciu triggered a short burst that flamed the Japanese. On his next run, in a matter of seconds he picked off two more flying in a loose formation.

Amid the confusion, another Judy broke formation, and Vraciu jumped on it. His .50-caliber rounds "went right into the sweet spot at the root of his wing tanks." The plane tumbled, burning, out of control.

By now the attackers were into the American flak zone. Nevertheless, Vraciu chased three more Judys. He lined up the nearest, fired, and it exploded before he could get off the trigger. The same thing happened on number six. Barely had Vraciu fired when the bomber disintegrated. "I had seen planes blow up before, but never like this," he said.

The remaining Judy had too much of a lead for Vraciu to reel it in, but he needn't have worried. The bandit took a direct hit, probably from five-inchers, and exploded. In eight minutes, Al Vraciu had run his score from twelve to eighteen. Later he said, "That was my payback for Pearl Harbor."

Meanwhile, other F6Fs were adding to the execution. *Yorktown's* VF-1 piled in with thirteen F6Fs, while the remainder of the Tophatters were retained to backstop the play. Skipper "Smoke" Strean immediately hosed two fighters, claiming a Zeke and a "Tony." Throughout the day Hellcat pilots reported downing twenty of the Kawasakis even though they were known Japanese Army types. It wasn't a unique error: *Enterprise* Wildcats had reported tangling with Messerschmitt 109s at Santa Cruz in October 1942.

The Tophatters' top gun was Lieutenant Richard Eastmond, who rolled in from his twenty-five-thousand-foot perch and chopped up a Zeke at seventeen thousand. He narrowly avoided collision with his second victim, then flamed a third and exploded a fourth. When he had time to look around, Eastmond noted seventeen smoke plumes still in the air. By then Fighting 1 had notched more than twenty "meatballs."

Subsequently *Yorktown's* CAG, Commander Jim Peters, arrived with his division in time to glimpse two planes splash. He quickly gunned two Zekes, and his three pilots claimed four more kills and a probable. Ensign Cyrus R. Garman disappeared somewhere in the hassle, and Lieutenant William C. Moseley couldn't stretch it back to the Fighting Lady. He plunked down on her teammate, *Hornet*, and gratefully climbed out as maintenance men surveyed his flying wreck. They decided it had "strike" damage and shoved it overboard.

Bataan also had CAP duty, but her fighters had one of the longest runs to the intercept. Leading four Hellcats at twenty thousand feet was Lieutenant Junior Grade Daniel Rehm Jr., who received a call from the 58.1 fighter director, sending him west with the word "Your signal: Buster." Rehm knew what that meant: "I immediately firewalled the throttle and turned on my guns." He climbed to twenty-four thousand and in about twenty minutes he eyeballed the intruders in formation at eighteen thousand feet—with no top cover.

"I placed my formation in a right echelon and made a high side pass at the nearest Zeke, gave a burst, and the left wing folded and began to burn. At this point I did not observe any other F6s or other burning Japs. I pulled back hard and climbed to the left, graying out. I did a hard right turn and bore down on the formation again, firing at the nearest fighter, burning him as he fell away. At this point I did observe other F6s and burning Japs. I turned back and fired at another Zeke and burned him, too. About this time there was just a big gaggle of F6s and burning Japs falling out of the sky. Not wanting to be hit by one of the fireballs, I began to fly back toward the fleet, since I was getting very low on fuel."

Rehm's mention of seeing no other Hellcats is instructive. VF-50 was among the last squadrons on the scene (just ten minutes after VF-16), but the cerulean arena was so vast—thirty miles long and four miles high—that scores of other aircraft went unobserved.

Despite appalling losses, the Japanese pressed in. At 1145 an estimated twenty raiders that survived the Hellcat gauntlet closed on Lee's force. One of the picket destroyers was *Stockham*, which reported a lively twenty minutes or so as her skipper, Commander Ephraim P. Holmes, reported "fighting off numerous attacks from all directions."

Other planes made individual or small group attacks on four battlewagons and four flattops, but only *Indiana* was tagged, shrugging off an eleven-thousand-pound Jill that destroyed itself against her thirty-five-thousand-ton bulk. It could have been a major hit, but the B6N's torpedo was still aboard and therefore not armed.

Two Jills went for *South Dakota*, steaming unimpeded after her Raid I bomb hit. *Alabama*'s gunnery apparently dissuaded them, as they veered away to seek other sport. However, the wavetop attack succeeded in diverting the bluejackets' attention from overhead, where a dive-bomber stooped unobserved. Its bomb splashed alongside *Alabama*, probably not scratching the paint.

Half a dozen Judys were obviously led by someone astute enough to pass up the battleships. Though prestigious targets, they could not hurt Ozawa from 350 miles' distance, and they were nearly impervious to bombing. Therefore, the Judys pressed ahead twenty miles southwest to Montgomery's Task Group 58.2. They arrived at high noon.

Wasp's gunnery department was on them, reporting two bogeys ten miles off the starboard bow. At that distance their identification was unknown, so they were classed as "not friendly." Passing astern without attacking, they were assumed friendly—prematurely. Abruptly one peeled off and dived, drawing the attention of Captain Clifton A. Sprague's Bofors and Oerlikon gunners. The Judy lasted long enough to release a phosphorous bomb that detonated over the flight deck, killing one sailor and injuring a dozen. Having fulfilled its destiny, the D4Y crew attained exalted status of "broken gems."

Swedes and Swiss

THE MOST EFFECTIVE CLOSE-IN AIR defense weapon was the Swedish-designed Bofors, a 40mm cannon that the British called "pom-pom" for its slow, rhythmic sound. It came in single, twin, and quadruple mounts. Fleet carriers and battleships used the Mark 4, a quad mount with two pairs. Most mounts had an eleven-man crew: gun captain, pointer, trainer, and eight loaders (two per barrel). Pointers controlled elevation on the port-side mount while trainers controlled azimuth on the starboard pair, both on tractor-type seats with foot-pedal "triggers."

Fed from four-round clips, each barrel fired 2.6 rounds per second, so sustained fire was a function of ammo supply. On some ships, cooks and bakers were the favored loaders, since they tended toward the beefy side: useful in manhandling the twenty-pound clips for sustained periods. Each full round weighed 4.75 pounds, with the shell itself just under two. Starting at 2,890 feet per second, the projectile (explosive or armor-piercing tracer) arrived with authority, and a couple of solid hits could wreck a single-engine aircraft. But time was always tight. Though rated at 11,200 yards maximum range at forty degrees elevation, nearly all shooting was inside 4,000 yards—two nautical miles. An attacker making 250 knots (290 mph) covered that distance in under half a minute. The final half mile, where automatic weapons were most effective, took seven seconds.

The final protective line was another foreign-designed weapon, the Swiss Oerlikon Mark 10 20mm cannon. In single and twin mounts, it was in effect an oversize machine gun firing a quarter-pound projectile at twenty-seven hundred feet per second. Its impact energy was one-eighth of the Bofors round, but rate of fire was nearly three times greater. Fed from sixty-round drums, the Mark 10 did not need to be reloaded nearly as often.

An *Essex*-class carrier's gunnery department was divided into five divisions. The first and third divisions manned the two forward and two aft five-inch turrets; second division handled all 40mm mounts (typically seventeen), while the fourth and fifth took the port and starboard 20mms, some sixty-five Oerlikons.

A single Oerlikon mount had a crew of five to seven sailors (starboard battery) or Marines (port side). The gunner was harnessed to the weapon, snugged up tight against the concave shoulder stocks lest the big gun's recoil dislodge him. He saw the target through a Mark 14 gyroscopic sight that greatly simplified aiming: Just place the reticle on the airplane and swing the gun smoothly. The rate of precession was translated into correct lead for target speed.

The trick to effective AA gunnery was volume of fire: a wall of steel and explosives in the sky. It was more barrage than aimed fire, but the attacking pilot had to survive the churning cauldron to reach his bomb or torpedo release point.

Volume of fire was a function of rounds per minute. Gun crews drilled relentlessly as team captains focused their men on specific jobs. The temptation to look around was enormous—after all, survival was at stake. It was hardest on the loaders, who had to block out the noise and excitement and keep their gun fed.

Despite frequent combat, some ships never got a shot at enemy aircraft. As late as August 1944, *Hornet*'s gunnery division remained unblooded, to the ambivalence of the shooters:

"That this should come to pass is undoubtedly due to good management on the part of the powers that be and good shooting on the part of our air group. This state of affairs makes everyone very happy, even the gunners, who—although anxious to try their skills, laboriously and noisily acquired shooting at towed sleeves—are reasonably acquainted with the laws of chance and have no desire to see their happy home messed up by a bomb dropped from a Val who, ignorant of the *Hornet's* reputation at sleeve shooting, refuses to cooperate by getting itself shot down."

Despite conscious efforts at recognition training, some mistakes were inevitable. During June 19, shipboard gunners shot down one or two Hellcats, including Ensign P. A. Neill off the *Wasp.*

Leakers

RAID II PROGRESSED AGAINST 58.2 as two more Judys selected *Bunker Hill,* broad on *Wasp's* starboard beam. Their bombing was decent, with hits close aboard that inflicted seventy-six casualties, though just three were killed. Bomb splinters and concussion caused a variety of damage, blowing a VF-8 Hellcat overboard and igniting three small fires. More important, the portside aircraft elevator was damaged and the hangar deck avgas fuel lines had to be repaired. Nevertheless, Captain Tom Jeter's damage control crews kept "the Holiday Inn" open for business.

Two of the six bombers got away, one heading directly for Guam and the other finding sanctuary on tiny Rota. Of the other crews, task force sailors saw two parachutes and marveled at the scene of one flier ejected from his plane as it impacted the water.

Defending 58.3, Fighting 10 got a vector on the inbound Jills. But the geometry was in the attackers' favor, and shipboard gunners had the responsibility. They began filling the sky with 20mm tracers, 40mm explosive rounds, and five-inch bursting stuff. The air became polluted with smoky speckles: dirty brown eruptions and gray-white explosions. Shell fragments churned the water with geysers large and small, adding alabaster contrast to the dark spots blossoming in midair.

Then another half dozen Judys flew onward, targeting *Enterprise* and *Princeton.* Lookouts saw them coming, resulting in a lively several minutes as Black Jack Reeves directed his group's evasive dance. Captains often experienced an urge to maneuver independently, but that was folly: A loner lost the immense AA support of its teammates.

At 1154 the call went out: "Torpedo planes [bearing] 270 at eleven [miles], closing." Within three minutes other sightings came from the southwest quadrant, prompting Reeves to order, "Emergency turn four." His group heeled into a formation turn to port, steady up on 040.

With the Nakajimas closing fast, Reeves almost immediately called another turn, "Mike Corpen 150" ("My course 150"), informing the group that *Lexington* was veering into a hard reversal to starboard. At that moment, apparently, he lost contact with his escort commander, as there were repeated requests for Destroyer Squadron 50 to acknowledge.

A Judy was first to attack, closing the Big E's starboard quarter from three thousand feet. He released his bomb and recovered at about fifteen hundred feet, where automatic weapons tagged him. Emitting smoke, targeted by at least three carriers, the D4Y limped about two miles before crashing ahead of the ship. Gunners on *Enterprise*, *Princeton*, and *Lexington* all cheered the splash.

But at 1203 Japanese fish were swimming toward American hulls at forty-plus knots. The warning came over the command net: "Look out for torpedoes on starboard hand." More evasive turns followed, varying between 060 and 100 degrees.

Then more Jills glided in for torpedo runs. *Enterprise* gunners noted with disapproval that their ship was the sole objective, with the B6Ns "disregarding the *Princeton*, which was two thousand yards on our starboard beam."

The *Tenzan* attack was pressed home but accomplished nothing, thanks to sharp ship handling and straight-shooting gunners. In a concussive cacophony, the five-inchers and quad forties deterred or destroyed the Jills before they could launch their torpedoes in a full spread.

The lone Type 91 known dropped had boiled toward *Enterprise*, but the 240-kilogram warhead detonated in her wake. It was a situation well-known to the Japanese naval arsenal, which willingly accepted the trade-off of reliable detonators in exchange for the low hit probability of an "up the kilt" shot. (The torpedo explosion may account for the report of a mysterious "bomb" 750 yards astern, while no bombers were observed.)

The Big E's 40mm mounts contributed to the splashing of two of the Jills, while her five-inch "put the kill on the last plane." The pilot chose a high-angle approach that placed him in the zone of Gun Group III, the starboard aft battery, whose crews were ready. In its straight, slanting dive the AA directors quickly obtained a firing solution at fifty-five hundred yards. The first three shells burst close by; the next severed the starboard wing. Now with asymmetrical lift, the Jill rolled over and careened into the water as its wing fluttered down behind it.

While her teammate was dealing with bombers and torpedo planes, *Princeton* was evading three attackers. Captain William Buracker had to dodge violently to avoid the floating wreckage of another B6N.

It was over in six minutes.

During the attack, aboard *Lexington*, Lieutenant Junior Grade Sims was eavesdropping on the Japanese strike coordinator, who had just expressed his intention to attack after he surveyed the results of his subordinates.

Despite damage to some American ships, perhaps the best performance on Raid II was provided by a nonshooter: *Taiho's* lone D4Y1-C dropping aluminum chaff. The "window" Judy skirted the northwestern edge of the task force, penetrating the CAP to a point some thirty-five miles north. It was a gutsy move, as the solo deception bird, sans escort, stood little chance of escape if intercepted.

Nevertheless, the D4Y came hard about and, shortly before noon, began a seven-minute run to the southwest. Along the way it released fifteen bundles of aluminum "deceiving paper" that strobed on American radar scopes. The 58.4 controller was sufficiently impressed to pull fourteen *Cowpens* fighters off the inbound raiders and divert them in the opposite direction. FitRon 25 orbited twenty miles north until the bogus bogey faded from the screen. Seven Hellcats spotted the culprit egressing the area and gave chase, but he bent his throttle, beat the odds, and got away.

Though a few singles hung around after the attack, they kept a respectful distance. Harrill's screens were clear by 1211, but Reeves's

radar operators tracked bandits and bogeys for another thirty-five minutes. Meanwhile, ForceCAP was reinforced as Montgomery's controllers directed twenty fighters of VF-14 and -28 to take station.

Monterey's Fighting 28 claimed six Jills and a Zeke, with the hard-
nosed skipper bagging two. Lieutenant Commander Roger Mehle, yet
another *Enterprise* alumnus, hailed from the Annapolis class of 1937.
He barely tolerated reservists, but he knew his way around the Pacific:
His first kill had been near Wake Island in February 1942. His
"USNRs" included Ensign George J. Barnes, who also splashed two
Jills, while Lieutenant Raymond G. Thorpe claimed a Zeke. Four
more VF-28 aviators split the remaining pair.

As was customary, returning fighter pilots taxied past the island and
displayed the appropriate number of figures for their kill claims.
When Alex Vraciu taxied up *Lexington's* deck, he glanced at the flag
bridge. The new ace of aces flashed six fingers, drawing an immediate
response. He had barely touched the deck when a ship's photographer
arrived, asking him to repeat the victory gesture. Vraciu didn't even
have time to pull his gloves off. The photo went into history as the
most enduring image of the battle.

Despite the adrenaline high, Vraciu was tugged in another direction. When he leaned down to unlock his wings prior to folding, he
discovered that the handle was not seated. He glanced out at the port
wing stub and saw the small red "barrel" protruding—a visual check
item prior to launch. He had flown the best mission of his life with his
wings only partly secured.

Fighting 16 ordnancemen found that Vraciu had fired just 360
rounds, which was world-class marksmanship. It averaged merely ten
rounds per gun per kill. Better shooting was simply not possible.

Task Force 58 had concentrated 162 fighters against 119 raiders. In
all, Hellcats claimed eighty splashes, which was exceptionally good
reckoning: They knocked down at least that many, not counting six to
eight AA kills. Of 119 raiders that gained the target area, merely
thirty-one reached Guam or returned to CarDiv One. Losses were
heaviest among the Jills (twenty-three of twenty-seven launched equals

85 percent) and Judys (forty-two of fifty-three launched equals 79 percent). The Zekes sustained "only" two-thirds attrition: thirty-two of forty-eight launched.

Returning to their task groups, many Hellcat pilots looked down on a twelve-mile stretch of ocean littered with wreckage and flotsam, oil slicks, and sodden parachute canopies. Even for the victors, postcombat reactions set in. Pilots directed to "pancake base" descended through ten thousand feet, removing their oxygen masks and clearing up the cockpit prior to entering the landing pattern. For most it was welcome relief: Sucking 100 percent oxygen for very long could turn the throat dry and raspy. A few pilots lit cigarettes, though it was contrary to regulations and common sense. Still, a smoke usually cleared out the tangy, rubbery scent of the mask. Everybody—well, almost everybody—reached down to the armament panel and safed the guns.

Descending to lower altitude, some pilots slid their canopies back, inhaling the fresh air. On clear days the Pacific sun beating down was magnified by the canopy glass, and the exertion of combat maneuvering could leave a pilot's flight suit damp and clammy with sweat. It was good to be headed home, maybe with one or two scalps on the belt.

It was good to be alive.

In CICs, FDOs identified the flights still "ammo plus" and usually kept them on station until relieved by fresh fighters. A Hellcat retaining more than half its load-out—twelve hundred rounds—still could do some useful shooting. Those who had been heavily engaged almost always had ammunition remaining, but entering another fight "ammo minus" might allow some new attackers to slip through.

The twenty Japanese pilots who returned to CarDiv One reported damage to at least three American carriers with twenty-five "certain" kills and nine possibles. In reality they inflicted small loss: moderate damage to *Bunker Hill*, slight damage to *Wasp*, and the armor belt impact on *Indiana*. Hellcat losses were a plane and pilot each from VF-1, -14 and -15, and a Fighting 8 aircraft.

* * *

Though a surface officer, Admiral Raymond A. Spruance won the war's greatest aircraft carrier victory at Midway in 1942 and rose to command the Fifth Fleet in 1944. His uncommon intellect and calm demeanor often appeared at odds with aggressive airmen, but he never lost a battle.

USN via National Museum of Naval Aviation

Commanding Task Force 58 was Vice Admiral Marc A. Mitscher, who had been flying since 1916. Only the thirty-third naval aviator to win his wings, "Pete" Mitscher was the most experienced carrier commander afloat in 1944.

USN via National Museum of Naval Aviation

Commander of the Mobile Fleet was Vice Admiral Jisaburo Ozawa, a prewar innovator in Japanese naval aviation. Following the Marianas battle, he led the ill-fated effort to defend the Philippines in October 1944 and helped American historian Samuel Eliot Morison compile a postwar account.

Courtesy of the Author

During the Marianas Turkey Shoot, some 450 Grumman Hellcats flew from the eleven carriers in Task Force 58. These F6F-3s belonged to Fighting Squadron One aboard USS *Yorktown* at the time of the battle. *Courtesy of the Author*

Plane handlers move VF-15 Hellcats forward on the flight deck of USS *Essex*. Deckhands were crucial to efficient carrier operations because they determined the pace of launching and recovering aircraft.

Courtesy of the Author

This rare view was captured by a photographer in a Grumman TBF during the search for Japanese carriers, likely on June 19. The Avenger's Hellcat escort has overshot its victim, a Jake floatplane from one of Ozawa's battleships or cruisers.

Courtesy of the Author

Chiyoda sailors watch Zero fighter-bombers prepare for launch against Task Force 58 on June 19.

IJN via Tatsuo Kaminou

Leading Air Group 15 from USS *Essex* was Commander David McCampbell, a thirty-four-year-old Alabaman who shot down seven enemy planes in two missions on June 19. He finished the war as the naval service's top scoring fighter pilot with thirty-four victories and the Medal of Honor.

Courtesy of the Author

Few Japanese aircraft got through the Hellcat combat air patrol, but those that did faced a wall of American gunfire. This Nakajima torpedo plane, having taken hits from shipboard gunners, streams flames amid flak bursts and water spouts. Seconds later, it crashed from its height of about 120 feet. *Courtesy of the Author*

The sisters *Shokaku* and *Zuikaku* fought every carrier battle except Midway. However, on June 19, *Shokaku* succumbed to the American submarine *Cavalla*, which scored at least three torpedo hits. In a few hours, the Pearl Harbor veteran was destroyed by uncontrollable fuel fires. *IJN via Tatsuo Kaminou*

USS *Cavalla*'s officers receive confirmation that they sank the Japanese carrier *Shokaku* off Saipan. From left: Ensign Ed Leeds, Lieutenants (jg) Art Rand and Jim Casler, Machinist Ray Nichols, Lieutenant Commander Herman Kossler (CO), Lieutenant Tom Denegre, Ensigns Vance Cathey and Zeke Zellmer. *USN via Zellmer*

Lexington's photographer caught Lieutenant (jg) Alexander Vraciu minutes after he landed from his spectacular mission the morning of June 19. The Indiana ace tackled a formation of Japanese dive-bombers and splashed six in about eight minutes. He ended the war with nineteen victories, fourth highest in the U.S. Navy. *USN via Tailhook Association*

One of the few Japanese squadron commanders to survive the Turkey Shoot was Lieutenant Zenji Abe. A veteran of Pearl Harbor, he led *Junyo*'s bombing attack on Task Group 58.2 and barely escaped. He landed his damaged plane on Rota, where he spent the rest of the war. *Courtesy of the Author*

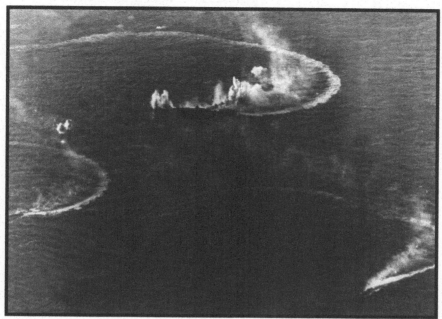

Zuikaku was the last survivor of the six carriers that attacked Pearl Harbor. In this strike photo during TF-58's attack on June 20, she is bracketed by two bombs off the bow and one off the starboard quarter, but is smoking from a direct hit. She succumbed to American airpower at Leyte Gulf. *USN via National Museum of Naval Aviation*

Among the most distinctive Japanese carriers was the twenty-five-knot *Junyo*, commissioned in 1942. She was easily identified by her rakish funnel, which slanted to starboard. Her only sister, *Hiyo*, was sunk on June 20. *IJN via Tatsuo Kaminou*

Among the six Japanese carriers surviving the Turkey Shoot was *Junyo*, seen here shortly after the battle. Items of note are the gauges on the console for pumping aviation fuel and the inclinometer mounted aft on the island. Though *Junyo* sustained only light damage, she never deployed again.

IJN via Jim Sawruk

Torpedo Squadron 28's Roland Gift imbibes in USS *Monterey*'s ready room after the June 20 mission. "Medicinal" alcohol was thought to help aircrew relax after combat and provide intelligence officers with more accurate information, though some fliers insisted that it "enhanced" mission results. *Courtesy of the Author*

That afternoon, Spruance was typically thinking ahead of the game. He contacted VP-16 at Saipan, requesting a seven-hundred-mile search that night. About the same time Mitscher ordered all groups to launch 325-mile searches along the same tracks as the day before. Clearly Ozawa was out there—likely within four hundred miles—and if the submariners could find him, presumably so could the aviators.

Raid III

RAID III WAS ALMOST A nonevent. Carrier Division Two's forty-seven planes (over half were Zero 21s) wandered around a goodly part of the Pacific Ocean, bedeviled by poor intelligence and poor communications.

Launched at 1000, the Air Group 652 squadrons had been briefed against the 7 I contact and therefore took a northwesterly track. Upon receipt of the 3 Ri report, Raid III (like Raid II) diverted to the newer contact, but evidently only about half of the pilots got the word. Whether pessimists or realists, most sailors would have reckoned it was the same in every navy.

Raid III was not only the smallest strike of the day; it was also the least capable. With forty Zekes (fifteen fighters) and just seven torpedo planes, it had almost no chance to inflict significant damage—even if it could find the target.

When it finally appeared on American radar, Joshima's strike was plotted well north, causing speculation that it had taken a devious route around Ching Lee's awesome ack-ack. In truth, most CarDiv Two pilots probably had little idea that the battle line existed.

Harrill's 58.4 made first contact at 1225, distance 110 miles. Clark's and Reeves's groups also tracked Air Group 652 during the next hour, watching its meandering progress. Twice the radar tracks stabilized as the Japanese again circled, uncertain of their intelligence or their navigation—or both.

Fighter directors were content to watch and wait for a while, unwilling to be drawn off by a possible diversion. It was a reasonable concern, because the enemy air group had split well to the north, with one segment dropping to a position sixty-three miles west of 58.4.

Finally 58.1 sent eight *Hornet* and four *Yorktown* F6Fs to investigate the northern threat, while twelve of *Langley's* were positioned to help. It was same song, umpteenth verse for the CVL pilots: Lieutenant Richard H. May of VF-32 eventually made ace, but he groused, "The big-deck squadrons mostly got the gravy."

At 1301 *Hornet's* two divisions got the tallyho fifty miles northwest of Harrill's 58.4. Ignoring two-to-one odds, the eight Hellcats jumped fifteen bandits at sixteen thousand feet, prompting a short, sharp dogfight that was resolved at 9–0 in favor of Fighting 2. Lieutenant Arthur Van Haren and Ensign Paul A. Doherty both got doubles.

Despite losses, at 1320 a handful of Zero fighter-bombers penetrated Harrill's screen and went for *Essex*. Just one reached an attack position, but his bomb fell six hundred yards wide. The inept but courageous rookie was chased by two *Langley* fighters; Lieutenant Junior Grade Jerome D. Keyser and his wingman split for a "bracket," making the Mitsubishi the meat in a Grumman sandwich. The Zero couldn't outrun the F6Fs, and if he turned to engage one, the other would be on his tail. Keyser's second burst flamed him.

Pursuing some strays, VF-1 claimed six kills but returned minus a night-fighter pilot, Ensign Warren F. Wolf. Happily, he was retrieved by a 58.1 destroyer later that afternoon. The two-phase intercept netted fifteen victory claims by Fighting 1 and 2, while actual Japanese losses were seven.

Raid III had ended—or had it? Shortly 58.1 sent other *Yorktown* Hellcats chasing a phantom radar contact. They found nothing, and subsequently the pilots suspected that radar returns had shown a large cloud. In another episode that day, a stationary blip hovering around longitude 145 was determined to be Guam. It was not an isolated incident: Fifty years later, with much better equipment, air traffic controllers still were mistaking moisture and mountains for airplanes.

After the 1000 launch, CarDiv Three hastily organized its remaining planes for a follow-up strike. The senior fighter pilot, Lieutenant

Kenji Nakagawa, counted five of his Zekes and nine Zeroes plus five *Tenzan* torpedo planes: nineteen in all, though a fighter spun in on takeoff. However, the mission was scrubbed due to returning survivors of Raid I and an uncertainty as to how much fuel could be allotted.

As Raid III petered out, Lieutenant Junior Grade Birkholm remained afloat in his raft near the site of Raid I's demise. He heard aircraft engines and looked up in time to see three Judys headed west at an estimated 180 knots. Abruptly one of them exploded for no apparent reason. Birkholm craned his neck, looking for some Hellcats, but there were none.

Bill Birkholm went back to musing on his prospects for rescue.

At 1120 a new player injected himself into the game. A Liberator patrol bomber out of Los Negros in the Admiralties had flown a thousand-mile search northward. It was worth the trip: The VB-101 crew spotted Carrier Division One some 450 miles west of Guam. The two big CVs were *Shokaku* and *Zuikaku* with cruisers and destroyers, but the report afforded no new info: It merely confirmed the previous submarine action.

Raid IV

At 1100 CarDiv Two began launching sixty-four planes: twenty-seven Vals and nine Judys plus ten Zero bombers and eighteen escorts. CarDiv One's contribution was fourteen *Zuikaku* fighters (ten Zeroes) and six Jills orphaned from *Taiho*. It totaled eighty-four aircraft, the second-largest raid of the day. Their target: the errant 15 Ri contact some 120 miles south of Task Force 58.

The scene that morning was not so different from the December launch against Pearl Harbor. The carriers bore into the easterly breeze, steam spouting from a vent in the flight deck forward so helmsmen on the bridge could hold the wind straight down the deck. From catwalks and islands, sailors waved their summer-weight caps in wide circles, cheering each imperial aviator on his takeoff run. Based on what little they had heard so far, they believed they were winning the battle.

The pilots ran up their engines to max rpm, then released the brakes and were on their way. With seats elevated for better visibility, the planes launched in turn: the simple elegance of the Zeroes; archaic fixed gear on the Vals; the rakish tails of the Jills; gaping radiators for the Judys' big liquid-cooled engines.

Lieutenant Zenji Abe led the bomber division from CarDiv Two, composed of his own *Junyo* squadron plus *Hiyo*'s and *Ryuho*'s. He sent three Val squadrons ahead, under Lieutenant Miyauchi, then followed with his nine faster *Suisei*s and six Zeroes.

The Americans called it Raid IV.

En route to the rendezvous, Abe grew increasingly nervous. He felt rusty after forty days out of the cockpit, "as if I were flying with another pilot's plane." Additionally, aborts plagued his formation: Two element leaders reversed course, unable to retract their landing gear. Then a Zero developed engine trouble and turned back. Abe pressed on, cruising at eighteen thousand feet.

An hour outbound, Abe shifted in his seat, turning his head to check the formation. Another dive-bomber and three fighters had disappeared. "I really wondered whether they retired . . . due to mechanical trouble or dove into the sea from mental confusion."

Reaching the expected intercept point sixty miles southwest of Guam, Zenji Abe found only open sea. He wanted a look beneath the clouds, so he retarded the throttle and put his Judy's pointed nose down. Emerging into the clear at twelve thousand feet, he found no target. He climbed back into formation, running the time-distance equation in his head. Standing orders were to attack the Americans, refuel on Guam, and return to the ship. Yet, with U.S. Marines offshore, each Mobile Fleet aviator knew better: Abe said, "Every Navy pilot understood that the instruction meant 'land on the enemy's base.' "

With fuel dwindling, Abe had little time to conduct his own search. It was almost a mirror image of Lieutenant Commander Wade McClusky's dilemma two Junes previously, off Midway. Reaching the expected contact point, the *Enterprise* CAG found only empty ocean, so he began a methodical box search. His reasoning was perfect, leading him to *Kido Butai*—and the turning point of the war.

But Raid IV had no such luck. After searching fruitlessly, the squadrons split up. *Zuikaku*'s eighteen planes turned for "Auspicious Crane" while the Air Group 652 squadrons proceeded to Guam and Rota.

Task Force 58 had to be to the north—there was no reason for the Americans to take their carriers south, away from Guam and Saipan. But with reduced forces and diminishing fuel, Zenji Abe turned his *Suisei*'s pointed nose toward the northeast, beginning a letdown to Guam.

Abruptly the intercom burst into life. "Sir! Big enemy formation, left forward," Ensign Nakajima's voice crackled over the circuit. Looking toward ten o'clock, Abe saw "a whole ring formation of ships was starboarding the helm with distinct white wakes." He wasted no time: The Grummans would pounce any moment. "Command was given to all aircraft to commence attack; then I myself accelerated immediately."

It was a bold move: At that point he personally led six Judys and two Zekes toward Task Force 58. Another eight aircraft were nearby but apparently out of sight.

Of course, the Americans saw them coming. At 1320 *Monterey* made first contact in 58.2, the southern carrier group. Several minutes later *Alabama*'s sharp-eyed radar watch got a 150-mile contact to the south-southwest; 'Bama consistently made the earliest or longest hits during the day. However, because the bogeys did not come straight in, it was uncertain whether they were friendly or hostile. The IFF transponder that printed three small dots around friendly blips was not always reliable, and its range was variable. Consequently, Air Group 652's small contingent got an unexpected reprieve. Sixteen Judys and Zekes lived long enough to reach an American carrier group.

The defenders were beset by complications. Since *Monterey* had the first contact, her controller tried to alert his own VF-28 but could not establish contact. It was one of the few communication failures of the battle, and while it did not lead to serious problems, it showed how important reliable "comm" could be.

Unable to talk to Fighting 28, *Monterey*'s FDO called *Wasp*'s VF-14, with no better results. Consequently, even though *Monterey* had the best radar picture, control of the intercept passed to *Wasp*. The resulting lapse allowed Abe's group to close the distance. He was not confirmed as hostile until 1413, barely fifty miles south of Montgomery's group.

Now events accelerated. With Raid IV distressingly close, more fighters were scrambled. *Cabot* launched two standby divisions whose Hellcats clawed for altitude.

At 1420—an hour after U.S. radar first "painted" the wandering Japanese—*Monterey* fighter pilots called the tallyho. But VF-28's three divisions were out of position, being held as high CAP against the last known enemy altitude—twenty-five thousand feet—while the raid came in at twelve thousand.

Wasp's fighters had the only shot at Raid IV. Fighting 14 knocked down two Zekes and a Jill, but it was too little, too late. And for some obscure reason, the "Iron Angels" failed to report the bandits' altitude— information the FDO badly needed.

Two minutes after the intercept, Yokosuka dive-bombers rolled in over 58.2. The first indication to most men was cruiser *Mobile*'s opening salvo on two Judys. Most ships immediately began maneuvering, complicating *Cabot*'s emergency scramble. Fighting 31 was still trying to get off the deck when the Japanese appeared at six thousand feet.

Abe picked the nearest large carrier and went for it: probably *Bunker Hill* on the engaged side of the disposition. He was quickly taken under AA fire, and the volume appalled him: "That was dreadful for me." Flak knocked down relatively few planes, but it often spoiled an attacker's aim; so it was with Abe. He dropped his bomb amid jostling concussion from five-inch shells, pulled out, and sped for the edge of the screen.

Air Group 652's bombing left something to be desired. *Bunker Hill* plotted three hits between fifty and two hundred yards off the mark, but the ship's high-speed maneuvering caused problems. A Hellcat parked near the deck edge went over the side with the plane captain in the cockpit. The youngster went for "a wild ride," but providentially he was rescued.

Meanwhile, Montgomery's AA gunners were hard at work. One of the Judys that assaulted *Bunker Hill* survived the torrent of flak over the carriers but crashed beyond the destroyer screen. *Cabot's* gunners shot the tail off another. A Judy aimed its bomb at *Wasp* and followed the ordnance straight into the sea.

Captain Sprague had already demonstrated his ship-handling ability during Raid II. Now, making twenty-two knots, *Wasp* heeled fifteen degrees to starboard in a port turn, spoiling the tracking of more Judys but not his gunners. They stayed on target and claimed three planes splashed. There was concrete proof of one: It crashed so close that four men of an Oerlikon crew were knocked off their feet by a large piece. They bounced back up and continued tracking and loading.

Wasp was repeatedly near-missed. One bomb threw up a fountain of water that cascaded over the catwalk, drenching several VF-14 personnel. Two more exploded close together about eighty yards off the starboard quarter, and then a phosphorous bomb erupted three hundred feet overhead. The greedy white tendrils looked eerily evil, but only one *Wasp* sailor was injured from any cause during the attack.

Raid IV was a vivid contrast to the other attacks. It was the main antiaircraft action, as shipboard gunners splashed five, maybe six, versus only three for the fighters.

When the attack was over, blunt-nosed silhouettes met the survivors. Beset by four Hellcats, Zenji Abe shoved everything to the firewall. There was no chance of reaching Guam, let alone returning to *Junyo*. He made for Rota, landing his shot-up *Suisei*, immensely grateful for the escape. Wide eyed, he exclaimed, "I never saw so many Grummans!"

Ozawa realized that he needed to open the distance between himself and Mitscher; even if his missing squadrons were safe on Guam, they could not protect him. Therefore, at 1430 he ordered a turn north. *Shokaku* had just erupted, and *Taiho's* survival looked doubtful, leaving A Force with only *Zuikaku*.

Shortly after 1700 Ozawa shifted his flag to cruiser *Haguro*, which offered the most immediate accommodations for staff work: an operations room and adequate communications. *Zuikaku* would have been preferable, but she was just over the horizon at that moment.

Shortly after leaving his flag, Ozawa was trying to make sense of the situation when *Haguro* experienced a low, rumbling sensation. That was *Taiho* departing. Rescue efforts were impeded by the terrific heat of her fires, and at least 660 men were blasted, drowned, or incinerated. She capsized to port and went down stern first, taking thirteen planes on the twenty-five-hundred-fathom voyage to the bottom.

Captain Ohmae's immediate task for his admiral was to restructure secure communications. As fleet flagship, *Taiho* was the only ship capable of sending and receiving the highest priority code. However, a lower-level flag officers' code was agreed upon, and eventually Admiral Toyoda learned the grim news.

The scorekeeping began that afternoon. Mitscher knew that his CAPs had badly hurt the Japanese, but he wanted a more specific idea of what he still faced. Around 1530 he asked each task group to report its tally of shoot-downs thus far. As of 1500, totals indicated over two hundred destroyed and a few dozen probables. With CAPs and searches still airborne and others scheduled, Montgomery's 58.2 reported seventy-eight splashes, led by *Cabot*'s twenty-six. Clark's 58.1 tallied over sixty with *Hornet* and *Yorktown*'s big bags. Reeves's 58.3 and Harrill's 58.4 both had notched fifty-plus, on strength of *Lexington* and *Essex*.

Forty to One

THE CARDIV TWO SQUADRONS WERE under orders: Jettison remaining ordnance before landing. Since few of Joshima's pilots had found a target, they began dropping bombs and torpedoes into the sea prior to landing on Guam. The extra few minutes required were not wasted by American fighter directors.

Lieutenant Commander Gaylord B. Brown had a dozen *Cowpens* fighters capping 58.2 when the low-level gaggle appeared on shipboard radar. The acting VF-25 skipper (Lieutenant Commander Rice was still MIA) approached Orote and gawked at the spectacle. Though he had splashed two planes earlier in the day, he could hardly believe his eyes. He keyed his mike: "Forty enemy planes circling Orote Field at angels three, some with wheels down."

The remainder of Air Group 652—nearly fifty planes—made for safe haven at Orote Field on Guam. Forty-one Hellcats dropped onto Orote and shot down at least thirty. The F6 pilots claimed twice as many, but the Japanese recorded another nineteen damaged beyond repair.

First to respond were three *Essex* divisions, launched at 1425 to cap Guam and Rota, preventing reinforcements from landing and others from getting airborne. Dashing Dave McCampbell coasted in at twenty-four thousand, keeping the invaluable advantage of height, and spotted pairs and singles winging toward Orote.

Some of the inbound Japanese had reached the end of a long tether. They included thirteen Zekes of Air Group 253, led by Lieutenant Commander Harutoshi Okamoto. After the long flight from Truk in the Carolines, they were low on fuel, and Okamoto was anxious to land. He should have known better: He had been flying combat since 1937.

With an altitude advantage, McCampbell picked off a Zeke with little trouble, but the others were flown by pros. Two Zeroes reversed and came up shooting. They damaged McCampbell's plane and shot his wingman's full of holes. Ensign Royce L. Nall's elevators were shredded and his engine began streaming smoke. The CAG tried to lead the stalkers away from "Bird's Legs" Nall, but the Zekes were too cagey for that. The only way out of the situation was through it.

McCampbell weaved with Nall, sliding across the turn to confront the nearest Japanese. A quick sight picture, a trigger press, and the Mitsubishi exploded, McCampbell's seventh of the day. Seeing his partner converted to heat and light, the other Zeke called it quits and put his nose down for Orote. McCampbell chased him, drawing a bead as the Zeke performed an elegant aileron roll. Reported the new ace, "It was so perfect [that] there was no need even for changing point of aim or discontinuance of fire." Miraculously, the Zero escaped destruction and let down for Orote. McCampbell declined to pursue; he went looking for Nall and gathered up other errant Hellcats.

At dawn McCampbell's score had been two; now it was nine.

One of the errant *Essex* pilots was the fighter exec, Lieutenant Commander James F. Rigg. He had a frustrating mission, plagued by gun malfunctions. He shot at five Vals and a Zeke, getting hits on each, but could claim only probables. As if that weren't enough, he drew the attention of a competent Zeke pilot who thoroughly perforated the Hellcat. Rigg decided to trap aboard *Enterprise* in 58.3 rather than risk the longer flight to 58.4.

Another senior VF-15 pilot was Lieutenant Commander George Duncan, erstwhile floatplane aviator. Sticking in the low-level dogfight, he gunned three Zekes—all flamers. His wingman, Ensign Wendell V. Twelves, splashed two with deflection shots barely two hundred feet off the water. Known as "Doz" (for Dozen), Twelves was a soft-spoken Mormon who had just turned twenty-three—a long way from Spanish Fork, Utah. But he and Duncan proved a potent team: Both finished their tour with thirteen victories.

One of Twelves's victims apparently was twenty-four-year-old Warrant Officer Sadamu Komachi, who had claimed eighteen victories in most of the major battles since 1942. Known as "a wild character," Komachi was a survivor: He had flown at Coral Sea, Eastern Solomons, Santa Cruz, and Rabaul. In the low-level scrap with VF-15, his Zero took hits in the fuel tank and burst into flames at 150 feet. Sitting in a burning airplane, he pushed the stick forward and splashed down offshore. Badly burned, he was evacuated by air a few days later.

Close behind McCampbell's slipstream were two *Hornet* divisions led by Lieutenant William K. Blair. All eight VF-2 pilots scored, Blair and three others claiming doubles, while Ensign William H. Vaughan Jr. got a triple for a total of fifteen.

Hornet produced two instant aces that day, including Ensign Wilbur

"Spider" Webb; barely twenty-four but no tyro. Before winning his wings and joining VF-2 he had been a scout-observation backseater at Pearl Harbor, Coral Sea, and Midway. Launched at midafternoon, Webb was covering a downed aircraft offshore when he noticed a Japanese air group orbiting overland. Closing to investigate, he found a shooter's dream. He keyed his mike: "Any American fighter pilot, this is Spider Webb. I've got about forty of 'em cornered over Orote Point and I could use some help."

The young Texan piled into a clutch of Val dive-bombers, following his victims over Orote Airfield. Then, despite malfunctioning guns and heavy return fire from Japanese rear gunners, he systematically attacked eight. By the time he pulled away his F6F was full of holes. He "trapped" safely aboard *Hornet*, but the deckhands judged his Grumman too shot-up to repair. They retrieved his gun camera before ditching the Grumman, but the film ended with "only" six kills. Webb was credited with two probables as well.

Also airborne was Lieutenant Russell L. Reiserer, an erstwhile Stanford student and two-victory *Enterprise* pilot of 1942 vintage. Now leading *Hornet*'s night-fighter detachment, he had not expected to fly during the day. It was a frustrating situation, as he related: "We spent the early part of the day watching the air group operate continuously with the VF pilots holding up the number of fingers of their victories as they taxied out of the arresting gear."

Finally, with VF-2 fully occupied, Reiserer and two of his VF(N)-76 pilots were assigned to suppress flak at Guam's Orote Field. Because the night owls used the torpedo ready room ("it wasn't as crowded or as boisterous as the fighters'"), they had no knowledge of Spider Webb's mission. However, Reiserer's trio flew Fighting 2 aircraft, including skipper Bill Dean's pet photo bird.

When Reiserer pulled up from his strafing run he noticed an SOC taxiing out of the bay with downed fliers on board. He directed Lieutenant Junior Grade Fred Dungan and Ensign William Levering to photograph Orote while he contacted the duty rescue team.

While orbiting, Reiserer noticed in the distance "a large number of planes coming in and circling Orote Field prior to landing." That was meat on the table. He went to "gate" speed, engaging water injection for a temporary boost in power, and called a quick Mayday to *Hornet*.

Years later Reiserer recalled, "Spider and I must have hit the group at the same time, because the formation was intact as I fired at a Zero and went on through as fast as I could. As I pulled up to make a turn for another run, I noticed a group of seven or eight Vals turning to the right, away from the field. I looked around and couldn't believe my luck. The rest of the formation was all over the sky, but my group stayed together."

Reiserer tagged on to the rear of the Val formation and hauled into range. While strafing he had switched off his two inboard guns as "get-me-home insurance" and chased the Aichis at treetop level. The first two fell within five miles of each other. The third was more elusive: After several minutes of a lethal game of tag, in and out of the clouds, Reiserer dropped it from dead astern.

With ammo remaining, the veteran pilot caught three more Aichis at the island's southern tip. He dropped wheels and flaps to avoid overshooting them, and killed one with the last of his ammo. Another evaded, but the remaining bomber fled out to sea. Reiserer made a few dry runs, hoping to force his quarry into the water. It worked. The Val splashed down in a successful ditching three miles offshore. As the instant ace flew past, he glimpsed the pilot and gunner shaking their fists at him.

Back aboard ship, Reiserer found that his wingmen, "Buck" Dungan and "Scoop" Levering, had added a Zeke, a Kate, and a Val between them. But both of their VF-2 "loaners" were badly shot-up—Levering's so badly that it was jettisoned, while Commander Dean was peeved at Dungan "for bringing back such a wreck."

The episode that began with Russ Reiserer's spotting the SOC ended later that afternoon. He had called fellow night fighters from *Enterprise*, as Lieutenant Commander Richard E. Harmer's Corsairs provided "ResCAP," protecting rescue aircraft that retrieved downed aviators. Four fighters were launched in the afternoon with two F4Us capping a downed floatplane while Harmer and VF-10's executive officer flew a mixed section on similar duty. At 1600 the Corsair and Hellcat found an SOC picking up two fliers off Guam. Burdened with two extra men, the floatplane could not take off and elected to taxi the long miles out to sea.

Approaching Orote Point, Harmer and Lieutenant Henry C. Clem heard a frantic call from the Curtiss biplane with the incongruous call sign "Ace." He was being strafed by a Zeke, and though other F6Fs tried to intervene, the Japanese proved elusive. As Clem bent his throttle to engage, Harmer arrived overhead the SOC, awaiting events.

The Zeke pilot was Lieutenant Shinya Ozaki, leader of Air Group 343, who saw the threat and climbed. Clem, overly aggressive, pulled his stick back in a high-speed zoom, trying to get a shot. Watching from a distance, Chick Harmer feared the worst. An old hand in fighters, he knew the Reapers' exec was vulnerable.

As the Hellcat bled off airspeed, Ozaki saw his chance. He was a veteran by 1944 standards, graduating in the sixty-eighth naval academy class four years before. He winged over, stooped like a hawk, and fired a well-aimed burst. Clem's F6F stalled, nosed down, and went into the water. "Ace" also saw the short fight: "They got one of our guys!"

Harmer wasted no time. He shoved throttle, prop, and mixture full forward and gave chase. Ozaki, seeing his chance, made for shore, offering the Corsair only a long-range shot. Firing from dead astern, Harmer triggered his five guns and drew smoke from the bandit, which never slowed. Frustrated, Harmer returned to his perch overhead Ace until relieved by *Princeton* Hellcats.

Years later it was learned that Chick Harmer's parting shot had struck home. Lieutenant Ozaki was hit by a .50-caliber round and, though he crash-landed in a swamp, he died of his wound.

Other Big E fighters were more heavily engaged. Lieutenant Richard O. Devine took his division to Guam, finding good hunting in the milling, low-level enemy formations. He selected from a smorgasbord of Japanese planes, ultimately reckoned to include Zekes, Vals, Judys, Kates, and even an ancient Nate (an Army type; the comparable Navy fighter was dubbed Claude). Whatever their types, they were ripe for plucking. Devine summoned help, then dived on Orote Field, trying to prevent more bandits from getting airborne.

Devine screamed in downwind, spotting a Zeke ready to take off. His .50-calibers churned the runway; he raised his sights and spattered the A6M. Pulling up, he picked off a Judy and a Zeke while Lieutenants Junior Grade Vernon R. Ude and Philip L. Kirkwood went after dive-bombers. Ude dropped his without difficulty; Kirkwood's maneuvered well, the rear gunner gamely popping away. But one 7.7 against six .50s was no contest.

Then "Rod" Devine caught sight of two Kates (recognition may have been in error) and went after them. He hammered one and Kirkwood the other. Next Devine climbed beneath a Val at two thousand feet and executed it.

But the Reapers weren't finished. When another Zeke and Kate cruised through the area, they were downed by Devine and Ude, respectively. It rounded out Devine's four-plane "flush," doubling his previous score. Ude reported that he dropped a fixed-gear Nate-cum-Claude fighter, but it was almost certainly a Val.

Early in the fight Devine's wingman became separated. However, Lieutenant Junior Grade James F. Kay formed up with Robert F. Kanze and Peter Long, forming a dangerous trio. Kay sent a Val burning into the water, then claimed a Zeke. Long matched the toll with two fighters over Orote Field, where planes were still trying to land. Kanze had the most cost-efficient kills: He gunned a Val and, when he aimed at its partner, the pilot abandoned ship.

In something under twenty minutes, seven Reapers claimed sixteen shoot-downs without loss.

From 1510 to 1645 elements of six Hellcat squadrons had plucked the feathers of Air Group 652. Total claims amounted to sixty kills, and though "only" thirty were shot down, as many as nineteen more were unserviceable on landing. Some piled up while landing on Orote's cratered runway, a residual of Task Force 58 bomber attacks earlier in the day.

* * *

The lead Hellcat rolled wings-level low in the groove as *Essex's* LSO picked him up. Ordinarily an approach below optimum glide slope would elicit a "low" signal, but "Paddles" knew better. After waving the air group for several weeks, he recognized each pilot's style; this was Commander McCampbell. Himself a former LSO, Dashing Dave certainly knew the error of his ways. But he was CAG and liked to do things his way. Low at the ramp, he took the perfunctory cut signal and snagged a wire.

Upon reaching the fighter ready room, McCampbell found Nall safely back, reporting a kill. Meanwhile, Commander Charles Brewer was briefing another hop to Guam and the CAG told the fighter skipper to take his sweep in high "and be extra cautious."

On station at 1825, Brewer spotted some planes landing at Orote. He led his wingman down to attack and bagged one for his fifth kill of the day. But he lost his altitude advantage, and high-flying Zekes dropped on the Grumman pair, killing the CO and Ensign Thomas Tarr. Other VF-15 pilots claimed eight more kills but considered it a poor exchange. *San Jacinto* also lost a pilot, Ensign Thomas E. Hallowell.

The Searchers

As THE SCOPES BEGAN TO clear, Mitscher's Japanese linguist overheard a farewell on the enemy radio circuit. Lieutenant Junior Grade Sims reported that the strike coordinator was about to return to base, prompting a suggestion from the flag staff that a division be vectored out to kill him. Mitscher shook his head, recalling the wealth of information on Japanese dispositions and intentions obtained by radio intercepts during the day. "No indeed! He did us too much good!"

When things eased up after 1330, Mitscher ordered additional searches; he still yearned for a shot at Japanese carriers. Therefore, *Lexington* launched five teams at 1350, and though they found no ships, they did tangle with several Japanese planes. In all, Air Group 16 Hellcats and Avengers splashed three more of Ozawa's own searchers, and a brief dustup resulted when two teams tangled with bandits in adjoining sectors.

About 170 miles outbound in the 245–255-degree sector, two Zekes were spotted, but they had company. Soon eight or more rolled in on the *Lexington* "Minutemen," caught at an altitude debit. Nevertheless, Lieutenant Junior Grade Zeigel W. Neff turned to engage, knowing that the two Avengers would have to defend themselves against three-to-one odds.

The bandits were homing *Zuikaku* fighters, residue of her abortive contribution to Raid IV. They had found no American carriers, but they seemed to have three Grummans at their mercy.

The *Hikotai* 323 Zekes executed low-side runs on the TBFs, attacking from starboard. Lieutenant Junior Grade Harry C. Thomas stood on his right rudder pedal and laid the stick over, meeting each pass nearly head-on. The Avenger, though big and heavy, had enormous wing area and could maneuver reasonably well. Foolishly, the Japanese recovered from their dives below and ahead of the Avengers, presenting almost no deflection shots. Thomas used his forward-firing .50-calibers to good effect, splashing one. His wingman, Ensign Earl P. Baker, also got some shooting, claiming another kill and a probable, while turret gunner AMM1c Grady L. Stanfill scored another probable. The two cripples made off slowly, trailing smoke, a good 150 miles from the Mobile Fleet.

While the TBFs were acquitting themselves so well, fighter pilot Neff also fought a lopsided battle. In succession he gained the advantage on two Zekes and shot them into the water, bringing the odds closer to parity.

But more *Zuikaku* Zekes still lurked around, and they wanted to fight. Consequently, welcome help arrived from the 235–245 sector as Lieutenant Junior Grade Alexander V. McPhillips pitched in. During the milling, churning aerial furball, McPhillips got three Zekes in his reflector sight and dropped each in turn. The *Lexington* fliers had scored six kills and two probables in exchange for a 20mm round in one Avenger's tail.

Less than half an hour after the dogfight, Ziggy Neff got another chance to shoot. His team encountered a Jake headed west at fifteen hundred feet, and he pounced on it. Three kills during one search mission was some kind of record.

Nor was that all. Lieutenant Junior Grade John W. Bartol was escorting two TBFs in the next sector north when he found three Jills headed northwest about a thousand feet off the water. With no threat to the bombers, Bartol gave chase and hauled within range of two. Both went down. The survivor fled southerly "ten feet off the water."

Despite the lopsided results of *Lexington*'s combats, other searchers were far less fortunate, as a *Bunker Hill* Helldiver-Hellcat team never returned from the 205–215 sector. Lieutenant Junior Grade Palmer I. Touw and his gunner, ARM2c William Hamner, were lost with an F6F pilot, Lieutenant Junior Grade Norman "Doc" Davisson. They were probably jumped by the same *Zuikaku* fighters that Neff and company encountered.

In the Groove

THE LAST COMBAT OCCURRED THIRTY-FIVE minutes later as, at 1900, a VF-51 division made an intercept thirty miles from the task group. Lieutenant Junior Grade Stuart H. Bobb got a shot at a single-engine bandit and claimed a probable. Shortly thereafter, dusky shadows stretched across the 145th meridian.

The last homing Hellcats dropped into the racetrack patterns over their ships, steaming upwind to receive them. Four to a division, the pilots took landing intervals—about thirty seconds apart—and flew down the starboard side, dropping tailhooks and slowing to 120 knots.

The landing checklist had been learned at Pensacola or Corpus Christi, shortened to the acronym GUMP. Gas: fuel selector on most full internal tank. Undercarriage: wheels down and locked. Mixture: auto rich. Prop: low pitch, yielding twenty-three hundred to twenty-four hundred rpm.

Pilots locked their canopies back and cinched up their shoulder harnesses. A perfect carrier landing was a violent sensation: It was widely described as "a controlled crash."

Crossing ahead of the ship, pilots lowered flaps and wheels, the F6Fs' noses bobbing downward slightly in response to the increased drag. Throttles came back, airspeed dropping toward a hundred knots.

A good carrier landing began with proper speed in the pattern. Flying aft down the port beam, division leaders were careful to provide sufficient distance from the ship so a steady, descending turn would place them "in the groove" for landing approach. Too close and the pilot had to roll hard left to avoid overshooting the groove. That could lead to other corrections that might result in a wave-off. Too far out and time was lost, upsetting the interval and perhaps running somebody out of fuel.

Turning final, the Hellcats made about ninety knots, slightly nose-high over the churning white wake. On the LSO platform, spotters put their binoculars on each plane in turn, calling out the litany: "Wheels down. Flaps down. Hook down. All down, sir." A glance behind him told the sailor the most important thing of all: "Clear deck."

The LSO extended his arms from his shoulders, beginning the pantomime routine with the Roger signal.

Judging the approaching plane in the groove, the LSO had seconds to signal any changes in attitude or altitude. With wings level, a quarter mile out, the pilot lost sight of the ship beneath his nose. His focus was entirely on the LSO, waiting for the slashing Cut signal.

When it came, the pilot chopped his throttle, bunted the nose slightly, counted "One potato," and brought the stick back. If his timing was right, seven tons of Grumman dropped onto the wood deck and the tailhook snagged a wire. The plane was lurched to a stop, tossing the pilot forward against his straps. Feet off the brakes, he allowed the aircraft to roll backward under tension of the retracting cable while a teenaged "hook runner" sprinted from the catwalk to disengage the tailhook. Then the sternmost plane director was signaling in the "Come on" motion, directing the pilot out of the landing area, as the next aviator was rolling wings-level half a minute behind him.

The greatest air battle of the Pacific War was over. It was a lopsided victory for radar, communications, and the Grumman Hellcat.

Options

WITH VICTORY CAME CONFLICT. AMID the excitement of air attacks and the concern that Ozawa might escape, a command decision was required. A rare opportunity had developed: The Imperial Navy had been brought to battle, and pursuit was on everyone's minds. Therefore, Spruance had to decide whether to unleash the fast carriers from their Saipan tether to complete Ozawa's destruction. But Nimitz's orders were clear—defend the landing beaches—so his two subordinates sought a means of having their Japanese cake and digesting it, too.

The brownshoe aviators—from ensign to admiral—badly wanted to pursue the Mobile Fleet. Enemy airpower had been shot to pieces, but thus far no American pilot had seen a flight deck covered with Ancient Pine. Raymond Spruance shared that sentiment, but he had other responsibilities. It was a replay of his Midway dilemma: whether to finish off a beaten foe or follow Chet Nimitz's prime directive to protect the islands—Midway in 1942; Saipan now.

Finally Spruance and Mitscher arrived at a compromise: They really could have it both ways. Mitscher was permitted to plan one long-range blow should the opportunity arise the next day. Hedding and Widhelm eagerly went to work.

By 1500 the task force had been bearing eastward since dawn, now drawing within twenty miles of Guam. The entire fleet—five task groups—could not simply put the rudder hard over and start chasing westward. It was still necessary to steam into the easterly wind to recover airborne planes, and hours would pass before each group could be ready. Even then, the task force would have to tack away from the pursuit heading to launch and recover CAPs and searches.

But two problems could be solved simultaneously. Spruance decided to allow Mitscher to detach 58.4 to cover Saipan while beating down Guam and Rota. Harrill had missed the chance to refuel his destroyers the day before, and that lapse offered Mitscher the excuse he needed to cut loose his least aggressive group commander. Though Ralph Ofstie's very productive *Essex* was included with *Cowpens* and *Langley*, Mitscher and his staff concluded that the force would move faster and more productively without William "Keen" Harrill.

The mood in flag plot improved at 1630 when Spruance signaled, "Desire to attack enemy tomorrow if we know his position with sufficient accuracy." The carrier brain trust went to work, doping out search patterns, allocating assets, using protractors and dividers to solve the two-dimensional puzzle laid out on light blue charts with oceanic squares defined by grids of latitude and longitude.

"An Old-time Turkey Shoot"

By EVENING OF THE NINETEENTH it was apparent that a significant victory had been won. Task Force 58 had absorbed repeated air attacks—the most concentrated yet launched against U.S. carriers—and repulsed them all. Aircraft losses amounted to only thirty-one—less than one-tenth of Ozawa's. Twenty-one of the U.S. losses were Hellcats, including four in operational accidents.

About forty Japanese planes penetrated the CAP during the day—one-eighth of those launched in the four raids. However, the actual proportion was somewhat higher owing to the Japanese aircrews who never found Task Force 58.

At the end of the day Mitscher and Spruance tallied the results. Two carriers—*Bunker Hill* and *Wasp*—had sustained minor damage from dive-bombers, while battlewagons *South Dakota* and *Indiana* took bomb and "kamikaze" hits, respectively. Cruiser *Minneapolis* was dinged by bombers, but the only other battle damage hardly scratched any ships' paint. In Lee's group, destroyer *Hudson* took some AA hits from U.S. guns.

At sundown, Ozawa's carefully crafted formations were shredded. Losses among his greatest asset—experienced formation leaders— were catastrophic. In addition to losing eight of Rear Admiral Obayashi's nine in Raid I, the other three raids cost nine of fourteen leaders in Air Group 601 and "only" five of twelve in 652. Overall, Ozawa wrote off twenty-two of his thirty-five unit commanders, both pilots and observers.

Additionally, *Junyo* bomber leader Zenji Abe sat hors de combat for the duration on Rota. Decades later he wrote, "I was snatched from the jaws of death."

The Japanese airmen, though persistent and courageous, could make no headway against Task Force 58's layered defense. Said Commander Okumiya, "They never stood a chance against the determined defense of the Hellcat fighters and the unbelievable accuracy and volume of the ships' antiaircraft fire."

In air combat throughout the day, Zekes claimed twenty-five Grummans shot down plus nine "uncertain." It was a far better assessment than normal with the Imperial Navy's "sea eagles," as the actual figure was seventeen. Conversely, available *Kaigun* records acknowledge loss of twenty-three senior fighter pilots on the nineteenth.

Then there were the carrier losses.

Taiho took eighteen planes to the bottom, including three *Shokaku* scouts and four *Hiyo* fighters. *Shokaku* took nine of her own on the fifteen-thousand-foot trip.

The Japanese also lost at least eighteen Guam-based aircraft in combat and sixty or more bombed or strafed to destruction.

A few of the missing Japanese turned up later. For example, two *Shokaku* scouts originally were unaccounted for, but a Jill managed to land at Guam, refuel, and find its way back to CarDiv One. The errant Judy eventually fetched up at Yap in the Carolines, 550 miles southwest.

* * *

Task Force 58 ready rooms and wardrooms pulsed with an electric atmosphere. Fighter pilots—high-strung by nature—avidly recounted the day's hunting by "shooting their wristwatches" (the world over, the left hand is the bogey). Intelligence officers toted up the growing score, hard-pressed to jot down the backlogged narratives of CAPs, sweeps, and searches. Pilots savored their two bottles of beer, which were permitted on such occasions, though some fliers were still too young to drink. But in less public places such as bunk rooms, fifths of Old Overholt and Jack Daniel's appeared: officially forbidden but not unknown aboard aircraft carriers.

Sometimes, however, amid the raucous celebrations and the chatter and the laughter, a few pensive men looked inward and remembered absent friends. A huge victory had been won; a bigger one lay in the offing. But fourteen fighter pilots and thirteen other fliers were missing or known dead.

At least thirty sailors also were killed during the day. *Wasp*'s sole casualty was her first death: Gunner's Mate Alfred B. Bridges, a popular twenty-three-year-old New Yorker. His shipmates collected $2,352 for his wife and six-month-old son, as interim income before GI insurance kicked in. Bridges's young widow, June, wrote a heartfelt letter of gratitude, saying that her husband intended Alfred Jr. to have a college fund. She also exhorted the Stingers to keep up the fight.

Meanwhile, among the celebrants on board *Lexington* was Lieutenant Junior Grade Zeigel Neff. During two missions he had claimed four kills—his only score of the war. Yet Ziggy Neff is credited with establishing the tone of the victory by declaring, "It was just like an old-time turkey shoot" back in Missouri. Fighting 16 skipper Paul Buie overheard the comment and passed it along. Thus did the air battle pass into history as the Great Marianas Turkey Shoot.

Stern Chase

AT 2000, SOME FIVE HOURS after Spruance agreed to the pursuit, three carrier groups had collected their airborne chicks, set the night watch, and reversed course. Preceded by Lee's battleships, ninety American men-of-war began the long stern chase to overhaul forty-eight Japanese combatants plus their vital oilers.

It was going to be a one-shot affair, if at all. Mitscher had to judge maximum rate of advance against remaining fuel: Slowing to conduct "unreps" would cost any chance of getting within 250 miles of Ozawa, provided he could be found. Duke Hedding consulted the engineers and reported to his boss, recommending twenty-three knots as the best compromise.

At the end of the skull session Pete Mitscher got up and stretched his wiry frame. Then he yawned and said, "Tomorrow I'm going to get a haircut."

Late that night, the Mobile Fleet received updated orders from Tokyo. Admiral Toyoda, whether suffering from poor information or residual "victory disease," dictated further offensive action on the twenty-second. Ozawa would continue attacking the U.S. task force, cooperating with the land-based air units. Thereupon the Mobile Fleet would dispatch its aircraft to Guam for Kakuta's further use while the carriers proceeded to home waters.

As if that were not enough, the Navy commander exhorted additional efforts "in mopping-up operations around Saipan." It is not recorded how the orders were received in the Mobile Fleet, but Japan's German ally had a perfect expression for such perspectives. Soemu Toyoda clearly resided in the fabled "cloud-cuckoo-land."

Just before midnight the Mobile Fleet shaped course northwest.

The Score

IT TOOK A WHILE AS Task Force 58 toted up the score, which originally ran more than four hundred shoot-downs, including nearly twenty by AA. With benefit of hindsight, it's possible to narrow the gap, though some discrepancies remain.

Of Ozawa's forty-three scouts in the three morning searches, only twenty-two returned. Nearly all the missing were destroyed, though a handful proceeded to Guam or even Yap. Nevertheless, American claims for known or likely recon aircraft amounted to only nineteen during the day, so those figures were extremely accurate.

The biggest diversion between U.S. claims and Japanese losses occurred on Raid I. Elements of seven Hellcat squadrons engaged 69 raiders and claimed 105 splashed. Excluding fifteen probables, that was two and a half times the forty-two that failed to return to CarDiv Two. The biggest claimants were *Princeton*'s VF-27, *Essex*'s VF-15, and *Cabot*'s VF-31, each with more than twenty.

Hellcat pilots were far more accurate on Raid II. The 119 Japanese who reached Task Force 58 were nearly annihilated by Grummans from ten carriers: 98 destroyed against U.S. claims of 107. Again *Essex* figured prominently, though *Yorktown*'s VF-1 and *Lexington*'s VF-16 both edged out Fighting 15, all with twenty-plus credited.

As noted, Raid III was largely a nonevent, as Jocko Clark's VF-1 and -2 reported fifteen splashes against seven actual. The 100 percent error in two small dogfights is difficult to explain, though some squadrons overclaimed more than others.

Ironically, the lengthy, potentially confusing donnybrook in Raid IV was perhaps the most accurately reported. Despite the prospects for multiple claiming and simple error, the low-level shoot-out over Guam was resolved almost perfectly. Hellcats from six carriers reported seventy-two kills against an acknowledged loss of seventy-three (including those destroyed on the ground or damaged beyond repair). *Hornet* pilots, paced by instant aces Russ Reiserer and Spider Webb, got twenty-nine, while *Essex* and *Enterprise* each bagged nearly twenty.

Overall, the record for all four raids was some 220 Japanese losses compared to 299 Hellcat claims: a 35 percent exaggeration well within the historic 50 to 100 percent margin of error. However, shipboard gunners contributed nineteen to the total, which rightly should be deducted from the fighter score.

The day's CAPs over the islands and the search encounters also raised the tally. Kakuta's base air force wrote off some fifty aircraft, largely during the morning fighter sweeps, which closely matched U.S. claims. However, Japanese records specifically mention eighteen destroyed overland. That may represent a partial figure, to which should be added shot-up planes that never flew again.

The final hassle that evening contributed nine more Hellcat victories, raising the day's toll to 380 confirmed plus 55 probables. But as scorekeepers have long known, the truth lies in reducing the "destroyed" and ignoring the probables.

Accepting acknowledged Japanese in-flight losses from all ships and from ashore, the likely toll was about 261 (224 carrier and 18 known land-based planes downed by U.S. fliers, plus 19 splashed by shipboard gunners). Therefore, Mitscher's pilots likely overclaimed by 57 percent—a decent showing, considering that far smaller one-day combats often produced 100 to 200 percent errors. Adding "grounders" to the Japanese figure brings losses to over 290, plus 24 aboard the carriers equals 314.

Aviation historians love to calculate cockpit-to-cockpit matchups, playing "Who Got Whom?" Because of the scale, it's almost impossible for June 19, but some trends can be observed. Generally, individual fighter pilots likely got what they claimed on Raids II and IV.

The magnitude of Task Force 58's victory was immediately apparent. *Life* correspondent Noel Busch compared the U.S. Navy's figure of nearly four hundred shoot-downs to the RAF's one-day record claim in the Battle of Britain, 185 on September 15, 1940. Only after the war did Luftwaffe records reveal the actual toll of 61, but a comparison could be made between the two events. Both were defensive victories for fighter aircraft under radar control, confirming the importance of electronics in air defense. But Vice Admiral Marc Mitscher and Air Marshal Sir Hugh Dowding reckoned their success not in raw numbers but in the vital question: Who controlled the air? As it was over England in the summer of 1940, so it was over the mid-Pacific four years later: Whether cockaded Spitfires and Hurricanes or white-starred Hellcats, Allied aircraft reigned in their respective domains five miles high.

However, the difference between the two victors was substantial: Dowding had no means of depriving Reichsmarschall Hermann Göring of his bases, whereas Mitscher yearned to put Vice Admiral Jisaburo Ozawa's on the bottom of the Marianas Trench.

PART FOUR

"Launch 'Em"

A VICTORY HAD BEEN WON. Now Mitscher's aviators wanted more.

Ironically, in the greatest naval air battle of the war, all the offensive action had been conducted by American submarines. In contrast, Task Force 58's victory thus far was wholly defensive. Fleet air defense methods and equipment had been validated beyond all doubt, but the brown-shoe fliers desperately wanted their own shot at Ozawa's beaten ships.

When Monday rolled over to Tuesday, the Mobile Fleet was 460 miles west of Guam, scurrying northwest. Ozawa believed he had hurt Mitscher at a cost, but Tokyo broadcast claims of sinking eleven American carriers and perhaps a battleship with scant reference to *Kaigun* losses. Whatever his assessment that night, it is doubtful that Ozawa felt such optimism. Having lost two flattops, some 240 aircraft, and most of his formation leaders, he was in no position to resume the battle, even if he believed that Guam retained some airpower.

Task Force 58 was some 320 miles astern, continuing the chase while computing the inexorable factors: distance, fuel, time, and the great imponderable—Ozawa's position. Each hour took Mitscher about twenty miles farther from the vital beachhead at Saipan, and "Bald Eagle" knew that "Blue Jacket" took that responsibility extremely seriously. The decision to pursue or disengage lay with Spruance.

June 20

AMERICAN PILOT LOSSES HAD BEEN blessedly small on the nineteenth, but some were still out there, afloat literally in the middle of the Pacific

Ocean. Shortly past midnight, in Task Group 58.1, destroyer *Boyd*'s watch reported a flashing light in the darkness. A signalman made out the pattern: three short, three long, three short. SOS.

The ship turned to the bearing, rang down to dead slow, and stopped. A line was tossed over the side and the weight at the end evolved into a *Lexington* fighter pilot. He was Lieutenant Junior Grade William C. B. Birkholm, who had spent fourteen hours in his raft. Five minutes later he was "drinking coffee and telling sea stories." He was saved by his waterproof flashlight.

Later in the early blackness of June 20, *Essex* launched Hellcat night fighters on her first nocturnal mission. Two F6F-3Ns each prowled Rota and Guam, as the detachment commander of VF(N)-77, Lieutenant Commander Robert M. Freeman, took Ensign George L. Tarleton on a shadowy tour of enemy airfields. Orote was in blackout but Agana had landing lights, evidently expecting reinforcements. After a strafing pass the lights were doused; Freeman and Tarleton pulled off to await events. Five minutes later the lights flicked on again and the nocturnal prowlers found game.

Freeman tagged on to a Val and, hanging nose-high at eighty-five knots, opened fire from fifty yards. Hard hit, the dive-bomber nosed down, but Freeman lost sight at five hundred feet. He said, "I am certain that he could not have survived." Freeman was credited with a kill.

Tarleton also hunted Vals, clobbering two, leaving Orote Airfield dark and quiet. In their debrief the VF(N) pilots said they saw no explosions from delayed-action bombs dropped during the day. Therefore, they advocated "night caps" as the best method of keeping Japanese airfields inoperable. After the predawn excitement, enemy aircraft were extremely scarce around Guam; VF-15 dropped one and a probable throughout the day.

There wasn't much more activity for task force CAPs: just two snoopers splashed during the day, credited to VF-31 and -50.

Meteorologically nothing had changed on June 20. The wind still favored the Japanese, forcing Mitscher to reverse track for air operations, as Task Force 58 remained between Ozawa to the west and the invasion beaches to the east. At 0530 Mitscher's undetected target was still 330 to 350 miles downwind of him, making knots to the northwest. Ozawa's goal was Okinawa, more than eight hundred miles away.

Searchers found much more activity farther afield. During the morning, *Hornet* teams slew five Jakes, Kates, and Rufes, while *Wasp's* Ensign Carl E. Smith, a naval aviator just seven months, splashed a Jake about 250 miles out.

After missing the fighter pilot's paradise the day before, *Enterprise* CAG Killer Kane put himself back on the flight schedule for the 0530 launch. Rising with the sun, the Big E's four search teams stretched their wedge-shaped sectors to the west, hunting the Mobile Fleet. They found no ships, but Kane, escorting a section of TBFs, shot down a Jake and a Jill from 50 to 110 miles west of the task force. By the time the searchers returned they had been airborne five hours.

Patterns

THE MOBILE FLEET ALSO PUT up search planes that morning. Despite the grinding attrition of the day before, Kurita managed to fling nine Jakes off battleship and cruiser catapults at 0530, while CarDiv Three launched six carrier-based scouts. The search pattern afforded overlapping coverage of the 040–140 sector with floatplanes probing 300 miles and tailhook birds to 350.

Like their American counterparts, the Imperial Navy searchers found no ships. However, several crossed paths with Grumman search teams, resulting in three Jakes shot down.

While the searchers were airborne, Ozawa proceeded with consolidating his forces. He had to assume that Mitscher might find him during the day, which would bring an inevitable rain of bombs upon the Mobile Fleet. Consequently, at 0800 A and B Forces turned north to link up with C Force and the two oiler groups.

At the same time, Mitscher—or at least his staff—was thinking one or two moves ahead. Like chess grand masters, they anticipated their opponent's likely moves, but also needed to keep their fingers on their own pulse. The blood in their veins was Bunker C, and it was running low. Therefore, Task Force 58 requested that the oilers head west "as soon as possible" with Harrill's 58.4 covering them.

Spruance, still mindful of his responsibility off Saipan, granted cautious approval. From his flagship *Indianapolis* he signaled, "Desire to push our searches today far to westward if possible. If no contact with enemy fleet results, consider it indication fleet is withdrawing and further pursuit after today will be unprofitable." Being polite, he added, "If you concur, retire tonight toward Saipan."

Mitscher and the melee-minded aviators still had their prospective chance. If only Ozawa could be found.

Perhaps indulging in wishful thinking, some staffers concluded that the enemy floatplanes encountered were from a cruiser force escorting "the damaged *Zuikaku*." *Cavalla*'s attack on *Shokaku* had produced a juicy damage report, but her loss would not be confirmed for months. (U.S. Naval Intelligence often had trouble with *Nihon Kaigun* ship names, occasionally assigning nonexistent names to questionable ships. In this case, the analysts got the names right but assumed that *Zuikaku* was first ship of the class.)

While the morning search was still out, *Lexington*'s air group commander had an idea. Commander Ernest M. Snowden had huddled with Gus Widhelm about the damaged "*Zuikaku*-class carrier" and sought an audience with Mitscher. The CAG proposed something novel: a dozen Hellcats, each toting a five-hundred-pound bomb, to fly to the limit of their endurance, a butt-numbing 475 nautical miles. That was 150 miles beyond the normal "maximum" search range. However, if they found the reported cripple, they would have something to use against her.

Mitscher thought it over, then agreed, adding, "You'd better take a bomber with you." Aside from extra navigation support, an Avenger could use its radar to extend the horizon. But the admiral withheld immediate permission, preferring to see if the scheduled searches found anything.

Snowden trotted off the flag bridge, headed for Fighting 16's ready room to find eleven volunteers. Addressing the Airedales, he said, "Chances are less than fifty-fifty you'll get back." He chalked a dozen numbers on the blackboard with his name in the first spot. Thirty minutes later he returned to find every slot taken.

Ernie Snowden was part of the reason for *Lexington*'s sky-high morale. Graduating in the upper half of the Annapolis class of 1932, he had married into a prominent Army family five years later. His wife of seven years was Lois (née) Arnold, daughter of General Henry H. Arnold, chief of the Army Air Forces. Snowden's relationship with his four-star father-in-law was marked by good-natured bantering along Army-Navy lines as well as the exchange of favored liquor. Both men appreciated fine whiskey, and Snowden frequently sent bottles of White Horse as a warrior's "payment" for marrying the "chief's" daughter.

When the regular search teams turned up empty-handed, Snowden returned to flag country, suited up for flight. Confirming orders for the longest U.S. carrier-based search of the war to date, he headed below to man up and launch. As insurance, he had eight VF-51 escorts from *San Jacinto*.

Almost six hours later, headed back to *Lexington*, Snowden heard a faint radio report. Obviously it came from far away, but apparently an *Enterprise* team had found Japanese ships.

Rendezvous

OZAWA'S FLEET ACHIEVED RENDEZVOUS DURING the noon hour, but refueling was delayed. Part of the problem was his dispersed forces, as underway replenishment required orderly assembly for maximum efficiency, but communications also suffered. Ozawa and his staff transferred to *Zuikaku* around 1300, where at last he began learning of the appalling losses among his *hikokitai* from all three divisions. However, an excessively optimistic message from Kakuta on Guam led the fleet commander to believe that he retained useful assets there. Jisaburo Ozawa was willing to continue the battle, even though he was steadily drawing away from his "surviving" aircraft ashore.

At the same time Ozawa and company transferred to *Zuikaku*, Obayashi's B Force launched at least three scouts to cover the 100–130-degree sector to a distance of three hundred miles. Most likely the searchers were *Chitose* and *Zuiho* Kates, though there's evidence that cruiser *Maya* contributed a floatplane.

About eighty minutes after Ozawa transferred his flag—at 1420—Spruance reconsidered his options. He informed Mitscher, "Would like to continue pursuit of enemy to northwestward tonight if this afternoon's operations give any indication it will be profitable." He also asked for amplification of the fuel situation.

After checking with Hedding and the operations shop, Mitscher responded that his "smallboys" would be very low on fuel in the morning, but he could replenish them from the carriers while continuing the pursuit. Then he addressed an "allcon" to the task force: "Indication that our birdmen have sighted something big." He called for continuing on course at twenty-three knots. Though the "indication" was imaginary, harder information was forthcoming.

"Many Ships . . ."

FOUR *ENTERPRISE* SEARCH TEAMS FANNED out, each taking their assigned ten-degree sectors. The lead Avenger in each team flew unusually low, about seven hundred feet, in deference to haze above. The second TBF and the F6F escort were echeloned higher on either side, scanning the far horizon between breaks in the cumulus.

There was little to report—at least nothing worth breaking radio silence for. In the southern sector Lieutenant Junior Grade Charlie Henderson's team spotted a submarine that quickly pulled the plug. In one of the middle sectors Lieutenant Robert S. Nelson's trio saw an enemy aircraft—likely a Kate—on a reciprocal heading. Nelson was an old head, a second-cruise pilot, and knew there was no point pursuing. He continued on course.

About half an hour later, at 1538, Nelson was peering to port when he noticed a ripple on the horizon. Rain squalls interfered with visibility, but Lieutenant Junior Grade Robert R. Jones's team also turned up something in the adjoining sector. "Railroad" Jones's wingman, Lieutenant Junior Grade Edward Laster, eyeballed their quarry within minutes of Nelson.

Nelson's and Jones's teams were looking at something no American aviator had seen in nearly two years: a Japanese carrier force.

The TBF pilots pulled their plotting boards from beneath their instrument panels and went to work. Hunched over the "Ouija boards" the aviators spun the circular grids, checked the time-distance equation, and factored in the wind. Then they sent the all-important information. Nelson was first off the mark with a voice radio report: "Enemy fleet sighted. Latitude 15-00, longitude 135-24. Course 270, speed 20." He repeated the message three times.

In the adjacent sector Jones's radioman, ARM1c Robert Grenier, sent an immediate Morse code message via long-range continuous wave (CW): "Many ships, one carrier 134-12E 14-55N." The difference in the two plots was seventy nautical miles east-west, a little more than one degree of longitude. Both contacts were south of the actual track, but the five-minute northerly variation was irrelevant.

Meanwhile, Nelson's wingman, Lieutenant Junior Grade James S. Moore Jr., double-checked the plot. He had been doing his own navigation and unknowingly concurred with Jones that the original report had a one-degree easterly longitude error. Nelson's radioman, ARM1c James Livingston, then sent a Morse code amplification.

Both search teams broadcast follow-up reports; then Jones scooted for home to deliver the message in person. Meanwhile, Nelson closed in for a better look.

Nelson said, "My most vivid recollections of the search flight are [of] the Japanese carrier leaving a circular wake as it turned after we had been in view for four or five minutes . . . double-checking the plot of our position. As we were returning after transmitting the contact report, I also recall the sight of fighter pilot Ned Colgan's F6F as it swooped down and away in pursuit of the Japanese plane we spotted heading on an opposite course, possibly carrying a contact report of its own. The splash of the Jap plane, shot down by Colgan in the distance, was in a way anticlimactic."

Headed for the Big E that afternoon, Nelson got visual confirmation that the scouting reports had been received. Approaching the task force, he saw one air group after another passing high overhead, blunt noses pointed west. It was, he said, "most impressive, and the most clearly remembered event of the day."

Meanwhile, the Mobile Fleet was onto Task Force 58. Radio monitors aboard cruiser *Atago* in C Force heard Nelson and Moore's contact report and notified Ozawa. Realizing that he was likely to be hit, he canceled the unrep scheduled for that afternoon. Fleet speed was increased to twenty-four knots, putting every possible sea mile between Ozawa and the inbound Americans.

An hour later, at 1715, Japanese airmen got another visual on Mitscher. Launched from B Force four hours previously, apparently a Jake floatplane from *Maya* (she of the Kure Zoo's pet monkey) reported American carriers three hundred miles to the east—an equal distance west of Guam. The report was accurate within several miles: further good work by *Nihon Kaigun's* often maligned recon crews.

Nobody received the VT-10 report with greater enthusiasm than that inveterate gambler Gus Widhelm. The contact came none too soon for Widhelm, who was just musing whether he should try to sell his standing bet for fifty bucks. Having won his thousand-dollar wager on a fleet engagement, he had doubled down, betting two air group commanders equal amounts that the Japanese carriers would be found. Now there was no doubt: The enemy carriers were pegged. He grinned his toothy smile, exuding confidence again.

Comparing the two "different" contact reports, Mitscher concluded that the *Enterprise* pilots were looking at the same ships. Consequently, just before 1600 he signaled, "Expect to launch everything we have. We will probably have to recover at night."

Gus Widhelm was working at the plotting table, measuring the geometry of the situation: courses out and back, but more critically the all-important distance. At length he looked up and said, "We can make it, but it's going to be tight."

Marc A. Mitscher did not hesitate. In his almost feminine voice he merely said, "Launch 'em."

Launching late in the afternoon was a serious consideration, as few air groups were night-qualified. Landing on a straight-deck carrier was hard enough in daylight; getting aboard in reduced visibility, running low on fuel, posed even greater problems. Mitscher knew that he risked losing some of his striking power in a night recovery.

The original plot looked like 230 miles—a bit of a stretch. In some squadrons there was a last-minute shuffle to fill out the "dance card" determining who went and who stayed. In Bombing 8's ready room aboard *Bunker Hill*, skipper James D. Arbes decided to lead the first-launch Helldivers. His most experienced pilot was Lieutenant Martin D. Carmody, a square-jawed *Enterprise* alumnus who had sunk his first ship at Guadalcanal. Red Carmody was so ruggedly handsome that he was occasionally mistaken for a Marine—and did not object to the comparison. Because of his experience and reputation as an exceptional navigator, Carmody suggested that he take the mission, but Arbes wanted him available for the second deckload, if necessary. Carmody slumped into his reclining chair and pondered his misfortune.

Aboard the Big E, Carmody's erstwhile shipmate Jig Dog Ramage told his Dauntless pilots, "We're going to be gas misers." Behind him, in Bombing 10's ready room, an officer had inscribed in six-inch block letters, "Get the carriers!" It was a widespread sentiment in the task force.

On the blackboard in VT-28's ready room a *Monterey* sailor had chalked, "Get the carriers!"

Aboard *Belleau Wood* some fliers had raised a banner inscribed, "Get the carriers!"

Task Force 58 intended to get the carriers.

Torpeckers

FOR THE LARGEST SHIP-KILLING MISSION in American history, the ordnance load-out was peculiar.

Of fifty-four Avengers attacking the Mobile Fleet, only twenty-one carried torpedoes. The reason had to do with recent history: Nearly all the carrier killing in the 1942 battles was accomplished by dive-bombers. Of six enemy flattops sunk at Coral Sea, Midway, and Guadalcanal, only two had torpedoes in them; all felt the weight of Dauntless bombs. Furthermore, three TorpRons had been destroyed at Midway, with no damage inflicted on the enemy. The record did not inspire confidence in "torpeckers."

Consequently, on June 20 bombs were the weapon of choice: In addition to dive-bombers and thirty-three bomb-toting Avengers, a dozen or more F6Fs lugged single five-hundred-pounders.

Hornet Avenger pilot Harry Lewis typified the frustrated torpedo fliers. "I had four five-hundred-pound bombs when I needed a torpedo," he recalled sixty years later. "But our torpedoes were no good. I only dropped one, and that was later in the Philippines."

The U.S. Navy's scandalous torpedo problem was the result of prewar complacency, bureaucratic inertia, and absurd budget restraints—no empirical tests were conducted until six months after Pearl Harbor.

Apart from technical problems with torpedoes themselves, it was extraordinarily difficult to mount a combined bombing-torpedo attack against an alerted force. In fact, the U.S. Navy had managed it only twice: at Coral Sea, with an enormous numerical advantage, and on a smaller scale at Eastern Solomons.

The Japanese had been more successful. In 1942 their Nakajima Kates had contributed to the loss of three carriers with namesakes in Task Force 58: the original *Lexington* (CV-2), *Yorktown* (CV-5), and *Hornet* (CV-8). Besides more effective tactics, the Imperial Navy possessed far better torpedoes: reliable weapons that could be dropped higher and faster than the "fish" issued to U.S. squadrons in 1942.

Nihon Kaigun's Type 91 aerial torpedo was a 45-centimeter (17.7-inch) weapon that entered service in 1933. It was upgraded throughout the war, most notably increasing safe dropping speed from 200 to 350 knots. The 519- to 679-pound warhead contained a German-developed explosive with a 60:40 ratio of TNT and hexamine, producing 7 percent greater power than pure TNT.

The American torpedo scandal of World War II still is not widely appreciated. Armed with the Mark 13, U.S. aviators began the war with unreliable weapons delivered by obsolescent Douglas Devastators. Avengers replaced the latter in mid-1942, but the egregious Mark 13s were the only option. Torpedo crews repeatedly risked their lives to attack enemy fleet units with "fish" that ran too deep, veered off course, or failed to explode.

The Navy's ordnance bureaucracy ("BuOrd") was easily the most hidebound in the service. From the 1920s onward the Newport Torpedo Station committed a series of astonishing errors (ultimately investigations exposed a dozen problems) that went not only uncorrected but unpunished. Apparently the engineers who developed a magnetic detonator in the North Atlantic never reckoned that the Navy might fight elsewhere on planet Earth—where the magnetic field was different. In combat, when submariners reported consistent failures to hit or detonate, BuOrd blamed the shooters. Furthermore, the bureau arrogantly refused tests to determine the actual running depth, declaring it unnecessary. Finally, in June 1942, ComSouthwestSubPac ran empirical tests, shooting through submarine nets. The results proved that the torpedoes were running eleven to fifteen feet lower than the settings. The last "fix" was not made until October 1943.

The scandal was suppressed during the war, even though some officers held the failure of submarine torpedoes partly responsible for loss of the Philippines. Meanwhile, more time and opportunities were lost curing the many faults of the Mark 13. Bill Martin, skipper of Torpedo Ten, reported that during his deployment, of thirty-one torpedoes launched, none ran "hot, straight, and normal."

It took civilian industry to plug the torpedo gap. Aside from increasing production, private contractors produced all the innovations in torpedo technology during the war. Probably the most notable was General Electric's excellent Mark 18, which accounted for 65 percent of submarine firings in 1945.

Some of the ordnance bureaucrats who inflicted faulty torpedoes upon the U.S. Navy made admiral. (One was Fleet Admiral William Leahy, FDR's naval aide.) In Germany, those responsible for similar lapses went to prison.

But improvements were made and results improved. When the torpeckers launched that Tuesday afternoon, the twenty-two-hundred-pound Mark 13 in the bomb bay of each Avenger had become a viable weapon. Shorter and bigger than other nations' torpedoes, the Mark 13 had a bulky, squat appearance: twenty-two inches in diameter and only thirteen feet long. But at least American torpedo crews could trust their "fish" to go where they were pointed, and explode upon arrival.

Deckload Strike

LEADING *BELLEAU WOOD*'S FOUR AVENGERS was Lieutenant George Brown of Rochester, New York. "Brownie" was known as "a very aggressive aviator." During the briefing in VT-24's ready room he declared he would torpedo a carrier "or else."

In addition to four Avengers, eight Fighting 24 Hellcats also contributed to the largest light-carrier contingent. The TBMs were filled with 301 gallons of fuel. It would not be enough.

For many pilots on the mission, it was their second sortie of the day. Lieutenant Junior Grade Ben Tate and other *Belleau Wood* pilots had already flown a four-hour antisub patrol, but the prospect of a shot at "Jap CVs" overwhelmed his fatigue.

Hornet's new CAG was Commander Jackson D. Arnold, a southerner who lettered in tennis at Annapolis. He became a torpedo pilot and, like his *Enterprise* counterpart, Killer Kane, had been at Pearl Harbor. Arnold was absolutely determined to get a lick at the Mobile Fleet, even if he had to lose every plane on the mission. Upon receiving the amended contact report, he said that regardless of how far west the enemy force was found, he would lead an attack, regroup as many planes as possible, and fly eastward until fuel ran out. Before the mass ditching, Morse code messages would pinpoint the location for Mitscher. "Ripper Leader" felt that a group landing in the water would allow pilots and aircrewmen to support each other until the task force arrived.

Task Force 58 manned aircraft at 1610. Pilots and aircrewmen jogged onto flight decks, clambered into Hellcats, Avengers, Helldivers, and Dauntlesses, and settled into the practiced preflight routine. Deckhands already had pulled the props through several blades, distributing oil in the big cylinders of Wrights and Pratt & Whitneys. Within minutes 240 engines were throbbing on eleven flight decks: more than four hundred thousand horses powered by eighty-one thousand gallons of high-octane fuel, bearing 115 tons of ordnance. The Hellcats alone loaded nearly a quarter million rounds of machine-gun ammunition, and the Helldivers' wings held over thirteen thousand rounds of "twenty mike-mike."

From carrier bridges, engine telegraphs rang far below in the engineering spaces. In man-made heat sometimes reaching 130 degrees, the B Division sailors running oil-fired boilers supplied power to the M Division main engine rooms. There, each flattop's screws were turned at an increasing rate as the ships worked up to twenty-two knots. The last thing the aircrews heard from Mitscher was a typical exhortation: "Give 'em hell, boys. Wish I were with you."

Three task groups began launching 240 aircraft at 1624. However, as always there were aborts. The "airborne duds" reduced the total to 226: 95 Hellcats, 54 Avengers, and 77 dive-bombers, including 26 Dauntlesses from *Enterprise* and *Lexington*.

* * *

The outbound strike was heavily weighted toward the CVs, which launched two-thirds of the sorties. *Yorktown*, for instance, contributed forty planes, while CVL *San Jacinto* provided two TBMs.

Flagship *Lexington*'s contribution was representative of Task Force 58 aviators, as her thirty nonaborting pilots and twenty-seven aircrewmen hailed from twenty-five of the forty-eight United States, including nine from California, six from Massachusetts, five from New York, and four from Ohio. They averaged twenty-four years of age with extremes from nineteen to forty-three.

Many fliers were superstitious: Some indulged in prelaunch rituals such as donning clothes in a particular order. Some carried lucky totems ranging from Saint Christopher medals to an unused handkerchief. Probably the record was held by a dive-bomber gunner who would not fly without his lucky charms: a pipe, an ivory die, a screwdriver, two nuts and bolts—and a pinecone "worry bird."

Though the briefed distance to target was fairly long, that was less a concern than fading daylight. Years later, some pilots confessed that when they taxied past the island and tossed a salute to the bridge, they felt they were saying good-bye. Few air groups had conducted night-carrier qualifications, and none had operated much after twilight. It was understandable: nobody expected that two hundred planes would ever be airborne after dark.

On *Lexington*'s flag bridge, as 226 planes disappeared into the late-afternoon sky, Pete Mitscher pondered the time-distance equation and the inexorable rate of fuel consumption. Apart from the Japanese Imperial Navy, fuel was the admiral's biggest concern for the 411 men winging westward. Marc and Frances Mitscher had no children, and intimates wondered whether "Pete" transferred that yearning to the young men flying from his decks. Meanwhile, his chief of staff anticipated problems getting scores of planes back aboard at night. Arleigh Burke checked plans for illuminating the task force to assist homing pilots in the dark.

The flag bridge was not the only place where stay-behinds watched shipmates departing for harm's way. Aboard *Belleau Wood*, twenty-year-old Quartermaster John Di Fusco watched George Brown's

Avengers and fighter escort headed for the far horizon. With infinite sadness, he recalled, "We did not think we would ever see them again."

While elements of eleven air groups climbed outbound, a second deckload strike was being prepared on most of the engaged carriers as well as the stay-at-homes: *Essex, Langley,* and *Princeton* in Harrell's 58.4. However, as darkness approached, Mitscher had second thoughts. Losses were bound to be heavy in the first strike, and extending the recovery time farther into the night would only increase the casualties.

Sitting in his SB2C ahead of "the pack" on *Bunker Hill* was VB-8's Lieutenant Red Carmody. He was warming up his Wright engine, anticipating the prospects of hitting the Mobile Fleet with the follow-up attack, when one of the plane directors got his attention. The sailor was making emphatic gestures including a hand at the throat: the "Cut engine" signal. Carmody knew what it meant. He wasn't launching into a three-hundred-mile mission with the certainty of a black Pacific recovery. He added some throttle, pulled back the red-knobbed mixture handle to idle-cutoff, and watched his three-bladed propeller spin slowly into stillness. Behind him, eleven other "Beasts" followed suit. The pilots and aircrewmen secured their cockpits and descended from the Helldivers' high fuselages. They returned to the ready room to wait some more.

Course Two-niner-zero

THE AIR GROUPS CRUISE-CLIMBED INTO the westering sun, conserving fuel at the outset. With mixture in auto lean, the pilots watched their gauges, keeping cylinder head temperature below 232 degrees Celsius. Hellcats climbed at 140 to 145 knots, the Double Wasp engines pulling no more than thirty-four inches manifold pressure.

The outbound leg was flown on 290 true, en route at twelve thousand feet. In each formation the bombers were the limiting factor, and the SBDs were slowest of all. The *Enterprise* and *Lexington* air groups had the last Dauntlesses in the fleet, as Ramage and Lieutenant

Commander Ralph Weymouth watched the other groups pass them en route to cruise altitude. Leading the Big E's formation was Killer Kane, cloth helmet tugged over his bandaged head. It wasn't enough that he had shot down two planes on the morning search. After missing the turkey shoot the day before, he intended to get in as much flying and shooting as possible.

About twenty minutes after launch, formation leaders began receiving priority radio messages. Some air groups had not received the corrected "lat-long" report before launch, and the update was a shocker. The *Enterprise* search team's amplification had been confirmed: An additional seventy miles put Ozawa fully three hundred miles from Mitscher's launch position. Pilots immediately recomputed their fuel situation.

During the westbound leg, Alex Vraciu's fighter division flew lazy S-turns to avoid outrunning *Lexington*'s SBDs. The Hellcat escorts were deployed above the bombers, layered between 13,500 and 17,000 feet. As mid cover for the base element, he was mainly concerned with keeping position and did not know about the extra degree of longitude between Air Group 16 and the Mobile Fleet.

For planes heavily laden with bombs or torpedoes, facing gas-guzzling combat maneuvers over the enemy fleet, that was an eye-watering prospect. The U.S. Navy had never launched a major strike over such an extreme distance. Avengers and Hellcats would be tight; the dive-bombers had no margin for error.

Leading Bombing 10 in the *Enterprise* formation, Lieutenant Commander Jig Dog Ramage nursed his "slow but deadly" SBDs at 140 knots:

"Strike groups were passing us until we were all alone in the rear of some two hundred and twenty aircraft. We had our own game plan. I began to even out the fuel in my wings by shifting tanks about every fifteen minutes. I did not want to have an asymmetrical load in my dive. Also, we had been warned that one wanted some fuel in each tank. A completely empty tank was considered more likely to explode because of residual vapor."

Some 260 miles out, trailing along in his Dauntless, Ramage saw

about three dozen planes veering to port. He spotted the Japanese refueling group and guessed the unknown pilots' intention. He broke
radio silence, calling Lieutenant Van Eason, the *Enterprise* Avenger
leader. "Eighty-five Sniper from Forty-one Sniper. We will not attack.
The Charlie Victors [CVs] are dead ahead." Then Ramage opened up
on VHF "guard" channel, hailing the attackers: "Unknown strike
leader from Forty-one Sniper. The Charlie Victors are dead ahead.
What are you trying to do? Sink their Merchant Marine?"

Ramage felt that every striker should go for "the fighting Navy" but
his call went unheeded. Later he learned that *Wasp*'s SB2Cs were low
on fuel at that point, but as he commented, "Who wasn't?"

Wasp's deckload strike was led by the bomber skipper, Lieutenant
Commander Jack Blitch. En route westward, his group was lured
south of the track by radio calls and curious radar returns. Returning
to the base course, *Wasp*'s aviators felt they had too little fuel to continue on to the Mobile Fleet. Consequently, when the refueling group
hove into view, Blitch opted to attack Ozawa's oilers.

The supply force counted thirty-five attacking aircraft, which—for
a change—was exactly right. Blitch assigned three Helldivers to each
of four oilers and four Avengers to a fifth. Thus, he retained four
TBFs to strike any targets that were missed or only damaged. He also
kept his sixteen Hellcats for flak suppression or top cover.

The SB2Cs produced spectacular results. Bombing 14 saw one oiler
"explode and disintegrate," with another afire and a third dead in the
water. The fourth was damaged, leaking oil, but under way.

While reorganizing after the attack, *Wasp*'s bombers were beset by
at least six Zeroes that unexpectedly turned up, apparently from
Zuikaku. With the Hellcats poorly positioned to intervene, the Mitsubishis shot one bomber into the water. Two other SB2C pilots were
wounded, and may have been killed but for the timely intervention of
three unidentified F6Fs. In the brief dogfight a VF-14 Hellcat also
went down, while VB-14 gunners claimed hits on two Zekes.

The *Wasp* air group sank two oilers: *Seiyo Maru* and *Genyo Maru*. A
third ship survived thanks to excellent damage control.

* * *

Two hours after launch the U.S. strikes found Ozawa's force thirty-five miles west of the oilers. The carrier divisions were arrayed roughly northeast-southwest, partially hidden by two huge cumulus clouds that glowed yellow-red in the lowering light. The sky over the Mobile Fleet was five-tenths cloud cover between three thousand and ten thousand feet. Visibility was fair: fifteen to twenty miles.

In some air groups, radio discipline began breaking down as excited pilots exclaimed at something they had never seen: enemy warships maneuvering at sea. Snippets of conversation crackled over the VHF radios:

"Look at that oil slick!"

"Haven't got time to look around."

"We've got to attack immediately if we're going to get back."

Jig Ramage had never seen so marvelous a sight, either, but Bombing Ten's mission-oriented skipper considered the outbursts "completely unwarranted transmissions."

Meanwhile, Ozawa had time to put up a strong combat air patrol. He managed to launch some seventy-five planes, including forty Zeke fighters and twenty-eight fighter-bombers. The other half dozen apparently were Vals. It was a substantial number but too few to defend three carrier groups and the oilers spread across forty miles of ocean.

Though many of the Japanese pilots were novices, they fought hard for their ships. But, unlike army pilots whose bases could not be destroyed, naval aviators either won their battle or hoped for an intact flight deck other than their own.

Some of Joshima's B Force scouts spotted Mitscher's force shortly before the lead American air groups sighted the Mobile Fleet. Within minutes Ozawa—now riding *Zuikaku*—dispatched three "pathfinders" to relieve the scouts tracking Mitscher while seven torpedo planes were launched. What they were expected to accomplish is speculative, but fortunately for the crews, they received word of the inbound Americans and returned to their ships.

Knowing what was coming, the Mobile Fleet deployed in air defense formation. Bugles blared the call to action, and it was none too soon. Nine minutes later, at 1803, CarDiv Three radar plotted hostile aircraft inbound, and elements of Air Group 653 eyeballed more than two dozen blue airplanes. About twenty minutes thereafter, the U.S. strike leaders began calling visual contact with the Mobile Fleet. High-speed wakes were clearly visible as Ozawa steered northwest, churning the Philippine Sea at twenty-four knots.

Beneath the three-thousand-foot lower cloud layer, visibility was twenty-five miles. Strike leaders quickly sorted their options and assigned targets. It had to be done quickly: Less than a half hour of daylight remained.

In the twenty minutes between 1840 and 1900, elements of seven U.S. air groups exchanged gunfire with the Japanese CAP, and twenty American aircraft were lost to fighters and flak—one-fifth of the Japanese claims. Curtiss Helldivers proved especially vulnerable, as eight of the fifty-one launched were shot down. So were seven Hellcats, four Avengers, and a Dauntless, including write-offs from battle damage.

The resulting action was understandably confused, given the numbers of attackers and defenders, the expanse of ocean, and fading daylight.

Carrier Division One

NORTHERNMOST OF THE THREE CARRIER divisions, Ozawa now retained only *Zuikaku*, flying her own surviving Zekes, plus some overage from *Shokaku* and *Taiho*. At the time of the attack, A Force was steaming north-northwest between the two prominent clouds as the strike from 58.1 closed in. The attackers were from *Hornet*, *Yorktown*, and *Bataan*.

Among the pilots attacking CarDiv One was Lieutenant Harold E. Buell of Bombing 2. A veteran of most of the 1942 battles, Buell now led one wing of *Hornet*'s Helldivers down on *Zuikaku*.

"As I pushed over into my dive at about twelve thousand feet, the AA fire became so intense that I saw no way of getting through it. My dive brakes were already open and I was well into a good dive, but because of the potent defensive fire, I felt like I was moving in slow motion in quicksand . . . At this point I did something I had never done before in a dive—I closed my dive brakes. My plane responded by dropping like a stone toward the target below, leaving the heavy AA fire behind.

"My speed was building up and, in the clean condition without flaps, I could never expect to pull out of the dive. . . . Shouting a prayer to my guardian angel, at six thousand feet I placed the dive-brake selector back into the open position. The wing brakes did what no manufacturing specs said they would—they opened! It was as if a giant hand grabbed my plane by the tail; my headlong plunge slowed, and there was the enemy carrier dead in my sight below me, turning into my flight path along its lengthwise axis. At a point-blank range of two thousand feet, I fired my bomb."

Buell's choice of words is instructive. He regarded a dive-bomber as a precision weapon much like a sniper's rifle, but in the dusk and confusion he could not "call his shot." However, his Helldiver took a hit— a heavy-caliber round that set the starboard wing afire and sent a splinter into the pilot's back.

Reducing airspeed, Buell got the fire extinguished and concentrated on navigating back to the task force.

The strike coordinator over A Force was *Hornet*'s aggressive CAG, Jack Arnold. After his Helldivers attacked, he ordered *Yorktown*'s bombers onto *Zuikaku*, then directed *Hornet*'s Avengers to the target. None of the torpeckers claimed hits, but the two bombing squadrons claimed eight. Then some *Bataan* Hellcats piled in for good measure. As the aviators pulled away, "Zui" seemed done for. She gushed so much smoke that two dive-bombers diverted to other targets rather than expend their ordnance on a "doomed" ship.

Air Group 601 retained eight *Zuikaku* Zekes under the senior fighter pilot, Ensign Yoshio Fukui. Most of the survivors had to land in the water after dark, and few of those were recovered.

Hornet's was the only Avenger squadron not intercepted, permitting a clear shot at A Force. But the ordnance load-out and mechanical problems conspired to prevent any hits. Torpedo Two's six planes included four armed with bombs, and *Zuikaku*'s slippery evasive maneuvers proved effective. Of the two torpeckers, one aborted its run on the carrier because the bomb bay doors were jammed, forcing Lieutenant Junior Grade K. P. Sullivan to resort to manual control. He lined up a cruiser and was able to drop, but his intended victim turned safely to port.

The other VT-2 pilot was Ensign Van G. Stauber, who forgot to open his doors during the run. Belatedly realizing his error, he turned and flew down the big carrier's starboard beam, looking for another target. Like Sullivan, he chose a cruiser and made a good drop. Glancing backward past the tail, his gunner gleefully reported an explosion on the ship's stern. However, it was likely an errant bomb, as no A Force cruisers were hit.

After aborts, Commander James Peters's *Yorktown* group totaled thirteen bombers, eight Avengers, and fourteen fighters, the latter all packing five-hundred-pound bombs. Passing the large clouds, the *Yorktown*ers split up. The torpeckers and fighters diverted to B Force, while the bombers remained focused on A Force.

Somewhere in the *Yorktown* group's breakaway circle, Lieutenant Commander Joseph W. Runyan spotted a more lucrative target and took his thirteen bombers to the north, where he had spotted *Zuikaku*. CarDiv One put up a lot of flak, but the *Yorktown*ers nosed over from twelve thousand feet. The Bombing One Helldivers pressed the attack, most releasing below two thousand feet and some as low as a thousand. As a result, they confidently claimed three hits or more. At one point fliers saw through Zui's flight deck, "a large hole, rimmed with fire apparently emanating from the hangar deck."

The attackers made a lasting impression on *Zukaku*'s bridge watch. A division of Hellcats—likely from *Yorktown* or *Hornet*—pushed through CarDiv One's flak to strafe the island. Standing together, Ozawa and his chief of staff openly admired the American fighter pilots' determination to press in close for maximum accuracy. Captain Ohmae said, "The . . . strafing planes were very brave and came in low." Another staff officer, Commander Ishigura, was wounded by a fractured .50-caliber round.

The Americans inflicted far worse damage, however, and Ozawa very nearly lost *Zuikaku*. His new flagship took at least one direct hit and seemed smothered in a carpet of near misses. She dodged two or more torpedoes; otherwise she undoubtedly would have gone down. As it was, the aviation fuel system split open, dousing the hangar deck with high-octane gasoline that quickly ignited. The Imperial Navy had belatedly installed foam in its capital ships to smother fires, but damage-control crews reported that the "bubble extinguishing equipment" was insufficient. With fires spreading out of control, Captain Takeo Kaizuka decided to save the crew and ordered his men to abandon ship.

Whether they did not hear the order or they simply refused to quit, *Zuikaku*'s sailors fought and won a valiant battle to save their "Auspicious Crane." Before the abandon-ship drill could be implemented, engineers reported to the bridge that the hangar deck fires were coming under control.

The Japanese pilots still airborne faced a serious dilemma. Some, like Lieutenant Hideo Katori, became seagoing nomads. Launched from *Hiyo* on the nineteenth, he landed on *Taiho*. After the flagship was torpedoed, he high-lined to a destroyer and was delivered to *Zuikaku*. Now he took off to intercept the American strike but had to recover aboard *Ryuho*. He was fortunate: Few imperial aviators landed with their shoes dry that evening.

Carrier Division Two

IN JOSHIMA'S DIVISION, Commander Shoichi Suzuki's Air Group 652 launched all twenty-six operational fighters, including seven Zero bombers. They made good use of height and clouds, claiming seven Avengers "confirmed" as well as two probables and two more probable Hellcats. Eleven A6Ms were shot down and three more ditched, leaving twelve to find sanctuary with dry feet.

The strike from Reeves's Task Group 58.3 was composed of *Lexington*, *Enterprise*, and *San Jacinto* contingents, plus the *Belleau Wood* tagalongs from 58.1. The Avengers and Hellcats glided off Jig Ramage's and Ralph Weymouth's SBDs, skirting the north end of the largest cloud formation, then turned abruptly port to approach B Force from the east.

But first in line were the "orphans" from the 58.1 formation.

When the *Yorktown* group split up, Lieutenant Charles W. Nelson led Torpedo One's TBMs and SB2Cs between A Force and B Force. He took his Avengers in a hard port turn, away from his intended target, setting up the attack geometry he wanted. But in descending through the lower cloud deck, he emerged twenty-five hundred feet over B Force. Nelson liked what he saw—three carriers instead of one—and took his five-plane division down for a torpedo attack; the other three "Turkeys" trailed with bombs. Smoke Strean's Hellcats followed, wanting to keep the group together.

Nelson led his torpedo attack against *Ryuho*, making a good drop at about a thousand yards. Rather than turn away, exposing his white belly to enemy AA gunners, he pressed ahead, into the guns, and hopping over the target. The Japanese could hardly miss—and didn't. They riddled the Avenger with automatic weapons, setting it afire. Nelson and his crew died in the crash. The other torpeckers also dropped, but *Ryuho* dodged all five "fish."

The rest of VT-1 executed glide-bomb runs against *Hiyo* or *Junyo*: In the flak and fear and confusion, identification was often impossible. Strean's fighter-bombers rolled in on the same target or targets. Results were optimistically pegged at three hits and five near misses, a score disputed by CAG Jim Peters, orbiting overhead.

Japanese gunners had no shortage of targets. Helmets cinched down, straps secured in bows tied beneath the chin, gun captains tried to identify the most likely target and pointed their white canes in the appropriate direction. It was an ineffective system, especially against a coordinated, multiaxis attack. American aircrews reported more volume than accuracy: Japanese gunners shot down only six planes among 199 that attacked Mobile Fleet ships.

When Air Group 16 cleared the huge anvil-shaped cumulus, B Force lay in the distance beneath the tricolor Grummans and Douglases. It would have been a memorable sight under any circumstance: three carriers, a battleship, a cruiser, and eight destroyers trailing twenty-four-knot wakes across the cloud shadows highlighted by the evening's slanting rays on a sun-dappled sea. But for aircrew who had never glimpsed an enemy fleet unit, the sight was entrancing.

Leading the base element of SBDs at twelve thousand feet was Ralph Weymouth, a Guadalcanal veteran who had flown from big, aged *Saratoga* in 1942. At twenty-seven he was an old-timer in the literal and figurative sense: Only one other pilot among the thirty in *Lexington*'s formation was older.

Quickly assessing Joshima's force, Weymouth selected "the southern *Hayataka*" as his target. There never was a Japanese carrier by that name—nor likely any other ship, either. No matter. The intended victim was probably *Junyo*, which was not the most southerly flattop (actually it was *Hiyo*).

Like so many pilots on the mission, top gun Alex Vraciu was struck by the huge cumulus buildup, which likely topped thirty-five thousand feet. *Lexington*'s strike skirted the northern edge of the towering cloud formation, which blocked much of the sky from view. Consequently, Joshima's CAP was able to approach largely unseen, and initiated a well-executed bounce on Air Group 16. Vraciu recalled, "I became aware of the attack when I saw a burning TBF's crew bailing out. Then, all of a sudden, my wingman and I were surrounded by more Zekes than we could handle." He thought, "I don't see how we can get them all." The Airedales had to fight for their lives.

Vraciu's team started at a disadvantage, as the number four man had aborted. With three Hellcats against eight Zekes, "We were purely defensive." The dogfight was hard-fought and short-lived. Vraciu scissored with his wingman, Ensign Homer W. Brockmeyer, trying to meet each slashing attack, but the odds were too great. Again coming abeam of Brockmeyer, Vraciu saw the young Ohioan temporarily straight and level, taking hits from astern. The Indiana ace rolled hard right, drew a bead on the offending Zeke, and fired from about 45 degrees off the nose. The Mitsubishi exploded on the second burst, but Brockmeyer's Hellcat went down streaming smoke.

Vraciu dived after his wingman, hoping to mark the splash if "Brock" got out. But two Zekes intervened and Vraciu had to pull up to avoid them. Jamming stick and rudder, he cross-controlled, forcing his F6F into a speed-killing snap roll that placed his guns on a third assailant. He fired, saw hits, and glimpsed the Zeke dropping away inverted.

When he looked around, the sky seemed empty.

The Avenger that Vraciu had seen was Lieutenant Junior Grade Warren E. McLellan's. The VT-16 crews had been alerted to fighters ahead, and kept their eyes peeled in that direction. McLellan was raptly watching an attack on a big carrier when "about fifty tracers appeared to pass through my plane and go directly out ahead and slightly upward." Nearly a dozen Zekes had executed a six-o'clock attack from above and below, taking the Americans by surprise. McLellan's assailant had dived below the Grumman, hiding beneath the tail to shoot into the vulnerable underside.

In seconds the Avenger called "61 Gimlet" was afire. McLellan, his gunner, and radioman rang up the "for-sale" sign and abandoned ship. They delayed pulling their rip cords in order to clear the combat area, then tugged the D-handles. Yards of silk blossomed overhead, yielding the welcome violence of opening shock.

Descending toward the water, McLellan took a professional interest in the scene below. He observed further attacks on what he thought was a *Shokaku*-class carrier, then busied himself with his water landing. He lost his inflatable raft when it sank with his waterlogged parachute. Buoyed only by his Mae West, facing a night in the ocean, the twenty-two-year-old flier was a long way from Arkansas.

Meanwhile, Torpedo 16 evened the score. As the squadron pulled off target, AMM1c Jack W. Webb in Lieutenant Norman A. Sterrie's plane shot down a Zeke that got too close. As the Japanese turned away from his ineffectual run, Webb got a good burst into the belly and saw the hostile nose into the water and explode. The sharpshooting Ohioan got a Distinguished Flying Cross for his gunnery.

Weymouth's Dauntlesses—lower and slower than the Avengers—got most of the Zekes' attention. The skipper's backseater, ARM1c William A. McElhiney, saw unidentified aircraft closing from astern. He pushed his mid canopy section forward, folded the rear section down, stepped on the pedal opening his gun bay, and pulled his twin

.30 mount up and back. A quick tug on the charging handles and he was ready to shoot. The lead Zekes reached firing range as Bombing 16 nosed over from 11,500 feet.

Other gunners also took up the challenge. Their twin Brownings began chattering, trying to keep Air Group 652's fighters at arm's length while the last miles swept past. But some fliers were still absorbed with the entrancing sight of so many enemy warships. ARM2c Richard L. Van Etten in Ensign Henry M. Moyers's plane was manhandling a camera in the 160-knot slipstream, trying to steady the viewfinder for a prestrike photo. Abruptly streaks of light flashed past: Japanese tracers. Van Etten deposited the camera in the bilges of his SBD and deployed his guns.

Three SBDs were hit by Japanese gunfire, but no serious damage was done. In turn, VB-16 gunners put enough .30-calibers into three Mitsubishis to deter them from further attack. Weymouth signaled for a shift from vees into right echelon preparatory to diving. Heavy flak now was bursting nearby, jostling the Dauntlesses in their descent, but the transition was smoothly made. Bringing the formation around to the west, with the setting sun behind him, Weymouth had a nearly perfect setup: down-sun, upwind, along the target's axis.

The Minutemen rolled in at 1904, raining one-thousand- and five hundred-pound bombs down on *Hiyo*. Ralph Weymouth had put a Japanese carrier in his sight once before: Nearly two years earlier he had near-missed *Ryujo* at Eastern Solomons. Now he was determined to get a hit. In his brief dive he played the SBD's controls with the deft touch so beloved of dive-bomber pilots. It was the gift that Douglas design genius Ed Heinemann had bestowed upon aviators of the U.S. Navy: inherent stability coupled with light control responses to keep on target. Helldiver pilots could only envy those who flew the "obsolete" Dauntless.

Weymouth had "Wandering Falcon" squarely in his illuminated sight when he pressed the red button atop his stick at fifteen hundred feet. Then he moved the flap selector lever rearward, pulled in his dive brakes, and hauled back on the stick. Despite the heavy g load, gunner

McElhiney looked back in time to see a smoke puff erupt beside the island.

Most of the other *Lexington* pilots pressed their attacks on *Hiyo*, but some shifted targets on the way down. A few were deprived of a clear view of the objective, so they went after *Junyo*, pounding along off *Hiyo*'s port beam. Others were bounced around by bursting flak, finding it easier to settle on *Junyo* than the primary target. One was Lieutenant Cook Cleland, an extroverted, fun-loving Ohioan with three Air Medals and the Purple Heart. His Dauntless, faithful old Number Thirty-nine, took hits from 20- and 40mm shells, knocking him off course. Thanks to the SBD's marvelous ailerons, he quickly rolled back on target and claimed a hit just forward of the stern. Then he tugged back on the stick, praying that his wing with a two-foot hole would hold together.

It did. That was the good news.

The bad news: He had just regained level flight when a Zeke initiated a high-side run from five o'clock, then wrapped around in a continuing turn. But gunner William J. Hisler was quick on the draw. He swung his .30s, got a quick bead on the assailant, and put sixty rounds into the Mitsubishi's undersides. The fighter threw off a smoke trail, dropped one wheel, and managed a ditching alongside a destroyer.

Seconds later a Val rushed in from port, firing its nose guns as it came. Cleland's wingman, twenty-one-year-old Ensign John F. Caffey, swung into the threat and exchanged gunfire head-on. Two 7.7s against two .50s was no contest. The Aichi veered off and was lost to sight.

Later, *Lexington*'s Dauntlesses claimed seven half-ton hits on *Hiyo* and/or *Junyo*, while the high-speed, shallow-angle Avengers pickled their five-hundred-pounders as high as three thousand feet, claiming three or more hits. In truth, *Hiyo* sustained one bomb hit and *Junyo* two from all attackers. Fading light, normal combat confusion, excitement, and youthful optimism combined to produce the treble overestimate.

Whatever the bombing results, there was definitely a running gunfight to the rendezvous. By singles and sections, Bombing and Torpedo

16 shot their way clear of the vengeful Japanese CAP, and there were losses on both sides. Several Zekes slashed vertically at Weymouth and some of his SBDs, barely pulling out above the darkening water. One fighter was especially persistent: It survived the attention of three Dauntless gunners to fire one well-aimed burst before it pitched up, stalled, and dived into the sea. But that burst killed Weymouth's twenty-two-year-old wingman, Lieutenant Junior Grade James A. Shields. His twenty-three-year-old gunner, ARM2c Leo O. LeMay, was still firing when their SBD smashed into the waves.

Overhead Carrier Division Two, the Big E's fliers went to work with other squadrons. Jig Dog Ramage coordinated his SBDs with Torpedo Ten's Avengers to attack the two nearest flattops.

Ramage set up VB-10's attack on the center group, selecting *Junyo*, flanked by *Hiyo* and *Ryuho* off each quarter. Satisfied with his pilots' disposition, he reduced power with his left hand, moved the diamond-shaped flap-selector lever with his right, and felt the drag as his dive flaps split top and bottom.

Nose over and the attack was on.

To a dive-bomber pilot, the standard seventy-degree angle seemed nearly vertical. The pilot tilted forward against his shoulder harness, concentrating on the picture in his reflector sight. From roll-in at 14,000 feet to release and pullout at about 2,500 was perhaps thirty seconds. In that time, much had to be done right for any chance of a hit.

First, the airplane had to be balanced for a smooth dive. Too much elevator trim or too little imparted excess stick pressure up or down. Also, the aircraft had to track straight, without veering port or starboard. The reflector sight had a ball in a housing much like that in the turn-and-bank indicator. By rudder trim or physical finesse, the bomber pilot kept the ball centered, exactly the way a fighter pilot did in aerial gunnery.

Next, the pilot selected his desired point of impact, or POI: the spot on the vessel where his bomb would do the most damage. Center of the flight deck was favored on carriers, or perhaps somewhat aft if enemy aircraft were spotted for launch. But the sight's aiming dot or "pipper" had to be offset to allow for ship's motion and wind. Because a warship under attack was likely making thirty knots or better, the aim point or POA was moved ahead of the desired POI. If the ship was steaming upwind, the bombing solution was simplified: Put the pipper on the bow and wait as long as you dared before toggling the bomb.

But if the attack was made crosswind, the bomb's fall line would be affected. In that case, the pilot juggled rudder feet and stick hand, moving the pipper accordingly.

Despite the technology, dive-bombing was more art than science. One pilot compared it to playing the violin: Everybody knew the basics but individuals had their own techniques. Because range errors exceed deflection, most pilots liked to dive from the bow. Diving from behind, the tendency was to go shallow toward the end of the dive, resulting in a miss astern.

Several feet behind the pilot sat the radioman-gunner. The seventy-degree dive angle placed him nearly flat on his back, looking at the upper air. Usually he had his canopy open and twin .30-caliber machine guns deployed against interceptors. But some pilots liked the backseater to face forward, calling off the altitude that unwound at the rate of about three hundred feet per second.

Nearing 2,500 feet, when things looked right—or even if they didn't—the pilot pressed his bomb release. In the SBD it was a red button stamped "B" on top of the stick. But there was also a manual release below the throttle quadrant. Some pilots pressed the button, then immediately leaned forward and left, grasped the two-handled manual release, and gave it a tug. They had to keep the plane properly aligned with the aim point or the bomb would be skewed off target. To avoid slewing the bomb, some pilots advocated hitting the "pickle," then counting "One potato" before beginning a pullout.

When experience and intuition told him the time was right, the motivated pilot dropped, then waited one or two potatoes longer.

Below and behind him, the bomb was released from its shackles. The bomb displacing fork or "trapeze" arced downward and forward, tossing the bomb clear of the propeller before retracting under pressure of a heavy coil spring. The weapon was on its way, accelerating at thirty-two feet per second per second, acting on its particular ballistic characteristics.

Then it was time to pull. Hard.

At about 240 knots from twenty-five hundred feet, the ocean was filling the windscreen with breathtaking speed. The effort required to change the vector of ten thousand pounds of airplane was considerable, especially in the days before boosted controls. Typically a pilot wrapped both hands around the black plastic stick handle and tugged it toward his stomach.

Then gravity's elephant stepped on his head.

The force of six to eight times normal g descended on him, from the head downward. With a 160-pound aviator temporarily weighing 960 to 1,280 pounds, the body reacted adversely. The chin was forced onto the chest. Blood was pushed toward the lower extremities, and the eyes suffered first. Pilots experienced grayout as color bleached away, or full blackout: temporary blindness. The thorax felt constricted, limiting breathing.

Then consciousness returned. Most pilots found themselves with the nose on the horizon and began cleaning up the airplane. They shoved up the power, pulled in the flaps, and turned toward the rendezvous while scores of sailors they'd never seen before earnestly tried to kill them. The huge majority made it: An unlucky few fell to enemy gunners. A handful never recovered from the high-g pullout and went straight into the water.

Ramage divided his dozen Dauntlesses between *Ryuho* and *Junyo*. Pushing toward the roll-in point at twelve thousand feet, they drew heavy flak, accurate in altitude but wide in deflection. As per doctrine, the leader took the closer ship, which, according to the Japanese disposition, was *Ryuho*. The second division leader, Lieutenant Louis L. Bangs, proceeded to *Junyo*.

Ramage was about to pop his dive brakes when he heard his gunner, Chief Radioman David Cawley, on the intercom: "Zekes overhead."

Looking around, the skipper saw a Zero make a halfhearted pass at the SBDs. As it turned away, Ramage thought, "No guts."

Meanwhile, Killer Kane took his Hellcat division down ahead of the SBDs, enthusiastically strafing to help suppress flak. The CAG triggered long, satisfying bursts that pelted the deck and gun tubs with eighty .50-caliber slugs per second. Kane had brought twenty-four hundred rounds three hundred miles; there was no point taking them home.

The timing was excellent. As Ramage nosed into his dive, the carrier steadied upon an easterly heading. Ramage led his first division in a near-vertical attack, diving from the bow, which was the preferred method. Another *Enterprise* bomber leader, Richard H. Best, had advocated that approach at Midway: "It forces you to get steep."

Peering through his reflector sight, Ramage saw the enemy flight deck outlined in sparkling muzzle flashes. Tracers and bursting stuff flashed ahead of him as he plunged downward at three hundred feet per second. The heavy shells were exploding behind him now, though the tracers seemed curling into his sight. But he hung on: This was the day and hour and minute that his first CO had anticipated when he pledged to make James D. Ramage the second-best bomber in the Pacific Fleet.

At point-blank range of fifteen hundred feet, Jig Ramage toggled his bomb. Freed of half a ton, the Dauntless leaped as his right hand went to the flap-selector handle.

Several things happened at once. Ramage's bomb exploded close astern in the ship's wake. The explosion rocked his plane. Then Dave Cawley's twin .30s were firing: a bad sign.

Ramage looked up and almost flinched. An equally astonished Zero pilot gaped from "about fifteen feet away." The Japanese honked back on his stick, climbing at "an impossible angle." The CO began looking for his chicks: A quick rendezvous was essential if anybody was getting home.

Three of Ramage's other five pilots dropped close aboard; one claimed a peripheral hit through the deck edge. The fifth pilot experienced "hung ordnance" and was unable to release.

Lieutenant Van Eason's four VT-10 Avengers also went for *Ryuho*.

Her CAP objected to their intentions, but Grim Reaper Hellcats ran interference. In all, Torpedo 10 saw a dozen bandits, and two gunners fired at those that got past the F6Fs. One Zero dropped toward the water; the big Grummans proceeded unimpeded.

Making glide-bombing attacks on *Ryuho*, the Avengers drew heavy flak from the battleship *Nagato*, which even unlimbered her sixteen-inchers. But the big bursting shells did no damage, and the "Buzzard Brigade" TBFs dropped their sixteen bombs largely undeterred. The pilots and aircrewmen squinted through the smoke and spray to count eight hits; Captain Tokio Komei merely logged "slight damage" from near misses.

Meanwhile, Lou Bangs took his VB-10 division and fighter escorts toward *Junyo*. Descending toward the target, Bangs extended his dive flaps earlier than expected, prompting his section leader to dive on the most immediate flattop. Lieutenant Junior Grade Harold F. Grubiss therefore attacked *Hiyo* with his two pilots, including a *Lexington* tagalong, Lieutenant Junior Grade Jack Wright, who had diverted to the Big E the day before. Bangs claimed a hit that blew several aircraft off *Junyo*'s flight deck, while his two wingmen reported hits near his. Meanwhile, Grubiss saw his bomb strike *Hiyo*, which in fact reported such damage.

As the *Lexington* squadrons attacked, their junior partner was also on hand. *San Jacinto* had been able to allot only two planes to the mission, but Torpedo 51's Lieutenant Commander Donald J. Melvin and his wingman, Ensign Jack O. Guy, followed Air Group 16. Targeting *Hiyo*, they opened their bomb bay doors and attacked from altitude, but Melvin's quarter-tonners refused to release, compelling him to pull up and try again. Guy dropped from about five thousand—an extremely optimistic endeavor—but the skipper thought his youngster may have scored.

Upon recovering from his abortive run, Melvin found himself positioned over a destroyer. He went down to 2,500 feet and dropped manually, claiming 75 percent hits with one bomb just off the bow. In fact, no imperial destroyers were damaged on June 20, and no cruisers in B Force were struck.

* * *

Two aborts depleted *Belleau Wood*'s outbound formation, but the remaining six Hellcats and four Avengers tacked onto 58.1, trailing *Lexington*'s air group, which went after the center carrier force. When Bombing 16 circled the area to tighten formation before attacking, Lieutenant George Brown, apparently thinking the attack had begun, took his Avengers down into a maelstrom of flak, largely unescorted. Brown drew a bead on a large carrier, and his squadron mate Ben Tate recalled, "We had everybody shooting at us."

Brown split his division to execute an "anvil" attack on His Imperial Japanese Majesty's ship *Hiyo*. Approaching from the north, Brown went wide to the right, then turned in to attack from the bow. Lieutenants Junior Grade Benjamin C. Tate and Warren R. Omark broke port, attacking from the starboard beam and quarter, respectively.

During the approach, Ensign William D. Luton made his torpedo attack on *Junyo* or *Ryuho* as Brown led the other two toward *Hiyo*. One of Brown's wingmen, Lieutenant Junior Grade Warren R. Omark, described the attack on the two-year-old flattop:

"Brownie, Ben Tate, and I fanned out to approach from different angles. The attack course took us over the outlying screen of destroyers, then cruisers, and finally the battleships. This screen had to be penetrated in order to reach the proper range for launching torpedoes against the carrier. The antiaircraft fire was very intense, and I took as much evasive action as I could.

"During the attack, Brownie's aircraft was hit by AA and caught fire. I think one of the remarkable stories of the war then took place. AMM2c George H. Platz and ARM2c Ellis C. Babcock were Brownie's crewmen, and, knowing their plane was afire and unable to reach Brownie on the intercom, they parachuted and witnessed the attack from the water.

"We came in at about four hundred feet from the water to get a satisfactory launch of our torpedoes and dropped them on converging courses, which presumably did not allow the enemy carrier to take effective evasive action."

It worked. Captain Toshiyuki Yokoi was unable to thread his twenty-four-thousand-ton carrier through the Neptune's web that

VT-24 flung at him. At least one torpedo hit the target: *Hiyo* took a Mark 13 in the starboard quarter, and maybe another as well. Her hull was opened to the Pacific Ocean, which immediately began filling the available space inside. With her steering gear wrecked, "Wandering Falcon" was fatally crippled.

Obviously upset at the successful attack on *Hiyo*, Zekes chased the Avengers in futile anger. However, Tate and Omark evaded the CAP and independently came across Brown's blackened, battle-damaged Avenger. Brown was flying slowly, just off the water. "He held up his right arm," recalled Tate, "which was all bloodstained. I tried to keep him on my wing to guide him back. I called him on the radio but he didn't answer with anything understandable. I lost him in the dark."

Omark was the last to see George Brown. "He acted stunned, like a football player who had been hit in the head. I turned on my lights to help him, but evidently his light system was shot, because he didn't turn on his. I lost him in the dark about an hour later."

George Brown was never seen again.

Japanese gun crews were frantic to fend off the attackers, but Imperial Navy flak left something to be desired. It had nothing to compare with American fire-control radar, let alone the VT fuse.

Main batteries on battleships and cruisers could fire "incendiary shrapnel" rounds with time fuses, but the phosphorous eruptions were far more impressive than effective. Comparable to the American 5.38 dual-purpose weapon was Japan's 5.40: a similar round of lower velocity.

The most numerous Japanese AA gun was the 25mm cannon of French origin. Deployed in single, twin, and triple mounts, it was an effective weapon firing 220 rounds per minute per barrel. It could be controlled by mechanical director but probably was more often fired under "local control," with gun captains choosing their own targets. Consequently, though Imperial Navy ships were capable of throwing a lot of steel into the air, *Nihon Kaigun* lacked in accuracy throughout the war. Over B Force that evening, only three Avengers fell to Japanese flak—small consolation to the crews killed or ditched.

The American air combat claims over B Force were unusually accurate. Air Group 652 lost eleven Zekes in dogfights plus three more ditched afterward. The three Hellcat squadrons escorting the attackers claimed eleven kills, bomber gunners four more. Conversely, the attackers lost five planes to Joshima's pilots, who claimed nine "confirmed" and two probables.

Carrier Division Three

THREE AIR GROUPS FROM 58.2 tackled Kurita's C Force: *Bunker Hill*, *Cabot*, and *Monterey*. Avengers dominated the strikers, since only Air Group Eight had Helldivers.

Knowing that Americans were inbound, Obayashi launched available aircraft to intercept. Lieutenant Ito led four fighters and ten fighter-bombers, while two *Tenzans* also took off. They had little chance of defending themselves, but they could serve as airborne sentries to alert Force C of the U.S. disposition.

Obayashi deployed his ships into antiaircraft disposition at 1754, and less than ten minutes later his Type 21 radars detected something to the south. That was likely a phantom blip, as Montgomery's air groups bore down on him from the starboard quarter. However, at 1830 his CAP spotted the tricolor blue raiders, reporting them splitting into four groups for a multiaxis attack.

Shortly lookouts aboard cruiser *Maya* gave the alarm. They reported no fewer than fifty Avengers inbound (there were sixteen, plus other types), but the warning did little good. Eight minutes after the CAP report, bombs began falling around *Chiyoda*, southernmost of the three CVLs in a north-south line of bearing.

Obayashi faced the same problems as the other division commanders, and then some. He had recalled the ministrike launched three hours before, but the sixteen aircraft were caught with gear and flaps down. According to one source, seven planes of Air Group 653 were shot down in the landing pattern, but no matching U.S. claims were made. The more likely culprit was "friendly fire."

Lieutenant Commander James D. Arbes's Bombing 8 jumped *Chiyoda*. He took his *Bunker Hill* SB2Cs down on the light carrier, splitting the defenses with six bombers from the southeast and six more from the north. With four battleships escorting the carriers, C Force put up a wall of flak. Rolling into his dive from thirteen thousand feet, Arbes saw holes sprout in the top of his wing. Nevertheless, he kept the CVL in his sight and dropped at about two thousand feet. In all, Bombing Eight claimed six hits on *Chiyoda* and three more on two escorts. The assessment was clearly optimistic: As combat films revealed, it was often impossible to distinguish between hits and near misses.

Monterey and *Cabot* each contributed four Avengers to the strike, selecting *Chiyoda* to receive their thirty-two bombs. The TBMs slanted into their dives from six thousand feet, splitting to bracket the flattop port and starboard. Lieutenant Roland P. Gift's VT-28 pilots double-checked their master-arm switches, lined up the maneuvering carrier, thumbed the red button on the stick, and spaced their ordnance across the flight deck aft, probably scoring two hits. Twenty men were killed and two planes destroyed, but the seven-month-old carrier remained operational.

Almost simultaneously Lieutenant Edward E. Wood directed VT-31's attack, claiming bomb hits as a result of smoke and flames. As often occurred, astute young aviators saw what appeared to be heavy damage to the primary target and switched to other ships. The second section went after the thirty-year-old battleship *Haruna*, allegedly sunk by B-17 hero Colin Kelly in December 1941. Three five-hundred-pounders found the mark, striking the aft turret and quarterdeck, killing fifteen men, and threatening a magazine. Captain Shigenaga Katazuke took the precaution of flooding the area, but the old battlewagon kept station, her thirty-one thousand tons making twenty-seven knots.

The name "Torpedo 8" earned reverential glory at Midway, but *Bunker Hill*'s TorpRon had no relation to the original VT-8. Nevertheless, Lieutenant Commander Kenneth F. Musick's Avengers continued Commander John Waldron's legacy from two years before. With nearly half the torpedoes on the entire mission, Musick took his two divisions in an approach on *Chiyoda*'s port beam, prompting Captain Eiichiro Joh to order hard a-starboard. With a stern aspect on the target, closing at 220 knots relative speed, the five leading pilots were denied time and geometry to set up an anvil attack on both bows. Still, they did what they could. Satisfied with the sight picture, the pilots reached down to the right and tugged the red torpedo-release handle. All their Mark 13s made safe water entry after a four-hundred-foot or more drop, churning toward the speeding flattop. During the breakaway, closing their bomb bay doors, some Avenger crews saw two eruptions against the hull.

As often was the case, however, *Chiyoda* escaped the spread of torpedoes. The warheads may have detonated in the roiling wake, or the explosions could have been bomb near misses.

Musick's other three aviators saw the same detonations and optimistically concluded that the carrier was doomed. They shifted targets to a cruiser and battleship, made good drops, but also missed.

Eight minutes after attacking, the Americans began withdrawing, though Japanese gunners reported three "SBDs" resuming the assault shortly thereafter. The account has little credibility, especially since no Dauntlesses belonged to Task Group 58.2. Kurita's AA crews checked fire at 1910, having failed to down any Americans. But plenty of Zekes waited beyond the flak belt, looking for opportunities.

Five of *Bunker Hill*'s SB2Cs that raced past the Japanese destroyer screen were attacked from six-o'clock low. At least five Zekes got within range unseen by the rear gunners and shot down two Helldivers. One "Beast" hit the water like a wing-shot duck, and the other went down burning. The other three bombers were holed by 7.7- and 20mm rounds but got away.

At the rendezvous east of the force, other Zeroes belatedly tried to intervene. *Bunker Hill* CAG Ralph L. Shifley and Lieutenant Gerald R. Rian each claimed a destroyed and a probable about ten miles east of the enemy fleet. None of the other 58.2 squadrons (from *Monterey* and *Cabot*) reported intercepts.

The Japanese consistently underestimated the American strength over each force, an unusual event in the Pacific War. Ozawa's staff pegged the total strike at 140 to 150 aircraft, well under the two hundred that actually engaged.

The dubious prize for greatest disparity went to B Force, which reckoned it was jumped by forty Americans. In truth there were more than twice as many, owing to the *Yorktown* fighters and torpeckers who diverted from the crowded airspace over *Zuikaku*.

Hits and Misses

As THE AMERICANS DEPARTED, JAPANESE crews took stock of their situation. Four carriers had been struck by bombs, but those ships would survive; *Hiyo* was another matter. A year previously, en route to Truk, she had survived two torpedoes from the submarine *Trigger*. But now she was in extremis. Torpedo 24's well-executed attack left her crippled from one hit in the starboard engine room and possibly another to port. Barely two hours later, with fires spreading her length, a catastrophic explosion racked her hull. Some Japanese assumed that the culprit was yet another American submarine, but the cause was internal. The same sequence that slew *Shokaku* and *Taiho* now destroyed *Hiyo*: fuel-fed explosions. The flames ignited other explosions that compounded the damage. George Brown's crewmen watched her death throes; she sank by the stern only six minutes later. Destroyers rescued a thousand men; 250 died with her.

Ozawa was understandably shaken: In two days he had lost three carriers and most of his aircraft. Mustering his resolve, he briefly considered prospects for a night surface action but lacked knowledge of Mitscher's position. The rest of the Mobile Fleet continued its westward retreat.

The battle "results" reported to Tokyo looked gratifying on paper, perhaps even in exchange for *Taiho*. Ozawa's perennial optimists calculated that the CAP had splashed more than forty Americans (they got eleven), while AA gunners accounted for seventy more (they got six). In other words, the Mobile Fleet reported destroying 110 of the 140 or so aircraft that supposedly attacked Japanese ships.

The other side of the ledger was all in the debit column.

Zuikaku survived one serious bomb hit aft of the bridge and six near misses. Pilots who attacked "Zui" refuse to believe her damage report, and it's easy to see why. Color combat footage of the attack shows repeated explosions that cannot be distinguished as hits or near misses. However, there is no cause to doubt the veracity of the Japanese assessment, and it's worth remembering that the big carrier was nearly abandoned.

Junyo took a pounding: two hits near the smokestack and six near misses. Though her stack was "utterly crushed" and her mast destroyed, she remained under way but canceled flight operations.

Chiyoda sustained a hit on the flight deck aft, destroying two fighters but otherwise producing only moderate damage.

Ryuho received slight damage from near misses, but her operating ability remained unimpaired.

The oft "sunk" battleship *Haruna* took two bomb hits aft plus near misses that warped her hull. The captain flooded magazines to prevent further problems.

Cruiser *Maya* had some fires owing to a bomb exploding close aboard the port torpedo tubes. However, the damage was minimal.

Wasp's diversion to the supply group deprived the Mobile Fleet of two oilers. Three near misses badly damaged and flooded *Genyo Maru*'s engines; after the crew was removed she was sunk by gunfire from the destroyer *Usuki*. *Seiyo Maru*, set afire and abandoned, was torpedoed by her escorting destroyer *Yukikaze*. Another oiler, *Hayasui*, recorded one bomb hit and two near misses resulting in slight damage.

The disparity in U.S. and Japanese claims for aircraft destroyed over the Mobile Fleet cannot be resolved. Mitscher's pilots and gunners were credited with twenty-six kills, nineteen probables, and thirty-one damaged, while Ozawa acknowledged the loss of nineteen in combat plus others lost operationally. The gap between nineteen and twenty-six is easily accepted as the price of doing dogfight business: Anything under a 50 percent error is unusually good.

But at the end of the action, the Mobile Fleet's aircraft inventory was depleted well beyond the total of American claims. As the Task Force 58 aircraft winged into the gathering eastern gloom, the Mobile Fleet counted merely thirty-five carrier planes and a dozen floatplanes still operational. Therefore, presumably forty-six tailhook aircraft and fifteen scouts—sixty-one airplanes—were lost or badly damaged by other than combat causes on the twentieth. That strains credulity: It is far more likely that American aerial marksmen were more accurate than the debriefers allowed, and Japanese "friendly fire" may have been a factor.

Hotshot Charlie Henderson was at it again. Having surprised the Jake on an early-morning flight two days before, the VT-10 aviator drew a late-afternoon search. Nearly three hours along his track (less than ninety miles southeast of Ozawa) he spotted a Jill. The *Tenzan* crew saw the Avenger and escorting Hellcat, then immediately shoved the throttle in a westward direction. Henderson did the same. "After a long tail chase, he finally burned," Henderson recorded, adding, "This was more credit to Grumman than to me."

En route to the Big E that evening, Henderson began hearing voice radio calls. They were disconcerting: Apparently something had gone wrong.

PART FIVE

"Turn on the Lights"

Course Zero-niner-zero

FOLLOWING THE SHORT, INTENSE COMBAT over the Mobile Fleet, 209 American aircraft headed east into the growing dark, at least 240 miles from base.

Those who survived fighters and flak over the target now faced an even greater ordeal. With the sun on the horizon behind them, pilots leaned on their fuel mixtures for maximum efficiency. Many realized that they would not reach a flight deck. Fuel problems were especially acute among the Helldivers: fifty-one launched on the "mission beyond darkness." Of forty-three that departed the Mobile Fleet, thirty-two splashed or crashed. Meanwhile, the older Dauntlesses limped along, milking every gallon of gas for maximum efficiency.

Most gas-shy pilots decided to ditch while they still had power for a controlled landing. Some splashed in small groups for mutual support and better prospects of rescue. The others pushed their fuel and their luck to the limit, straining for the first tentative glimpse of the task force.

Nearing the expected position of "point option," some pilots began receiving the task force's electronic homing beacons. From about seventy miles out the YE-ZB homers indicated a plane's position relative to the emitter by broadcasting a Morse code letter. Pilots refined their headings, tuning the homer for maximum clarity and the straightest course home.

In CICs throughout the force, radar operators began noticing blips around 2015. Most were clustered in a gaggle to the west, but strays meandered north and south of the course.

Fifteen minutes later the carriers reversed helm and turned into the easterly breeze. Captains called for more "turns" of the screws, accelerating to twenty-two knots in order to provide the required thirty over the deck.

As luck had it, June 20 was the first night of a new moon, and the first phase provided no illumination at all. Much of the return trip was "on the gauges," as pilots relied on their red-lit instruments to remain in level flight. If the artificial horizon failed, it was back to basics: needle, ball, and airspeed, or "needle, beedle, speedle," cross-checking compass for course, turn and bank indicator for wings level, and airspeed indicator to show climb or dive. Even so, the constant threat of vertigo seemed perched on a pilot's shoulder, his inner ear often belying what his instruments told him. Undoubtedly a few aviators succumbed to the siren song—pull up or level your wings—when nothing was wrong. Sometimes it helped to maintain position on another aircraft's lights, but whoever was out front had nothing but his mechanical references and his potentially fatal instincts.

Before long, idle radio chatter began cracking the normal discipline of carrier aviators. It increased as darkness descended and some pilots became disoriented. Others called for their squadron mates; a few broke down and began sobbing. Some pilots heard enough and turned off their radios.

The sun set shortly before 1900, and minutes later the first returning aircraft arrived over the task force. In the four hours and twenty minutes between launch and start of recovery, the task force had made good ninety miles, with two course changes to launch or land patrols. That distance was crucial: For some fliers it meant perhaps forty minutes of lifesaving air time. For others it was inadequate.

At least from the day before, Mitscher's staff contemplated the potential of a mass recovery after dark. Whether the admiral himself had laid plans or Arleigh Burke discussed it with Gus Widhelm, the contingency was anticipated. With advance notice of the air groups' return via radio relay aircraft and radar, the word went down from Lex's flag bridge: Prepare to illuminate the fleet. The hazard posed by Japanese submarines and land-based aircraft was acknowledged, accepted, and filed.

In the end, there was little controversy, if any. Task Force 58's striking arm was its aircraft; without bombers and fighters it was a hollow fleet.

The expected procedure was fairly routine: Carriers would show their running lights, masthead truck lights, and deck-edge glow lights. As an extra measure, Mitscher directed each task group flagship to shine its largest searchlight vertically as a visual beacon.

On *Hornet*'s flag bridge, Jocko Clark listened to the aviators' chatter. The high-pitched voices told him that nerves were getting ragged. A calamity was brewing, but he could help alleviate some of the concern. At 2030, without word from Mitscher, he ordered his carriers to turn on their brightest beams: the carbon arcs, big searchlights with lenses two feet across. He also had his cruisers shoot star shells. Whether by direction or enthusiasm, screening destroyers aimed their searchlights on the four flattops. From there, things quickly got out of hand. The night over Task Group 58.1 erupted into man-made illumination that blasted garish blotches against the black, moonless sky.

Nearing the briefed position of "point option," astonished pilots gawked at the task force, lit up like a carnival. After Jocko Clark's premature action, Pete Mitscher had given the word: "Turn on the lights."

That was the good news. The bad news: the illumination plan reflected more zeal than coordination. Pilots found chaos in all four task groups: Every ship was burning lights, including destroyers and cruisers. It was not always possible to distinguish carriers amid the chaos. Mitscher had overdone it: Pilots didn't need to see every ship in the task force—just those with flight decks. Air discipline began breaking down.

Many planes were flying on fumes. Desperately, pilots sought any carrier with a clear deck, seldom knowing whether they were approaching their ship—nor did they care. Landing signal officers with illuminated wands repeatedly had to wave off planes when two or even three crowded the final approach in "the groove."

Still, fuel shortage and deck crashes far exceeded the efforts of the Japanese, as some seventy carrier planes went into the water that night. Of all the air groups flying the mission, probably none was shorter on fuel than *Wasp*'s.

After hitting the oilers, Air Group 14 was keenly aware that it was not night-qualified. Jack Blitch had problems of his own, reporting: "The last thing I remember was being about twenty-five miles from the nearest searchlight. Apparently I passed out and crashed. I came to underwater with the cockpit closed. I do not remember getting out . . . but remember being on the wing and then getting in the rear cockpit to look for my gunner. He was not there, and, as the plane sank, I reached for the life raft, which was not in its holder, so I was only able to get out of the plane just as it was sinking."

Blitch spent a trying forty hours afloat before rescue by a floatplane from cruiser *Canberra*. One of Blitch's eleven other dive-bomber pilots who snagged a wire that night was the junior aviator, Ensign K. P. Fulton. His landing aboard *Enterprise* was the first time he attempted a night trap.

The VF-14 history distilled the factors into a terse account of "the mission beyond darkness."

"Now began the most dramatic part of the entire action as our planes commenced their long homeward trip, for by this time it was already beginning to get dark. Fighters, bombers, and torpedo planes joined up as best they could. . . . To those who remained aboard, that night will forever remain unforgettable as the planes came straggling back one by one to land aboard whichever carrier they could pick out of the darkness. Many of the bombers were forced to make water landings as they ran out of gas, some of them within sight of the fleet. . . . A number of planes crashed and burned within sight of the ships, and of course there were many barrier crashes and accidents aboard the carriers.

"Five of our fighter pilots made it safely back to the *Wasp*; four landed on the *Bunker Hill*; two each on the *Cabot* and *San Jacinto*; and one each on the *Enterprise* and *Monterey*. One of our pilots landed aboard the *San Jacinto* without the compass or generator operating in his plane, and with no signal officer, barrier or landing lights on the ship—and only three gallons of gas left!"

Dozens of other pilots were not so fortunate. However, they had the unseen eye of radar watching over them, as recalled by Lieutenant Junior Grade Richard Morland in *Lexington*:

"I particularly remember the two hours of night landings. Those of us in CIC were finding and trying to guide the planes in while keeping track of the approaching planes. I was on the dead-reckoning tracer. We plotted the approach of a plane through its IFF until it disappeared from the scope. Then we circled the spot, noted the latitude and longitude, and sent the information to the flag staff. Fortunately, they did not need it. The destroyers in the screen had the info on their radars and initiated rescue procedures. . . . With the floatplanes and PBMs that came in after daylight they did a remarkable job in rescuing the pilots. They deserve all the credit in the world."

Radar played another role in guiding aircraft home. Lieutenant Commander Richard E. Harmer commanded *Enterprise*'s night-fighter detachment. At 2050 he launched in his radar-equipped Corsair (which still was not cleared for daytime operations) and intercepted some errant fliers who otherwise may have died in the ocean. Searching through the moonless sky, Harmer found three groups of aircraft on his AIA radar set. In succession he led each formation to the task force, where the pilots were able to take their place in the churning confusion of each ship's traffic pattern. With ample fuel, Harmer remained airborne until most of the homing planes were back. He considered the two hours airborne that night more satisfying than the three times he downed Japanese aircraft.

Another night-flying shepherd was Pete Aurand, aloft in his *Bunker Hill* Hellcat. He had splashed a Jill for his third victory the previous afternoon, but, like Chick Harmer, he did more good in the frantic, horizonless sky over his own force. Following radio vectors, he used his AIA aerial intercept radar to locate small groups and singles, then led them home.

One of those saved was Torpedo 24's Warren Omark. Upon reaching what he considered point option, Omark found "nothing but pitch-black sky." With fuel running out, he needed a direct course to the task force, pronto. Deciding "to hell with radio silence," he called *Belleau Wood*, asking for a steer. He was surprised to get a reply from Lieutenant Jim Alston, CO of TorpRon 24, who was monitoring the proceedings in radar plot. Alston told Omark to hold on—a night fighter was being vectored to lead him back.

In a few minutes a dark silhouette appeared off Omark's wingtip, running lights aglow. The "VF(N)" pilot indicated by hand signals to follow him, and took the errant Avenger to Task Group 58.3, perhaps fifty miles away. Within sight of the spectacular light show, the fighter waggled its wings and the pilot gave the "kiss-off" signal.

Omark made a straight-in approach to the closest carrier. He dropped hook, wheels, and flaps, and motored up the big ship's wake, hoping that he still had a few gallons. His fuel gauge had long since registered empty. Settling in the groove, Omark was aware of another plane beside him: a hazardous situation and completely against regulations. He thought, "We may have a midair collision but I'm not giving up." The other pilot veered away, leaving the Avenger to attempt its chance at the deck.

The LSO gave Warren Omark the one cut he needed to have, and the TBF snagged a wire. When Omark climbed out he learned he was aboard *Lexington*. His two crewmen didn't care what ship they were on: They bent down and kissed the deck. The big Grumman had two gallons remaining.

Among the other homing *Belleau Wood* planes were the survivors of George Brown's division. Ben Tate and Bill Luton both successfully ditched their shot-up Avengers near the task force; Tate was rescued by the destroyer *Knapp*.

Other pilots were still airborne. Not bothering with call signs, anonymous voices crackled over the radio frequencies, either plaintive, angry, or boastful.

"I'm out of gas and going in the water."

"I got a hit on a carrier; that's about all."

"I'm going in the drink. . . . All I can say is that you're losing a god-damned good pilot!"

For those who did reach the task force, the peril was even greater. Tired, frightened aviators made mistakes. They landed with gun switches on; they failed to watch their altimeters and flew into the water. Others were greedy: They flew nonstandard patterns or crowded other planes out of the groove. Bringing off a water landing was trouble enough in daylight; nobody relished ditching on a moonless night.

Several pilots nursed damaged aircraft while others, like "Hal" Buell of VB-2, were wounded as well. One such was Lieutenant Clifford Fanning, a *Bataan* fighter pilot who had good cause to adore the "Grumman Iron Works." In two dogfights over *Zuikaku* he had gunned a Zeke, but another hit him solidly, sending splinters into his forehead and shoulder. Additionally, the F6F had lost partial use of its rudder and right aileron; a portion of the port flap was gone; and most of the starboard stabilizer had failed. Nevertheless, without an operable radio or compass, Fanning continued boring east at 140 knots, tacking on to a straggling formation. He was all right for the moment, but wondered how he could get aboard with his shot-up fighter when the controls grew lax at ninety-eight knots.

Anticipating the nocturnal recovery, task force LSOs made preparations. They traded their daytime attire (sometimes floral swim trunks or skivvy shorts) for night operations: flight suits with fluorescent stripes. The paddles already had fluorescent panels, but some LSOs preferred lighted wands. They were heavier than paddles but much more visible to pilots slanting down the groove toward the ramp.

The two-hour recovery resembled nothing before or since. One of the best descriptions came from Pete Aurand, who likened it to "a combined Hollywood premiere, Chinese New Year, and Fourth of July."

In addition to the man-made light show, nature provided one as well. About sixty miles south a well-developed thunderstorm strobed the sky with lightning flashes. Some pilots wandered in that direction, prompting Harmer and Aurand to overtake them and fetch them home.

Landings began at 2045 and continued until about 2252. By that time, everybody was home who was coming home. Destroyers turned their biggest searchlights on the water, relentlessly scanning for the source of blinkered messages and whistles. The impetus was urgent: Scores of men were in peril of being drowned, lost, or worse.

Task Group 58.1: *Hornet, Yorktown, Bataan, Belleau Wood*

A *YORKTOWN* PILOT WAS HEARD calling "Coal Base" requesting a vector to "the Fighting Lady." He was told, "Land on any base."

In the confusion, some pilots asked seemingly peculiar questions. A *Yorktown* flier snagged a wire, lurched to a halt, and asked a deckhand which ship he was on. "The *Yorktown!*" he was told.

On *Yorktown*'s platform, LSO Dick Tripp (of the famous floral swim trunks) had his hands full. At one point, two and even three planes were responding to his signals. The pattern became exceedingly crowded, and the winner wasn't always the pilot closest to the ramp. Some just bulled their way into the groove, letting the others take their chances. Tripp logged a virtuoso performance that night, intentionally cutting two Helldivers simultaneously: the first onto the one wire, the other onto the eight wire. It wouldn't have been possible without the slavishly devoted "deck apes," the plane handlers who pushed several tons of airplane up the deck.

Fighting 1's Lieutenant Junior Grade M. M. Tomme Jr. got the cut from Tripp and caught a wire. With his tailhook disengaged, "Mad Dog" added power and taxied up the deck to clear the landing area. Behind him a *Hornet* fighter pilot failed to see Tripp's "no hook" signal or the violent wave-off. With no hook to stop him, the VF-2 pilot hit the deck and bounced over the barrier. Seven tons of Hellcat dropped onto Tomme, killing him and fouling the deck. *Yorktown* pulled the plug, dousing lights while deckhands worked frantically to clear the wreckage. Meanwhile, more planes went in the water.

Only about 150 of the planes that reached the Mobile Fleet snagged an arresting wire that night, and barely half "trapped" on their own flight deck. *Yorktown*'s homing brood was even more varied: She recovered ten of her own "chicks" plus fifteen more from six other carriers.

One example was Jig Ramage, who navigated back to the task force with the help of his radioman-gunner, ARM1c David Cawley, who prepared for the worst:

"I concentrated on our radar, which had a maximum range of seventy-five miles. Our ship could send a homing signal that we could receive on the radar. At ninety miles this signal began to show clearly in the pitch dark. We adjusted course only a few degrees and continued on. It was about 2030, and lots of planes were going in the water, out of gas. The radio was chaos."

Ramage and Cawley went over their ditching checklist, agreeing to fly as long as fuel permitted. Cawley grabbed his one-cell flashlight and hung it around his neck, then stripped to his shorts, socks, and helmet. Finally, he loaded his .38 revolver with tracers and put on his shoulder holster.

"Forty-one Sniper" flew directly to the Big E, which was running lights and landing planes. Cawley continued, "We made a standard squadron breakup and entered the landing pattern. About this time there was a bad crash on the *Enterprise*'s deck. The skipper called and advised our squadron of the problem and told them to land on any base.

"Our radar was still on and all the ships appeared clearly. If they were carriers, I could even see if there were planes in their landing pattern. We picked a big one about two miles away and went over to land. There was no one in her pattern and we entered. As we slowed to approach attitude in our SBD, the big radial engine blocked most all of the skipper's forward view. He pulled down his goggles, opened the canopy, and stuck his head way out to the port side. As he did, everything went dark. He had the polarized lenses; in his effort to get everyone briefed and started this day, he forgot to change to clear lenses. The skipper asked me to help so I read the LSO signals; he made a perfect approach and we got the cut. As the power came off, we started a beautiful three-point drop and I thought we were falling into a black hole. The deck was so big it seemed we had to fall three times normal to get down to it. We had landed on the new *Yorktown*."

It was an extremely close call. Ramage's VB-10 pilots averaged four gallons remaining: perhaps five minutes' flight time. *Lexington*'s SBD squadron fared somewhat better, as VB-16 returnees had roughly twenty gallons in their last tank.

Amid the concern for returning errant aviators to their rightful ships, paperwork suffered. Aboard *Yorktown*, Chief of Staff John Crommelin eagerly sifted through pilots' reports. Seeing Jig Dog Ramage in the ready room, he welcomed his former shipmate. "I think we got 'em all," the Alabaman enthused. Ramage shook his head. "I don't think so, Captain."

Jig Ramage never was debriefed, either aboard *Yorktown* or upon return to *Enterprise*. Consequently, he felt that an accurate assessment of the mission was not compiled.

Also in Clark's group, light carrier *Bataan* barely got into the action. Two *Yorktown* "chicks" landed; the second crashed into the barrier. *Bataan*'s deck crew scrambled to disentangle the mashed Hellcat but it was too big a job. No more planes trapped aboard her that night.

For ten frantic minutes only 58.1 was illuminated. Not surprisingly, many fuel-shy pilots diverted there rather than risk the dark saltwater miles to their own ships. Therefore, at 2040 Mitscher directed each task group to have one destroyer shine its searchlight vertically. In a few minutes the entire force was running illuminated and firing star shells. Navigation was no longer a problem.

Ship identification was.

Pilots became desperate. Some made passes at anything showing a light, including destroyers' truck lights.

Belleau Wood's senior LSO was Lieutenant John A. Harper, known to all aboard as "Harpo." He recalled, "It was a very dark, moonless night with the inky sea showing no whitecaps in the light breeze, and the wake fluorescence was at a minimum. The strike against the Japanese fleet, launched over five hours earlier, would be returning with very low fuel state."

Harper left VT-24's ready room, where a large banner remained: "Get the carriers!" Emerging onto the flight deck, he was startled at what he found. "Whoa! This looks like a big city at night!" Every ship in the task group was running illuminated, with carriers' flight decks spotlighted. Harper and his friends realized the risk: "We're still only a couple hundred miles from Jap bases on Guam."

Harper zipped up his "zoot suit" with the fluorescent stripes, then pulled a pair of filtered goggles over his eyes. One of his assistants stood by with the ultraviolet "black light" that would make him more visible to pilots approaching the stern.

Hornet and *Yorktown* were already landing aircraft, prompting *Belleau Wood*'s crew to wonder "where the hell our guys are." At length a Hellcat appeared broad on the starboard beam, rolled left, and proceeded around the racecourse pattern. As the fighter turned crosswind, Harper's crew began the litany:

"You've got a clear deck, sir. Barriers up."

Harper pantomimed the circular "fast" signal. Otherwise the plane's landing lights looked good: proper attitude. The stern-mounted spotlight illuminated the F6's belly, permitting the spotter to run his verbal checklist. "Gear, flaps, hook, all down, sir."

Harper's paddles slashed downward in the "cut" signal: right hand to the throat, left hand across the body. The pilot chopped throttle and allowed the Hellcat to scrunch onto the deck, snagging a wire and lurching to a halt. A teenage "hook runner" dashed from the catwalk to disengage the tailhook so the pilot could taxi forward. Shortly Harper brought another Hellcat aboard; it too taxied forward over the lowered woven-steel barriers, which then popped back upright.

The third plane into the pattern made a straight-in approach. "This SOB must be real low on fuel," a sailor murmured.

Harper picked up the homing pilot with an initial Roger signal—arms extended outward from the shoulders. The plane drifted upward and the LSO responded with a "high." Harper was perplexed: The proper response to a high approach was to reduce power and settle onto the glide slope.

The assistant LSO, Lieutenant Junior Grade Walter Wujcik, had a chilling thought: "Japs have opposite signals. I said we're too close to Guam to turn the lights on!"

Harper had just given a "low" and watched the plane settle. That did it: "Gimme the searchlight . . . now!"

The white light pierced the gloom, showing a rust-red *hinomaru* on the wings. Wujcik exclaimed, "Look at those meatballs! Looks like a Val!"

Instantly *Belleau Wood* vanished into darkness. Every light was extinguished as the loudspeaker and klaxon competed in a *bong-bong* and "Man your battle stations!"

The stranger's alien engine nose passed overhead and disappeared into the black sky. Only later did the Americans learn that the Imperial Navy had no LSOs; the assumption that Japan used British landing signals was invalid, since imperial carriers used visual landing lights rather than paddles.

When it was over, *Belleau Wood* sorted out the chicks in her nest. She had launched sixteen planes, and "Harpo" Harper gave the cut to just three of her own. Some of the deficit was made up by three Grummans from *Lexington*, *Hornet*, and *Yorktown*.

Task Group 58.2: *Bunker Hill*, *Wasp*, *Cabot*, *Monterey*

WASP LANDED PLANES FOR TWO HOURS, interrupted by two crashes that stopped recovery due to a fouled deck. Even so, she snagged five VF-14 Hellcats and nine other planes from *Lexington*, *Enterprise*, *Bataan*, *Yorktown*, and *Bunker Hill*. Only one of the latter was even from Montgomery's task group.

Included in the visiting birdmen was Lieutenant Cliff Fanning of VF-50. After coaxing his crippled Hellcat back from two dogfights over the Mobile Fleet, he made repeated approaches at *Wasp*. Either the pattern was choked, the deck was fouled, or he got a wave-off on six consecutive passes. Finally, it was a matter of lucky number seven before he got aboard. However, he was high at the ramp when he got the "cut" signal, and he piled into the barrier. The battered F6 tumbled inverted, the engine mounts failed, and the R2800 was torn off. The wreck slammed to a stop upside down, requiring *Wasp*'s mobile crane to lift the remains. All the while, Fanning remained strapped in his seat, looking outside into a harshly lit, upside-down world. When he finally had room to exit, he released his seat belt and fell on his head, adding to the combat injuries.

Among the officers watching the fascinating recovery was thirty-year-old Lieutenant Commander Gerald Ford, *Monterey*'s assistant navigator. He recalled the tension in the ship following launch of four Avengers at 1613:

"The wait was long, as it was 2030 that night before the formation turned into the wind to recover the returning planes. No one in task Force 58 will ever forget the spectacle of those night landings that were seldom undertaken. All blackout measures were suspended. The task force ships were lighted almost as if they were peacetime ocean liners. The carriers had flight deck, landing signal, and glow lights burning. A destroyer in each task group had her twenty-four-inch searchlight pointed up into the clouds to serve as a beacon, while others fired star shells periodically for the same purpose. From time to time a horrid illumination was afforded by the yellow flames of planes crashing into the water and catching fire.

"Aircraft landings on a carrier are always exciting, but that night to stand on the bridge, watching pilots bring their planes to the deck in the worst of conditions, was an unforgettable experience.

"Three of *Monterey*'s planes were gotten safely aboard. . . . The plane piloted by Ensign R. W. Burnett was seen in the landing circle, but failed to come in."

Ensign "Pappy" Burnett's missing crew included radioman ARM2c W. E. Trego and gunner AOM2c A. J. Rogers. With three other *Monterey* Avengers they attacked *Chiyoda* and sustained flak damage but made it back to Task Group 58.2. However, after failed attempts to find a clear deck, their TBM's Wright engine quit cold—out of fuel. Allen Rogers recalled what happened next:

"The landing wasn't particularly hard, and we had only minor problems exiting. Previously, I had returned to my turret, so I jettisoned the escape hatch, flipped the buckle of my seat belt, and attempted to crawl out through the hatch. However, we were flying a 'borrowed' aircraft, and the assigned crew had neglected to adjust the belts . . . so I sat back down and methodically pulled on the belt until the overlap was completely out through the buckle. Then I exited onto the port wing.

"At the time it seemed as if my difficulty in getting free of that damn belt had taken an eternity. But I'm sure it didn't take more than five or six seconds. Even so, knowing that a ditched TBM usually floats for only forty-five to sixty seconds, I was in sort of a hurry.

"By this time Pappy had left the cockpit and was on the starboard wing. We removed the life raft stowage plates, he pulling while I pushed the three-man raft out on the wing. I then scrambled over the canopy and looked around for Trego. He had jettisoned the main tunnel hatch and was peering out at Pappy and me.

"Pappy was attempting to inflate the raft and, after a moment, I told him the aircraft was settling by the nose and I thought we should get clear. He agreed and tossed the rolled-up raft into the water and jumped after it. I followed him and Trego joined us. As we swam clear the plane's tail rose high in the air, paused for a moment, and slipped beneath the waves.

"The destroyer *Owen*, which we learned had been the object of our last two landing approaches, had hove to about a hundred yards away with a searchlight on us the whole time."

Bunker Hill's two-acre flight deck was chaos in a small space. As deck crews slaved away, clearing the way for homing planes, a *Hornet* Helldiver drove up the groove, obviously intent on landing. The LSO gave a frantic wave-off, and his assistant even fired a warning flare. To no avail: the "Beast" dropped onto the deck, lurched violently, and tumbled tail over nose. The propeller slashed into the Douglas fir planks and remained embedded in mute tribute to the pilot's folly. While sailors grappled with the wreckage, a *Cabot* TBF turned on final approach. Like the SB2C, it ignored the vigorous wave-off and smacked down off center. The starboard wing snagged on a gun turret, careening the Avenger into the Helldiver. The impact knocked down six men trying to move the '2C, killing three, including *Bunker Hill*'s air officer, Commander Wayne O. "Wingover" Smith.

All the Helldiver squadrons were hard hit, but none so badly as Bombing 8. Twelve had launched; one returned. Jim Arbes lost two planes over the Mobile Fleet and put nine in the water, out of fuel.

Meanwhile, the same meandering Val that alarmed *Belleau Wood*'s LSOs turned up in 58.2. Reportedly he made two approaches at *Bunker Hill*, then sought other sport elsewhere.

Task Group 58.3: *Lexington*, *Enterprise*, *Princeton*, *San Jacinto*

ALTERNATING BETWEEN *LEXINGTON*'S BRIDGE and radar plot, Commander Jimmie Thach monitored the building crisis. A meticulous observer, he noted procedures, errors, and questions in his ever-present notebook for later dissection. He had established a good rapport with Burke and opined that in the future, concern over lights would be misplaced when the enemy had radar comparable to America's. In that case, he advocated lighting carrier decks "like an airport runway."

Mitscher ordered the interval between task groups extended to fifteen miles, almost twice the usual distance. On a moonless night with a couple of hundred homing aircraft, the black sky was going to be crowded enough without risking overlapping traffic patterns.

Lexington recovered twenty-one aircraft that night. The air department found only nine of its own planes among them.

Approaching *Lexington*'s ramp, *Hornet*'s Hal Buell fought for control of his stricken "Beast." His right landing flap was partly shot away, ruining the '2C's stability, and his back was still bleeding from the shell fragment. On the ragged edge of control, he anticipated the LSO's "cut" signal when he received a last-second wave-off: fouled deck. But "with no power reserve and staggering just above the stall . . . to turn away would put me into the ramp, the 'spud locker,' or an uncontrolled spiral dive into the ocean."

With nowhere to go but down, Buell chopped his throttle and settled straight ahead. He probably would have been safe but for a phenomenon called "hook skip." His tailhook bounced over the arresting wires, and the impact of his landing gear with the deck bounded him over two woven-steel barriers. The wounded Helldiver impaled itself on the third barrier, broke loose, and smashed into the plane just ahead. It was the SB2C of Buell's wingman, Lieutenant Junior Grade David Stear. Buell's wreckage destroyed the tail of Stear's plane, killing the gunner, ARM2c Winifred E. Redman. Flying debris also killed a sailor in the catwalk.

Sick with grief, still in pain from his untreated wound, Buell was called to flag country. There he was grilled by Arleigh Burke and Gus Widhelm until Mitscher intervened. "Gentlemen, you have questioned the lieutenant enough." The admiral ordered Buell to sick bay for treatment, brandy, and a bunk. Buell wound up rooming with a VF-16 pilot: Lieutenant Jim Seybert, a former high school friend from Ottuma, Iowa.

Meanwhile, *Enterprise* air group commander Killer Kane went around after a wave-off for a fouled deck and flew into the water. "Everybody else ran out of ideas," he quipped. "I just ran out of altitude." It was his second dunking in a week.

The madhouse scramble to get aboard any carrier turned most formations to hash. For example, that night *Enterprise's* returning planes were spread among five other carriers. In return, the Big E recovered seventeen planes from *Lexington, Hornet, Yorktown, Wasp,* and *Bunker Hill.* Ten were from other task groups. Though one Reaper Hellcat was shot down and five other Big E planes made water landings, all the fliers were recovered.

Enterprise was always blessed with gifted LSOs, dating to Lieutenant Robin Lindsey's virtuoso performance after the sanguinary Santa Cruz battle in October 1942. With the rear elevator jammed in the down position, Lindsey cut plane after plane onto the three wire, then the two wire. By the time he cut the last Wildcat, only the one wire was available. Lieutenant Swede Vejtasa—perhaps the finest carrier aviator afloat—believed in Lindsey's eloquent paddles and snagged the cable. After that, the deck was "locked."

Inheritor of Lindsey's mantle was Lieutenant Horace "Hod" Proulx, a former SBD pilot who "forgave a lot of bad approaches that night." Intervals were cut thin, then sliced some more. Instead of the normal twenty to thirty seconds between planes, Proulx gave two cuts fifteen seconds apart.

Then it got closer.

The notorious "double cut" was the bugaboo of LSOs: It was more theoretical than factual, but two pilots eager to get aboard might crowd the pattern, responding to the same cut. It nearly happened on the Big E when Proulx landed a Hellcat that snagged the five wire— next to last up the deck. As the grateful pilot powered out of "the gear" his hook reengaged, bringing him to a halt. Meanwhile, Proulx gave a Roger to Lieutenant Junior Grade Cecil R. Mester, who had splashed on launch nine days before. This night his division leader had just ditched astern, but Mester had fuel for one pass at the deck. Shaving seconds, Proulx judged it nicely, cutting the SBD onto the three wire. Lieutenant Walter L. Chewning Jr., the arresting gear officer, was helping disengage the F6's hook when he looked back and saw Mester's prop churning several feet away. Chewning had survived two planes in the wires simultaneously.

Amid the confusion and mayhem were vignettes of humor. A Torpedo 10 pilot, Lieutenant C. B. Collins, made a pass at the first ship he saw: It turned out to be a destroyer. Next he identified the Big E's distinctive funnel and turned into the groove. Sucking fumes, he was "lookin' good" when the deck became fouled. With his last pints of fuel "Crossbow" Collins set down alongside the destroyer *Dortsch*; it was a good ditching.

Collins and his two aircrewmen scrambled out of the sinking Avenger. His turret gunner opened the port-side life raft access while Collins retrieved the emergency kit from starboard. Both men pulled, to no avail. Neither the raft nor the survival pack would budge. Finally the fliers discovered the problem. "There was a line connecting the two, and a tug-of-war took place until I finally gave in and pushed the emergency kit back through the compartment," Collins confessed. Hauled aboard the "tin can," they watched the big Grumman submerge with its white dorsal light still burning.

When *Lexington*'s Cook Cleland landed aboard *Enterprise*, a director urged him to get out of the shot-up Dauntless: "We've got to push this thing overboard!" Cleland and old Number 39 had been through too much together for that. He reached for his pistol: "This airplane stays aboard." He won the argument.

After the combat near the Mobile Fleet, *Lexington* ace Alex Vraciu found himself alone. He had been so preoccupied in the dogfight that he never caught sight of the enemy force. He came across a strange TBF limping along with its bomb bay doors open and escorted it to a circle of Helldivers. Then he set course easterly, musing whether the conventional wisdom would be disproved: "Fighter pilots can't navigate." He nursed his fuel, tweaking the throttle and mixture settings for "max conserve" as the legendary Lieutenant Commander Butch O'Hare had taught him.

The upcoming landing did not bother Vraciu as much as some pilots. He had not logged a night trap in more than six months, but few fliers had any nocturnal landings in their logbooks.

Nearing the expected return point, Vraciu picked up "dit-dah" in his earphones. It was the Morse code letter *A* (Able), telling him he was in the right quadrant for an approach to the flagship. Once over the force, however, he set aside any early intentions of landing. "It was a mess," he recalled. "Planes were everywhere, every ship was lit up, and some carriers had lost position. They had overlapping traffic patterns; the upwind leg of some carriers seemed to merge with the downwind leg of others. I don't know why there weren't any collisions." Casting a longing glance at his fuel gauge, the former premed student decided to bide his time, letting the short-legged planes get aboard first. Finally he dropped into *Lexington*'s pattern but got a fouled-deck wave-off and slid over "next door." Flying *Enterprise*'s pattern—he recognized the distinctive funnel—he got the cut.

One of *Lexington*'s missing was Ensign John F. Caffey of VB-16. Waved off from Lady Lex, Caffey resigned himself to getting wet. He shucked his parachute harness and advised his gunner to prepare for a ditching. Moments later AOM2c Leo Estrada felt the Dauntless lurch to a stop, so he jumped overboard. He was astonished to find himself standing upright, facing an equally surprised deckhand. Estrada played it cool, quipping, "This water landing business isn't as bad as I thought it'd be!"

Caffey appeared, explaining that he had seen a chance to get aboard *San Jacinto* and took it. But the CVL sailors were unacquainted with the stiff-winged Dauntless. When told to fold his wings, Caffey replied, "This is an SBD." The angry retort: "God damn it, fold 'em anyway!"

Shortly thereafter another mysterious aircraft appeared. "San Jac's" LSO reported waving off a strange plane that neglected to lower its tailhook. It was a Val. After the third abortive attempt the wandering Japanese disappeared into the gloom.

Other ships in 58.3 reported the Val, while at least one called a warning of a Zeke overhead, running red lights. Destroyer *Caperton* identified a Val four minutes after the initial sighting, and so did an *Enterprise* pilot trying to get aboard. Apparently no Japanese documentation exists, but competent observers on four ships plus an airborne aviator reported the same thing.

Apparently there was just one Aichi pilot in the pattern, but he made landing approaches on four carriers in three task groups, including three at *San Jacinto* alone. Men on the LSO platform wondered why the stranger hadn't lowered his tailhook. Finished with "San Jac," he flew through *Enterprise*'s traffic pattern en route to his ultimate destination. Judging by radio logs, the amazing Aichi spent some twenty-five minutes over the task force. The meandering Val disappeared around 2245, but no night fighter engaged it.

Presumably one highly amused Aichi pilot enjoyed bragging rights on Guam that night.

Torpedo 10's Lieutenant Junior Grade Ernest J. Lawton Jr. called the landing spectacle "a Mardi Gras setting fantastically out of place midway between the Marianas and the Philippines." Like nearly half the homing pilots that night, he snagged a wire on a ship other than his own—in this case, *Princeton*.

Even while the frantic recovery was under way, debriefs were held in a catch-as-catch-can fashion. Mitscher and Burke were eager for firsthand reports from returning aviators, and the staff tried to make sense of the partial, confused accounts: some contradictory, some almost incoherent. Therefore, strike photos were treasured. Lieutenant Junior Grade William A. Schroeder Jr., a *Yorktown* fighter pilot, had flown a camera-equipped F6F-3P, and by happy coincidence he landed aboard *Lexington*. There, awaiting his film to be developed, he received three or four small bottles of medicinal brandy from the flight surgeon. By the time the visiting flier was escorted into Mitscher's presence to view the photos, "Tank" Schroeder was so wobbly that the admiral put a paternal arm around him. Mitscher finally turned to a staffer: "You know, I think this young man could stand a cup of coffee." Years later Schroeder said with a grin, "That just made me a wide-awake drunk!"

As decks filled up and elevators failed to keep pace with the traffic, more wave-offs ensued. The night sky was alive with the earsplitting moan of high-performance engines, props in low pitch, as one pilot after another went around.

Too often there were crashes. Some pilots ignored wave-offs and landed anyway. Frequently they struck the previous aircraft that had not yet taxied forward. In all, six sailors were killed and more injured; everybody's nerves were jagged.

Probably the last man down was *Yorktown*'s CAG, Commander Jim Peters. He had flown the mission with two extra drop tanks beneath his wings, extending his endurance beyond six hours. Orbiting overhead the churning traffic patterns, occasionally caught in random searchlight beams, he surveyed the chaos and bided his time.

Finally the sky grew quiet. CAG Peters dropped into the Fighting Lady's landing pattern, lowered hook, wheels, and flaps, and flew a Roger pass. Everybody who was coming home was down.

In pondering the shambles of the nighttime recovery, *Hornet*'s Captain Bill Sample commented, "I have been flying for something over twenty-one years now, and I've never seen such a hectic night before, and hope to never see one again. Our planes were crashing through the barriers almost as rapidly as we could get them repaired and up again; going into the catwalks, and landing in the water around us. Our ships were winding in and out in quest of an elusive wind or picking up survivors, with the urgency of time pressing on us throughout the entire operation, as every minute might mean another plane out of gas and into the water; it was certainly a weird, confusing, and most hectic experience."

Search and Rescue

EXCLUDING ABORTS, SOME 226 PLANES had launched on the afternoon of the twentieth; the next morning 140 of those were back aboard. The missing 172 pilots and aircrew were strewn over a large tract of ocean, but search and rescue efforts began before sunup.

Some two dozen ships, including four light cruisers, picked up about ninety pilots and aircrewmen that night. Fliers fished from the water were greeted aboard the "blackshoe" vessels as conquering heroes. One squadron recorded the rescue of a junior officer, saying, "They liquored him up, swiping most of his flight gear. The hospitality was high-class throughout the force that night, except for the souvenir hunters." Some fliers returned to their ships minus flight suits, pistols, knives, and even wallet photos. Nobody minded.

However, nearly as many fliers remained missing, with only rubber rafts or life preservers between them and watery eternity. Consequently, Montgomery's 58.2 detached Destroyer Division 104 to search along the strike group's westerly track. The four ships did well, rescuing ten fliers.

Destroyer skippers reported their experience, noting that they obtained best results with aircraft orbiting downed fliers and guiding ships to the position. In turn, pilots said that the bright-green dye marker made the search much easier, especially when cresting waves could obscure even three-man yellow rafts. A Hellcat pilot's one-man raft could easily be missed: a tiny yellow spot adrift on a slate-gray sea.

Task Force 58 aircrews reported sixty-seven Japanese planes destroyed or damaged over the Mobile Fleet, one-third by Air Group Sixteen. One Zeke brought Alex Vraciu's tally to nineteen, a figure that would remain tops in the Navy for another three months. In all, the Americans claimed twenty-seven shoot-downs, though Morison computed the number at forty, while the Japanese figure of sixty-five undoubtedly was a lump sum including operational losses. Obviously, few of the survivors got back aboard.

Falcon Flies Away

HIYO WAS SINKING.

Four hundred miles northwest of *Shokaku* and *Taiho*'s crypt in the abyss, "Wandering Falcon" reeled from the inrushing water. Captain Toshiyuki Yokoi wandered dazed and in pain, having seen his navigator torn to pieces by a bomb—the same explosion that blinded Yokoi's left eye.

Meanwhile, the Imperial Navy's unyielding ritual was played out. A staff officer removed the gilt-edged portraits of the emperor and empress and lowered the imperial battle flag; both were transferred to a destroyer. The photo portraits would be returned to storage and presumably reissued to a new ship in the weeks or months ahead.

With the ceremonial requirements observed, the wounded were settled in rafts and eased over the side. Survivors mustered on the flight deck in preparation to abandon ship. Despite his painful wounds,

Yokoi delivered a short speech in parting. The sailors responded with "*Banzai!* Ten thousand years' life to the emperor!"

Hiyo's abandon-ship drill was orderly. As the last men filed past, someone sang the old refrain, "Seafaring may we lay our bodies deep. . . ." Yokoi heard the words and mused, "Now is the end. And the beginning?"

A few diehards were not ready to concede the obvious. At least one ensign drew his sword and stood before a group of antiaircraft gunners who, not unreasonably, concluded that their obligation ended when the Pacific Ocean reached their ankles. The earnest young officer ordered the sailors to sing *Umi-Yukaba*, the battle anthem glorifying death for the emperor. The men accelerated the usual two-four tempo, finished the last refrain, and made to rush past the ensign. Dissatisfied, he insisted upon a rendition of "The Naval March," which was interrupted when inrushing water rose to knee level. At that point the songfest ended.

Yokoi watched through his right eye as the last officers went over the side. He saluted each in turn, then found an empty ammo box. He sat down, contemplating his 126 days in command, and waited to die.

At 1926—barely two hours after being torpedoed—a violent explosion rent the ship. It was the same lethal process that had slain *Taiho* and *Shokaku*: Gasoline vapors ignited within the hull. More than twenty thousand tons of steel began settling with frightening speed.

Sailors floating nearby heard *Hiyo*'s death throes. Bulkheads collapsed with a high, eerie screeching followed by "a great sigh of escaping air." Yokoi went under, his box pitched upward before the final plunge. Debris, crates, wrecked gear, and corpses rolled down the deck. Yokoi was aware of a sharp pain, swirling water . . . then nothing.

In six minutes, HIMJS *Hiyo* had dropped from sight. The Mobile Fleet had lost three prime carriers in less than thirty hours.

A couple miles away, two Americans watched *Hiyo*'s demise. AMM2c George H. Platz and ARM2c Ellis C. Babcock had bailed out when George Brown's TBF was set afire during the run-in. Now they observed the fruits of VT-24's sacrifice.

An underwater eruption rocked the lifeboats and rafts. Men in one of the boats saw an officer ejected to the surface. They pulled him aboard. He rolled onto his back, opened his eyes, and saw only stars overhead. Toshiyuki Yokoi had been forcefully ejected back into the world of men. Years later he mused, "To an old-fashioned sea captain like myself, it was my duty to go down with my ship. But what was I to do when it sent me back up?"

While Japanese sailors mourned their loss, American bluejackets marveled at so many fliers' salvation. Aboard *Hornet*, some "Stingers" attributed their good fortune to divine intervention. Certainly the ship's "sky pilots" worked overtime that night. *Hornet*'s Catholic chaplain, aboard for most of the war, was Lieutenant Commander Terrence Patrick McMahon. Immensely popular, he forged a formidable alliance with his Protestant counterpart, Lieutenant Allan A. Zaun.

Said the skipper, Captain Bill Sample: "Some of you will say that this was certainly a stroke of Providence, or that Lady Luck was really smiling on us that night. Well, she certainly was, but I would like to put it another way. I would like to say that the Lord is with this ship. With the Lord on our side, and the *Hornet* fighting spirit, there is nothing that can stop us. And so . . . I hope that we will have the opportunity of letting the Japs feel the sting of the *Hornet* again. I hope that we can keep letting them feel that sting until the day that they can no longer do harm to anyone; then we can go back and enjoy our homes the way we would like to. Until that day, I hope that we will be in there slugging as long as there is a Jap to be slugged."

Nobody was more dedicated to destruction of the Japanese empire than Marc Mitscher. Late that night off Saipan, it was said that he did what no Japanese or German admiral would have done: risked his ships on behalf of his fliers. True or not, only the U.S. Navy was ever placed in such a position, and hundreds of pilots and gunners lived to sing Marc Mitscher's praises.

Searchers in the Dark (June 21)

DURING THE WEE HOURS OF JUNE 21 a VP-16 Mariner tracked oil slicks leading to many ships westering through the darkness. The plot was about seven hundred miles west of Saipan. In Task Force 58, deckload strikes were fueled and armed in case the range closed.

However, the day did not go well for the PBMs. One was misidentified by U.S. destroyers, who, not reading the IFF code, opened fire. The Mariner was lost with all eleven men.

While the mayhem of recovering the strike unwound, plans were proceeding for another nocturnal mission. Not surprisingly, it involved Bill Martin, the *Enterprise* night-flying evangelist commanding Torpedo Ten.

In the first hour of June 21, Martin huddled with his available Avenger pilots, plotting a four-plane torpedo attack on the fleeing Japanese. As originally planned, the mission was to launch at 2200, but the prolonged recovery scotched that. Consequently, the schedule was rolled back to 0100. Two TBFs were already on the catapults, launch bridles affixed to the shuttle that would slingshot them into the moonless sky. They were the pathfinders who would locate Ozawa on radar and guide the attackers to the target. A night torpedo attack on a fleet at sea had never been attempted, which was exactly the reason that Bill Martin wanted to do it.

As Martin was about to conclude his briefing, word arrived from flag plot. The strike was scrubbed. Mitscher felt that the risks outweighed the potential benefit, and with so many splashes that night, he wanted to conserve his strength. Years later Vice Admiral Martin admitted that it was the greatest disappointment of his career. In the 1960s, any number of officers were capable of commanding the Sixth Fleet, but only a handful were ever positioned to torpedo enemy capital ships maneuvering at sea on a moonless night.

The stand-down was met with ambivalence. The aircrews assigned to the strike knew the odds, but they also knew their business and believed in their skipper. However, there was still work to be done that night. The daylight search team that had found Ozawa was dispatched to find him again. Lieutenant Bob Nelson was playing acey-deucy in ready room six when he got the word. At 0230 his and Jim Moore's crews manned the waiting Avengers and were flung off the Big E's deck, armed with a patrol plane contact report.

Tracking westward into the dark, the VT-10 team searched for three hours along the westerly course. In the cramped interior of each Grumman the radioman fine-tuned his radar set, looking for the green phosphor trace.

The blips appeared at 0530. ARM1c Thomas T. Watts in Jim Moore's plane was first to note the glowing phosphors. The pilots dropped smoke lights to verify the wind drift, then tweaked their navigation. They placed Ozawa 252 nautical miles from *Enterprise*'s 0300 position.

Nelson and Moore had ample time to compose their contact reports. Without fear of enemy night fighters, the Avengers used darkness and cloud cover to snoop the Mobile Fleet, practically counting each ship. There were four task groups arrayed in a diamond formation, steaming west.

The snoopers did not go undetected. Alert Japanese skywatchers pointed out the blunt Grumman silhouettes, and Ozawa's ships took action. Destroyers began making smoke, while gunners opened an optimistic long-range fire at the Big E's fliers. One battleship even chimed in with its concussive heavy guns, to no effect.

Nelson and Moore remained on station for an hour, broadcasting details of Ozawa's strength, course, and speed. They got close enough to confirm the identities of *Yamato* and *Musashi*, which bore a pleasant resemblance to the ONI recognition sheets. However, they concluded there was no point trying to identify the light carriers, which looked alike, especially in the dark.

Periodically the Avengers passed updated information to an airborne radio relay team orbiting far to the east, ensuring that the reports were passed to the task force in legible form.

In Task Force 58, the men were exhausted, spent. That morning, Wednesday the twenty-first, it seemed as if the smaller ships were carpeted with bodies. The "hot bunk" system made for maximum efficiency of limited space, permitting two or even three men to share the same "racks" in sequence. Now, after forty-eight hours of general quarters alarms, repeated air attacks, and the chaos of the night recovery, sailors slumped in slumber wherever there was space. From Arleigh Burke's perspective, "unless performing indispensable duties, [they] simply went to sleep. They fell asleep on decks, on tops of ammunition lockers, in corners or passageways—wherever they found a little empty space."

Regardless of the difficulty in keeping their eyelids open, thousands of other men still had work to do, both routine and exceptional. Among the latter were Hellcat pilots from each task group, bombed up with five-hundred-pounders and launched by 0615. They were briefed to fly three hundred miles and attack any Japanese ship—crippled or otherwise—they found along their track.

A good part of the twenty-first was spent sorting out the mixed-up air groups. Some carriers had nearly empty decks and hangars, while others were chockablock with the overage. Much of the morning involved refueling aircraft and getting them headed for their own ships. Some squadrons had pilots on half a dozen carriers. But even the mundane task of returning errant chicks to their "bird farms" had routine risk.

In the process of launch and recovery that morning, some squadrons staged mini reunions in the air. Three of VF-16's Airedales unexpectedly came across one another: Lieutenant Henry M. Kosciusko didn't know that his wingman, Ensign William J. Seyfferle, was still alive until *Lexington*'s number thirty-three Hellcat joined him over the task group. Grinning broadly, they exchanged exaggerated gestures of relief. Then another familiar F6 appeared with Alex Vraciu, just launched from *Enterprise*. Flashing thumbs-up, he joined them overhead *Lexington*, happy to see two other survivors from his squadron.

As senior member of the trio, Kosciusko led the fighters into the pattern and trapped on his first pass. He was climbing from the cockpit when he heard the warbling notes of the crash alarm. Looking astern, the Floridian saw Vraciu turning away from the groove. Beneath him the water was churned white with an expanding patch of brilliant green dye marker. Bill Seyfferle apparently had not dropped his fully fueled belly tank and turned too tight in lining up with the deck. His Hellcat stalled and went straight in; the twenty-two-year-old flier left a widow in Cincinnati.

Fighting 16 had launched nine planes and got seven back. When the pilots finally compared notes, they found that each had landed on a different carrier.

Far to the west, *Enterprise's* tireless search team of Nelson and Moore was still at it, having tracked the Mobile Fleet during the night. Just before 0700 one of the light carriers with planes remaining on deck seemed to be turning into the wind, and the Big E's snoopers prudently decided to scram. En route home, Nelson sent amplifying reports from so far out that he needed a Hellcat radio relay team to get the messages back to home plate. Knowing that the long-range strike was airborne, Nelson radioed, "It's a beautiful day. I hope you sink them all."

Though Nelson and Moore had done their typical splendid job, ultimately they were disappointed. As they took up an easterly homing track, the "Bombcats" were headed west on their three-hundred-mile tether. In his narrative report Nelson gloomed, "Our striking planes would not be able to reach those sitting duck targets."

One advantage of a night launch on a seven-hundred-mile round trip: The weary pilots could land in broad daylight. Nelson and Moore logged eight hours, including three in green ink indicating instrument flight.

Their information was immediately absorbed aboard *Lexington* and *Indianapolis*. The plot put Ozawa 360 miles west of Task Force 58, and Spruance ordered an increase in fleet speed, trying to close the distance.

Though keyed up after two significant finds in two days, eventually the VT-10 scouts logged some well-earned sack time. One crewman slept for thirty-six hours—a near-impossible feat on a crowded, noisy aircraft carrier.

Throughout the day, the cockeyed optimists in flag country hoped for a chance to finish off some limping Japanese ships. Even Spruance caught the spirit: At midmorning he directed Lee's battle line to take up the chase, supported by *Bunker Hill* and *Wasp*, detached from Montgomery's group.

Meanwhile, the 0600 strike returned with nothing to report. By then the Mobile Fleet had extended the distance from its pursuer, and though the enemy was still being tracked by *Enterprise* and *Bunker Hill* TBFs, it was clear that the game was up. Task Force 58 could not gain enough headway to haul within the optimum 250 miles to launch a useful air strike.

Nor could Lee hope to press ahead with any chance of overhauling some cripples. He needed to refuel his destroyers along the way, a task that consumed most of three hours stretching into early afternoon. At a regulation twelve to fourteen knots, the process only allowed Ozawa—who had no cripples—to add to his lead.

Perhaps mindful of the criticism he knew was building, Spruance permitted the hunt to continue. A second contingency strike tucked its wheels in the wells at 1500, not knowing that the fleet commander allotted them four hours to find something worth killing. When the clock ticked over at 2030, Blue Jacket hailed Bald Eagle and called off the chase, six hundred miles west of Saipan.

The Battle of the Philippine Sea was over.

Adrift

BUT THE RESIDUE REMAINED AFLOAT. One benefit of the task force's stern chase was that it largely steamed through the track the strike groups had taken the night before. Scores of fliers still bobbed in their tiny rafts in the midst of a vast ocean.

Two years previously, Spruance and Mitscher had faced the dilemma of launching aircraft for a night recovery. At Midway Spruance had approved a long-range strike against the retreating Japanese fleet but only after assuring himself that the risk was acceptable. Later he said, "If the tactical situation is such that the commander is unwilling to do what is required to get the planes back safely, then he has no business launching the attack in the first place." Mitscher, then captain of the first *Hornet* (CV-8), had sweated the return of his aircrews and never forgot the incident.

The lesson was taken to heart. In December 1943 a Pacific Fleet summary had addressed the issue of air-sea rescue. The AirPac staff conceded that "distances are great, atolls relatively few, and the drift resulting from prevailing wind and current is in the direction of enemy-held islands rather than our own."

Nevertheless, Vice Admiral John Towers, ComAirPac, endorsed a plan to establish search and rescue procedures and an organization dedicated to that mission. He felt it essential "to have a plan and to let pilots know that the problem has been fully considered in advance." Towers's philosophy was endorsed by several operational commanders, including *Essex*'s skipper, Captain Ralph Ofstie, who urged "active, immediate, and continuous follow-ups on all information received on downed pilots and crews." Apart from the military advantage of retrieving valuable "assets," Ofstie noted the salubrious effect on aircrew morale.

Washington heeded AirPac sentiments. In March 1944 CNO Ernest J. King authorized establishment of a dedicated rescue squadron designated VH-1. It was activated the next month at San Diego, equipped with Martin PBM-3Ds. The twin-engine Mariners were an excellent choice: The big flying boats could land at sea, pick up downed fliers, and return them to safety. The first VH-1 aircraft arrived at Saipan on June 20, supported by the seaplane tender *Onslow*.

Aircraft picked up nine fliers, including seven by floatplanes from the cruisers *Boston*, *Canberra*, and *Wichita*.

Boston and *Canberra* OS2Us rescued three men each; a *Wichita* SOC from the battleship group retrieved one. A *Boston* pilot, Lieutenant Junior Grade Fred W. Rigdon, picked up two *Belleau Wood* fliers, one of whom bore important information. AMM2c George Platz had been George Brown's gunner. He and radioman Ellis Babcock had watched *Hiyo* sink: news that Mitscher and Spruance eagerly received. Babcock was fetched back aboard a *Canberra* Kingfisher, corroborating Platz's observation.

Lexington torpedo pilot Warren McLellan and his crew spent twenty-two hours in the water. Part of the time he wielded his shoes to beat off nosy sharks.

The crew had become separated on bailout over the Mobile Fleet and spent much of the night linking up. That helped a lot: The only thing worse than being down in the Pacific at night was being alone. "Mac's" gunner was AMM2c John S. Hutchinson, whose middle initial stood for Seaman. Time would tell whether that would prove apt or ironic.

By afternoon of the twenty-first the three fliers felt much better emotionally than physically. During the day Hellcats had circled the spot, and Avengers had dropped extra rafts, so obviously the crew's position was known. Radioman Selbie Greenhalgh had been able to sleep a bit, but all the men were sunburned, and they continually retched from swallowing seawater. Their tongues had swollen, making swallowing and speaking difficult.

Late that afternoon McLellan's educated ears detected a low drone. He identified it as an F6F. In minutes four OS2Us motored into view, escorted by a division of Hellcats. Three Kingfishers splashed down and taxied toward the raft. The first pilot leaned out, grinning hugely, and asked rhetorically, "Want a lift?"

Warren McLellan rasped, "You're the best thing I've seen since I've been living!"

Meanwhile, the Navy's first dedicated air-sea rescue squadron went to work immediately. Three Mariner flying boats of VH-1, operated by forty-three officers and men, began flying searches upon arrival on the twentieth. However, the rescuers suffered frustrating failure the first two days of operations. On the twenty-first one of the PBMs logged a ten-hour search without result. The next day's sortie was aborted barely half an hour after takeoff when the normally reliable Pratt & Whitney engines proved balky.

That same day Ozawa's diversion force and main force arrived at Nakagusuku Bay, Okinawa. That evening Ozawa called for his chief of staff and dictated a resignation letter to Captain Ohmae. The admiral accepted responsibility for the defeat, then directed that the message be sent to Naval General Headquarters.

In Tokyo, Admiral Toyoda scarcely bothered to read the communication. He remarked, "I am more responsible for this defeat than Admiral Ozawa, and I will not accept his resignation."

It took a while for several hundred survivors of the three sunken carriers to get sorted out. *Taiho* and *Hiyo*'s crews went to *Zuikaku*, while *Shokaku*'s boarded cruiser *Maya* (where presumably some were diverted by the Kure Zoo's saluting monkey).

Upon returning to base and pulling together pilot and ship reports, the First Mobile Fleet compiled its record for A-Go. It concluded with certainty that four or five carriers and a battleship or large cruiser were sunk or damaged, optimistically adding, "It is not possible to assert that others did not blow up or sink." Additionally, Zero pilots and AA gunners presumably shot down 160 enemy airplanes.

Actual Task Force 58 losses to enemy action June 19 and 20: no ships and forty-two aircraft.

American aviators were disappointed: They badly wanted to pursue Ozawa to destruction. But Spruance had priorities. Guarding the amphibious landing was more important than chasing Japan's empty flattops. Four would reappear off the Philippines in late October, offering themselves as sacrificial bait. Again in command, Jisaburo Ozawa would find Bull Halsey an easier mark than Ray Spruance.

June 22

ON THE TWENTY-SECOND, TASK FORCE 58 reversed course, steaming eastward along the general track of the strike group two evenings before. There was ample evidence of "the mission beyond darkness." Searchers found empty life rafts, some of which were sunk to avoid confusing reports later on. Six fliers were rescued during the day, but it was not entirely dull.

That morning destroyer *Miller* in 58.2 had finished refueling when she received an emergency signal on her SC-2 radar set. Checking with Rear Admiral Montgomery, Commander T. H. Kolberg turned toward the electronic beacon to investigate. He was told that a TBF was orbiting over a raft, marking the position.

About half an hour later the destroyer detected a low-level aircraft which turned into a Kawanishi H8K, largest flying boat in the world. Americans knew her as "Emily."

Kolberg, one of the few non-Annapolis skippers, turned his ship to bring his guns to bear. The five-inch .38s trained outboard and opened up in their authoritative bark, but the range was too great. The snooper kept a respectful but watchful distance.

Shortly two Hellcats arrived, and *Miller* indicated the Emily's presence by firing in her direction. Then a signal mirror flickered and flashed a few miles away, closer than the orbiting TBF. *Miller* investigated and fetched a Helldiver crew from the *Wasp*.

However, the Emily was nothing if not persistent. Operating only three hundred miles from her Carolines base, she reappeared in the noon hour, but the destroyer ignored her. Instead, *Miller* continued to the patient Avenger and found a *Bunker Hill* dive-bomber crew.

Amazingly, the Japanese flying boat remained in the area for some four hours. However commendable the crew's dedication, it proved ultimately foolhardy. At midafternoon a Fighting 8 pilot, Lieutenant Junior Grade Lloyd P. Heinzen, caught sight of the persistent Emily and shot her down in "a great column of flame and smoke." It was his third kill en route to a career total of six. The destroyer hove to, launched a boat, and searched for intelligence. Among several floating corpses some useful information was retrieved, including maps and a navigator's kit.

The emperor's air arm got in a last lick on June 22. At dusk two torpedo-packing Bettys of 755 *Kokutai* at Truk skimmed low across the island, making for the roadstead off Guam. There they found two battleships anchored: a marvelous target of the sort not seen since Pearl Harbor.

Standing watch in *Pennsylvania*'s "sky control forward" was a Marine officer, Captain John D. Cooper, a devoted marksman trained as a gunfire spotter. He glanced up, saw a twin-engine Japanese aircraft crossing the bow, and exclaimed, "Look at that!" Nobody else had reported the intruder.

The nearest G4M drew a bead on *Maryland* and released its torpedo. It ran hot, straight, and normal (as Type 91s were wont to do) and smashed into her port bow. The damage, though not extensive, resulted in five weeks of repairs at Eniwetok. Oddly, the successful Japanese airmen apparently did not recognize their achievement, as they made no claim upon return to Truk.

Over the previous day, much of the Mobile Fleet dispersed to its home ports or commands. At 0515 Operation A-Go was formally concluded, with the remaining carriers and escorts reverting to Third Fleet, still under Ozawa. Meanwhile, most of the battleships and cruisers, with their destroyers, returned to control of Second Fleet in Singapore. The exceptions were battleship *Haruna* and cruiser *Maya*, which needed time in a repair yard.

June 23

THE CARRIER BATTLE WAS CERTAINLY over, but land-based Japanese airmen continued fighting. On the twenty-third a Jill of Air Group 551 attacked a convoy west of Saipan and reported sinking a large transport. However, throughout June, the 22nd Air Flotilla lost twenty-eight land attack crews, fifteen fliers from Air Group 253, and five other individuals. The crippling losses might have been partially offset had any of the claims proved valid, but in fact, Kakuta's island-based squadrons were expended in a fruitless effort to stem a rising tide of American steel.

In home waters, the Mobile Fleet continued its dispersal as the supply forces were ordered to western Naiki. Cruiser *Maya* returned to Yokosuka on June 25; her irreverent aircrew went ashore with the Kure Zoo's monkey still saluting senior officers by way of parting.

Destroyer *Boyd* under Commander U. S. Grant Sharp made a specialty of fishing stranded aviators out of the Pacific Ocean. The 58.1 escort had found *Lexington*'s Bill Birkholm early on the twentieth, and on the afternoon of the twenty-third came across a skinny, sunburned flier 150 miles from Guam. He was *Cowpens*'s CAG, Lieutenant Commander Bob Price, shot down during the original strikes on June 11. He had survived twelve days in his tiny rubber raft, and could find no better way to celebrate his daughter's birthday.

In bitter irony, Price survived only six months. Retained as "Mighty Moo's" air officer, he was swept overboard during "Halsey's typhoon" in December.

On the twenty-third the VH-1 detachment commander was airborne, searching his assigned sector. Lieutenant Junior Grade Robert L. Sharp was a newcomer, having joined the squadron only three months before. However, he was a determined young Nebraskan who stretched his flight pattern (and his orders) by more than forty miles. It was a good decision; late that afternoon his crew spotted a yellow raft with two men aboard, and the twenty-three-year-old aircraft commander decided to make an open-ocean landing. The dive-bomber crew gratefully scrambled aboard the PBM and enjoyed the hospitality of the tender *Onslow* for a few days.

It was the last rescue.

The searches were more successful than anybody could have hoped: 80 percent of the downed fliers were rescued. Task Force 58's superb search and rescue effort eventually recovered all but seventeen pilots and seventeen aircrew. Of the 138 fliers rescued, 85 percent were picked up by vigilant "smallboys," the hardworking destroyers. They had played little part in the sweeping drama of the Battle of the Philippine Sea: Their appointment with history lay four months hence, off Samar. But the tin-can sailors took justifiable pride in their successful search for downed aircrews. Recorded Lieutenant Commander William B. Brown of *Knapp*, "This was a source of great satisfaction. We could not catch the Japs ourselves; the next best thing was to look after the boys who did."

A last "casualty" was Rear Admiral Harrill. Largely bedridden, ten days after the turkey shoot he underwent surgery for appendicitis. Some *Essex* veterans felt that Captain Ralph Ofstie, in concert (and perhaps in cahoots) with the chief of staff, recommended the operation as a way of sidelining the reluctant warrior. Whatever the facts, Harrill entered the Pearl Harbor Naval Hospital in early July and proceeded to San Diego. Within days he was replaced by the pugnacious, astute Rear Admiral Gerald F. Bogan, a flier's flier who led an escort carrier group supporting the troops on Saipan.

June 24

FOUR DAYS AFTER THE "MISSION beyond darkness," Task Group 58.1 was back in the Bonins. Clark's and two other groups were ordered to Eniwetok for a brief rest and refitting, but the ever-aggressive "Jocko" decided to revisit his old hunting grounds en route.

By the twenty-fourth Clark's airmen and sailors had adopted a proprietary attitude toward the Bonins, calling them "the Jocko Jimas." Knowing a morale builder when he saw one, Clark had his print shop turn out certificates in the "Jocko Jima Development Corporation . . . only five hundred miles from downtown Tokyo." As "corporation president," Clark signed enough of the documents to distribute to all concerned.

Clark reckoned—correctly—that Japanese reinforcements would have arrived since his first visitation on June 15. Tokyo's intent was to funnel new squadrons into Guam and Tinian via Iwo and environs. However, the same kind of weather that had bedeviled the carrier aviators on that occasion now hampered Imperial Navy efforts to get off the ground in the home islands. Consequently, the new units trickled into Iwo, creating a shortage of ramp space with some 120 planes waiting there by the twenty-fourth. But despite the impressive numbers, the quality was lacking. By one reckoning, about 30 percent of the pilots were fully trained; the others were rookies.

At 0600 on the twenty-fourth, *Hornet*, *Yorktown*, and *Bataan* launched fifty-one bombed-up Hellcats 235 miles southeast of Iwo. The strikers circled their ships, forming into sections, divisions and squadrons, and proceeded on course into blustery, cloudy skies. The other CVL, *Belleau Wood*, handled ForceCAP in case the Japanese came out to investigate.

As the raiders would learn, the defenders already had done so.

A patrol plane found 58.1 that morning, and immediately passed the word to Rear Admiral Sadaichi Matsunaga, commanding the 27th Air Flotilla on Iwo. He scrambled all fifty-seven Zekes and several bombers in time to greet the inbound raiders about ten miles offshore. Less than two hours after launch, a terrific dogfight erupted beneath scudding gray clouds.

Emerging from a storm front, the F6F pilots immediately recognized that they had their hands full. With master armament switches selected, they hit the red "B" button, depositing their five-hundred-pounders in the spume-tossed sea, and prepared to shoot it out. However, one division kept its bombs and ignored the interceptors to attack Iwo's main airfield, cratering the runway.

Fighting 1's flight officer had been solicitous in assigning pilots to the mission. The lineup included mostly "combat virgins" who had not yet scored, and they got plenty of opportunity.

The Yokosuka Zekes were led by Lieutenant Sadao Yamaguchi, who had survived a shoot-down at Guadalcanal and tangled with Spitfires over northern Australia. He took his half of the force up through the cloud layer while the others staked out the airspace below.

At the head of sixteen Tophatters, Lieutenant Harry J. Mueller glimpsed an estimated forty bandits at about eleven thousand feet, turned into them, and broke up their formation. From there on it was a rat race. Mueller, with one scalp to his credit, chased down two "Oscars," but the enemy fighters were unusually well flown. They shot down the popular Ensign Carl C. "Whitey" Reinert almost immediately. Another Hellcat survived with thirty nonregulation holes in its tough hide.

Other Tophatters quickly turned the tables. Flying in Lieutenant Robert R. Baysinger's division, slim, dark-haired Lieutenant Junior Grade "Tank" Schroeder (who had overimbibed during Mitscher's debriefing on the twentieth) was belle of the brawl. He had an "assist" on one of the squadron's early successes while based on Tarawa six months before, but since then had gone scoreless. Now he locked onto one Zeke right away and exploded it from astern. Then another crossed his sights, slightly high. Schroeder nosed up, got his lead, and triggered a burst into the Mitsubishi's wing root. The fuel tank ignited, turning the bandit into a spectacular flamer. Minutes later "the Tank" scorched another Zeke in a similar setup. Three other Tophatters who had never scored emerged with doubles.

The churning furball turned inward upon itself as blue Hellcats and green Zekes sought temporary advantage. In wrapped-up, mindblurring turns, pilots caught glimpses that etched themselves on the retinas of their memories: tracers glowing through the atmosphere, striking sparks where the APIs struck enemy airframes. One pilot looked around and saw three parachutes in the air; he couldn't tell if they were American, Japanese, or both.

Hornet's Fighting 2 claimed thirty-three kills among thirteen pilots, paced by two jaygees: Everett C. Hargreaves and Merriwell W.

Vineyard with quadruples. In his first fight, Hargreaves very nearly made ace with four confirmed and a probable. Meanwhile, Lieutenant Robert R. Butler and Lieutenant Junior Grade Robert W. Shackleford each claimed triples.

Between them, Fighting 1 and 2 claimed fifty-one kills and likely got twenty-nine: two dozen Zekes or Hamps and five Judys, though VF-2 claimed nine D4Ys. In exchange, the Americans lost five planes and pilots.

While VF-1 and -2 shot their way clear, VF-50 pressed on to Iwo. There Lieutenant Commander Johnnie Strange and six of his *Bataan* pilots each scored double kills en route to a seventeen–two score.

Not all the Zero pilots were pushovers.

The prime example was Warrant Officer Saburo Sakai, a twenty-seven-year-old veteran with six years' experience. He had claimed his first kills in China, then sharpened his aim in a series of spectacular combats over the Philippines, Borneo, Java, New Guinea, and the Solomons. Consequently, Sakai's victims included Chinese, American, Australian, and Dutch airmen. But his winning streak ended at Guadalcanal on August 7, 1942, when he was severely wounded attacking U.S. Navy dive-bombers. His survival was rated near miraculous: Blinded in one eye and bleeding from other wounds, he lapsed in and out of consciousness. Yet his determination took him 550 saltwater miles back to Rabaul, New Britain. From there he was invalided to Japan, seemingly beached for the duration.

However, Sakai lived by an ironclad rule: Never give up. And he didn't. After nearly two years of convalescence and home service he insisted that his experience was too valuable to waste, and his argument had merit. Having destroyed or damaged some seventy Allied aircraft, he talked his way back into combat, and in June 1944 he fetched up at Iwo Jima. There he and the Yokosuka Wing prepared for the Americans' inevitable appearance. They weren't long in coming.

When Yamaguchi took his formation on top of the cloud layer, Sakai's portion went low. The Mitsubishis and Grummans merged at nine thousand feet: head-on runs shredded both formations as four-plane *shotai*s and divisions broke down into singles and pairs.

Hampered by limited vision, Sakai slipped out of his shoulder harness. He needed all the agility he could manage to maintain situational awareness. But in the violence of the dogfight, he lost his wingmen. Looking around, he found himself alone in a skyful of hungry Hellcats. He fired at one and missed; his shooting eye had failed him. But he latched onto another and shot it into the water. Then the roof fell in.

Attacking by sections and divisions, the F6Fs repeatedly rolled in on Sakai. The Americans were probably *Hornet* pilots of VF-2. The imperial ace needed every ounce of his extensive skill and knowledge to survive. Repeatedly he timed his evasive maneuvers to perfection, avoiding pass after pass. His right arm ached; his good eye fogged with sweat. Rolling, turning, and slipping, he skidded to one side and the other, foiling the Americans' tracking. As the fight continued, other Hellcats passed nearby. A couple of *Bataan* pilots flew overhead, noting four F6s in a Lufbery circle with one Zeke. Ensign William A. McCormick said, "I flew over it and decided it wasn't the place for me." Rather than get embroiled in a low-level turning contest, McCormick wisely kept going.

However, McCormick's squadron mate Ensign Clarence E. Rich already claimed two kills and saw an opportunity for a third. From a thousand-foot perch he rolled in, tracked the olive-green A6M in his Mark VIII sight, and fired at full deflection. He seemed to score; the Zeke dropped away, apparently out of control. Rich intended to finish the "meatball" when tracers sparkled past his canopy. Keeping his speed up, he rolled, pulled hard, and eluded the unseen assailant.

After perhaps thirty agonizing minutes, Sakai got a break. The fight had unwittingly strayed within range of Iwo's AA guns, and the Hellcats disengaged. Sakai managed a decent landing on Motoyama Number One and achingly climbed out. Part of his epic battle had been seen from the ground; mechanics were astonished to find no bullet holes in the Zero.

A quarter century later, meeting Sakai at a fighter pilot reunion, Clancy Rich expressed surprise and delight to find his erstwhile opponent on the golf course.

The battle was resumed with more combat near the task force. The 27th Air Flotilla's next wave included some twenty unescorted torpedo planes that had almost no chance against the Jocko Jima Development Corporation. The CAP had been reinforced with night fighters that chopped up the Kates piecemeal, starting at 1000. *Hornet's* VF(N) detachment was prominent as Russ Reiserer—who had joined the Orote traffic pattern on the nineteenth—splashed two. His enterprising young wingman, Lieutenant Junior Grade Fred L. Dungan, went one better. Eight other Fighting 2 pilots added fifteen more, though it wasn't always easy. Some of Rear Admiral Matsunaga's torpedo crews were exceedingly persistent, hanging around the periphery of the task group for well over an hour, seeking an opportunity. But it never came, as alert fighter directors put *Hornet* and *Belleau Wood* F6Fs on their trail. No torpedomen returned to base.

During the interception, the gunfire was interspersed with some heated radio debates. A *Hornet* night-fighter pilot requested permission to strafe a parachuting enemy, but Russ Reiserer, who had been fighting Japan since 1942, would not endorse murder. When the youngster began his run, another flier broke in, "Cut it out, you son of a bitch, or I'll shoot you down!"

Under the circumstances, there was no military reason for gunning parachutes. The enemy fliers were more than two hundred miles from base, and it was unlikely that any would be rescued by American ships. The main motivation was revenge, as the Japanese routinely killed Allied fliers who had bailed out. But "shooting chutes" was poor policy for other reasons. In order to line up a parachute, a fighter pilot had to slow down and fly a predictable course, which could make him vulnerable to other enemy aircraft. There was also the possibility of mistaken identity.

Some other Kate pilots had jumped during the interception, and the heated transmissions apparently prompted a cease-fire. Then the task group fighter director opened up. Using Clark's call sign, he said, "CAP is authorized to shoot any Jap in the silk." *Hornet's* fighter pilots shredded three parachutes; a destroyer in the screen recovered one corpse riddled with .50-caliber rounds.

That precedent paid a ghastly dividend some months later when a *Hornet* pilot killed a squadron mate who had bailed out.

Matsunaga's second attack force—the third wave of the day—comprised twenty-three Zekes, nine Jills, and nine Judys. Clark's CAP intercepted them at about dusk near Urachus Island. Japanese assessment conceded that the results were "vague" owing to Jocko Clark's efficient defense. They fell afoul of VF-2 about sixty miles from the task group, and the Rippers lived up to their name. For once the results exceeded the claims as *Hornet* Hellcats splashed ten Zekes and seven Jills against claims for nine fighters and five "Kates." Among the shooters were Lieutenant Roy M. Voris with two Zekes; Lieutenant Junior Grade Byron M. Johnson with two torpeckers; and Lieutenant Lloyd G. Barnard with one—he of the five-plane mission at Iwo on June 15. A great deal had happened in nine days.

Belleau Wood's VF-24 splashed a Kate on ForceCAP during the day, but one snooper was extremely cagey. *Hornet's* fighter director, Lieutenant Charles D. Ridgway III, spent a frustrating ninety minutes trying to position his Hellcats to trap the elusive Japanese, who changed course and altitude every ten minutes or so. When the VF-2 division ran low on fuel, *Yorktown's* Lieutenant Alexander Wilding thought he saw an opportunity. He had been studying the snooper's pattern and had a good radar picture, so he asked his counterpart to pass the conn. Ridgway consented, with a bottle of Scotch weighing in the balance.

Controlling a *Bataan* division, Wilding sent the VF-50 pilots to Angels 20, flying astern of the bandit. Having timed the Jill's breaks, Wilding anticipated that the enemy pilot would turn starboard and, at the appropriate moment, he sent the fighters on a cutoff vector. The *Tenzan* crew saw them coming and scooted for the clouds, but Ensign Robert H. Veach Jr. hauled into range and opened fire. Topside lookouts in the task group saw the flaming streak twenty miles away.

Charlie Ridgway paid his debt to Alex Wilding at Christmas 1951: a bottle of Chivas Regal.

Several minutes later Wilding dispatched two *Bataan* divisions against an estimated twelve Zekes and six Judys inbound from eighty miles. Fighting 50 splashed seven planes but lost the Hellcat leader, Lieutenant Rolla S. Lemmon.

That was not the end of it. In the evening sixteen Yokosuka P1Ys took off, led by Lieutenant Obuchi. The fast, twin-engine "Frances" attack planes were capable machines but they accomplished nothing. One managed a run on the American force; seven failed to return. None were intercepted, so it was presumed that the crews became lost and ran out of fuel.

Throughout the day Clark's squadrons fought half a dozen combats over and around Iwo Jima, yielding an optimistic tally of 116 destroyed and 14 probables. The Japanese acknowledged losing twenty-three Zekes, twenty-one Kates, and at least seven Jills. The seven Frans that disappeared raised the toll to nearly sixty, though Morison cites a total of sixty-six. Eight of the Zero pilot losses were senior aviators, including five commissioned officers—a very high ratio.

Conversely, the Yokosuka, 252 and 301 *Kokutai*, celebrated twenty-seven "certain" kills and ten "uncertain." In truth, half a dozen Hellcats were lost.

Eniwetok

THE NEW BASE AT ENIWETOK, at the extreme northwest rim of the Marshalls, offered advantages over Majuro in the southeast. Not only was Eniwetok a larger anchorage; it was 660 miles closer to Saipan. With its beautiful lagoon fifty miles in circumference, Eniwetok was a logical attraction as a naval operating base. However, the Japanese brigade dispatched to defend it had hardly unloaded its gear before Operation Catchpole descended. The Americans seized the atoll in one week of February 1944 and began developing facilities. The work was well under way when Forager kicked off, and Task Force 58 would steam to Eniwetok from Saipan.

Clark's group slid into Eniwetok on the twenty-seventh, joining Task Groups 58.2 and 58.3. It seemed incredible that so much had occurred since Mitscher led the task force outbound from Majuro on June 6, only three weeks before. But the post–Philippine Sea respite was short-lived. On June 30 the force raised steam and hoisted anchors, headed for the western horizon. Clark arranged yet another visit of the Jocko Jimas, and beyond them lay the Philippines . . . and more.

In July Halsey relieved Spruance in the Fifth Fleet/Third Fleet turnover, while Vice Admiral John S. McCain took the helm of 38.1, anticipating his eventual replacement of Mitscher. When Task Force 38 sortied for the Philippines in October, the lineup was even greater than Forager's: seventeen carriers, including four new ships and six new air groups.

In the ultimate confrontation in Leyte Gulf, Japan's last four deployable carriers would be sunk and the world's last battleship slugfest would occur. The process begun at Coral Sea in May 1942 took two and a half years to complete, but at length the work was done.

The world will never see its like.

PART SIX

Final Cut

Reckoning

As OzAWA'S BEATEN FORCE FLED westward, critics were already condemning Spruance for "letting the CVs get away." However, the Fifth Fleet commander had fulfilled his orders: Prevent the Imperial Navy from interfering with the landings. The situation reflected his triumph at Midway two years before. In defending the island base he defeated a stronger enemy force but was chided for not pursuing it. In the end, history's verdict on Raymond Spruance is two thumbs up.

After the appalling meat grinder at Tarawa, where one Marine in six was killed or wounded, Saipan went smoothly. Fatalities amounted to 5 percent of the landing force, with 335 total casualties per square mile. Guam went even better, with half the death rate and slightly fewer losses per mile.

Saipan was secured on July 9 after three weeks of fighting. However, Mitscher kept the pressure on, revisiting the Bonins July 3 and 4, and the western Carolines July 25 through 28. Japanese airpower was given no respite, no breathing space to rest and regroup.

Meanwhile, amphibious troops completed seizure of the other islands: Guam (July 21–August 10) and Tinian (July 24–August 1).

In Tokyo, loss of the Marianas prompted the ouster of Premier Hideki Tojo. But it was far too late for Japan. American engineers quickly built large bomber bases in the Marianas, shortly receiving hundreds of B-29s of XXI Bomber Command. The first Superfortress mission from Guam was flown in November, and Japan began to reap the whirlwind.

The course of the Pacific war was irrevocably set. America returned to the Philippines in October, seized Iwo Jima in February 1945, and landed at Okinawa in April. U.S. carrier aircraft owned Japanese airspace, and B-29s methodically razed almost every large city in the home islands. Surrender came in August, but only after two atomic bombs and a Soviet declaration of war.

In the aftermath of A-Go, efforts to itemize the Mobile Fleet's losses and compare them with American claims are doomed to failure: The inevitable confusion of combat is bad enough, but incomplete or contradictory Japanese records preclude a precise accounting. Nonetheless, the bottom line is known:

At midnight on June 18, Jisaburo Ozawa commanded nine carriers embarking 430 aircraft, while his screening vessels tallied forty-three floatplanes. Twenty-four hours later he was returning to base with six carriers retaining thirty-five operational fighter or attack aircraft and a dozen floatplanes.

Gone with 476 planes were 445 pilots and aircrewmen.

American losses are known with precision: on the nineteenth, fourteen fighter pilots died in combat, while thirteen other pilots and aircrew were lost over Guam or on searches. Thirty-one sailors were killed in action aboard *South Dakota*, *Bunker Hill*, and *Wasp*, plus at least two from "friendly fire."

After the search and rescue operations, missions on the twentieth cost sixteen pilots and twice as many aircrew. The two-day battle therefore resulted in the deaths of seventy-six American fliers.

Japanese shipboard losses will never be fully known: They likely ranged between two thousand and three thousand, depending upon *Taiho*'s actual toll. Another 440 or more aircrew also perished in combat.

The Marianas and related Bonins combats destroyed several Imperial Navy air groups. Five of the seven were disbanded in July and never re-formed. For example, by June 21 Guam's Air Group 261 contingent (already depleted by transfers for Operation Kon) had merely two planes left. Air Group 265 lost most of its remaining planes on June 11, while 263 had almost no planes by the end of June 19. Air Groups 301 and 341 had been exterminated at Iwo. The activities of some units remain unknown because there were no survivors after the Americans seized the islands.

Many surviving pilots were evacuated in Bettys or by submarine, though some aviators perished in sunken submarines.

The Japanese after-action report said, "It reads in Chapter 49 of the *Combat Sutra* that 'Tactics is like sandals. Those who are strong should wear them. A cripple should not dare wear them.' The plan in Operation A is minutely worked out and the strategy of the operational unit has also been checked in great detail. But the training for combat duty in each detachment is not complete. Therefore, it looks, as said in the *Combat Sutra*, as if well-made sandals were allowed to be worn by a cripple."

Postscript

PHILIPPINE SEA IS OFTEN COMPARED with Jutland: Both were historic naval battles that produced spectacular losses without war-winning results. But that is a narrow interpretation of the carrier battle. Destruction of the Japanese fleet was not a primary goal of Operation Forager: Occupation of Saipan and other islands was. Phil Sea contributed to Forager's success and, in so doing, helped topple the Tojo government and convinced realists in Tokyo that the war was lost, though the zealots held sway.

There was no successor to Jutland, but the Turkey Shoot was followed by Leyte Gulf only four months later. Historians speculate whether U.S. losses at Leyte would have been as heavy if the four Japanese carriers off Cape Engano had not escaped Mitscher off Saipan in June. Ozawa's ability to lure Halsey north, leaving Seventh Fleet escort forces vulnerable to Kurita's battleships, unquestionably increased American casualties. Although A-Go veterans *Zuikaku*, *Chitose*, *Chiyoda*, and *Zuiho* all perished as decoys in October, *Junyo* and *Ryuho* survived the Marianas to become aircraft ferries, and could have appeared off the Philippines. Two spanking-new imperial carriers missed A-Go and could have deployed to Leyte: *Unryu* and *Amagi*. Therefore, by reallocating its new air groups, *Nihon Kaigun* still could have dangled four flight decks as live bait in the Philippines. Consequently, Spruance's "failure" in June likely would not have affected later events as long as Halsey commanded Third Fleet.

Surviving Ships

MOST OF THE FORAGER WARSHIPS had postwar careers. *Cimarron* finished the war with ten battle stars, a record matched by just three other oilers and exceeded only by the second *Neosho* and *Platte*. In 1963 AO-22 became the senior vessel in the U.S. Navy, with more commissioned service than any active ship. She deployed to Korea and Vietnam but suffered damage in a 1968 collision with another Marianas veteran, the antisubmarine carrier *Hornet* (CVS-12). "Cim" was judged too badly damaged to repair and was sold for scrap in 1969, nearly thirty years after commissioning.

The Iowa-class battleships also proved long-lived. *Iowa* and *New Jersey* fired their sixteen-inchers off Korea; *New Jersey* returned to Asian waters during the Vietnam War.

Among the Forager carriers, *Enterprise* built a unique legacy. She earned twenty battle stars—only two short of the possible total—and no other ship matched her record. She became a night carrier in 1945, again with the irrepressible Bill Martin leading her Avengers. However, a daylight kamikaze knocked her out of the war in May, and Tokyo capitulated before she could return to harness.

With so many new flattops on hand, it made no sense to retain the Big E in service, and she was decommissioned in 1947. Bull Halsey led a valiant effort to preserve his old flagship as a museum, but the effort failed: The Enterprise Association was allowed only six months to raise two million dollars. To its eternal shame, the United States Navy did not care enough to save "the one vessel that most nearly symbolizes the Navy in this war," and she was sold for scrap in 1958. Less than two years later the wrecking yard had completed its task. The Navy tossed a fillip to her men and the cause of history by perpetuating her name in CVN-65, the first nuclear-powered carrier, in 1961. As of this writing the current *Enterprise* is entering her forty-second year with the fleet.

Mitscher's flagship, *Lexington*, enjoyed an exceptional career: In 1969 she became the Navy's training carrier, a role she retained almost until decommissioning in 1991. "The Blue Ghost" thus became the last combat flattop of World War II in commissioned service.

Other carriers of the Marianas campaign enjoyed long postwar careers, including *Yorktown*, *Hornet*, and *Wasp*, which became antisubmarine carriers. *Yorktown* picked up *Apollo VIII* after its 1968 lunar orbit, while the latter two retrieved six *Gemini* or *Apollo* capsules between 1966 and 1972.

Today only three Marianas carriers remain. *Yorktown* has been preserved at Charleston, South Carolina, since 1976; *Lexington* at Corpus Christi, Texas (1992); *Hornet* at Alameda, California (1998); and their sister *Intrepid*, which missed Forager, receives visitors in New York. *Midway* (CV-41), commissioned in late 1945, became a San Diego attraction in 2004.

The last surviving CVL was *Cabot*, sold to Spain in 1967 and returned in 1989. Though intended for preservation, the project lacked funding and the ship was sold for scrap in 1999.

One carrier name stands out. In August 1944, Bethlehem Steel in Quincy, Massachusetts, laid down CV-47. In May 1946 she was commissioned with the name USS *Philippine Sea*. She was among the last of the long-lived *Essex* class, serving until 1958. "Phil Sea" was stricken from the Navy roster eleven years later and sold for scrap in 1971. A successor, CG-58, was the twelfth *Ticonderoga*-class guided-missile cruiser, commissioned in 1989.

Spruance's flagship, cruiser *Indianapolis*, did not survive the war. She carried the first atom bomb to the Marianas in the summer of 1945 but fell prey to a Japanese submarine after delivering components for the nuclear weapons that would pulverize Hiroshima and Nagasaki. She was sunk on July 29, but owing to a colossal communications screwup,

"Indy" was not missed for days. Hundreds of her crew survived the sinking but succumbed to thirst, exposure, and the unspeakable horror of shark attack. In all, 883 of 1,200 men perished. Captain Charles B. McVay III was persecuted (it is not too strong a word) by CNO Ernest King, who reportedly held a grudge against McVay's father. The captain, well regarded by his crew, was so despondent that he committed suicide in 1968.

One of the submarine stars of the battle still remains: Herman Kossler's *Cavalla* is preserved in Galveston, near Task Force 58 flagship *Lexington*.

Albacore was lost on her eleventh patrol five months later, after Jim Blanchard departed.

Of Lee's seven battleships, four remain. *Alabama, Iowa, North Carolina*, and *New Jersey* all are preserved or scheduled for preservation.

Few of the remaining Japanese ships survived the war. Of fifty-eight that returned from A-Go, nine lasted til VJ-day. *Zuikaku* succumbed to a concentrated air attack at Leyte Gulf, as did CVLs *Chitose, Chiyoda*, and *Zuiho*. *Ryuho* and *Junyo* escaped the Marianas but never deployed again; they were scrapped in 1946–47. Only five other Japanese combatants off Saipan (and two oilers) remained afloat fourteen months later.

Ironically, the only known surviving aircraft from Operation Forager is Japanese. Lieutenant Shinya Ozaki, mortally wounded on the nineteenth, force-landed his Zero (serial number 4685, tail code 43-188) on Guam. The abandoned fighter was reclaimed from a swamp in 1963, shipped to Japan, and restored for display. Debuting in 2000, it occupies an honored place at Hamamatsu Air Base.

Most World War II aircraft went to the smelters. Today, roughly twenty-five of twelve thousand Hellcats remain; fewer than a hundred of ten thousand Avengers; nineteen of six thousand Dauntlesses; three of seven thousand Helldivers; and thirty-four of eleven thousand Zeroes. The numbers change almost monthly due to losses, restorations, and even retrievals of sunken aircraft.

What Became of the Americans?

FOLLOWING THE BATTLE OF JUNE 19–20, Forager's veterans experienced most of the vagaries of wartime life. Most advanced in their professions, living well into old age. Some did not.

Chester Nimitz was one of four naval officers promoted to fleet admiral. He was postwar CNO, retired in 1947, and became the United Nations' goodwill ambassador. He died in San Francisco in 1966, but the National Museum of the Pacific War was built in his hometown, Fredericksburg, Texas. The U.S. Navy honored him upon launching the nuclear-powered supercarrier USS *Nimitz* (CVN-68) in 1972. Every subsequent carrier has been named for mere politicians, including USS *Truman* (CVN-75), named for the most anti-Navy president of the twentieth century.

Ray Spruance continued leading Fifth Fleet until November 1945. He succeeded Nimitz as Commander of the Pacific Fleet and retired as president of the Naval War College in 1948. He was ambassador to the Philippines during the Eisenhower administration and finally retired to California, where he passed away in 1969, age eighty-three. Like Nimitz, he declined to write his memoirs. Nevertheless, Samuel Eliot Morison got it right when he said, "There was no one to equal Spruance."

Marc Mitscher remained in the Pacific for most of the remainder of the war. He continued leading the fast carriers until well into 1945 and subsequently rose to the four-star rank of full admiral. He died as commander of the Atlantic Fleet in 1947, age sixty. Friends felt that he had worn himself out during the war.

Willis "Ching" Lee, the flint-eyed leader of Task Force 58's battleships, also died in harness. He was commanding the organization conducting fleet air defense studies when stricken in August 1945. Appropriately for a devoted seadog, he died on the water, approaching one of his beloved big-gun ships at Casco Bay, Maine. He was only fifty-seven.

The last of Mitscher's Philippine Sea group commanders was Jocko Clark, who characteristically went out fighting at age seventy-seven in 1971. The last three Forager carrier captains were *Bataan*'s Valentine Schaeffer and *Monterey*'s Stuart Ingersoll, who both died in 1983 and another CVL skipper, Stanley Michael of *Cabot*, in 1984.

Wasp's captain at Phil Sea, Clifton "Ziggy" Sprague, had a much bigger fight on his hands four months later. Commanding the escort carrier group immortalized as "Taffy Three," he collided with another Marianas admiral, Takeo Kurita, during the Battle of Leyte Gulf. He died young in 1955.

Bill Sample, *Hornet*'s popular skipper in Forager, was promoted to rear admiral. However, his aircraft disappeared after takeoff from Japan in October 1946.

Other veterans of the Marianas battle were heard from over succeeding decades. Two became president of the United States. Gerald Ford, *Monterey*'s assistant navigator, was elected to Congress from Michigan and succeeded Spiro Agnew as Richard Nixon's vice president in 1973. Following Nixon's resignation in 1974, Ford was sworn in as the thirty-eighth president but lost the 1976 election and retired to California.

George H. W. Bush was a twenty-year-old *San Jacinto* Avenger pilot, though he did not fly the June 20 mission. Winning a Texas congressional seat in 1966, he was later United Nations ambassador and head of the CIA before becoming Ronald Reagan's vice president in 1980. Bush handily was elected president in 1988. Despite his naval aviation background, his administration conducted the Tailhook witch hunt of 1991–92, which ruined or marred the careers of hundreds of innocent officers. He lost the presidency to Bill Clinton, who made no secret of his antimilitary sentiments.

Two officers in Forager rose to the top of their profession. Mitscher's chief of staff, Arleigh Burke, remained in the Pacific most of the war. Though already marked as a comer, he risked his career in the bitter postwar political battles with the Air Force but was "stashed" to preserve his enormous talent. Subsequently he was promoted over ninety senior admirals to become chief of naval operations, serving an unprecedented three terms from 1955 to 1961. He directed conversion of the Navy from oil to nuclear power, and died in 1996, age ninety-five. To this day sailors still boast, "I served in Arleigh Burke's Navy."

Far less known, but well regarded, was George W. Anderson Jr., who stood twenty-seventh in the class of 1927. As *Hornet*'s air officer he helped conduct operations during Forager. He followed Arleigh Burke as CNO in 1961, overseeing naval operations during the Cuban Missile Crisis the next year. Anderson died in 1992, preceded by two sons, George III and Thomas, who also became aviators.

Skipper of destroyer *Boyd* in Task Group 58.1 was Ulysses Grant Sharp Jr., a classmate of Anderson's. As commander in chief Pacific Forces early in the Vietnam War, Sharp opposed the Johnson administration's halfway measures. Following retirement in 1968 he authored a critical appraisal, *Strategy for Defeat*.

Another four-star admiral was *Hornet*'s air group commander, Jackson D. Arnold. In 1952 he received an MBA from Harvard, leading to commands in air matériel and ordnance roles. He retired in 1971 after thirty-seven years on active duty.

Pete Aurand commanded one of the Navy's first jet squadrons, then became Eisenhower's naval aide. The former night-fighter skipper retired as a vice admiral and died in 1989.

Helldiver pilot Hal Buell recovered from his wound over the Mobile Fleet and the shock of his deck crash. He remained in the Navy, commanded a jet fighter squadron, and earned a PhD. He wrote a memoir, *Dauntless Helldivers*, and at this writing lives in Florida.

Fighting 15's George Carr posted additional success after his five-plane debut on June 19. He finished the *Essex* tour with 11.5 victories and remained in the Navy during the Korean War. He died in an aircraft accident in 1952, age thirty-five.

Lexington pilot Cook Cleland, who prevented *Enterprise* deckhands from pushing his SBD overboard, continued flying after the war. He commanded a reserve squadron and, pulling appropriate strings, obtained surplus Goodyear F2G "Super Corsairs" and modified them for racing. He won the Thompson Trophy Race at Cleveland in 1947 and 1949, and took a fighter squadron to Korea.

Fighter director Joe Eggert left the Navy as a lieutenant commander and returned to Wall Street. He retired after a long, successful investment career and died in 1998.

Chick Harmer, who guided so many strays to the task force on June 20, remained in the night-fighter business well after the war. He commanded the Pacific Fleet VF(N) outfit during the Korean War, sending night detachments to Task Force 77 carriers. He died in 1999.

LSO John Harper had a postwar career in the Naval Air Reserve, commanding three squadrons and two air groups. Subsequently he earned an aeronautical engineering degree and worked in the aerospace industry until retirement. In 1999 he wrote *Paddles*, a memoir of his days and nights as a "waver." At this writing he resides in Colorado.

Hotshot Charlie Henderson, the Avenger pilot who narrowly missed acedom, continued his flamboyant ways after the war. He lived in China and the Philippines but eventually married a young Australian woman and fetched up in the outback. He was grooming one of his daughters for the world aerobatic championship when he died in 1986.

Dave McCampbell succeeded Alex Vraciu as the naval ace of aces. When he returned stateside in 1945, "Dashing Dave" had scored thirty-four aerial kills—the all-time naval record—and received the Medal of Honor. He commanded the carrier *Bon Homme Richard* in 1959, retired in 1964, and settled in Florida, where he died in 1996.

Bill Martin, the aggressive skipper of Torpedo 10, bounced back from his Saipan shoot-down. He returned for a third combat deployment in 1945, commanding an air group aboard his beloved *Enterprise*, and his record for night carrier landings stood for forty years. He commanded Sixth Fleet in 1967 and retired to Virginia, where he died in 1996.

"Ziggy" Neff, the VF-16 pilot credited with the Turkey Shoot analogy, earned a law degree and retired as a reserve captain. He was Missouri's assistant attorney general and served on the federal parole commission from 1964 to 1970. He died in 1999.

Belleau Wood torpedo pilot Warren Omark was headed for WestPac in a new squadron when the bombs were dropped in 1945. He joined the reserves after the war and commanded an award-winning unit. He also enjoyed a long career with Hammermill Paper, retiring as vice president of sales in 1984. In 2005 he maintains an active retirement in Pennsylvania.

Jig Dog Ramage remained in the Navy, commanded two aircraft carriers, and astonished himself by achieving flag rank. He left the service after thirty-three years, a victim of the Zumwalt purges, and lives in Coronado, California. A founder of the Association of Naval Aviation, he also inaugurated the enlisted aircrewmen's hall of fame and was among the prominent defenders of the Tailhook Association during the naval leadership failure of the 1990s.

Ramage's radioman-gunner, David Cawley, became a pilot and retired as a commander. He lives in California.

Russ Reiserer, the *Hornet* night-fighter pilot who had a very good day over Guam, finished the war with nine kills. Remaining in the Navy, he attended California Institute of Technology, where he received a master's degree in 1947. Subsequently serving in the regulars and reserves, he retired as a captain in 1969. Presently he lives in California.

Ben Tate, survivor of VT-24's attack on *Hiyo*, transferred to fighters and was due for a second deployment when the war ended. He made the Navy a career, retiring after thirty years, having commanded the carriers *Wasp* and *Kearsarge*. He died in 1998.

Hornet ace Butch Voris led a distinguished postwar career. Not only did he establish the Blue Angels flight demonstration team in 1946, he returned for a second tour in 1950. Additionally, he commanded two squadrons and an air group. He retired a captain in 1963 and pursued a second career in the aerospace industry and NASA. He too settled in California, where he died in 2005.

Alex Vraciu went home, got married, and returned to the Pacific. In

December 1944 he was shot down by AA fire in the Philippines. He evaded capture and turned up five weeks later sporting a beard, a pistol, and a samurai sword at the head of 180 Filipino guerrillas. At war's end he was the Navy's fourth-ranking ace. Leading his own jet squadron, he won the naval aerial gunnery championship in 1957 and, after retiring in 1964, he joined Wells Fargo. He had five children and named his youngest son after Marc Mitscher.

"Spider" Webb, who shot down six planes over Orote Point, was nominated for the Medal of Honor but, like Alex Vraciu, received a Navy Cross. After the war he resigned his commission to revert to his previous status of chief aviation pilot, a rate in which he had more seniority. Upon retiring in 1958 he worked in the aviation industry, and died in Fort Worth in 2002.

Gus Widhelm's diamond-in-the-rough persona was legendary, and he would spare no effort to help a friend. Upon hearing a fellow test pilot remark on the difficulty in moving his family to a new assignment, Widhelm piped up, "I can get you a B-29." Widhelm kept flying as a captain but was killed stunting in 1954, age forty-six. Like many Navy juniors, his son graduated from Annapolis in 1965.

Zeke Zellmer, Herman Kossler's plotting officer, retired as a captain in 1967. Residing in Florida, he is a moving force in the *Cavalla* museum.

Submarine ace Sam Dealey and *Harder* were lost in late August. Jim Blanchard, who sank *Taiho* and four other ships, turned over *Albacore* to Hugh R. Rimmer, who was sunk off Japan in November. Blanchard retired in 1957 and died in Dallas in 1968. James Jr. graduated from Annapolis in 1956 and also earned dolphins; he coauthored a submarine encyclopedia.

On VJ-day Herman Kossler was still skipper of *Cavalla*, patrolling off Japan with thirty-four-thousand tons to his credit. Subsequently he led a submarine division and squadron. He retired as a rear admiral commanding the Sixth Naval District in Charleston, South Carolina, where he was named outstanding citizen in 1970. He died of cancer in 1988.

The earliest recorder of the Philippine Sea battle was *Life* correspondent Noel F. Busch. His narratives first appeared in the July 17 issue, and subsequently he contributed to the Time-Life history of the war. Already recognized as an authoritative writer on Japan, he produced books about the 1905 Battle of Tsushima Strait and the 1923 earthquake as well as a biography of Theodore Roosevelt. Busch died in New York in 1985.

What Became of the Japanese?

JISABURO OZAWA REMAINED IN COMMAND of the Mobile Fleet. Despite the serious losses off Saipan, no one in Tokyo seriously expected anyone to do better, and Ozawa took Japan's four remaining flattops to the Philippines in October. There he succeeded brilliantly in decoying Halsey north, away from the landing areas in Leyte Gulf. After the war Ozawa provided much assistance to Samuel Eliot Morison in compiling the history of U.S. Navy operations in World War II. He died in 1966, age eighty.

Takeo Kurita, leader of Ozawa's C Force, returned to combat leading a powerful battleship group in October 1944. Within perhaps minutes of destroying the U.S. escort carriers in Leyte Gulf, he reversed helm and withdrew. He died at age eighty-eight in 1977.

Kurita's subordinate, Sueo Obayashi, survived the Leyte Gulf debacle, serving as Ozawa's chief of staff. He finished the war as commander of the First Special Attack Division, directing kamikaze operations from Japan. He also lived to eighty-eight, dying in 1983.

Takaji Joshima, leader of B Force, held five subsequent aviation commands. He finished as titular commander of Carrier Division Two, which never deployed after Leyte Gulf. Joshima died in 1964, age seventy-four.

Zenji Abe, *Junyo's* bomber leader, spent the rest of the war on Rota, and fifty years later he was still proud of the fact that he had surrendered to the United States Marines. He held a security position when the Japanese Self-Defense Force was established but spent most of his subsequent career in the plastic industry. At this writing he is ninety years old.

Captain Hiroshi Matsubara of *Shokaku* served ashore for the rest of the war, finishing his naval career as director of a torpedo school.

Hiyo's Toshiyuki Yokoi survived his injuries following loss of the ship and was promoted to rear admiral. He served on Admiral Ugaki's Fifth Air Fleet staff for most of the remainder of the war. In 1963 he contributed to translator Jay Gluck's anthology of postwar Japan.

The legendary Saburo Sakai survived two more Iwo Jima combats, then conceded that there was little future for a one-eyed fighter pilot. He ended the war as Japan's top surviving ace and established a printing business in Tokyo. His memoir, *Samurai*, was an immediate hit in 1956, gaining him admirers around the world. When he died in 2000, he was more widely mourned in America than in Japan.

The Marianas Today

IN ONE WAY, WORLD WAR II on Guam lasted thirty-one years. The final Japanese holdout, Sergeant Shoichi Yokoi, emerged from the jungle in 1972.

Today the Marianas are administratively divided. From 1947 to 1986 the chain was an American-administered U.N. Trust Territory. Residents voted the Northern Mariana Islands (Saipan, Rota, and Tinian) a self-governing U.S. commonwealth in 1975, leading to dissolution of the trust territory in 1986. The current population is about seventy-two thousand.

Guam (population 155,000) became a U.S. territory in 1950 with unincorporated status, as Guamanians are nonvoting American citizens. The island retains important air and naval bases that were especially valuable during the Vietnam War.

Today the Marianas are gloriously portrayed in travel brochures and Internet sites. Beautiful beaches, resort hotels, and sporting activities draw tourists from around the globe. Golf is especially popular, with at least sixteen courses on Guam, Saipan, Tinian, and even tiny Rota. Ironically—or perhaps not—the Marianas attract more travelers from Japan than any other nation.

APPENDIX A

UNITED STATES NAVY

Fifth Fleet Adm. Raymond A. Spruance USNA 1906*
Task Force 58 Vice Adm. Marc A. Mitscher USNA 1910

Task Group 58.1	Rear Adm. Joseph J. Clark '18	
298 CV a/c		
Hornet (CV-12)	Capt. William D. Sample '19	
Air Group 2	Cdr. Jackson D. Arnold '34	
VF-2	Lt. Cdr. William A. Dean '24	36 F6F-3
VB-2	Lt. Cdr. Grafton B. Campbell '32	33 SB2C-1C
VT-2	Lt. Cdr. Lewis M. D. Ford	18 TBF/TBM-1C
VFN-76 Det. B	Lt. Russell L. Reiserer	4 F6F-3N
Yorktown (CV-10)	Capt. Ralph E. Jennings '19	
Air Group 1	Cdr. James M. Peters '31	
VB-1	Lt. Cdr. J. W. Runyan, USNR	40 SB2C-1C
VF-1	Lt. Cdr. Bernard M. Strean '33	46 F6F-3
VT-1	Lt. Cdr. Walter F. Henry '35	17 TBM/TBF-1C
VFN-77 Det. B	Lt. Anthony C. Benjes '40	4 F6F-3N
Belleau Wood (CVL-24)	Capt. John Perry '20	
VF-24	Lt. Cdr. Edward M. Link Jr. '36	26 F6F-3
VT-24	Lt. Jim T. Alston, USNR	9 TBF/TBM-1C
Bataan (CVL-29)	Capt. Valentine H. Schaeffer '19	
VF-50	Lt. Cdr. Johnnie C. Strange	24 F6F-3
VT-50	Lt. Cdr. L. V. Swanson	9 TBM-1C
Cruiser Division 10	Rear Adm. Leo H. Thebaud '13	VCS-10
Baltimore (CA-68)	Capt. Walter C. Calhoun '17	1 OS2N-1, 1 OS2U-3
Boston (CA-69)	Capt. Ernest E. Herrmann '10	1 OS2N-1, 1 OS2U-3
Canberra (CA-70)	Capt. Alexander R. Early Jr. '14	2 OS2N-1
San Juan (CL-54)	Capt. Guy W. Clark '17	
Screen	Capt. Clark	
Destroyer Squadron 46	?	
Oakland (CL-95)	Capt. William K. Phillips '18	

* '33 = Annapolis Class of 1933
USNR: Naval Reserve
No notation: Regular Navy, not Annapolis

Destroyer Division 91   ?
Charrette (DD-581)   Cdr. Eugene S. Karp '26
Conner (DD-582)   Cdr. William E. Kaitner '27
Bell (DD-587)   Lt. Cdr. John S. C. Gabbert '35
Burns (DD588)   Cdr. Donald T. Eller '29
Izard (DD-589)   Cdr. Milton T. Dayton '27
Destroyer Division 92   Capt. William M. Sweetser '26
Boyd (DD-544)   Cdr. Ulysses S. G. Sharp Jr. '27
Bradford (DD-545)   Cdr. Robert L. Morris '28
Brown (DD-546)   Cdr. Thomas H. Copeman '31
Cowell (DD-547)   Cdr. Charles W. Parker '27
Destroyer Division 11   Capt. Edwin G. Fullinwider '21
Gridley (DD-380)   Cdr. Phillip D. Quirk '32
Craven (DD-382)   Lt. Cdr. Raymond L. Fulton '33
Helm (DD-388)   Lt. Cdr. Shelby K. Santmyers '33
McCall (DD-400)   Lt. Cdr. John B. Carroll '37
Maury (DD-401)   Lt. Cdr. Joseph W. Koenig '33

Task Group 58.2	Rear Adm. Alfred E. Montgomery '12	
246 a/c		
Bunker Hill (CV-17)	Capt. Thomas P. Jeter '19	
Air Group 8	Cdr. Ralph L. Shifley '33	
VF-8	Lt. Cdr. William M. Collins Jr. '34	42 F6F-3
VB-8	Lt. Cdr. James D. Arbes	33 SB2C-1C
VT-8	Lt. Cdr. Kenneth F. Musick '35	18 TBF/TBM-1C
VFN-76 Det. A	Lt. Cdr. Evan P. Aurand '38	4 F6F-3N
Wasp (CV-18)	Capt. Clifton A. F. Sprague '18	
Air Group 14	Cdr. Walter C. Wingard Jr. '30	
VF-14	Lt. Cdr. Edmund W. Biros	39 F6F-3
VB-14	Lt. Cdr. John D. Blitch '36	32 SB2C-1
VT-14	Lt. Cdr. Howard S. Roberts	18 TBF-1C/1D
VFN-77 Det. C	Lt. John H. Boyum '40	4 F6F-3N
Cabot (CVL-28)	Capt. Stanley J. Michael '20	
VF-31	Lt. Cdr. Robert A. Winston	24 F6F-3
VT-31	Lt. Edward E. Wood	9 TBM/TBF-1C
Monterey (CVL-26)	Capt. Stuart H. Ingersoll '21	
VF-28	Lt. Cdr. Roger C. Mehle '37	21 F6F-3
VT-28	Lt. Roland P. Gift	8 TBM-1C
Cruiser Division 13	Rear Adm. Laurence T. DuBose	VCS-13
Santa Fe (CL-60)	Capt. Jerauld Wright '18	2 OS2N-1

Mobile (CL-63)	Capt. Capt. Charles J. Wheeler '16	1 OS2N-1, 1 OS2U-2
Biloxi (CL-80)	Capt. Daniel M. McCurl	2 OS2U-3

Screen	Capt. George R. Cooper '22
Destroyer Squadron 52	Capt. Cooper
Destroyer Division 103	Capt. Cooper
Miller (DD-535)	Cdr. T. H. Kolberg
Owen (DD-536)	Cdr. Robert W. Wood '28
The Sullivans (DD-537)	Cdr Kenneth M. Gentry '30
Stephen Potter (DD-538)	Cdr. Leonidas W. Pancoast '27
Tingey (DD-539)	Cdr. John O. Miner '31

Destroyer Division 104	Cdr. H. H. Bell
Hickox (DD-673)	Lt. Cdr. J. H. Wesson '35
Hunt (DD-674)	Cdr. H. A Knoertzer '32
Lewis Hancock (DD-675)	Cdr. William M. Searles '28
Marshall (DD-676)	Cdr. Joseph D. McKinney '27

Destroyer Squadron 1	Capt. Ephraim R. McLean Jr. '27
Destroyer Division 1	Capt. McLean
Dewey (DD-349)	Lt. Cdr. C. Raymond Calhoun '38
MacDonough (DD-351)	Cdr. John W. Ramey '32
Hull (DD-350)	Lt. Cdr. Charles W. Consolvo '35

Task Group 58.3	Rear Adm. John W. Reeves '11	
227 a/c		
Lexington (CV-16) (TF Flag)	Capt. Ernest W. Litch '20	
Air Group 16	Cdr. Ernest M. Snowden '32	
VF-16	Lt. Cdr. Paul D. Buie '33	41 F6F-3
VB-16	Lt. Cdr. Ralph Weymouth '38	34 SBD-5
VT-16	Lt. Norman A. Sterrie, USNR	18 TBF/TBM-1C
VFN-76 Det. C	Lt. W. H. Abercrombie, USNR	4 F6F-3N

Enterprise (CV-6)	Capt. Matthais B. Gardner '19	
Air Group 10	Cdr. William R. Kane '33	
VF-10	Lt. Cdr. Roland W. Schumann '39	31 F6F-3
VB-10	Lt. Cdr. James D. Ramage '39	21 SBD-5
VT-10	Lt. Cdr. William I. Martin '34	14 TBF-1C
VFN-101	Lt. Cdr. Richard E. Harmer '35	3 F4U-2

San Jacinto (CVL-30)	Capt. Harold M. Martin '19	
VF-51	Lt. Cdr. Charles L. Moore '33	24 F6F-3
VT-51	Lt. Cdr. Donald J. Melvin	8 TBM-1C/1D

Princeton (CVL-23)	Capt. William H. Buracker '20	
VF-27	Lt. Cdr. Ernest W. Wood '38	24 F6F-3
VT-27	Lt. Cdr. Sebron M. Haley, USNR	9 TBM-1C
Indianapolis (CA-35)	Capt. Einar R. Johnson '18	VCS-4 4 SOC-1
Cruiser Division 12	Rear Adm. Robert W. Hayler '13	VCS-12 & 13
Cleveland (CL-55)	Capt. Andrew G. Shepard '17	1 SOC-1
Montpelier (CL-57)	Capt. Harry D. Hoffman '18	2 SOC-1
Birmingham (CL-62)	Capt. Thomas B. Inglis '18	2 OS2U-3
Screen	Capt. Ralph C. Alexander '18?	
Reno (CL-96)	Capt. Alexander	
Destroyer Squadron 50	Cdr. Charles F. Chillingworth Jr. '25	
Destroyer Division 99	Cdr. Chillingworth	
Clarence K. Bronson (DD-668)	Cdr. Gifford S. Cull	
Cotten (DD-669)	Cdr. Philip W. Winston '33	
Dortch (DD-670)	Lt. Cdr. Robert C. Young '32	
Gatling (DD-671)	Cdr. Alvin F. Richardson '31	
Healy (DD-672)	Cdr. John C. Atkeson '27	
Destroyer Division 90	Cdr. Fondville L. Tedder '26	
Terry (DD-513)	Lt. Cdr. John M. Lee '35	
Anthony (DD-515)	Cdr. Blinn Van Mater '27	
Braine (DD-630)	Cdr. William W. Fitts '31	
Wadsworth (DD-516)	Cdr. John F. Walsh '26	
Destroyer Division 100	Cdr. Wallace J. Miller '26	
Caperton (DD-650)	Cdr. Miller	
Cogswell (DD-651)	Cdr. Harold T. Deuterman '27	
Ingersoll (DD-652)	Cdr. Alexander C. Veasey '31	
Knapp (DD-653)	Lt. Cdr. William B. Brown	
Task Group 58.4	Rear Adm. William K. Harrill '14	
161 a/c		
Essex (CV-9)	Capt. Ralph A. Ofstie '19	
Air Group 15	Cdr. David McCampbell '33	
VF-15	Lt. Cdr. Charles W. Brewer '34	42 F6F-3
VB-15	Lt. Cdr. James H. Mini '35	36 SB2C-1C
VT-15	Lt. Cdr. Valdemar G. Lambert	20 TBF/TBM-1C
VFN-77 Det. A	Lt. R.M. Freeman	4 F6F-3N
Langley (CVL-27)	Capt. Wallace M. Dillon '18	
VF-32	Lt. Cdr. Edward C. Outlaw '35	23 F6F-3
VT-32	Lt. David A. Marks '40	9 TBF/TBM-1C

Cowpens (CVL-25)	Capt. Herbert W. Taylor '21	
VF-25	Lt. Cdr. Robert H. Price	23 F6F-3
VT-25	Lt. R. B. Cottingham, USNR	9 TBM/TBF-1C
Screen	Rear Adm. Lloyd J. Wiltse '14	
Cruiser Division 11	Rear Adm. Wiltse	
San Diego (CL-53)	Capt. Lester J. Hudson '17	
Cruiser Division 14	Rear Adm. Wilder D. Barker	VCS-14
Vincennes (CL-64)	Capt. Arthur D. Brown '19	2 OS2U-3
Houston (CL-81)	Capt. William W. Behrens	2 OS2U-3
Miami (CL-89)	Capt. John G. Crawford '19	1 OS2U-3, 1 OS2N-1
Destroyer Squadron 12	Capt. William P. Burford '23	
Destroyer Division 23	?	
Case (DD-370)	Lt. Cdr. Robert S. Willey '37	
Lansdowne (DD-486)	Lt. Cdr. William S. Maddox '34	
Lardner (DD-487)	Lt. Cdr. Jefferson D. Parker '35	
McCalla (DD-488)	Lt. Cdr. Edwin K. Jones '34	
Destroyer Division 24	Capt. John L. Melgaard '25	
Ellet (DD-398)	Lt. Cdr. Eugene C. Rider '34	
Lang (DD-399)	Lt. Cdr. Harold Payson Jr. '31	
Sterett (DD-407)	Cdr. Francis J. Blouin '33	
Wilson (DD-408)	Lt. Cdr. Colin J. MacKenzie '34	
Destroyer Squadron 23	Capt. Thomas B. Dugan '22	
Destroyer Division 45	Capt. Dugan	
Stanly (DD-478)	Lt. Cdr. John B. Morland '34	
Dyson (DD-572)	Lt. Cdr. James D. Babb '34	
Charles Ausburne (DD-570)	Lt. Cdr. Howard W. Baker '37	
Destroyer Division 46	Cdr. Robert W. Cavenagh '26	
Converse (DD-509)	Cdr. John B. Colwell '31	
Spence (DD-512)	Cdr. Henry J. Armstrong '27	
Thatcher (DD-514)	Cdr. Leland R. Lampman '27	

TF-58 cruisers: 20 OS2U/OS2N and 7 SOC = 27 VOS

Task Group 58.7	Vice Adm. Willis A. Lee '08	
Battleship Division 6	Vice Adm. Lee	VO-6
Washington (BB-56)	Capt. Thomas R. Cooley Jr. '17	2 OS2U-3
North Carolina (BB-55)	Capt. Frank P. Thomas '14	2 OS2U-3
Battleship Division 7	Rear Adm. Olaf M. Hustvedt '09	VO-7
Iowa (BB-61)	Capt. John L. McCrea '15	2 OS2N-1
New Jersey (BB-62)	Capt. Carl F. Holden '17	2 OS2U-3

Battleship Division 8	Rear Adm. Glenn B. Davis '15	VO-8
Indiana (BB-58)	Capt. Thomas J. Keliher '16	2 OS2U-3
Battleship Division 9	Rear Adm. Edward W. Hanson '11	VO-9
South Dakota (BB-57)	Capt. Ralph S. Riggs '18	2 OS2N-1
Alabama (BB-60)	Capt. Fred D. Kirtland '16	2 OS2U-3
Cruiser Division 6	Rear Adm. C. Turner Joy '16	VCS-6
New Orleans (CA-32)	Capt. Jack E. Hurff '20	4 SOC-1/2/3
Minneapolis (CA-36)	Capt. Harry Slocum '19	4 SOC-1
San Francisco (CA-38)	Capt. Harvey E. Overesch '15	4 SOC-1
Wichita (CA-45)	Capt. Douglas A. Spencer '17	4 SOC-3
Destroyer Squadron 45	Cdr. Edmund B. Taylor '25	
Destroyer Division 89	Cdr. Taylor?	
Guest (DD-472)	Cdr. Marvin G. Kennedy '29	
Bennett (DD-473)	Lt. Cdr. Philip F. Hauck '35	
Fullam (DD-474)	Cdr. William D. Kelly '32	
Hudson (DD-475)	Lt. Cdr. Richard R. Pratt '36	
Halford (DD-480)	Lt. Cdr. Robert J. Hardy '34	
Destroyer Division 12	Cdr. Karl F. Poehlmann '26	
Bagley (DD-386)	Lt. Cdr. William H. Shea Jr. '36	
Mugford (DD-389)	Lt. Cdr. M. A. Shellabarger '33?	
Ralph Talbot (DD-390)	Lt. Cdr. W. S. Brown	
Patterson (DD-392)	Cdr. Albert F. White '29?	
Conyngham (DD-371)	Lt. Cdr. Brown Taylor '34	
Selfridge (DD-357)	Lt. Cdr. Louis L. Snider '33	

(*Conyngham* replaced *Ralph Talbot*, damaged June 12.)

Destroyer Squadron 53	Capt. Harry B. Jarrett '22
Destroyer Division 106	Cdr. Thomas Burrowes
Monssen (DD-798)	Cdr. Bernhart A. Feutch
Twining (DD-540)	Cdr. Ellis K. Wakefield '30
Yarnall (DD-541)	Cdr. Benjamin F. Tompkins '26
Stockham (DD-683)	Cdr. Ephraim P. Holmes '30
Halsey Powell (DD-686)	Cdr. W. T. McGarry '27 TF-57/58
Renshaw (DD-499)	Cdr. J. A. Lark '32 TF-57/58

TF-57: 14 OS2U/2N, 16 SOC = 30 VOS

Patrol Squadrons
Seaplane tender at Saipan

Ballard (AVD-10)	Lt. Cdr. G. C. Nichandross, USNR	
VP-16	Lt. Cdr. W. J. Scarpino	5 PBM-5

Los Negros Island
VB-101   Cdr. Justin A. Miller '31   12 PB4Y-1

Picket Line Submarines
Task Force 17   Vice Adm. Charles A. Lockwood Jr. '12
Bonin Islands
Plunger (SS-179)   Lt. Cdr. Edward J. Fahy '34
Gar (SS-206)   Cdr. George W. Lautrup '34
Archerfish (SS-311)   Cdr. William H. Wright '36
Plaice (SS-390)   Cdr. Clyde B. Stevens Jr. '30
Swordfish (SS-193)   Cdr. Edmund K. Montross '35
Southeast of Formosa
Pintado (SS-387)   Lt. Cdr. Bernard A. Clarey '34
Pilotfish (SS-386)   Lt. Cdr. Robert H. Close '34
Tunny (SS-282)   Cdr. John A. Scott '28
West and Southwest of Marianas
Albacore (SS-218)   Cdr. James W. Blanchard '27
Seawolf (SS-197)   Lt. Cdr. Richard B. Lynch '35
Bang (SS-385)   Cdr. Anton R. Gallaher '33
Finback (SS-230)   Lt. Cdr. James L. Jordan '33
Stingray (SS-186)   Lt. Cdr. Samuel C. Loomis '35

Ulithi-Philippines
Growler (SS-215)   Cdr. Thomas B. Oakley Jr. '34
Flying Fish (SS-229)   Lt. Cdr. Robert D. Risser '34
Cavalla (SS-244)   Lt. Cdr. Herman J. Kossler '34
Muskellunge (SS-262)   Cdr. Michael P. Russillo '27
Seahorse (SS-304)   Lt. Cdr. Slade D. Cutter '35
Pipefish (SS-388)   Lt. Cdr. William N. Deragon '34

7th Fleet Submarines   Rear Adm. Ralph W. Christie '15
Southeast of Mindoro
Bashaw (SS-241)   Lt. Cdr. Richard E. Nichols '34
Hake (SS-256)   Lt. Cdr. John C. Broach '27
Paddle (SS-263)   Lt. Cdr. Byron H. Nowell '35
Tawi-Tawi
Bluefish (SS-222)   Cdr. Charles M. Henderson '34
Haddo (SS-255)   Lt. Cdr. Chester W. Nimitz Jr. '36
Harder (SS-257)   Cdr. Samuel D. Dealey '30
Redfin (SS-272)   Lt. Cdr. Marshall H. Austin '35
Off Luzon
Flier (SS-250)   Cdr. Jack D. Crowley '31
Jack (SS-259)   Cdr. Arthur E. Krapf '34

APPENDIX B

IMPERIAL JAPANESE NAVY

First Mobile Fleet	Vice Adm. Jisaburo Ozawa	
A Force	Vice Adm. Ozawa	
1st Carrier Division	Vice Adm. Jisaburo Ozawa	
Air Group 601	Cdr. Toshiie Irisa	
Fighter Leader	Lt. Yasuo Masuyama	
Bomber Leader	Lt. Cdr. Kenji Ono	
Torpedo leader	Lt. Cdr. Akira Tarui	
Scout Leader	Lt. Toyohiko Oyamada?	
CV *Taiho* (F)*	Capt. Tomozo Kikuchi	
Hikokitai 311		
Fighter Squadron	Lt Toshitada Kawazoe†	22 A6M5
Bomber Squadron	Lt. Masao Hirahara†	22 D4Y1/1C, 3 D3A2
Torpedo Squadron	Lt. Cdr. Tarui (o)†	18 B6N1
CV *Shokaku**	Capt. Hiroshi Matsubara	
Hikokitai 322		
Fighter Squadron	Lt. Yasuo Masuyama	34 A6M5
Bomber Squadron	Lt. Yoshiakira Tanaka†	10 D4Y1, 3 D3A2
Scout Squadron	Lt. Toyohiko Oyamada (o)†	10 D4Y1C
Torpedo Squadron	Lt. Tadotoshi Nire†	9 B6N1
Scout Detachment	Lt. Shizuo Fukagawa (o)	3 B6N2?
CV *Zuikaku*	Capt. Takeo Kaizuka	
Hikokitai 323		
Fighter Squadron	Lt. Ikuro Sakami†	24 A6M5
Fighter Bombers	Lt. Toshio Suzuki†	11 A6M2
Bomber Squadron	Lt. Masami Shimada†	18 D4Y1, 3 D3A2
Torpedo Squadron	Lt. Torizo Kishimoto	14 B6N1
Scout Detachment	Lt. Keizo Kitao (o)	2 D4Y1C, 3 B6N2?
Cruiser Division 5	Rear Adm. Shintaro Hashimoto	
Myoko (F)	Capt. Itsu Ishiwara	

* † Sunk or KIA in May–July 1944
(o) observer
Note: IJN referred to torpedo planes as attack aircraft (*Kogekikitai*) but U.S. terminology is employed for clarity. 653 AG referred to torpedo planes as search-attack.

Haguro	Capt. Kaju Sugiura	
Destroyer Squadron 10	Rear Adm. Masanori Kimura	
CL *Yahagi* (F)	Capt. Motake Yoshimura	
Destroyer Divs 10 and 17	Capt. Shizuo Akawaga[†] (KIA June 8)	
	Capt. Tamotsu Tanii	
Asagumo	Cdr. Kazuo Shibayama	
Urakaze	Cdr. Shoichi Yoshida	
Isokaze	Lt. Cdr. Saneho Maeda	
Tanikaze*	Lt. Cdr. Ikeda Shunsaku	Sunk by sub June 9
Destroyer Division 61	Capt. Shigetaka Amano	
Hatsuzuki	Cdr. Shoichi Taguchi	
Akizuki	Cdr. Tomoe Ogata	
Wakatsuki	Cdr. Yasuatsu Suzuki	
Shimotsuki	Cdr. Kenji Hatano	
Minazuki*	Lt. Kaije Isobe	Sunk by sub June 6

B Force   Rear Adm. Takaji Joshima
Carrier Division 2   Rear Adm. Joshima
Air Group 652   Cdr. Shoichi Suzuki
Attack Leader   Lt. Cdr. Jozo Iwami
Bomber Leader   Lt. Zenji Abe
Fighter Leader   Lt. Yasuhei Kobayashi
Fighter Bombers   Lt. Hiroshi Yoshimura
Torpedo Leader   Lt. Cdr. Iwami

CV *Junyo*	Capt. Kiyomi Shibuya	
Hikokitai 321		
Fighter Squadron	Lt. Hiroshi Yoshimura[†]	18 A6M5
Fighter Bombers	Lt. Ichiro Sato[†]	9 A6M2
Bomber Squadron	Lt. Abe	11 D4Y1
Bomber Detachment	Lt. Susumu Ikari (o)[†]	9 D3A2
Torpedo Squadron	Lt. Cdr. Iwami (o)	6 B6N1
CV *Hiyo**	Capt. Toshiyuki Yokoi	
Hikokitai 322		
Fighter Squadron	Lt. Hideo Katori	18 A6M5
Fighter Bombers	Lt. Takeshi Murakami	9 A6M2
Bomber Squadron	Lt. Yasunori Miyauchi	20 D3A2
Torpedo Squadron	Lt. Oji Edagawa (o)[†]	5 B6N1
CV *Ryuho*	Capt. Tokio Komei	
Hikokitai 323		
Fighter Squadron	Lt. Dai Nakajima	18 A6M5

Fighter Bombers	WO Fuijiki Azuma	9 A6M2
Torpedo Squadron	Lt. Yasuji Takeuchi[†]	5 B6N1

Screen		
BB *Nagato*	Capt. Yuji Kobe	
CA *Mogami*	Capt. Ryo Toma	
Destroyer Division 4	Capt. Kameshiro Takahashi	
Michishio	Lt. Cdr. Tomoo Tanaka	
Nowaki	Cdr. Setsuji Moriya	
Yamagumo	Cdr. Shirou Ono	
Destroyer Division 27	Capt. Masashichi Shirahama (KIA in *Harusame*)	
	Capt. Ichitaro Oshima?	
Akishimo	Lt. Cdr. Kotarou Nakao	
*Harusame**	Lt. Cdr. Tomita Toshihiko	Sunk by USAAF June 8
Hayashimo	Lt. Cdr. Toshio Hirayama	
Samidare	Lt. Cdr. Iokuta Nishimura	
Shigure	Lt. Cdr. Shigeru Nishino	
*Shiratsuyu**	Lt. Cdr. Matsuda Kuru	Sunk in collision June 14
Hamakaze	Cdr. Kazue Maekawa	

Carrier Division 3	Rear Adm. Sueo Obayashi	
Air Group 653	Cdr. Gunji Kumura	
Fighter Leader	Lt. Kenji Nakagawa	
Fighter Bombers	Lt. Keishiro Ito	
Torpedo Leader	Lt. Cdr. Masayuki Yamagami	

CVL *Chitose* (F)	Capt. Yoshiyuki Kishi	
Hikokitai 331		
Fighter Squadron	Lt. Hiroshi Shiozaka[†]	6 A6M5
Fighter Bomber Squadron	Lt(jg) Eiichi Furusawa[†]	16 A6M2
Torpedo Squadron	Lt. Michijiro Nakamoto[†]	3 B6N1, 6 B5N2

CVL *Chiyoda*	Capt. Eichiro Joh	
Hikokitai 332		
Fighter Squadron	Lt(jg) Kunio Nomura[†]	5 A6M5
Fighter Bombers	Lt. Takashi Ebata[†]	15 A6M2
Torpedo Squadron	Lt. Cdr. Yamagami (o)[†]	6 B5N2, 3 B6N1

CVL *Zuiho*	Capt. Takuro Sugiura	
Hikokitai 333		

Fighter Squadron	Lt. Nakagawa	6 A6M5
Fighter Bomber Squadron	Lt. Ito[†]	15 A6M2
Torpedo Squadron	Lt(jg) Taro Yukitake (o)[†]	3 B6N1, 6 B5N2

Battle Division 1	Vice Adm. Matome Ugaki
Yamato	Capt. Nobuei Morishita
Musashi	Capt. Bunji Asakura
Battle Division 3	Vice Adm. Suzuki
Kongo	Capt. Toshio Shimazaki
Haruna	Capt. Shigenaga Katazuke
Cruiser Division 4	Vice Adm. Takeo Kurita
Atago (F)	Capt. Tsutau Araki
Takao	Capt. Shigechika Hayashi
Chokai	Capt. Jo Tanaka
Maya	Capt. Ranji Ooe

Cruiser Division 7	Rear Adm. Kazutaka Shiraishi
Kumano (F)	Capt. Soichiro Hitomi
Chikuma	Capt. Saiji Norimitsu
Suzuya	Capt. Yuji Takahashi
Tone	Capt. Haruo Mayazumi

Destroyer Squadron 2	Rear Adm. Mikio Hayakawa
CL *Noshiro* (F)	Capt. Sueyoshi Kajiwara
Destroyer Division 31	Capt. Tokujiro Fukuoka
Asashimo	Lt. Cdr. Yoshirou Sugihara
Kishinami	Cdr. Toshirou Mifune
Okinami	Cdr. Hiroshi (or Akira) Makino

Destroyer Division 32	Capt. Kyuji Aoki	
Fujinami	Cdr. Matsuzaki Tatsuji	
Hamakaze	Cdr. Maekawa Kazue	
Shimakaze	Cdr. Hiroshi Uwai	
Tamanami	Cdr. Chihogi Tomiji	
*Hayanami**	Cdr. Itsurou Shimizu	Sunk by sub June 7

Oiler Group	
First Supply Force	?
Oiler *Hayasui*	Capt. Keizaburo Sugiura
Oiler *Nichiei Maru*	Capt. Ikaan Okano (ret.)
Oiler *Kokuyo Maru*	?
Oiler *Seiyo Maru**	?
CL *Natori*	Capt. Toshi Kubota

DD *Hibiki*   Cdr. Eikichi Fukushima
DD *Hatsushimo*   Lt. Cdr. Kouji Takigawa
DesDiv21
DD *Tsuga*   Lt. Masanobu Kuniya
DD *Yunagi*   Lt. Cdr. Goro Iwabuchi
DesDiv22

Second Supply Force   ?
Oiler *Genyo Maru**   ?
Oiler *Azusa Maru*   ?
DD *Yukikaze*   Lt. Cdr. Masamichi Terauchi
DD *Uzuki*   Lt. Yoshiro Watanabe

Land-based Air
Base Air Force Marianas Vice Adm. Kakuji Kakuta

61st Air Flotilla	Rear Adm. Ueno	
Air Group 121	Cdr. Iwao	Tinian
Hikotai T.1	10 C6N1	Palau
Hikotai T.2	10 D4Y1	
Air Group 261	Cdr. Ueda	Saipan
Hikotai S.1, S.2	80 A6M5	
Air Group 263	Cdr. Tamai	Guam
Hikotai S.3, S.4	80 A6M5	
Air Group 265	Cdr. Urata	Guam
Hikotai S.7, S.8	80 A6M5	
Air Group 321	Cdr. Kubo	Tinian
Hikotai S.801, S.802	30 J1N1	
Air Group 343	Cdr. Takenaka	Palau
Hikotai S.403	40 A6M5	
Air Group 521	Cdr. Yoshio Kamei	Guam
Hikotai K.401	40 P1Y1	Tinian
Hikotai K.402	40 P1Y1	
Air Group 523	Cdr. Wada	Tinian
Hikotai K.1, K.2	40 D4Y1	
Air Group 761	Cdr. Matsumoto	Tinian
Hikotai K.601	40 G4M2	Palau
Hikotai K.602	40 G4M2	

Air Group 1021	Cdr. Kurihara	Tinian
Hikotai U.1, U.2	20 L2D2	

22nd Air Flotilla	Rear Adm. Sumikawa	
Air Group 755	Cdr. Kusumoto	Guam
Hikotai K.701	40 G4M2	Truk
Hikotai K.702	40 G4M2	

S.1 *Sentoki* (fighter)
K.1: *Kogeki* (bomber)
T.1: *Teitsu* (reconnaissance)
U.1: *Unso* (transport)

Authorized strength:

280 A6M Zeke	240 in Marianas
160 G4M Betty	80 in Marianas
80 PY1 Frances	80 in Marianas
50 D4Y Judy	40 in Marianas
30 J1N Irving	30 in Marianas
20 L2D Tabby	20 in Marianas
10 C6N1 Judy	10 in Marianas
630 in region	500 in Marianas
Actual strength:	250–540 aircraft

Sixth Fleet (Submarines)	Vice Adm. Takeo Takagi	
I-5*	Lt. Cdr. Mareshige Doi[†]	Lost July 19
I-10*	Cdr. Seiji Nakajima[†]	Lost July 4
I-26	Cdr. Toshio Kusaka	
I-38	Lt. Cdr. Yoshiro Shimose	
I-41	Lt. Cdr. Mitsuyoshi Itakura	
I-53	Lt. Cdr. Seihachi Toyamasu	
I-184*	Lt. Cdr. Matsugi Rikihisa[†]	Lost June 19
I-185*	Lt. Cdr. Atsushi Arai[†]	Lost June 22
RO-36*	Lt. Cdr. Tatsua Kawashima[†]	Lost June 13
RO-41	Lt. Cdr. Keneo Sakamoto	
RO-42*	Lt. Yoshonosuke Kudo[†]	Lost June 10
RO-43	Lt. Masaki Tsukigata	
RO-44*	Lt. Sadao Uesugi[†]	Lost June 16
RO-47	Lt. Shoichi Nishiuchi	
RO-68	Lt Cdr. Kazuaki Uesugi	
RO-104*	Lt. Shikari Izubuchi[†]	Lost May 23
RO-105*	Lt. Junichi Inoue[†]	Lost May 31
RO-106*	Lt. Shigehiro Uda[†]	Lost May 22
RO-108*	Lt. Kanichi Obari[†]	Lost May 26
RO-109	Lt. Jun Toji	

RO-112   Lt. Fumitake Kondo
RO-113   Lt. Hisashi Watanabe
RO-114*   Lt. Yoshihiro Ata[†]   Lost June 17
RO-115   Lt. Chuzo Takema
RO-116*   Lt. Cdr. Takeshi Okabe[†]   Lost May 24
RO-117*   Lt. Cdr. Yasuo Enomoto[†]   Lost June 17

APPENDIX C

GLOSSARY

AA: Antiaircraft guns
API: Armor-piercing incendiary ammunition
ASI: Airspeed indicator
BB: Battleship
CA: Heavy cruiser
 CAG: Commander of Air Group; Carrier Air Group
CAP: Combat Air Patrol
CarDiv: Carrier Division
CIC: Combat Information Center, also radar plot
CL: Light cruiser
CV: Fleet carrier
CVE: Escort carrier
CVL: Light carrier
DD: Destroyer
DFC: Distinguished Flying Cross
FDO: Fighter direction officer
HF/DF: High-frequency direction finder
IFF: Identification, friend or foe (transponder)
JK: Submarine listening gear
JP: Long-range listening gear
LCI: Landing craft, infantry
LSO: Landing signal officer
ONI: Office of Naval Intelligence
PPI: Plan position indicator (overhead view)
QB: Supersonic listening gear
QC: Supersonic transmitter
RCAF: Royal Canadian Air Force
SC: Shipboard air search radar
SG: Shipboard surface search radar
SK: Shipboard air search radar with PPI
TBS: Talk between ship radio
TDC: Torpedo data computer
TF: Task Force
TG: Task Group
VB: Bombing squadron or aircraft
VF: Fighting squadron or aircraft
VF(N): Night-fighting squadron or aircraft
VP: Patrol squadron or aircraft
VT: Torpedo squadron or aircraft

APPENDIX D

AMERICAN AIRCRAFT

Consolidated PB2Y-3 Coronado. One of the most capable flying boats of the war, the big, four-engine PB2Y was a "theater asset" in later parlance. Though Coronados were based in the Marshalls, well east of the Marianas, their exceptional range and endurance suited them well for searches in the Pacific expanse, where twelve-man crews typically flew ten-hour missions. Top speed: 224 mph/195 knots.

Consolidated PB4Y-1 Liberator. With more than eighteen thousand copies, the U.S. Army's B-24 was the most-produced aircraft in American history. The Navy adopted the Liberator in 1942 and acquired nearly a thousand of the four-engine, twin-tailed bombers. A Liberator squadron operated from the Admiralty Islands during Operation Forager, augmenting the PBM flying boats on long-range patrol. Top speed: 287 mph/250 knots.

Curtiss SB2C-1C Helldiver. The dive-bomber meant to replace the Douglas Dauntless was a colossal problem for the U.S. Navy. Though bigger and faster than the SBD, with an internal bomb bay, the Helldiver failed its original carrier trials and was plagued with structural problems. First flown in 1939, it did not reach combat until late 1943. Helldivers suffered catastrophic losses on June 20, but the much improved SB2C-3 and -4 models made respectable records after the Marianas campaign. Top speed: 281 mph/244 knots.

Curtiss SOC-1/3 Seagull. Floatplane pilots said that SOC meant "Scout on a Catapult." The 1934 biplane was placed aboard American battleships and cruisers, employed for scouting and gunfire spotting. Launched from catapults, SOCs were recovered by crane and hoisted back aboard ship. Only 303 were produced, but the Seagull remained in service throughout the war, with twenty-six in the U.S. task forces off Saipan. Top speed: 165 mph/143 knots.

Douglas SBD-5 Dauntless. By mid-1944 the Dauntless was considered obsolescent, but it did more to win the Pacific War than any other aircraft. Its role in winning the 1942 battles was unapproached by other planes, let alone any other dive bomber. Dauntless pilots and gunners insisted that SBD meant "slow but deadly," and repeatedly proved that their airplane was competitive with the latest aircraft in the fleet. SBDs sank more carriers unassisted than any plane in history. Of 5,900 manufactured from 1940 to 1944, 950 went to the Army as A-24s. Top speed: 252 mph/220 knots.

Grumman F6F-3 Hellcat. The Hellcat was the most successful naval fighter of World War II. Upon replacing the F4F Wildcat in 1943, the F6F was largely responsible for destroying Japanese airpower over the next two years. With a rugged two-thousand-horsepower Pratt & Whitney engine and six .50-caliber machine guns, the angular fighter from Long Island produced more aces than any American fighter in history. Though less maneuverable, the "dash three" was notably faster and more rugged than the Mitsubishi Zero. In a notable industrial achievement, Grumman built 12,275 Hellcats at one factory in barely two years. Top speed: 375 mph/326 knots.

Grumman TBF-1C Avenger. The Avenger was the largest carrier-based aircraft of World War II. Designed as a torpedo plane, it flew far more missions with bombs against land targets. With a sixteen-hundred-horsepower Wright engine and three-man crew, the Avenger could perform a variety of missions, including attack, reconnaissance, and submarine patrol. Demand was such that Grumman turned over production to General Motors in 1943, and Eastern Aircraft Division built the TBM series. Nearly ten thousand Avengers were produced during the war. Top speed: 257 mph/223 knots.

Martin PBM-5 Mariner. The Mariner never quite rivaled the Consolidated PBY Catalina's reputation but still proved itself as a flying boat. First flown in 1939, the PBM entered service the next year and remained in the fleet until 1956. With twin radial engines on its gull wing, the Martin possessed considerable endurance, and a Mariner squadron was deployed to the Marianas to perform long-range patrol. Some thirteen hundred were delivered between 1940 and 1949. Top speed: 215 mph/187 knots.

Vought F4U-2 Corsair. The Corsair had the same Pratt & Whitney engine as the Hellcat, but in a sleeker airframe. However, the F4U's early promise was stunted by poor carrier landing characteristics, resulting in assignment to land-based squadrons. Corsairs did not begin routine carrier deployments until the end of 1944, but in the first half of the year two small detachments of radar-equipped night fighters operated with Task Force 58. When production ended in 1953 the Corsair held the all-time record for most naval aircraft: more than 12,570 from Vought, Goodyear, and Brewster. Top speed: 381 mph/331 knots.

Vought OS2U-3 Kingfisher. The observation-scouting mission of the Curtiss SOC was largely absorbed by the more capable Vought beginning in 1940. More than 1,500 Kingfishers were built through 1942, with a less powerful Pratt & Whitney engine than the SOC. The OS2U was also built as the OS2N-1 by the Naval Aircraft Factory; some thirty-four Kingfishers were aboard Fifth Fleet ships at Saipan. Top speed: 170 mph/148 knots.

APPENDIX E

JAPANESE AIRCRAFT
Aichi D3A2 carrier dive-bomber. The fixed-gear "Val" was another familiar player in the Pacific league. With fixed landing gear and an eleven-hundred-horsepower radial engine, it appeared ungainly in flight but proved deadly to Allied warships. First flown in 1937, the D3A made a name at Pearl Harbor and beyond, but by 1944 it was long in the tooth. Though it was an effective aircraft, with fifteen hundred built throughout the war, it was highly vulnerable to fighters. Hellcats snacked on Vals; at Philippine Sea Vals were used on antisub patrol as well as attacks. Top speed: 240 mph/209 knots.

Aichi E13A scout-observation floatplane. Doctrinally the Japanese Navy believed in concentrating attack aircraft in carriers, leaving much of the reconnaissance mission to floatplanes. One such was "Jake," a twin-float monoplane that entered service in 1941, scouting Pearl Harbor ahead of the strike force. It was still used three years later, flying from battleships and cruisers. Top speed: 234 mph/203 knots.

Mitsubishi A6M2/5 carrier fighter. Japan's signature aircraft, the Zero fighter was legendary for its range and performance. With 7.7- and 20mm armament, it first flew in 1939 and six years later was the most produced Japanese plane of all time, with nearly eleven thousand units; no other Japanese aircraft reached six thousand. In the Marianas it was land- and carrier based, assigned fighter and fighter-bomber duty. With 234 embarked, "Zekes" represented over half of Ozawa's strength, including early Model 21s as bombers. Top speed: 350 mph/305 knots.

Mitsubishi G4M2 land-based bomber. Big, fast, and long-legged, "Betty" posed a threat to Allied forces afloat and ashore. It flew two months before the Zero in 1939 and astonished the Anglo-Americans in the Philippines, Indian Ocean, and elsewhere. However, its lack of armor plate and self-sealing tanks prompted the nickname "Type One Lighter" from nervous crews. Nearly twenty-five hundred were built—more than any Japanese bomber. Top speed: 272 mph/236 knots.

Nakajima B5N2 carrier torpedo plane. The "Kate" came as an unpleasant surprise to the U.S. Navy. First flown in 1937, the three-seat attack aircraft outperformed every carrier-based torpedo plane on earth in 1941–42, also proving effective as a horizontal bomber. Though its radial engine was upgraded from 770 to a thousand horsepower, by 1943 it was useful mainly for reconnaissance.

Some eleven hundred were built, with eighteen aboard *Zuiho* at Philippine Sea. Top speed: 235 mph/204 knots.

Nakajima B6N1 torpedo plane. Nakajima's follow-up to the Kate was the *Tenzan* (Heavenly Mountain), which first flew in 1941. But development problems delayed production for two years, and "Jill" saw limited service. Though relatively fast, it was unable to outpace American fighters, and the twelve hundred manufactured achieved little success. Seventy-one were deployed with Ozawa. Top speed: 289 mph/251 knots.

Yokosuka D4Y1 carrier dive-bomber. With retractable gear (and nonfolding wings) the *Suisei* (Comet) was a modern naval strike design, unusual with its Daimler-Benz liquid-cooled engine. It entered fleet service in 1942 as a recon plane but made its name as a dive-bomber. At 298 knots (343 mph) "Judy" was the fastest carrier-based strike aircraft of the war. A little over two thousand were built, second only to the Zero among IJN carrier types. Fifty were ashore in the Marianas. Top speed: 343 mph/298 knots.

Yokosuka P1Y1 land-based bomber. Japan's interest in twin-engine medium bombers reflected America's production of the B-25 Mitchell and B-26 Marauder. Consequently the *Ginga* (Milky Way) was fast, with 295 knots (340 mph) top speed, but it proved difficult to maintain. The "Frances" was new in the summer of 1944, having first flown the previous year. Nearly eleven hundred were built, eighty of which were ashore in the Marianas. Top speed: 340 mph/295 knots.

APPENDIX F

AIR COMBAT CLAIMS, JUNE 19

Squadron	Ship	Destroyed	Probable	Damaged	Lost*
VB-8	*Bunker Hill*	0	0	0	1
VB-14	*Wasp*	1.5	0	1	1
VB-15	*Essex*	1	0	0	0
VC-10	*Gambier Bay*	1	0	0	0
VC-41	*Corregidor*	3	0	0	0
VF-1	*Yorktown*	37	5	0	2
VF-2	*Hornet*	43	10	0	1
VF-8	*Bunker Hill*	20	2	3	2
VF-10	*Enterprise*	20	0	0	1
VF-14	*Wasp*	11.5	0	4	0
VF-15	*Essex*	68.5	12.5	1	4
VF-16	*Lexington*	46	5	1	0
VF-24	*Belleau Wood*	10	3	6	0
VF-25	*Cowpens*	9	3	0	1
VF-27	*Princeton*	30	6	5	2
VF-28	*Monterey*	19	0	0	0
VF-31	*Cabot*	28	1	1	0
VF-32	*Langley*	2	0	0	0
VF-50	*Bataan*	11	2	0	0
VF-51	*San Jacinto*	7.5	3	0	1
VF(N)-76	*Hornet, Bunker Hill*	9	2	0	2
VT-16	*Lexington*	2	2	0	0

* Combat losses only

Top Scores
June 19

Pilot	Squadron	Destroyed	Probable	Damaged	Total Destroyed	
Cdr. David McCampbell	CAG-15	7	1	0	34	
Lt(jg) Alexander Vraciu	VF-16	6	0	0	19	
Ens. Wilbur W. Webb	VF-2	6	2	0	7	
Cdr. Charles W. Brewer	VF-15	5	0	0	6.5	KIA* June 19
Lt(jg) George R. Carr	VF-15	5	0	0	11.5	
Lt. Russell L. Reiserer	VF(N)-76	5	0	0	9	
Lt. Oscar C. Bailey	VF-28	4	0	0	5	
Lt(jg) William R. Bauhof	VF-16	4	0	0	4	
Lt. Richard O. Devine	VF-10	4	0	0	8	
Lt(jg) Richard T. Eastmond	VF-1	4	0	0	9	
Ens. Richard E. Fowler	VF-15	4	0	0	6.5	
Lt. William E. Lamb	VF-27	4	1	0	6	
Lt(jg) Zeigel W. Neff	VF-16	4	0	0	4	
Lt. Edward W. Overton Jr.	VF-15	4	1	0	5	
Ens. Claude W. Plant Jr.	VF-15	4	0	0	8.5	KIA September 1944
Lt. John L. Wirth	VF-31	4	0	0	14	KIFA† April 1945

*KIA: Killed in action
†KIFA: Killed in flying accident

Task Force 58 Losses
June 19

	Combat	Operational	Personnel
F6Fs	17*	4	14
Bombers	8	2	13
Shipboard	0	0	31?

* One to U.S. AA fire

June 20 Strike

	Sorties	Combat loss	Operational	% Loss
F6Fs	95	6	16	16.8%
SB2Cs	51	4	39	84.3%
SBDs	26	1	3	15.3%
TBF/TBMs	54	6	24	55.5%
Total	226+	17	82	42.9%

+ 14 aborts
Personnel losses: 16 pilots, 33 aircrew, 6 shipboard fatalities

APPENDIX G

U.S. Warships Commissioned 1941–42 to September 1945

1941	0 CV	0 CVL	3 CVE*	2 BB	1 CA/CL	27 DD	13 SS
1942	1 CV	0 CVL	27 CVE*	4 BB	8 CA/CL	103 DD	33 SS
1943	6 CV	9 CVL	37 CVE*	2 BB	11 CA/CL	128 DD	50 SS
1944	5 CV	0 CVL	31 CVE	2 BB	14 CA/CB	89 DD	80 SS
1945	1 CV	0 CVL	6 CVE	0 BB	13 CA/CL	53 DD	37 SS
	13 CV	9 CVL	104 CVE	10 BB	47 CA/CL	400 DD	213 SS

* CVE totals include 2, 18, and 13 for UK 1941–43 respectively = 33
583 surface combatants plus 213 subs = 796 warships

Warships in Commission May 1944

	CV/CVL	BB	CA/CL	DD	SS	Total
USN	22	20	49	356	197	644
IJN	10	9	27	60	69	165

Fifth Fleet Warship Construction

Type	Prewar*	1942	1943	1944	Total
Carriers	1	1	13	0	15
Battleships	2	3	2	0	7
Cruisers	5	5	10	1	21
Destroyers	19	6	41	2	68
Total	27	15	66	3	111

* Through Dec. 31, 1941

ACKNOWLEDGMENTS

First and foremost, I owe thanks to my agent, Jim Hornfischer, who suggested this book. Following close in the wake of his own *Last Stand of the Tin Can Sailors*, a reprise of the Marianas Turkey Shoot was a natural.

The Forager veterans and contributors are listed below, with ranks and assignments as of June 1944. I am indebted to Jim Sawruk, who (as always) was unstinting in his assistance with Imperial Navy material, and Henry Sakaida, who provided information and contacts in Japan.

The appendices include the most complete listing ever compiled of Forager/A-Go ship captains. However, the U.S. destroyer skippers were especially hard to nail down, and that could not have been done without Bob Cressman's extra efforts in the Naval History Office.

Two valued friends volunteered as de facto editors of an early draft, and I extend heartfelt gratitude to Richard Frank and Alex Vraciu. Jeff Cooper also reviewed segments of the text. With such splendid assistance, any residual errors are the fault of the author.

MARIANAS VETERANS
Lt. Zenji Abe, CO *Junyo* dive-bombers
Lt. Cdr. Evan P. Aurand, CO VFN-76, *Bunker Hill*. (d.1989)
ARM2c Ellis C. Babcock, VT-24, *Belleau Wood*.
Lt. Cdr. Fred A. Bardshar, CAG-27, *Princeton*. (d.1993)
Lt(jg) Norman Berg, VT-28, *Monterey*.
Lt. Harold L. Buell, VB-2, *Hornet*.
Lt. Martin D. Carmody, VB-8, *Bunker Hill*.
ARM1c David Cawley, VB-10, *Enterprise*.
Capt. John D. Cooper, USMC, *Pennsylvania*.
Coxswain John Cummings, *Hunt*.
Lt. Robert Dickey, *Dortsch*.
QM3c John M. DiFusco, *Belleau Wood*.
Lt. Cdr. George C. Duncan, VF-15, *Essex*. (d.1995)
Lt. Edward L. Feightner, VF-8, *Bunker Hill*.
Lt. Cdr. Gerald R. Ford, *Monterey*.
Lt. Donald Gordon, VF-10, *Enterprise*.
Donald Gritz, *San Francisco*
Lt. Cdr. Richard E. Harmer, CO VFN-101, *Enterprise*. (d.1999)
Lt. John A. Harper, LSO, *Belleau Wood*.
Lt(jg) Charles E. Henderson III, VT-10, *Enterprise*. (d.1986)
Lt(jg) Harry G. Lewis, VT-2, *Hornet*.
Cdr. David McCampbell, CAG-15, *Essex*. (d.1996)
Lt. Cdr. William I. Martin, CO VT-10, *Enterprise*. (d.1996)
Lt. W. Robert Maxwell, VF-51, *San Jacinto*.

Lt. Richard H. May, VF-32, *Langley*.
Lt. John Monsarrat, FDO, *Langley*. (d.1995)
Lt(jg) Richard G. Morland, FDO, *Lexington*.
Lt. Robert R. Nelson, VT-10, *Enterprise*.
Lt(jg) Warren R. Omark, VT-24, *Belleau Wood*.
Lt. Cdr. James D. Ramage, VB-10, *Enterprise*.
Lt(jg) Daniel R. Rehm Jr., VF-50, *Bataan*. (d.2004)
Lt. Russell L. Reiserer, VF(N)-76, *Bunker Hill*.
AOM2c Allen J. Rogers, VT-28, *Monterey*.
Lt. Richard J. Stambook, VF-27, *Princeton*. (d.2000)
Lt(jg) Benjamin C. Tate, VT-24, *Belleau Wood*. (d.1998)
Lt(jg) Richard C. Tripp, LSO, *Yorktown*. (d.1990)
Lt(jg) Alexander Vraciu, VF-16, *Lexington*.
Ens. Wilbur B. Webb, VF-2, *Hornet*. (d.2002)
Lt. John P. Wheatley, VP-13. (d.2006)
RM2c Jack Yike, *Dewey*.
Ens. Ernest J. Zellmer, *Cavalla*.

CONTRIBUTORS
Jason Abraham; Jim Broshot; Cdr. Pete Clayton, USN(Ret); Robert C. Cressman;
David Dickson; Ray Emory; Cdr. Vice Capt. Clayton Fisher, USN(Ret); Richard
Frank; Dick Fread, *Belleau Wood* Association; Capt. Roy Gee, USN(Ret); Hill
Goodspeed, Buehler Library; Bob Hackett; Cdr. Jan Jacobs, USNR(Ret); Tatsuo
Kuminou; Masao Kikuchi; James F. Landale; John B. Lundstrom; Paul McLean;
George W. McMullan; Jean-Francois Masson; Capt. Steve Millikin, USN(Ret);
Allyn Nevitt; Cdr. R. R. Powell, USN(Ret); Ron Russell and the Midway round-
table; Janelle Sahr, *Hornet* Museum; Henry Sakaida; James C. Sawruk; Linda
Sheeran; Cdr. Doug Siegfried, USN(Ret); Keith C. Smith; Bob Sourisseau; Don
Steffins, *Hunt* Association; Osamu Tagaya; Koji Takaki; Jim Timmons, USS *Nitro*
Association; Ron Werneth; Heidi Yefremov, Buehler Library; Capt. Akikiko
Yoshida, JMSDF (Ret); Jiro Yoshida; CombinedFleet.com J-Aircraft.com; Steve's
IJN Submarine Page; and of course the Tailhook Association.

BIBLIOGRAPHY

Blair, Clay. *Silent Victory: The U.S. Submarine War Against Japan.* New York: Lippincott, 1975.

Bryan, Joseph. *Mission Beyond Darkness.* New York: Duell Sloan Pearce, 1944.

Buell, Harold L. *Dauntless Helldivers.* New York: Orion, 1991.

Buell, Thomas B. *The Quiet Warrior: A Biography of Raymond A. Spruance.* Boston: Little-Brown, 1974.

Chesneau, Roger. *Aircraft Carriers of the World, 1914 to the Present.* London: Brockhampton Press, 1998.

Cressman, Robert J. *A Source of Great Satisfaction: The Rescue of American Aircrew after the Battle of the Philippine Sea.* Unpublished manuscript.

Dickson, W. D. *Battle of the Philippine Sea.* U.K.: Ian Allan, 1975.

Dull, Paul S. *A Battle History of the Imperial Japanese Navy (1941–1945).* Annapolis: Naval Institute Press, 1978.

Ewing, Steve. *Thach Weave: The Life of Jimmie Thach.* Annapolis: Naval Institute Press, 2004

Fahey, James C. *The Ships and Aircraft of the U.S. Fleet.* Victory Edition. New York: Ships and Aircraft, 1945.

Francillon, René J. *Japanese Aircraft of the Pacific War.* London: Putnam, 1979.

Glass, Kenneth M., and Harold L. Buell. *The Hornets and Their Heroic Men.* USS Hornet Club, 1992.

Grossnick, Roy A. *United States Naval Aviation, 1910–1995.* Washington, D.C.: Naval Historical Center, 1996.

Harper, John. *Paddles: The Foibles and Finesse of One World War Two Landing Signal Officer.* Atglen, Pennsylvania: Schiffer Military History, 1996.

Hata, Ikuhiko, and Yasuho Izawa. *Japanese Naval Aces and Fighter Units in WWII.* Annapolis: Naval Institute Press, 1989.

Hoyt, Edwin P. *McCampbell's Heroes.* New York: Van Nostrand Reinhold, 1983.

Mangold, Tom, and Jeff Goldberg. *Plague Wars.* New York: St. Martin's Press, 1999.

Mersky, Peter. *The Grim Reapers: Fighting Squadron Ten in WWII.* Mesa, AZ: Champlin Museum Press, 1986.

Monsarrat, John. *Angel on the Yardarm: The Beginning of Fleet Radar Defense.* Newport, RI: Naval War College, 1985.

Moore, Steven L., with William Shinneman and Robert Grubel. *The Buzzard Brigade: Torpedo Squadron Ten at War.* Missoula, MT: Pictorial Histories, 1996.

Morison, Samuel E. *History of United States Naval Operations in World War II. Vol. VIII: New Guinea and the Marianas, March 1944–August 1944.* Edison, NJ: Castle Books, 2001.

Naval Analysis Division. *United States Strategic Bombing Survey (Pacific).* Washington, D.C.: Government Printing Office, 1946.

Okumiya, Masatake, and Jiro Horikoshi. *Zero! The Air War in the Pacific from the Japanese Viewpoint.* Washington, D.C.: Zenger Publishing, 1956.

Olynyk, Frank. *USN Credits for Destruction of Enemy Aircraft, WWII.* Aurora, Ohio: 1982.

Peattie, Mark. R. *Sunburst: The Rise of Japanese Naval Air Power.* Annapolis: Naval Institute Press, 2001.

Potter, E. B. *Admiral Arleigh Burke: A Biography.* New York: Random House, 1990.

Ramage, James D. "A Review of the Philippine Sea Battle." *The Hook,* August 1990.

Reynolds, Clark G. *The Fast Carriers.* New York: McGraw-Hill, 1968.

———. *The Fighting Lady.* Missoula, MT: Pictorial Histories, 1986.

Sakaida, Henry. *Winged Samurai: Saburo Sakai and the Zero Fighter Pilots.* Mesa, AZ: Champlin Museum Press, 1985.

———. *Imperial Japanese Navy Aces 1937–1945.* London: Osprey, 1998.

Shores, Christopher F. *Duel for the Sky: Ten Crucial Air Battles of World War 2.* New York: Doubleday, 1985.

Stafford, Edward P. *The Big E.* New York: Dell, 1964.

Tagaya, Osamu. *Imperial Japanese Naval Aviator, 1937–1945.* Wellingborough, U.K.: Osprey, 1988.

Taylor, Theodore. *The Magnificent Mitscher.* Annapolis: Naval Institute Press, 1991.

Tillman, Barrett. *The Dauntless Dive Bomber of World War II.* Annapolis: Naval Institute Press, 1976.

———. *Carrier Battle in the Philippine Sea: The Marianas Turkey Shoot, June 19–20, 1944.* St. Paul: Phalanx Pub. Co., 1994.

———. *Corsair: The F4U in World War II and Korea.* Annapolis: Naval Institute Press, 1979.

———. *Hellcat: The F6F in World War II.* Annapolis: Naval Institute Press, 1979.

———. *Helldiver Units of World War 2.* London: Osprey, 1997.

———. *TBF-TBM Avenger at War.* London: Ian Allan, Ltd., 1979.

———. "Coaching the Fighters." *The Hook,* Summer 2001.

Toland, John. *The Rising Sun: The Decline and Fall of the Japanese Empire.* New York: Random House, 1970.

United States Naval Academy Alumni Assn. *Register of Alumni, 1845–1991*. Annapolis: 1990.

United States Government Printing Office. *United States Strategic Bombing Survey: The Campaigns of the Pacific War*. Washington, D.C.: 1946.

———. *Location and Allowance of Aircraft, June 13, 1944*.

Watts, A. J. *Japanese Warships of World War II*. Garden City: Doubleday, 1970.

Wildenberg, Thomas. *Gray Steel and Black Oil: Fast Tankers and Replenishment at Sea in the U.S. Navy, 1912–1992*. Annapolis: Naval Institute Press, 1994.

Y'Blood, William T. *Red Sun Setting: The Battle of the Philippine Sea*. Annapolis: Naval Institute Press, 1981.

Yokoi, Toshiyuki. "The Admiral That Davy Jones Didn't Want." *Ukiyo: Stories of the "Floating World" of Postwar Japan*. Jay Gluck, translator. New York: Vanguard Press, 1963.

NOTES

USSBS: U.S. Strategic Bombing Survey (Pacific).

PART I

9   "Try to avoid shooting down our fighters." W. D. Dickson, *Battle of the Philippine Sea*, 116.

11   "Older men . . ." http://bartleby.school.aol.com/73/1923.html.

18   "I believe . . ." Thomas B. Buell, *The Quiet Warrior*, 268.

19   "had his own convictions . . ." Steve Ewing, *Thach Weave*, 168.

19   "You can train . . ." Theodore Taylor, *The Magnificent Mitscher*, 242.

21   "they came out of the blue . . . tail gunner in a TBF . . ." E. B. Potter, *Admiral Arleigh Burke*, 110.

21   "It's a job . . ." Taylor, 194.

24   "You came up . . ." Kenneth M. Glass and Harold L. Buell, *The Hornets and Their Heroic Men*, 19.

25   "I have orders . . ." Potter, 139.

27   "Ozawa was probably . . ." Toshiyuki Yokoi, *Ukiyo: Stories of the "Floating World" of Postwar Japan*, 9.

29   *Maya*'s monkey: www.combinedfleet.com/maya.

31   Japan's thirty-five hundred naval aviators: Mark Peattie, *Sunburst*, 166.

31   Imperial Navy losses April 43–February 44: Paul S. Dull, *Battle History of the Imperial Japanese Navy*, 312.

32   "key to the situation . . ." Samuel Eliot Morison, *History of United States Naval Operations in World War II*, 5.

35   Tojo's "feverish" attitude: Masatake Okumiya, *Zero*, 316.

36   Operation Z orders: Morison, 12.

36   Fukodome capture: John Toland, *The Rising Sun*, 605.

37   Toyoda's personality: Ibid., 605.

38   "Realizing the gravity . . ." USSBS, 233.

39   Tarakan crude oil: Dull, 315.

41   Ozawa's units "expendable": William T. Y'Blood, *Red Sun Setting*, 25.

42   Plague vials embarked for Saipan: Tom Mangold and Jeff Goldberg, *Plague Wars*, 24.

43   "There'll always . . ." Morison, 228.

43   Japanese submarine losses: Morison, 230.

45   U.S. submarine commanders: Clay Blair, *Silent Victory*, Vol. 2 data.

47   U.S. submarine claims: Ibid.

48   ". . . hollering like hell . . ." Ibid., 576.

49   Hogan evaded: Ibid., 598–99.

PART II

53	"Thank God . . ." Wheatley correspondence, May 2004.
53	"It was all over . . ." Ibid.
55	"To hell with that." Clark G. Reynolds, *The Fighting Lady*, 141.
55	"Cut their damned throats." Edward P. Stafford, *The Big E*, 344.
58	"I had more use . . ." James D. Ramage, Naval Institute oral history.
58	"It was a losing battle . . ." Okumiya, 317.
60	"Heads up." Barrett Tillman, *Hellcat*, 72.
61	"I knew . . ." Ibid, 73.
62	Japanese pilot losses: Ikuhiko Hata and Yasuho Izawa, *Japanese Naval Aces and Fighter Units in WW II*, 390.
62	"On D – 3 . . ." *Enterprise* action report, June 12, 1944.
63	"The Japs had . . ." Reynolds, *Fighting Lady*, 142.
65	Clark's long-range strike: Ibid., 143.
67	". . . getting damn disgusted . . ." Y'Blood, 54.
69	Preinvasion ammunition expenditure: Morison, 347.
69	Over 40 percent: Ibid., 343.
69	"There was nothing . . ." Morison, Vol. VII, 103.
70	". . . a very difficult . . ." Reynolds, *Fast Carriers*, 177.
72	"We all know . . ." Thomas Wildenberg, *Gray Steel and Black Oil*, 182–83.
75	"If you do not join me . . ." Reynolds, *Fast Carriers*, 178.
75	"Get the shootin' irons . . ." Reynolds, *Fighting Lady*, 143.
77	"When you brag . . ." Captain Clayton Fisher, USN (ret), e-mail, May 2004.
77	"Welcome, Air Group Nineteen . . ." Commander W. E. Copeland, USN (ret), c. 1995.
77	"The Jap fleet . . ." Commander Alex Vraciu, USN (ret), c. 1990.
78	". . . part Cherokee . . ." Morison, 239.
79	June 15 Japanese losses: Hata and Izawa, 188, 190.
79	". . . all the mistakes . . ." Reynolds, *Fighting Lady*, 145.
80	". . . erratic and disorganized . . ." VF-2 action report, June 15, 1944.
80	"I'm a fighter pilot . . ." Captain George C. Duncan, USN (ret), c. 1990.
81	Harrill's distress: Reynolds, *Fast Carriers*, 178.
82	"I would have had . . ." Vice Admiral E. P. Aurand, USN (ret), "Quonset Point to Combat: The Hard Way." *The Hook*, Summer 1989, 20.
82	". . . convoy and task force . . ." USSBS, 254–55.
84	". . . plenty of battleships . . ." Blair, 624.
88	Major action annex: Buell, 264.
88	"Our air . . ." Ibid., 264.
89	"The . . . list . . ." Y'Blood, 75.
90	". . . listed heavily . . ." USSBS, 255.
90	*Fanshaw Bay*: www.ibiblio.org/pha/chr/chr44-06.html.
90	". . . a faint, fading pip . . ." Captain Ernest Zellmer, USN (ret), e-mail, August 2004.

92   "... figures that were exactly right." FN Busch report: www.rb-29.net/HTML/81/lexingtonstys.

92   "... 660 miles west ..." Taylor, 218.

92   "Do not, repeat not ..." Taylor, ibid.

93   "... which apparently is Sunday ..." Busch, op. cit.

94   "Suddenly there was a Jake ..." Tillman, *TBF-TBM Avenger at War*, 115–16.

97   "... 'regular' *Saratoga*-class ..." Y'Blood, 84.

97   Attack on TG 50.17: USSBS, 255; www.seacadets.us/dd.552_history.htm.

99   "I will pound ..." Gluck, 9.

99   "We had never assembled ..." Okumiya, 318–19.

99   "In only ..." Okumiya, 322.

100   "We were completely undetected ..." Gluck, 9.

100   "Their attitude ..." Buell, 267.

100   "The way Togo waited ..." Ibid, 268.

100   "We knew ..." Potter, 151.

PART III

108   End run: Y'Blood, 93.

108   Gardner's cap: Stafford, 361.

109   Carriers sunk by U.S. subs: *Nautilus* was erroneously credited with a share of *Soryu* at Midway. *Sailfish* sank CVE *Chuyo* in December 1943.

111   "Airborne radar ..." Peattie, 341.

111–12 Japanese naval aviators: Osamu Tagaya, *Imperial Japanese Naval Aviator*, 27.

112   Flight class attrition: analysis of Hata and Izawa, 419–23.

113   "This unbelievable situation ..." Zenji Abe correspondence, July 1993.

113   "... to my amazement ..." Gluck, 10.

113   "The degree of training ..." USSBS, 264.

114   "... totally unusable ..." Ibid.

115   Fujita comments: *Hunters in the Sky*, video, 1992.

115   Voris comments: Ibid.

116   "The Marianas defense ..." Okumiya, 315–16.

118   *Ishin denshin*: Peattie, 137.

118   Evidence indicates: W. D. Dickson, e-mail, June 2004.

118–19 Land-based air: Morison, 261.

121   "The American tactics ..." Tsunoda, *Hunters in the Sky*.

121   "I respected the Japanese ..." McCuskey, ibid.

122   Service to service: Author study based on Olynyk sources for World War II, Korea, and Vietnam.

123   "I can't take this ..." Vraciu, c. 1980.

123   "I grabbed ..." Captain David McCampbell, USN (ret), interview, June 1991.

123   Task Force 58 radios: Morison, 261.

126   "One of the things . . ." Richard Morland, correspondence, August 13, 1993.

128   Assistant FDO: USS *Lexington* roster, June 1, 1944, supplied by Alex Vraciu.

128   Japanese radar: www.warships1.com/index_weapons.htm.

130–31 Search aircraft losses: Morison, 265, and Olynyk, 55–56. Morison says that *Langley* searchers accounted for most of the enemy scouts, but Air Group 32 claimed only three kills during the day.

132–34 Carrier dimensions: Roger Chesneau, *Aircraft Carriers of the World*, 157, 198.

137   Ebata's vow: Dickson, 151, places Ebata aboard *Taiho* but he was Air Group 653's fighter-bomber leader on *Chiyoda*.

138   "Hey, rube!" Tillman, *Hellcat*, 78.

139   "Back in time . . ." Otis Kight, e-mail, June 2004.

141   TF-58 bomber sorties: *Analysis of Pacific Air Operations, June 1944*. Com-AirPac, September 20, 1944.

142   "Radar was picking up . . ." www.ussbelleauwood.com/stories.

142   "The day was so clear . . ." Morland, op. cit.

144   "We had shoe clerks . . ." Ralph Clark interview, 1978.

148   "I remember . . ." Vice Admiral Frederick A. Bardshar, USN (ret), correspondence, March 1977.

149   "Air and communication . . ." Ibid.

151   ". . . an attractive, lethal target . . ." Captain Donald Gordon, USN (ret), ms., 1991.

151   *South Dakota* casualties: Morison, 269, reverses the figures, but the ship's roster lists twenty-three KIA this date. Y'Blood, 112, cites 27 and 24.

151   ". . . my most memorable scene . . ." Gordon, op. cit.

153   ". . . definitely scored hits . . ." *U.S. Strategic Bombing Survey*, 244.

153   7 I, 15 Ri, and 3 Ri contacts: Morison, 271–72, and Dickson, 111. The 7 I contact obviously matched the northerly U.S. groups, but still contained an error. At the time of the report, Mitscher's flagship was a good fifty miles to the southeast, placing Harrill's 58.4 about thirty-five miles southeast of the reported position.

        Though Morison and Dickson attribute the 15 Ri contact southwest of Guam to uncorrected magnetic variation, in 1944 Guam's variation was barely one degree east. Some commentators speculate that the Japanese aircrews lacked navigation experience, but a 120-mile error strains credulity. The Nakajima B6N2-R was the number fifteen scout in the number fifteen sector and clearly went where assigned. It is far more likely that the scouts observed American ships and saw what they expected: carriers where there were none.

        Unaccountably, Morison describes 3 Ri as "correct" when it was forty-five miles farther north than 7 I.

154   Strips of aluminum: www.vectorsite.net/ttwiz9.html.

157   "The battle . . ." Dickson, 129.

157   Blanchard's commendation: Blair, 628.

157   "There was the rising sun . . ." Morison, 281.

158   "On the last observation . . ." Zellmer, e-mail, August 2004.

159   Zellmer counted fifty-six depth charges: Ibid.

160   Two-thirds of the crew: www.combined fleet.com/shokaku.html, with a thorough postmortem by Anthony Tully, Jon Parshall, and Richard Wolf.

160   "It was necessary . . ." Zellmer, e-mail, August 2004.

161   "For the next . . ." Ibid.

161   "Heard four terrific explosions . . ." www.cavalla.org.

163   "I practiced . . ." McCampbell interview, June 1991.

164   Birkholm narrative: Air Group 16 ACA, June 19, 1944.

164–65   Vraciu narrative: Alexander Vraciu, "Battle Off Saipan." *The Hook*, Summer 1994; correspondence, September 2004.

165   "That was my payback . . ." Vraciu correspondence, September 2004.

166–67   Rehm narrative: Daniel Rehm correspondence, July 2003.

167   ". . . fighting off numerous attacks . . ." Morison, 270.

169   "That this should come to pass . . ." Glass, 17.

170   *Wasp* account: VF-14 history, 1944.

170   Two of the six: Dickson, 121.

171   "Torpedo planes (bearing) 270 . . ." Ibid., 121–22.

171   "Look out for torpedoes . . ." TG-58.3 radio log: Ibid., 122.

171   ". . . disregarding the *Princeton* . . ." *Enterprise* AA action report, June 19, 1944.

172   ". . . put the kill . . ." Ibid.

173–74   Raid II losses: USSBS, 245–53.

176   "The big-deck squadrons . . ." Commander Richard H. May, USN (ret), c. 1990.

176   Japanese lost seven versus fifteen. The history of Air Group 652 is specific: Losses were two fighters, four fighter-bombers, and one torpedo plane. Hata and Izawa, 81.

177   CarDiv Three's canceled launch: The composition of this portion of Raid III is usually cited as sixteen Zekes. Hata and Izawa, 84.

178   ". . . as if I were flying . . ." Abe correspondence, op. cit.

178   "I really wondered . . ." Ibid.

178   "Every Navy pilot . . ." Ibid.

179   "Sir! Big enemy formation," Ibid.

180   "That was dreadful . . ." Ibid.

181   ". . . a wild ride . . ." Y'Blood, 134.

181   *Wasp* casualties: Ibid., 133.

181   "I never saw so many Grummans!" Abe interview, 1994.

182   *Taiho* casualties: www.combinedfleet.com/taiho.html; Morison, 282. The usual figure for *Taiho*'s personnel loss is 1,650, cited by Minoru Genda to the distinguished naval historian Norman Polmar. But the

authoritative compilations at Combinedfleet.com cite specific sources as 660. The fact that *Taiho* sank slowly, on an even keel, may offer support for the lower figure.

183   "Forty enemy planes . . ." Morison, 273.

184   "It was so perfect . . ." VF-15 action report, June 19, 1944.

184   ". . . a wild character . . ." Hata and Izawa, 265.

185   "Any American fighter pilot . . ." Webb interview, 1994.

185   "We spent . . ." Captain Russell L. Reiserer, USN (ret), e-mail, September 2004.

185   ". . . it wasn't as crowded . . ." Ibid.

185   ". . . a large number . . ." VF-2/VFN-76 action report, June 19, 1944.

186   "Spider and I . . ." Reiserer, op. cit.

186   ". . . for bringing back . . ." Ibid.

187   "They got one of our guys!" Peter Mersky, *Grim Reapers*, 112–13.

187   Ozaki's fate: Shores, *Duel for the Sky*, 202.

189   ". . . and be extra cautious . . ." McCampbell correspondence, 1978.

189   "No indeed!" Morison, 274. It has been theorized that the strike coordinator was Lieutenant Commander Akira Tarui, CarDiv One's torpedo unit commander. But he was killed early in the action and in any case could not have remained airborne throughout the day. Mitscher's eavesdroppers apparently mistook two or more commanders for one.

191   ". . . ten feet off the water . . ." VF-16 action report, June 19, 1944.

194   "Desire to attack . . ." Taylor, 229.

195   "I was snatched . . ." Abe, op. cit.

195   "They never stood a chance . . ." Okumiya, 318.

195   Japanese fighter losses and claims: Hata and Izawa, 391–92; USSBS, 245.

195   Guam aircraft losses: Morison, 320.

195   Missing Japanese aircraft: James Sawruk, e-mail, July 2004.

196   Bridges fund: www.cv18.com/hist/bridges.html.

196   ". . . an old-time turkey shoot . . ." www.cannon-lexington.com/Pages/Airedales.html. Morison (256) attributes the phrase to VF-16 skipper Paul Buie, but squadron accounts stress Neff's authorship.

197   "Tomorrow I'm going to get a haircut." Taylor, 229.

197   ". . . mopping-up . . ." Dickson, 139.

PART IV

201   Tokyo's claims: Morison, 287.

202   ". . . drinking coffee . . ." VF-16 action report, June 20, 1944.

202   "I am certain . . ." Edwin P. Hoyt, *McCampbell's Heroes*, 80.

204   ". . . as soon as possible . . ." Dickson, 140.

204   "Desire to push . . ." Ibid.

204   ". . . damaged *Zuikaku* . . ." Potter, 163.

205   "Chances are . . ." Taylor, 230.

206   *Maya* search: www.combinedfleet.com/maya.html.

206   "Would like to . . ." Dickson, 145.

206   "Indication that . . ." Ibid.

207   "Enemy fleet sighted . . ." Stafford, 371.

207   "Many ships . . ." Ibid.

207   "My most vivid recollections . . ." Robert R. Nelson correspondence, 1993.

208   *Maya* report: www.combinedfleet.com/maya.html.

208   Widhelm's bet: Potter, 165.

209   "Expect to launch . . ." Joseph Bryan, *Mission Beyond Darkness*, 149.

209   "We can make it . . ." Dickson, 146.

209   "We're going to be . . ." Ramage oral history.

210   "I had four five-hundred-pound bombs . . ." Harry Lewis interview, May 2004.

211   Type 91 torpedo specs: www.warships1.com/weapons/WTJAP_WWII .html.

211   U.S. torpedo tests: Blair, 252.

212   VT-10 results: Tillman, *Avenger at War*, 6.

212   German officers to prison: www.uboat.net/history.

212   ". . . a very aggressive aviator . . ." Captain Benjamin Tate, USN (ret), correspondence, May 1978.

213   "Give 'em hell . . ." Morison, 291.

215   "We did not think . . ." www.ussbelleauwood.com/stories.

216–17 "Strike groups . . . fighting Navy . . ." Ramage oral history, U.S. Naval Institute.

217   "Who wasn't?" Ibid.

217   ". . . explode and disintegrate . . ." VF-14 history, 1944.

218   Radio calls: Ramage oral history and Dickson, 150.

219–20 Buell account: *Dauntless Helldivers*, 298–99.

221   ". . . a large hole . . ." Reynolds, *Fighting Lady*, 159.

221   "The . . . strafing planes . . ." Morison, 298.

222   ". . . bubble extinguishing equipment . . ." Dickson, 151.

223   Japanese AA results: compiled from Y'Blood, 234–35.

224   ". . . the southern *Hayataka* . . ." Bryan, 34.

224   "I don't see . . ." Alex Vraciu, telecon, July 2004.

225   McClellan account: Bryan, 51–52.

231   "No guts." Ramage oral history.

231   "It forces you . . ." Lieutenant Commander Richard H. Best, USN (ret), interview, 1993.

231   ". . . about fifteen feet . . ." Ibid.

232   ". . . slight damage . . ." USSBS, 246.

233   "Brownie, Ben . . ." Tate correspondence, May 1978.

233   "We came in . . ." Warren Omark correspondence, 1993.

234   "He held up . . ." Tate, op. cit.

234   "He acted stunned . . ." Omark, op. cit.

235   Air Group 652 losses: Hata and Izawa, 82; USN Air Operations Analysis.

235   Fifty Avengers: www.combinedfleet.com/maya.html.

235   Air Group 653 losses: Dickson, 157.

236   *Chiyoda* damage: www.combinedfleet.com/chiyoda.html.

237–38 Japanese estimates of U.S. attackers: USSBS, 243.

239   Mobile Fleet claims: USSBS, ibid.

239   ". . . utterly crushed . . ." www.combinedfleet.com/junyo.

239   Japanese ships damaged: USSBS, 246.

240   Mobile Fleet aircraft on June 21: Morison, 321.

240   "After a long . . ." Tillman, *Avenger at War*, 116.

PART V

243   Task group flagships: Potter, 166–67.

244   Blitch account: Tillman, *Helldiver Units*, 37–38.

244–45 "Now began . . ." VF-14 history, 1944.

245   "I particularly remember . . ." Morland, op. cit.

245–46 ". . . nothing but pitch-black . . ." Omark telecon, August 22, 2004.

246   "We may have . . ." Ibid.

246   "I'm out of gas . . ." Reynolds, *Fighting Lady*, 164.

247   Fanning account: Y'Blood, 179.

247   ". . . combined Hollywood premiere . . ." Aurand, op. cit.

248   "Land on any base." Reynolds, *Fighting Lady*, 163.

249   "Our radar was still on . . ." Commander David Cawley, USN (ret), "Review of the Philippine Sea." *The Hook*, special issue, 1990.

250   "I think we got . . ." Ramage, May 2004.

250–52 Harper narrative: Harper, *Paddles*, 222–25.

252   "Man your battle stations!" Ibid.

253   Ford narrative: Gerald R. Ford correspondence, November 1993.

254   Rogers narrative: "The View from TorpRon 28." *The Hook*, August 1990.

255   ". . . like an airport . . ." Ewing, 118.

256   "With no power . . ." Buell, 306.

256   "Gentlemen . . ." Ibid.

256   "Everybody else ran out . . ." Stafford, 385.

256–58 *Enterprise* landings: *Enterprise* action report, www.cv-6.org.

257   ". . . forgave a lot . . ." Stafford, 380.

258   "There was a line . . ." Ibid., 382.

258   "We've got to push . . ." Bryan, 96.

258   "Fighter pilots . . ." Vraciu, telecon, June 20, 2004.

258   "It was a mess . . ." Ibid.; correspondence, September 2004.

259   "This water landing . . ." Y'Blood, 97.

259   "This is an SBD . . ." Bryan, 98.

260   ". . . a Mardi Gras . . ." Morison, 303.

260   "You know . . ." Reynolds, *Fighting Lady*, 165.
261   "I have been . . ." Glass, 19.
261   "They liquored him up . . ." Reynolds, *Fighting Lady*, 165.
263   A few diehards: Toland, 630.
263   ". . . a great sigh . . ." Gluck, 14.
264   "To an old-fashioned . . ." Ibid., 15.
264   "Some of you . . ." Glass, 19.
265   PBM loss: Morison, 242.
267   ". . . unless performing . . ." Potter, 170.
268   "It's a beautiful day . . ." Y'Blood, 197.
268   "Our striking planes . . ." Ibid.
270   "If the tactical situation . . ." Buell, 278.
270   ". . . distances are great . . ." Robert J. Cressman, *A Source of Great Satisfaction: The Rescue of American Aircrew after the Battle of the Philippine Sea*. Unpublished manuscript.
270   ". . . to have a plan . . ." Ibid.
272   "Want a lift?" Bryan, 125.
272   "I am more responsible . . ." Dickson, 165.
272   "It is not possible . . ." USSBS, 244.
274   ". . . a great column . . ." Cressman, op. cit.
274   "Look at that!" Lieutenant Colonel J. D. Cooper, USMC, interview, August 2004.
274   755 *Kokutai* report: Tagaya, e-mail, August 2004.
275   June 23 claims and June losses: USSBS, 255.
276   "This was a source . . ." Cressman manuscript.
277   ". . . Jocko Jimas . . ." Morison, 311.
277   By one reckoning: Ibid.
280   "I flew over . . ." Henry Sakaida, *Winged Samurai*, 115.
281   "Cut it out . . ." Reynolds, *Fighting Lady*, 171.
281   "CAP is authorized . . ." Ibid.
282   Ridgway and Wilding bet: Ibid.

PART VI
286–87   IJN overall losses: Morison, 321.
286–87   IJN land-based losses: Hata and Izawa, 393, 431.
287   Evacuation by sub: Sakaida, *Imperial Japanese Navy Aces*, 101.
287   *Combat Sutra*: USSBS, 264.

INDEX

Photo by Nyle Leatham

Barrett Tillman, an aviation historian for the past thirty years, has written more than five hundred articles for leading military journals, as well as four novels, a novella, a screenplay, and thirty works of non-fiction. He has received numerous awards for his work and is an honorary member of three navy squadrons and the American Fighter Aces Association.